101 Sportbike
Performance Projects

Evans Brasfield

MOTORBOOKS
INTERNATIONAL

First published in 2004 by Motorbooks International, an imprint of MBI Publishing Company, Galtier Plaza, Suite 200, 380 Jackson Street, St. Paul, MN 55101-3885 USA

ISBN 0-7603-1331-8

Printed in China

Titlepage: GSX-R 600 built by Hypercycle. Photo courtesy of *Kevin Wing*

Editor: Peter Schletty
Layout: Sara Grindle

Evans Brasfield is a writer and journalist specializing in motorcycles. Before setting out on his freelance career, he was Feature Editor at both *Motorcycle Cruiser* and *Sport Rider* magazines. While in graduate school, he supported himself by teaching motorcycle safety for the California Motorcycle Safety Program. In pursuit of his passion for two wheels, he has ridden everywhere he can (including all the way up to the Arctic Ocean) and gets a perverse pleasure out of riding in the rain. Although he loves all things related to motorcycling, sportbikes have always held a special place in his heart. He club-raced for five years and has participated in two WERA 24 hour endurance events. Track riding is at the top of his list of favorite activities.

Evans lives in Burbank, California with his wife, Karin, and their daughter, Minna.

For Karin,
who gave me our beautiful daughter
and other blessings too plentiful to count.

CONTENTS

CONTENTS

CONTENTS

HOW TO READ THIS BOOK

While I'd be gratified if you read this book from cover to cover, we all know that our busy schedules will prevent that. So, the sections cover groupings of projects based on a sportbike's different systems. For the most part, maintenance projects are listed at the beginning of the section. These projects are usually the easier ones and offer novice mechanics an opportunity to get comfortable wrenching. To assist you in your planning for a project, each begins with an easy-to-read listing of information to give you an idea of what challenges you face. The items listed are:

Time: Many projects can be finished in a couple of hours. Others can take days. Wouldn't you like to know in advance? If you're a complete novice, you might want to factor in additional time. Old pros will probably breeze through some projects in significantly less time.

Tools: Although the majority of projects can be completed with the basic mechanic's tools listed in this section, each project requires a different subset of those tools listed here. Any special tools required will also be noted. You should still check your factory manual to make sure that your bike doesn't require a tool specific to it. Use this listing to justify your forays into your local tool store.

Talent: While bikes can vary from model to model, projects can be categorized into a broad range of difficulty. Each additional 🏃 marks an increased level of difficulty.

Cost: The dollar signs each indicate approximately $100. So, beginning with a single dollar sign, expect to pay up to $100 for the parts necessary to complete the project. If you see five dollar signs, the required components for the project will set you back $500 or more.

Parts: The listing of parts required to perform the modification. However, you should still check your factory manual to ascertain that your bike doesn't require anything special.

Tip: Knowledge comes from experience. The tip will have some information to make the project easier, keep you from overlooking a little detail, or give you information about how the modification may affect your bike. You won't find this information in your factory manual.

Performance Gain: What to expect from your time, money, and effort.

Complementary Modifications: This listing will point to other projects that could help you get even more out of the current project. Again, you won't find this information in your factory manual.

  Heads a project that a novice still could complete.

 Lets a novice know that a little help may be needed.

  Indicates a project that requires you have a fair amount of mechanical expertise and be comfortable with complex assemblies.

Implies that you are well versed in wrenching. Perhaps you've even had some training. A project at this level could be attempted with the assistance of a more experienced mechanic.

 Marks a job best left to the pros, but those who aspire to professional tuner status could press ahead.

ACKNOWLEDGMENTS

I suppose I should begin my thanks with those who endured the most during the creation of this book. Darwin Holmstrom, my long-suffering editor, first suggested this project to me as we stood in the cramped closet that passes for the motorcycle group archives at Emap USA (soon to be Primedia). Now, an embarrassingly long time later, as I type these final words, Darwin deserves much of the credit for getting me here—working even when he was laid up from a high-speed racing accident. Next in line is my wife, Karin Rainey, whose sacrifice while I wrote this book was immeasurable. She worked long hours bringing home the paycheck, while I appeared to sit around fondling the motorcycle parts that the UPS man dropped off almost every day. I can't wait to place a bound copy of this book into her hands to show her what her faith in me helped to create. The last member of my base of support was Andrew Trevitt. He fielded questions big and small, stifling the laughs (I'm sure) at some of the concepts I asked him to help me clarify. Andrew was also the first person besides myself to read every word of this book. Andrew's assistance went way beyond that of mere friendship. He deserves the credit for the technical accuracy of the book, while I can honestly state any mistakes are mine. I hope that I can repay the favors I owe the three of you.

The other folks directly involved in the production of the book also deserve thanks. Peter Schletty, the Motorbooks International associate editor working with Darwin, helped me through the hurdles of finishing my first book. Debbie Trevitt used her Photoshop skills to remove the safety wire supporting the parts in the section lead shots. Pat Hahn plowed through the book in record time, contributing immensely to the clarity and tone.

Attempting a book of this scale would have been impossible without the wholehearted support of the sportbike manufacturers. Honda, Kawasaki, Suzuki, and Yamaha all were generous enough to loan me bikes to use for photography. I can't thank these companies enough for entrusting their machinery to me. A couple of representatives were so supportive that they deserve a special mention. Honda's Jon Siedel came through with bikes when I was in dire need. Also, you may notice the plethora of Yamahas in these pages. Brad Bannister always managed to find a spare bike for me, no matter how tight the time frame, and for that I am truly grateful.

Motorcycle aftermarket companies are the heroes of this undertaking. Without the huge community of creative people devoted to improving sportbikes, there would have been no reason to write this book. Similarly, I can't think of an industry in which the trust is so great that a few phone calls and faxes could result in the loan of thousands of dollars' worth of parts. I feel honored to associate with people of this caliber. To see the complete list of companies supporting this endeavor, simply flip to the Resources Directory in the back of the book.

Again, a few individuals deserve a special mention. Craig Erion of Two Brothers Racing has been helping me out for years. Chuck Graves opened up the Graves Motorsports race shop, giving me access to his team's mechanics on several occasions—once just two days before a preseason test! Similarly, Paul Thede gave me the run of Race Tech, enabling me to shoot his technicians in action. Sandy Kosman of Kosman Specialties pulled some of his talented staff off their regular jobs to fabricate parts. Mike Mangan acted as my liaison with Craftsman Tools. Marc Salvisberg made me think a lot after his information-drenched phone conversations. Thanks to Kent Riches for the bodywork and the Bonneville stories. APE Race Parts' John Nave helped me out with both product and contacts. Thanks to Josh Alverson, Alan Butts, Tom Cates, Glenn Cook, Jeff Crago, Chris Curnen, Brandon Baldwin, Michael Belcher, Dale Berg, Aaron Brock, Geoff Cesmat, Steve Davie, Dave Dewey, Paul English, Jeff Favorite, Gohar Fayyaz, Rick Gero, Al Gillian, Andy Goldfine, Mike Golightly, Sean Gutierrez, Andy Horton, Jeff Johnson, Garrett Kai, Chris Kasey, Kent Kunitsugu, Larry Langley, Matt Lapaglia, Chris Macpherson, Eddie Melendreras, Doug Meyer, Mel Moore, Rich Munson, Chris Pickrell, Bill Rhode, Ryan Schnitz, Karl Steinwachs, Chris Taylor, John Ulrich, Ted Waibel, David Wolman, and anyone else I've neglected to mention. Also, a big high five to Mansoor Shafi, my Prudhoe Bay, Alaska, riding buddy (and the unstoppable force behind Roadgear), who was, as always, a constant source of enthusiasm for the book and motorcycling in general.

Looking closer to home, I want to thank my parents for, well, being my parents. I wouldn't be here without you. On the other end of the generational spectrum, my little girl, Minna, has taught me quite a bit—not the least of which is that some projects never end; they just keep progressing seamlessly from one stage to another. The trick is to keep looking ahead.

Finally, I'd like to thank my two mentors in the writing game. During my stint in graduate school at California State University Northridge, Professor Jan Ramjerdi helped me to find that I had something to say. Art Friedman, who claims he "ruined another productive life" by luring me away from academia, actually did me two favors. He introduced me to the motorcycle industry, and then he gave me enough freedom to learn for myself how to write for a magazine.

Now, if I could only figure out deadlines . . .

Evans Brasfield
www.101sportbikeprojects.com
March 2004

9

Deciding to perform your own modifications to your bike is the first step in a long, fascinating journey. As with any endeavor, you need to plan the initial portion of your route. From the most basic perspective, you need a place to work on your bike, you need a factory service manual to guide you through the intricacies of the modern sportbike, and you need the tools—including special-use ones—to do the actual work. With the right attitude, you'll soon find yourself comfortable with just about any excursion into your motorcycle's inner workings.

Setting Up Shop

The days of shade-tree mechanics are over. The advancement of sportbike technology killed them off long ago-though some claim they still do exist. The truth is that you need a dedicated space to work on your bike if you really want to do more than maintenance. I once selected an apartment because it had a "bike cage," really a glorified storage area located under one apartment with a locking chain-link fence on the two exposed sides. A peek into the dark and dusty interior revealed about five bikes in various stages of decomposition and a couple that were actually ridden. I knew that with a little creative rearranging, I'd have a great spot to wrench. So, after a few hours of cleaning and two flea bombs to make the space habitable for more than the two stray cats holed up in the corner, I had my garage.

The importance of having someplace indoors should be obvious-especially for a novice mechanic. You're going to get stuck and need to go out for more parts, advice, cold beer, or all of the above. Also, some projects require multiple days. You don't want your engine internals to be open to the elements do you? Your garage doesn't need to be the Taj Mahal-although we can always dream. My brother used an aluminum garden shed quite effectively for a few years while working on his race bikes. At the bare minimum, you need a cement floor (clean and level are nice extras). Electricity and good light are vital. A workbench is also good but not necessary if you're just starting out.

Most importantly, you need a secure place where you can leave the myriad of parts out in an arrangement that works for you as you wrench. (In my last apartment, I had a neighbor's potbellied pig walk up to my bike and actually eat the exhaust manifold nuts I had set in front of the bike while I reinstalled the system.) As you acquire more and better tools, you'll also want to be able to leave them in your shop too.

Factory Service Manual

As you go through this book, you'll see constant references to the factory service manual. Every bike is different, and while I've tried to outline the bulk of the information you'll need to perform the 101 projects here, you'd be foolish to attempt

Factory service manuals are vital to the successful completion of any work on your bike. After a while, they'll be dog-eared, grease-stained, familiar friends.

many of them without your bike's factory service manual. Not only does the service manual give you important tips on how to access parts on your particular motorcycle, but also it lists all of the specific measurements (gap, length, runout, thickness, etc.) as well as torque figures used for reassembly. A factory service manual will itemize any special tools you need to perform specific maintenance chores on your bike. Since original equipment (OE) tools are usually quite expensive, you can use the information to see if you can find a third-party tool that will perform the same function at a considerable saving. Finally, a manual becomes a vital research tool as you move into more advanced projects.

Tool Time

If you've spent any time around club racing, you've most likely seen some fairly accomplished mechanics who seem to get by with what looks like a set of open end wrenches and a really big hammer. Of course, those mechanics look as if they have just crawled out of the engine, and they probably have notes on every jetting or gearing change they've made for the past three years. At the other extreme is the guy who has the toolkit to die for-each polished and in its proper place. What the average mechanic needs is something between these extremes.

When buying your first set of tools, don't succumb to the siren song of cheap, no-name tools. While a step above the pot metal atrocities usually included with your bike, cheap tools don't last long, and they damage parts much more frequently than quality ones. Also, tools do wear out and break, so having a lifetime warranty is a good idea. The top two brands of lifetime tools for a home user are Sears Craftsman and Home Depot Husky. Both offer a we-replace-it-if-it-ever-breaks warranty. Although I have no experience with Husky tools, I can say that Sears has never rejected a broken tool I've returned, no matter how stupidly it was being abused when it failed. Yes, Snap-on offers a lifetime warranty too, but you pay a premium for these tools. However, you always know where Sears and Home Depot are, unlike the Snap-on truck.

You can save a bundle by buying the tool sets, but you often end up with extras. Read the list of items carefully, since you don't need SAE tools to work on metric machinery. The absolute best time to buy tools are around "guy holidays" like Father's Day, the Fourth of July, and Christmas. (No offense to female mechanics!) You can save as much as 50 percent if you plan your purchases wisely. Also, Craftsman has a tool club that offers monthly discounts to feed your addiction.

Basic Tools

Sockets and drivers: At the very least, you need a 3/8-inch ratchet and 8, 10, 12, 14, 17, and 19-mm sockets. You'll also need a couple of socket extenders and a universal joint. These represent the absolute, bare minimum selection. Ideally, you should have 1/4- and 1/2-inch ratchets and sockets too. The 1/4-inch ratchet needs correctly sized sockets ranging from 6 to 10 mm. A similar scope is recommended for 1/2-inch sockets, only at the big end of the spectrum in the 14- to 19-mm range. As you get further involved in wrenching, you'll find you need a set of deep sockets. Another nice addition is sockets with a universal joint built in. You'll be amazed at how much easier you can access exhaust manifold nuts and all sorts of fasteners tucked away in the bowels of your motorcycle. A good rule of thumb when buying tools is that if you find yourself needing a single socket or wrench you should buy a set. Why? Simple arithmetic. When you buy the second one, you have usually paid the bulk of the cost for the entire set. So, if you find yourself needing that 17-mm deep socket, you can bet that before too long you'll want the 19-mm or the 14-mm. Go ahead, you know you want the set anyway.

Torque wrenches: Another absolute must for a mechanic is a torque wrench-or two. You need a torque wrench because if you don't torque a fastener down tight enough, you risk having it vibrate loose. Go too far when tightening something, and you'll strip the threads or break the fastener. Torque wrenches

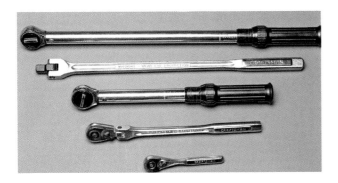

The more you get into wrenching, the more uses you'll find for different rachets. A nice, basic selection consists of (from top to bottom) a torque wrench in foot-pounds, 1/2-inch breaker bar, torque wrench in inch-pounds, 3/8-inch flex rachet, and 1/4-inch rachet.

come in a couple varieties. The least expensive (and least useful) is a wrench that has two bars. The first is the handgrip and the second is the pointer. As you tighten a bolt, you bend the bar with the handle, moving a gauge under the pointer. Don't waste your money on this type. You want to use a wrench that you can set the value you wish to torque a fastener to achieve. As you crank on the wrench, it will release with a click when you reach the specified torque. While you can buy torque wrenches with either foot-pounds or Newton-meters (SAE or metric), I recommend getting a torque wrench that has both measurement scales. Often, you will get instructions with one torque figure but not the other. A dual-scale wrench saves you from having to convert the figures. If you can only afford one torque wrench, get one ranging from 20 to 100 or more ft-lbs. Buy one in in-lbs (with a range up to 20 ft-lbs) as soon as you can. Motorcycle fasteners are expensive, so don't count on "feel" when you're wrenching.

When you're using a torque wrench, you still have to use common sense when tightening nuts. For example, torquing down the nuts securing a rear sprocket should be done in stages. Set your first torque value at about the halfway point, torque all the nuts in an alternating pattern, and then repeat at the full value. If you try to go for the full value at once, you can strip the studs embedded in the hub. Bigger nuts, such as axles, don't need the intermediary step. Also, unless otherwise stated, torque values are for dry threads. If you lubricate the threads, the lowered friction between the threads can allow you to exceed the recommended stretching force of the fastener, which can lead to damaged threads or broken fasteners.

One final word about torque wrenches: They are precise, expensive instruments. Don't use them as a breaker bar. It's tempting to turn the torque wrench all the way up and use the extra length to crack loose a stuck fastener. Unfortunately, you can ruin your torque wrench if you're not careful. Breaker bars have been designed solely for this purpose and are considerably cheaper, to boot. Although they're usually as long as a torque wrench, you can lengthen them with a piece of pipe for those times you need even more leverage. Just be careful not to twist the head right off the bolt.

Wrenches: You can't work on a motorcycle without a set of combination wrenches. Again you need them in the same sizes as the sockets mentioned above. Don't try to save money by buying wrenches that have two different-sized open ends on the same wrench. Combination wrenches have one open end and one closed end. The closed end has the same shape as a 12-point socket, making wrenching in tight places much easier than using the open end. As your collection expands, you'll find yourself lusting after a set of shorty combination wrenches. Give in to your desire. You'll be glad you did. When you're really flush with cash, buy yourself a big honkin' adjustable wrench. Your buddies at the track will tease you about needing a big tool. (Mine did.) You'll have the last laugh, though. A big adjustable wrench can help you loosen any variety of axle nuts you may run into. Those same friends will thank you when you save their bacon. Finally, stay away from the multitools you see advertised on TV. Most of them don't live up to their claims of fitting multiple sizes of nuts and bolts. Instead, they are equal-opportunity fastener manglers.

Motorcycle Mechanics Institute Metric Tool List

The Motorcycle Mechanics Institute (MMI) is one of the preeminent mechanic-training programs in the country. Included in every student's tuition is a tool voucher that is redeemed for a set of Snap-on tools once classes begin. Since MMI teaches factory-approved courses for all five of the major motorcycle manufacturers (Harley-Davidson, Honda, Kawasaki, Suzuki, and Yamaha), the selection of tools listed below should be considered the gold standard for what a mechanic needs to start off as a professional in the motorcycle industry. Anyone considering a career as a motorcycle mechanic would be hard pressed to find a better environment for nuts-and-bolts training than MMI—or a better source of the industry contacts necessary for finding a job wrenching.

MMI Metric Tool Set

3/8-inch ratchet	13-mm combination wrench
3/8-inch 10-mm socket	14-mm combination wrench
3/8-inch 12-mm socket	15-mm combination wrench
3/8-inch 13-mm socket	17-mm combination wrench
3/8-inch 14-mm socket	18-mm combination wrench
3/8-inch 15-mm socket	19-mm combination wrench
3/8-inch 17-mm socket	2-inch standard screwdriver
3/8-inch 18-mm socket	4-inch standard screwdriver
3/8-inch 19-mm socket	3-inch No. 1 Phillips screwdriver
3/8-inch 10-mm deep socket	4-inch No. 2 Phillips screwdriver
3/8-inch 12-mm deep socket	6-inch No. 3 Phillips screwdriver
3/8-inch 13-mm deep socket	Metric hex key (Allen) set
3/8-inch 14-mm deep socket	Pliers
3/8-inch 15-mm deep socket	Needle-nose pliers
3/8-inch 17-mm deep socket	16-ounce ball-peen hammer
3/8-inch 18-mm deep socket	Air pressure gauge
3/8-inch 19-mm deep socket	Feeler gauge set
3/8-inch No. 2 Phillips socket	Valve core tool
3/8-inch No. 3 Phillips socket	Socket rail and socket clips for 1/4- and
3/8-inch 3-inch extension	3/8-inch sockets
3/8-inch impact driver	Three-drawer toolbox
3/8-inch to 1/4-inch adapter	
1/4-inch ratchet	
1/4-inch 4-mm socket	
1/4-inch 5-mm socket	
1/4-inch 6-mm socket	
1/4-inch 7-mm socket	
1/4-inch 8-mm socket	
1/4-inch 9-mm socket	
1/4-inch 10-mm socket	
1/4-inch 11-mm socket	
1/4-inch 12-mm socket	
1/4-inch 13-mm socket	
1/4-inch 4-inch extension	
13/16-inch plug socket	
5/8-inch plug socket	
10-mm combination wrench	
11-mm combination wrench	
12-mm combination wrench	

Additional tools:

Scientific calculator
Safety glasses
Digital multitester

Reprinted with permission from the Motorcycle Mechanics Institute

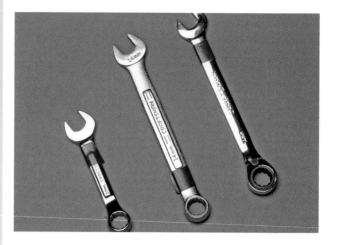

These wrenches are among my most commonly used tools. From right to left: stubby combination, regular combination, and ratcheting combination wrench.

Allen wrenches: While you can get by with a set of 3/8-inch Allen sockets, variety is a good thing to have in this class of tools. Personally, I prefer T-handle Allen keys for everything that doesn't require torquing. However, you'll find the time when you need an Allen socket with a ball end. These allow you to operate the tool at a slight angle to the bolt head, allowing you to access some truly evil locations. Until recently, Snap-on was the only vendor I could find that made ball-end Allen sockets. However, Sears has just started selling a non-Craftsman branded set. (Meaning: no lifetime warranty.) Since smaller Allen keys tend to wear out, you'll definitely want to make sure you have the warranty for your main set. Unfortunately, ball-end Allen keys tend to snap off if you get too aggressive with them. So, be careful and be prepared to buy more as they wear out.

Screwdrivers: This may sound crazy, but the shape of a screwdriver's grip plays an important role in how easy it is to use. Go to your local tool store and sample a few. Ones shaped with the natural curve of your palm with no edges to dig into your hand offer the best grip. The Craftsman Professional

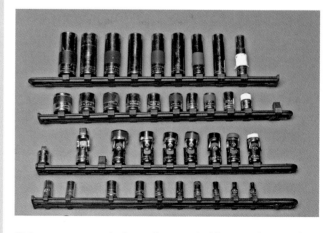

While you can survive with a basic socket set, each of these items has a specific use. Note the colored tape used to mark the most commonly used sizes for easy identification.

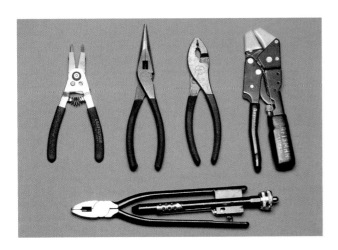

Each of these pliers fulfills a specific need: Circlip pliers, needle nose pliers, standard pliers, locking pliers, and safety-wire pliers. Note the Soft Jaws slipped over the teeth of the locking pliers to prevent them from marring delicate surfaces.

series of screwdrivers are my favorite. The grips are composed of a grippy, slightly soft material that makes it possible to really crank on a stubborn screw. When the tips wear out, just take them back for replacements. Buy a set with at least three sizes of both flat heads and Phillips heads. You'll also find jewelers screwdrivers invaluable for working with tiny parts-even helping to pry out ornery circlips.

Hammers: Be wary of any time you're tempted to reach for a hammer when working on a motorcycle. A good rule of thumb is: If you are breaking a sweat or considering using brute force on a part, stop what you're doing, step back from the bike, and make sure you're not overlooking something. Always use the muscle between your ears before you start flexing the ones in your arms. You'd be surprised how many times you find something little that's keeping you from your goal. Still, you will occasionally find that you need a hammer. A ball-peen hammer is ideal for rapping on an impact driver. You'll also find many uses for a rubber mallet or dead-blow hammer. Sometimes a little tap from one of these is just the trick for removing a stubborn side cover.

Pliers: While you should use a socket or a wrench to tighten and loosen fasteners, pliers have a multitude of uses. Invest in a quality set. You need, at least, one standard, one needle-nosed, and one arc-joint pliers. Locking pliers (Vise-Grips) are versatile and handy and can perform a variety of jobs. I've even pressed a chain master link into place with a pair when I had no other tools available. If you plan on safety-wiring your bike, invest in a set of locking safety-wire pliers.

Electrical tools: Troubleshooting electrical problems requires only a few tools. You need a good multimeter and continuity tester. In many cases, connectors are too far apart to use a continuity tester, and a homemade test light will do the trick. Also, you need a pair of wire cutters/strippers and a wire-crimping tool-although, for truly permanent connections, you should solder the wires together. Electrical tape and zip-ties will be called into action on more than just electrical jobs, so buy a bunch.

Drill: A hand drill-be it cordless or corded-plays a vital role in the home mechanic's toolkit. You'll also want to buy a variety of bits. Don't buy the supercheap ones either. (Unless, that is, you're buying bits for safety wiring, then get them by the dozen. They'll break before they dull.) A Unibit (with several stepped sizes on a single bit) makes mounting bodywork a breeze. If you plan on using your drill for extracting stuck fasteners, you'll need something that generates some torque. I alternate between a light-duty battery-powered drill for track use and a beefy corded model for major projects in the garage. As with any tool that spins, always wear safety glasses.

Impact driver: Sometimes the only way to remove a stripped screw or stuck bolt is to give an impact driver a good whack with a ball-peen hammer. The force of the blow presses the driver into the fastener, thereby increasing the friction available to the bit, which is being mechanically rotated by the impact. This is a brutal and inelegant, but somehow satisfying, tool . . . when it works. Wear eye protection.

Measuring tools: Most basic maintenance work can be done with just a steel metric ruler, tape measure, and feeler gauges. Once you move into more advanced projects, you'll find a dial or vernier caliper invaluable. If you're delving into your engine's internals, you definitely want to buy the higher-end models. While dial calipers are fairly easy to use, digital versions can often change from SAE to metric at the flip of a switch. Expect to spend some money on these. The same is true of dial indicators, which come in varying quality levels and measurement ranges. For most applications, a 1-inch range at 0.001-inch increments will suffice. For a dial indicator to work, it needs to be solidly mounted to something. A magnetic base works great for this.

Cutting tools: Sometimes you have to cut parts. If you don't have a rotary tool, a hacksaw makes removing an endless drive chain much easier. Also, a mat knife and other assorted blades will find frequent use in your garage. Files are also useful for deburring metal or plastic parts.

Toolbox: Big surprise, you need a place to keep your tools. Besides, it makes a great place to display all those stickers you get from the aftermarket companies when you buy their parts. While you can get by with a three-drawer toolbox with a basic tool set, you really need a way to organize your tools. Otherwise, you lose valuable wrenching time looking for a tool. Also, a great way to regain focus when you're stymied is to pick up the tools scattered around under the bike and return them to the toolbox while you noodle over what the problem is. So, get a freestanding rolling toolbox with a portable three- or four-drawer box on top of it. You can also buy a variety of shelves and other doodads to increase your workspace.

Little, necessary extras: You will never run out of little things (some obvious, some not) that make working on your bike easier. You'll need latex gloves. You're going to use some toxic chemicals, and your progeny will thank you for cleaning the parts, and not your hands, with contact cleaner. Also, a good set of work gloves will serve two purposes. You'll keep your hands cleaner-and stand a better chance of ever laying hands on your significant other again-and, like riding gloves, you'll have a better grip. While we're on the topic of hands, a tub of abrasive hand cleaner will make your transition from the garage to the dinner table a little easier.

Funnels of various sizes make fluid-related jobs easier. A big syringe lets you suck hydraulic fluid out of reservoirs or excess oil out of the crankcase if you overfill it. A dedicated oil drain pan is a must. It should seal so that you can take the dirty oil to a recycling center. A plastic dishwashing tub that will fit under your bike is nice for messy work. Similarly, small metal baking pans make sense for carburetors and other leaky parts while they sit on your workbench.

You never run out of uses for shop rags. While rags will come clean in a washing machine, you should just trash the dirtiest ones. Disposable shop towels work much better than regular paper towels. Also, during messy jobs, like changing oil, put something under your bike to catch the splatter. Newspaper will work in a pinch, but little parts can roll under individual sheets only to be thrown away with the paper. Finish Line makes a great rubber-backed work matt to put under your bike. When it gets dirty, take it to your local pressure wash and give it a good spray.

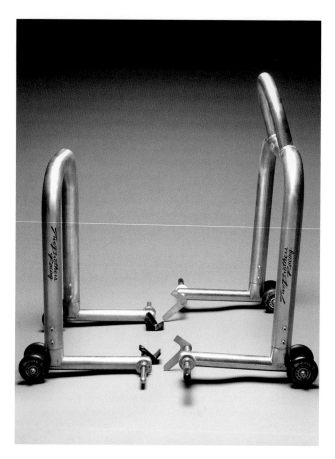

For many projects, you need a secure way of supporting your bike while you're working on it. Every sportbike enthusiast should have at least a set of front and rear stands.

You can fill up several shelves in your garage with the consumables you use regularly when working on your bike. These are some of the most important ones.

One drawer in your toolbox will most likely begin to collect the smaller necessities. Mine has X-Acto knives of varying styles, single-edged razor blades, Easy Out bolt extractors, and film canisters with miscellaneous nuts, bolts, washers, and cotter pins. I also have a collection of pens, pencils, Sharpies, and even grease pencils. Notepads are vital to keeping track of the order in which you removed parts. Paper tape (often found in photographic-supply stores) works great for labeling parts and wires without leaving a sticky residue when you remove it. Also, a box of plastic sandwich bags will help you group parts when you remove them. Take the time to label the bags. You'd be amazed what you can forget overnight.

Bike supports: In a perfect world, we'd all have pneumatic bike lifts to raise our machines to a comfortable working height. The reality is that simple front and rear stands offer the stability for the majority of our basic maintenance chores.

As your skills advance, you'll find that you need to support your bike with the suspension off it, so regular stands won't work. The Craftsman motorcycle jack (bottom) can lift your bike almost two feet off the ground. You will need to fabricate some wooden chocks to fit between the bike and jack. The Kawasaki bike jack (top) has a variety of adapters that mount on the top posts of the jack, enabling the jack to be used for multiple purposes.

However, some instances will require you to support your bike without those stands. Sears sells a hydraulic motorcycle jack that can work quite well, although you may need to fashion some chocks to keep the stand from pressing on vulnerable exhaust headers. Kawasaki sells a jack that can also support a variety of bikes via a selection of adapters. Home mechanics have survived for years using a piece of wood and a scissor jack bought from a salvage yard. If you choose this method, make sure you have a backup system, like a tie-down thrown over a garage rafter, to keep gravity from winning over.

Nice-but-Not-Necessary Extras

Work light: A variety of compact fluorescent units are available today. So, there's no reason you should ever have to use the annoying hot ones that rely on household lightbulbs. If you don't burn yourself on the metal housing, you'll probably drop it and break the filament at an inopportune time. Fluorescents are lightweight, cool, and tough.

Parts washer: Many maintenance tasks require cleaning parts as an initial step. Hunching over the utility sink in your garage is tedious work. Consider buying a parts washer. While full-service shops have parts washers that sit on top of 50-gallon drums and pump cleaning fluid into a basin, you can buy a much less expensive home washer. Finish Line has a self-contained washer that holds a citrus-based solvent that you pump into a little tub with a hand-sprayer. When you're done cleaning, pull the plug and let the dirty solvent mix back with the rest inside the washer. When not in use, the washer can stand on end under your workbench.

Vise: While the need might not seem obvious at first, a bench-mounted vise plays a vital role in fork and shock work. If you drill nuts and bolts for safety wire, you'll want a vise. Aluminum soft jaws are a nice addition.

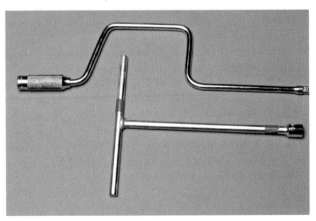

When you have several nuts or bolts to remove, a speed wrench or T-handle socket will speed things up tremendously. Which of these you choose depends on personal preference.

T-handle sockets or speed wrench: Removing a series of bolts goes much easier with a tool that allows you to spin it. Look in the pits at a national race, and you'll see T-handle sockets or speed wrenches. The T-handle allows you to spin

a nut free by holding the center and spinning the T. A speed wrench operates in a similar way by giving you a rotating end and a handle in the middle to crank. Once you get used to either of these tools, ratchets seem painfully slow.

Tap and die set: Threads get stripped or damaged, but often you can clean them up with a tap or die. When all else fails, you can drill out the hole and tap it with the next-larger-sized threads. Tapping oil will make these tools last longer.

Screw removal kit: Sooner or later fasteners break, and you'll have several options available to you. The ubiquitous Easy Out has been around for years, and when it works, can save your hide. Be forewarned, though, when an Easy Out breaks, you'll usually need to take the damaged part to a machine shop. Craftsman has recently introduced a line of Drill-Out extractors. These tools, on my initial experience, offer a solid alternative to Easy Outs. Craftsman's Bolt-Out removers that fit over the heads of nuts and bolts are also particularly effective.

Rotary tool: From grinding off the rivets on a chain to trimming your aftermarket fairing to deburring drilled parts to cutting the heads off of stripped fasteners, a rotary tool and a variety of cutting wheels and grinding stones will see more use than you can imagine. Don't forget eye protection.

Pop rivet gun: This versatile tool can help you repair crash damage quickly at the track. Some exhaust systems need to be reriveted after repacking the canister.

Air compressor: At the very least, you want a refillable 3- to 5-gallon auxiliary air tank in your garage to top off your tires before a ride. But forget about necessity: Have you ever seen how excited mechanics get over air tools? So, for a basic garage setup, you need about a 15-gallon-capacity compressor and 150-psi maximum pressure. The most important specification is the Standard Cubic Feet per Minute (SCFM) rating. Check to make sure that your compressor can handle your tools' requirements. However, you can get by on

You'll know you're really getting into wrenching when you decide you can't live without a set of air tools. Start with the basics: a compressor, a rachet, an impact driver, a blower and an air chuck.

the low side of the requirements for intermittent use such as a ratchet and impact driver. Painting, on the other hand, requires that your compressor be able to exceed the requirements. If you can't afford a complete air setup, cordless ratchets and corded electric impact drivers are available.

Specialty tools: Depending on how far you get into this wrenching habit, you'll also find yourself collecting narrowly focused tools. At the top of the list would be a chain breaker/rivet tool. Although the initial price may seem steep, consider how many chains you'll replace in your riding career. A bead breaker and wheel-balancing tool also fall into this category-only a little further down the list. Specialty tools aren't all expensive, though. Fork oil level tools, for example, come in a wide range of prices. Throughout this book, I've listed the tools required for a particular task in the "Tools" section at the beginning of each project.

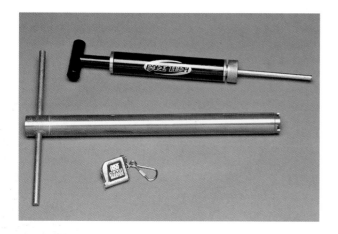

If you are planning to tune your bike's suspension, you'll probably need these: an oil-height tool, a fork cartridge tool, and the all important Sag Master.

Some jobs require extremely specialized tools. For example, to change your own tires and balance the wheels you'll need this collection of tire irons, bead breaker and balancer.

GENERAL MAINTENANCE

Maintenance chores need to be executed on a daily, weekly, monthly, yearly, or mileage basis, and although they rank fairly low in the sex-appeal department, a properly maintained motorcycle is the cornerstone of all the performance projects contained in this book. Now that you've begun by outfitting your garage with the right tools, you're ready for the next step. Most of these tasks require little wrenching experience and offer a great opportunity to help you get your feet wet—and your hands dirty. Even old pros might want to take a gander here to see if they've overlooked something they could add to their maintenance routine.

Preride Check

Time: 2 minutes

Tools: Tire pressure gauge

Talent:

Cost: None

Parts Required: None

Tip: Make this part of your routine and you'll minimize surprises.

PERFORMANCE GAIN: A fully functional motorcycle ready for whatever modifications you have in mind.

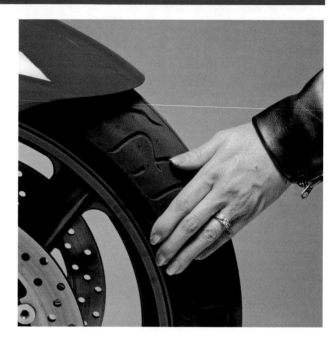

A quick visual check of your tires every time you park or get on your bike will help you spot that piece of metal in the tread before it has a chance to puncture the carcass.

Some people may question whether a preride check is a performance project. The simple reality is that if your bike is not in top condition, your performance is already suffering; all the modifications in the world won't help that. The condition of a motorcycle degrades over time and with use. Without daily, specific attention, the gradual shift in the performance of your bike's most basic systems can occur without you noticing. The lazy or overconfident riders among us may argue that a preride check takes too much time and that they just "wanna ride." However, when performed correctly and regularly, the process takes no more time than it does to don a jacket and helmet.

Start with the simple stuff as you approach your motorcycle. Do you see any fluid drips on the pavement? Does the fork look free of any leakage? Can you see anything stuck in the tire tread that could lead to a problem? (If your bike is cable locked, removing the cable is an opportunity to get a closer view of the tires.)

When was the last time you checked tire pressure? Do they look and feel like they're getting low? Motorcycles ridden regularly only need to have tire pressure checked twice a week or so—as long as they get a visual inspection of the tread condition before every ride. Bikes that sit for several days should have their tire pressure checked before hitting the streets. Finally, check your tires with a quick glance every time you park your bike. Not only do you get to see how far you cranked it over on that canyon run, but you may also notice the nail you picked up riding past a construction site.

Take a look at your chain. Does it need to be adjusted? Give it a quick test with your toe. Also, this is a good time to check your oil level, since it's all down in the oil pan. If your bike's engine has a sight glass, stand your bike so that it is level. The more fastidious will be tempted to use a rear stand to make sure the bike is straight up and down, but this raises the rear of the bike too high, giving an inaccurate reading. At the bare minimum, you should check your oil once a week.

Before starting the engine, test any controls operated by cables. A cable will rarely fail all at once. Instead, cables usually fray progressively until a complete breakage occurs. And by operating the controls with the engine off, you will notice the subtle but telltale grinding feel of torn strands. Another sign is a more difficult-to-operate throttle or one that must be closed manually instead of by the spring on the butterfly valves. By slowly rolling on the throttle a couple of times and squeezing the clutch lever, you can, in a matter of seconds, ascertain that the cables are in good working condition.

As you throw your leg over the seat, give the front brake lever a healthy squeeze. Is the pressure the same as yesterday? Does the lever come down to the grip? Give the rear brake pedal a press to see how it's doing.

Now you're ready to start the engine. While it warms up, check all your lights. In a garage, the job is easy. Just look at the light on the walls in front and behind you as you cycle through the high beam, low beam, front running lights, left and right turn signals, rear running light, and the brake light.

You'd be surprised how many bikes are out on the road with improper tire pressure. Having the right amount of air in your tires will improve your bike's handling and help you get the maximum life out of your tires. Improper pressure can lead to excessive wear or, in the worst-case scenario, tire failure.

If you're outside, holding a hand in front of the various lights will enable you to see their operation. Don't forget to check the brake lever and pedal individually to see that both trigger the stop lamp.

If you make this process part of preparing for a ride, you will find yourself checking automatically—just the way you reach for your motorcycle boots before a ride. Do it often enough, and you'll save yourself time and headaches—such as knowing you're on reserve *before* heading out for a ride.

Without brakes, you're dead. All it takes is a couple of test squeezes every time you mount your bike.

Roll the throttle on and off before starting the engine. After the second roll-on, release the grip to see if the throttle snaps closed. If not, don't ride until the problem is remedied.

Adjust Controls to Fit Rider

 Time: 1 hour

 Tools: Basic mechanical tools and rear stand

 Talent:

 Cost: None

 Parts Required: Possibly aftermarket replacements for the controls

 Tip: When you alter the controls, make sure the new position doesn't interfere with the operation of the motorcycle.

 PERFORMANCE GAIN: A more comfortable rider and, therefore, better control of the motorcycle.

No one should be surprised that consumer products come with certain compromises—one product must suit the maximum number of people. Motorcycles are no different. Riders come in a variety of shapes and sizes, so the OEMs (original equipment manufacturers) must determine the spatial arrangement of controls based on a complicated equation of performance, comfort, and a range of body types. Thus, the OEMs create an "average" rider for each model of sportbike.

What is that average? Is it based on Japanese median sizes, or American? Is the model directed primarily for the on-track market, or does it have a more real-world street environment in mind? How do you, and your plans for using your bike, compare to these averages?

Once you roll a bike off the showroom floor or pick it up used from another rider, average setups no longer apply to that particular machine. They should apply to you. In order to work in harmony with your dimensions and skills, some simple adjustments to the components you use to control the bike will make a huge difference in your riding enjoyment.

To get a feel for the current state of your bike, put it on a rear stand and get into your riding position. What type of riding do you do? Commuting and around town? Sit in a comfortable position for this riding. Mostly canyons? Then crouch down a bit. Do you have a different sport-touring position? When you extend your fingers flat from their natural position on the grips, do your fingers land right on top of the levers? Will raising or lowering them help you to operate them? Do you strain to reach the levers themselves? Maybe you need to adjust their distance from the grip. What about the positions of your feet? You get the picture.

Starting with the front brake, look at your wrist position when you cover the lever. If your wrist is tilted back awkwardly, you'll need to lower the lever. Loosen the two bolts on the master cylinder clamp and rotate the lever *slightly* down. Check your position again. Don't go too far down or you'll make it just as difficult to operate the brake as having the lever too high.

Although most of the current sportbikes come with adjustable brake levers, some older bikes and less exotic sporty bikes (GS500 and Ninja 250, for example) do not. If you find your reach to the lever is longer than you'd like, check the levers of other bikes or those from the same manufacturer. Often, one

Your ability to brake and control the throttle simultaneously can be dramatically affected by the brake lever position. If it's too high (left), your wrist is bent into an awkward position. If it's too low, the lever could make it difficult to fully close the throttle while applying the brake. Note the difference between the wrist positions when the brake lever is too high versus the proper height (right).

Little adjustments make big changes, so try moving the shifter a bit at a time, testing its position in the garage. Once you think it's right, go for a ride and take notes on how the changes improved the shifting. Or, better yet, toss a couple of wrenches in your tank bag and play with the position on a longer ride.

pedal so low that it drags in corners on track days, so don't go too crazy. If you feel the pedal is already too low, you may find controlling brake pressure is easier with the pedal raised slightly higher. Riders on bikes with drum brakes (yep, they're out there) can adjust the height with a bolt, but don't forget to reset the pedal free play by turning the nut at the end of the brake rod and drum. After any change to the brake pedal, check the brake light operation and adjust the switch if necessary.

As a rule, shift levers tend to have a bit more adjustability than brake pedals. Perhaps it's to allow for different styles of riding. Nevertheless, a properly adjusted shifter enables you to shift up or down without lifting your foot off the peg. You need to be careful when preparing to adjust the rod length of the shifter. Look closely at the threads above the locknut. One end of the rod is reverse threaded. Why? Well, you'll see once both locknuts are loosened. Raising or lowering the shifter is as easy as rotating the rod with a wrench or a pair of pliers. The reverse threads are what make this possible. Once you're happy with the position, check to make sure that plenty of threads remain engaged in the ball joints, and be sure to tighten the locknuts. If you don't, the rod may vibrate loose and possibly strand you 70 miles from home in third gear.

The adjustments listed here are just the beginning of the ways you can make your bike fit you better. Perhaps the footpegs aren't in the right position. Look for some adjustable rearsets. Too little wind protection? Take a gander at some of the aftermarket windscreens. Raising or lowering seat heights can be accomplished with either some creative foam trimming or a call to a seat manufacturer. Grips too hard or too soft? A world of options awaits you. Your interface with your bike improves not only your control, but also your comfort—which means you can ride longer too.

will fit. Another approach is to buy aftermarket items from companies such as Lockhart Phillips or Flanders. You may be surprised to find adjustable aftermarket levers made specifically for your bike.

Clutch levers are a little bit easier to adjust without any fancy aftermarket stuff. If your bike doesn't have an adjustable clutch lever, try loosening the thumb screw locknut where the cable enters the lever housing. Then simply screw the adjuster in, increasing the clutch lever's free play. Be forewarned that excessive free play can keep the clutch plates from fully disengaging and contribute to premature clutch wear—not to mention clunky gear changes.

While most of the clip-on handlebars on current sportbikes are affixed to both the fork legs and the triple clamps, some clip-ons can have their angle adjusted by simply loosening the pinch bolts and rotating the bar into its new position. If you find that the inward angle of the clip-ons makes you uncomfortable or strains your wrists, you may want to try altering the clip-on orientation outward to allow straighter access to the grips. When changing the bar location or angle, be sure to consider the tank, fairing, or instrument cluster clearance. Suppose you're riding your bike on a canyon road and decide to give the throttle a good twist entering a straight. A head shake that would normally be nothing to worry about could really hurt if you have the clip-ons in the wrong place and crunch your thumbs on the tank.

Foot controls are another consideration. Your riding style or the size of your feet may influence where the optimum pedal position is. The brake pedal needs to be low enough that you can cover it comfortably while you ride. If your ankle feels kinked after just a few minutes, try lowering the pedal. Hydraulic brakes usually allow the pedal to be adjusted on the master cylinder. Loosen the locknut and turn the bolt to lower the pedal. Remember, you don't want to adjust the

Notice how the rider's boot is in a comfortable position covering the brake pedal. Now, imagine commuting for 40 minutes with the brake covered. Would you rather have your foot in this position or bent upward?

PROJECT 3

Checking Vital Fluids

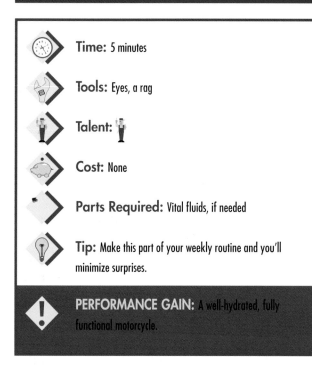

Time: 5 minutes

Tools: Eyes, a rag

Talent: 👤

Cost: None

Parts Required: Vital fluids, if needed

Tip: Make this part of your weekly routine and you'll minimize surprises.

! PERFORMANCE GAIN: A well-hydrated, fully functional motorcycle.

The secret to getting an accurate view of the fluid level from a master cylinder with an integrated reservoir is to turn the bar until the reservoir is as level as possible. Don't be concerned if the reading drops over time. The brake pads are wearing which requires more hydraulic fluid in the calipers. However, if the reading gets below the recommended height, check the brake pads before topping off the reservoir from a fresh container.

As motorcycles have gotten more reliable, many riders have become a bit lax in their preventive maintenance. The reason is obvious: When things usually work the way they are supposed to, we don't worry so much about checking for signs of impending failure. Still, if you consider the potential consequences of a major mechanical failure, you'll see the importance of spending a few minutes every week or so to make sure that all your bike's Precious Bodily Fluids are in satisfactory condition and available in enough quantity to do their job. After all, most of these checks require only a cursory glance.

You've probably heard the old saw about oil and internal combustion engines: Only two things matter when it comes to motor oil—so the saying goes. Make sure there is oil in the engine, and change it every now and then. While the problems with this argument won't be addressed at this point, the statements are true on the most basic level. You don't want to run your high-revving, manufactured-to-aerospace-tolerances, and extremely-expensive-to-replace engine without the proper lubricant.

Motor oil can give you important information about your engine's internal condition. If you check its oil daily or—at the bare minimum—weekly, you are more likely to notice symptoms of little problems before they get bigger. Back in the not-so-distant past when most bikes had center stands, a rider could glance at the engine's sight glass while strolling up to the bike before a ride. Today's lightened and compacted packages eschew frivolities like center stands.

Consequently, we have to work a bit harder to ascertain the status of the slippery stuff.

Before checking your bike's oil level, make sure the engine is warmed to operating temperature. Allow the oil to drain down from the top end by waiting a few minutes after shutting off the engine. Bikes with a sight glass require that you either have a good sense of balance, be double-jointed, or both. While holding the bike level—either from the saddle or beside the bike—look at the window conveniently located on the bottom of the engine to make sure the oil level is between the two marks on the case. For engines with a dipstick, check your owner's manual to make certain how the stick is to be inserted for an accurate reading. Usually, you will wipe the stick and insert it into the case until it makes contact with the filler plug's threads. Be sure the plug is straight or you may get an inaccurate reading.

So, how did the oil look when you checked it? Nice and amber like the day it was poured out of the bottle? Or was it dark black? The oil may need to be changed. Was it milky white? You've got coolant in the oil and a potentially major problem in your engine. Does it smell like gas? Another big deal is in the works.

Coolant is almost as vital to your bike's engine as oil. Run your engine without some kind of coolant and you risk extensive damage. (Yes, there are *true* stories of hapless racers who've run several laps around the high banks of Daytona with dry cooling systems and done no measurable damage to the engine, but would you like to gamble with your $10,000 investment?) A regular, cursory glance at the coolant overflow

Reading the fluid level on the rear brake of the R6 is easy. It's hanging out in the open on the subframe. Some sportbikes tuck the reservoir away behind bodywork, requiring you to look through a slot to view the reservoir.

The oil level on this bike is pretty obvious. Look a little closer to check the condition of the oil. To read the sight glass correctly, the bike must be held level on flat ground.

tank will tell you if everything is working right. You want the level to lie between the high and low marks when the engine is cold. The color should be a lovely fluorescent green. If oil or a rust-colored hue appears in the coolant, your engine may be telling you it has a problem that needs attention.

Similarly, your hydraulic fluid reservoirs need to be checked periodically. With the bike level, the fluid level should fall between the factory markings. Brake and clutch master cylinders with integrated reservoirs have sight glasses allowing you to view the contents. While checking the fluid levels, be sure to check the color of the fluid, which is usually clear with a slight yellowish tint. If you see any other color, you should flush the system before contaminants damage the hydraulic internals. The white plastic remote reservoirs should not be opened to check the color of the contents—hydraulic fluid absorbs moisture from the air. You can get a good idea of the brake fluid color through the plastic. Don't forget to check the rear brake system, which usually has the reservoir tucked away behind the bodywork.

Humans can only go a few days without fluids. Motorcycles aren't much better. Keep your bike hydrated and help it live a long, long time.

Although it is hard to read in this photo, the coolant level in the expansion tank is right where it should be. If you check your antifreeze frequently, you will notice when it starts to drop, signaling a leak somewhere in the system.

PROJECT 4

Rolling Gear Look-Over

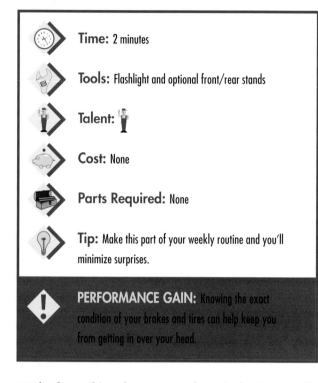

Time: 2 minutes

Tools: Flashlight and optional front/rear stands

Talent:

Cost: None

Parts Required: None

Tip: Make this part of your weekly routine and you'll minimize surprises.

PERFORMANCE GAIN: Knowing the exact condition of your brakes and tires can help keep you from getting in over your head.

The funny thing about wear and tear is that it generally happens slowly over time. Just like the frog that will jump out of a pot of hot water, but remain in a pot of water that's being gradually heated, we don't tend to notice small changes as they develop into big ones. You should make a rolling gear inspection at least once a week. Your brakes, suspension, and tires keep you on the road and deserve extra attention. If you don't provide it, you may run into a problem that makes your blood boil.

The most powerful force on a motorcycle is its braking system. Think about it: Your bike can accelerate from 0 to 60 in three seconds. Cut the time in half for braking. So, with a system this powerful—upon which your life depends—you don't want to come to a panic-stop situation and grab a handful of front brake only to find no pressure at the lever! Another undesirable scenario is hearing the screech of metal on metal as the last bits of brake pad material give way to its unforgiving backing. You're getting the picture, right?

Begin your brake check by looking at all the pads. This may sound easier than it actually is, though. With today's tightly packed front ends, getting your head in a position to see the pads is more of a contortionist's skill. To view the pads, try using a flashlight to sight along the disc. Some people resort to removing the calipers or covers. You want to look at the pads on both sides of the caliper. Do they have the minimum 2 to 3 mm of friction material or less? Replace them. If you've let the pads get down to 1 mm, you're skating

on dangerously thin ice. Once they arrive at the bitter end, brake pads have difficulty shedding heat and may fade on you when you need them most. Have the pads worn evenly? If not, you may have a problem with the caliper. (You've always wanted to learn how to inspect and rebuild calipers, right?) Don't forget to check the rear brake pads too.

While you're down on your hands and knees, give the rubber brake and clutch lines a quick flex to see if they're beginning to crack. While incidents of hydraulic lines rupturing are rare, a failure of the line will render either component inoperable. Although we've all wondered what it would be like to race on the Grand Prix circuit, do we really want to experience the thoughts Eddie Lawson must have had as he approached Laguna Seca's turn two at warp speed to find that the front brake wasn't working?

You can use this low-angle view of your bike to make a couple of other quick inspections. Despite the fact that the manufacturers do a good job of protecting the delicate parts of the fork, the sliders occasionally get dinged. Over time, the rough part on the slider will eat away at the fork's seal, leading to the annoying drip of fork oil seepage. In its most minor form, a weeping fork seal is nothing more than a messy nuisance, but it can quickly develop into a hazardous mess—particularly in the traditional fork arrangement, where the oil can contaminate the brake disc surface and brake pads — bringing us back to the Eddie Lawson nightmare. The shock can also develop its own leaks. A quick glance at the shock shaft with a flashlight will give you a visual clue as to whether it's time for a rebuild.

If you're going to get a glimpse of the brake pads, don't be afraid to get personal with your tires. The signs of problems are pad material less than 2 to 3 mm thick or uneven pad wear. If you see any fluid seepage around the calipers, one of the pistons may need its seals replaced.

Give the rubber portions of the hydraulic lines a bend to see if they're still flexible. If you notice any cracks, consider replacing them with shiny new braided stainless steel ones.

Wide rear wheels make the task of checking the pads a bit difficult. Get creative with your viewing angle.

The final stop in the tour of your bike's rolling gear is the tires. Although you take a glance at the visible portion of the tires every time you walk up to your bike (right?), a thorough inspection requires that you check the entire surface of both tires. Popping front and rear stands under the bike will make the process quicker (and allow you to easily check if the brakes are dragging), but you can make a complete inspection by rolling the bike forward a couple of feet at a time. You're looking for any foreign objects that may be lodged in the tire. If you find something, carefully pull it out. Check to see if the hole is leaking by rubbing a little saliva over the opening. If it bubbles, repair or replace the tire. If it doesn't bubble, still keep an eye on it for a few days. You may also find cuts in the tread caused by running over road debris. Closely inspect the depth of the slice to make sure it doesn't go deep enough to expose the cords. Slices on the sidewall are particularly dangerous. If you have any, have a professional look at the tire.

Finally, look inside the sipes (grooves) in the tire's tread. Tire manufacturers make it easy for you to gauge when a tire is worn to the point that it needs to be discarded. Spaced at regular intervals in the sipes you'll find little humps in the rubber. These "wear bars" should be below the top of the groove. If their tops are flush with the tread blocks, you need to replace your tires. Even if the wear bars aren't flush with the tread, you may want to replace the tires a bit early, especially if you have a long trip planned—say, to the American Motor Association (AMA) Nationals. Don't be cheap and try to nurse the absolute maximum mileage out of your tires. The shallow depth of the tread decreases the tire's ability to shed water on wet roads, as well as things like dirt or sand on the road surface. Also, the folks who build tires will tell you that the bulk of tire failures occur in the last 10 percent of the tire's life. If you think new tires are expensive, go take a look at the cost of replacement bodywork.

A new, just-scuffed-in tire will look like this. Note how deep into the sipe the wear bar lives.

While you try to find the wear bar, consider why this tire was on an F3 in a salvage yard. The center of the tread is worn down to the bottom of the sipes, giving the tire a square profile that could unsettle the bike when leaned over.

Adjusting Clutch and Throttle Free Play

Time: 30 minutes

Tools: Phillips screwdriver, open end wrenches, and maybe needle-nosed pliers

Talent:

Cost: None

Parts Required: None

Tip: If you run out of adjustment up at the lever, try adjusting the cables at the other end.

PERFORMANCE GAIN: Precise throttle control gives you maximum flexibility in the on/off/on throttle scenarios you encounter when entering a corner, or riding a series of them.

Rock the grip back and forth to measure the throttle free play. Use a metric tape measure for an accurate reading.

One hallmark of a skilled rider is the ability to precisely deliver the right amount of throttle at the right time. Smooth transitions on and off the throttle play a vital role in keeping the chassis stable in a corner. Since the throttle cables are the direct link between your hand and the butterfly valves in the mixers, minimizing slop in the system will pay big dividends.

To check the throttle free play, hold the grip between your fingers and roll it back and forth until you begin to feel the pull of the cable. Pick a spot on the grip and watch it to measure the free play. If you have trouble visualizing the measurement, hold a metric tape measure up to the grip. Most factory manuals will tell you that 2 to 3 mm is the correct amount of throttle free play.

Once you've determined that the free play needs adjustment, loosen the locking nut(s) near the throttle grip. Some bikes will only have one adjuster. For two-adjuster models, loosen the nuts until there is plenty of slack. Next, tighten the deceleration adjuster (the cable that pulls the grip into the throttle-closed position) so that there is no slack when the throttle is held closed. Tighten the deceleration locking nut. Now, adjust the acceleration cable's adjuster until the desired amount of free play is present in the grip and tighten its locking nut. Ensure that there are plenty of threads (at least three) engaged in the adjuster body. If you can't get the proper amount of free play with the

adjusters, see Project 6 for directions on adjusting the cables at the carburetors.

Food for thought: While 2 to 3 mm of free play may be the factory spec, many riders prefer even less free play, giving them the feeling of a seamless connection to the carburetors or injector housings. Experiment with different free play amounts to find the setting that suits your riding style. A word of warning about using less free play than the factory specifies: If the throttle cables are too tight, they can cause the throttle to stick or not close completely, so check thoroughly by rolling the throttle open and releasing it from a variety of settings. Finally, run the engine at idle speed and turn the handlebar to both the right and the left to make sure that the engine speed does not change. If it does, check the cable routing and free play again.

The clutch lever free play adjustment also can accommodate various rider preferences and hand sizes. To measure the free play, pull in the clutch lever to take up the slack in the cable. Now measure the gap between the clutch lever holder and the lever itself. Again, most manufacturers recommend 2 to 3 mm of free play.

To adjust the free play, loosen the knurled lock screw (if present) on the clutch lever holder. Now, unscrew the adjuster for less slack or screw it in for more slack. Riders with smaller hands will probably want to have a bit more slack than those with larger hands. Depending on where the clutch engages in the lever travel, you may want to adjust it to engage at a different

Set the free play with the cable adjusters on the throttle cables. If the bike has two adjusters, set the deceleration cable first.

Take up the slack in the clutch cable and measure the gap between the lever holder and the lever.

point. If you give the lever extra free play, make sure that the clutch releases fully when the lever is pulled all the way in. If it doesn't, your ability to shift smoothly will be compromised, and the transmission will undergo unnecessary stress when you downshift. If the free play is less than the recommended amount, the clutch may not fully engage, causing clutch slip and premature clutch wear.

Sometimes cable stretch makes it impossible for you to get the proper clutch free play. If this happens, turn the adjuster on the lever holder so that 5 to 6 mm of the thread is visible. Next, adjust the slack at the lower end of the cable. Slide the cable dust cover out of the way, if there is one. Loosen the nuts as far as they will go. Now, pull the cable tight by sliding it inside the bracket. Tighten the nuts firmly enough that they will not vibrate loose, and return the dust cover to its proper position. The free play can now be adjusted by the screw at the lever. You've just officially outsmarted your motorcycle.

Loosen the nuts holding the bottom end of the clutch cable (shown here out of the bracket for clarity). Pull the cable tight and retighten the nuts.

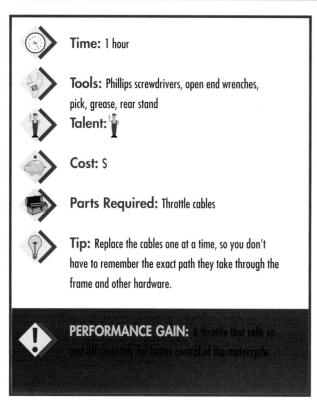

PROJECT 6

Replacing Throttle Cables

Time: 1 hour

Tools: Phillips screwdrivers, open end wrenches, pick, grease, rear stand

Talent: 🕴

Cost: $

Parts Required: Throttle cables

Tip: Replace the cables one at a time, so you don't have to remember the exact path they take through the frame and other hardware.

PERFORMANCE GAIN: A throttle that rolls on and off smoothly for better control of the motorcycle.

Your throttle cables form the vital connection between your wrist and the power delivered to the rear wheel. Get ham-fisted midcorner, and your sportbike could give you a nice view from 10 feet in the air. Consequently, a smooth hand and smooth operation of the throttle cables themselves are vital. If your throttle shows any signs of notchiness or becomes difficult to twist, you probably need new cables. Also, if you've lowered your clip-ons significantly, you may want to install shorter cables to keep them from rubbing against other components.

Begin by placing your bike securely on a rear stand to prevent accidentally knocking it off the side stand. Remove the tank and any bodywork that will interfere with your access to cables. On some bikes you may need to remove or disassemble the air box to reach the bell crank. Other components, like the radiator on this R6, may need to be loosened to allow the cables' adjusters to fit through the tight space.

Before disassembling the throttle, loosen all of the cables' adjusters to gain maximum free play. Unscrew the throttle's plastic cover and fold it back out of the way, being careful not to pinch the wires or stress any of the connectors for the kill switch and starter button. If you don't have enough free play, use a pick or small screwdriver to lift the cable into position to allow the fitting to slide out of the throttle grip body. Once one cable is free, the second one will be simple.

Resist the urge to remove both cables at once. While you may have a photographic memory, something may pull you away from this job, leaving you to decipher the line drawings in the service manual. In the tight confines of sportbikes, if you do not run the cables in the proper path, they may bind when you turn the bars or, worse, cause the bike to rev. Removing the cables one at a time will leave a path for you to follow while inserting the new ones.

When sliding the fittings into their positions, lube them as described in Project 7, since they move around in the mounting holes. Giving the cables a quick squirt of lubricant wouldn't be a bad idea either. Remove the throttle grip and give the clip-on a wipe and a spritz of WD-40 for lubricant. Once you have the cables run in the proper path, both ends secured, and the throttle body reassembled, set the adjuster near the throttle to the middle of its range. Now, adjust the free play to your liking with the locknuts down by the carburetor. Any final fine-tuning to get the free play to your to your personal preferences can be done at the throttle grip end. Using this method is time consuming, but pays dividends when you need to correct the free play in the future. When you are satisfied with the cable settings, tighten the locknuts firmly to prevent them from vibrating loose.

Check the cable routing one last time, and turn the bars from lock to lock to make sure nothing binds. Once you have the bike back together, warm up the engine and set the idle speed to the factory specification. One last time, turn the bars from lock to lock with the engine running to make sure that the idle speed doesn't change. If you're happy with it, stop wrenching and go ride.

Even with the cable adjusters loosened all the way, you may need to use a pick to help get the fitting free of the grip.

Space is tight, so exercise a little patience to get the cables free of the carburetors.

Sometimes you can use the idle speed adjuster (right) to move the bell crank into a position that makes removing the fitting a little easier.

Even if you didn't change the idle speed while swapping cables, you'll need to set the idle to the operating temperature spec.

General Lubrication

Time: 30 minutes

Tools: Assorted wrenches, cable lubrication tool, cable lube, chain lube, chain cleaner, molybdenum-based grease, WD-40, small paintbrush

Talent:

Cost: $

Parts Required: None

Tip: Lube the chain when it is warm for maximum penetration.

In most owner's manuals, the maintenance chart lists general lubrication as one of the activities. Since few people actually read their owner's manual, and even fewer follow the periodic maintenance intervals, some important motorcycle parts degrade quicker due to simple neglect. For the average rider, lubing your bike three times a season (the beginning, middle, and end) will suffice. If you ride the wheels off your motorcycle, give it a quick lube job every 7,500 miles. By performing this simple maintenance on a regular basis, you prolong the life of the bike's components, ensure that everything works the way it should, and may even catch a problem as it starts.

Lubing your motorcycle's cables should take no more than 15 minutes, and pays dividends every time you operate a control. For the throttle cables, unscrew the throttle housing on the grip and adjust the cables for maximum slack. After you release one of the cables, the other will slip right off. For the clutch cable, screw the adjuster all the way in for maximum slack but line up the slot in the adjuster with the slot of the lever holder. You should be able to pull the end of the cable free of the adjuster and release the cable.

For quick work on the cables, nothing beats a pressure cable luber from accessory companies like Motion Pro or Lockhart Phillips. Basically, you clamp a rubber stopper over one end of the cable, insert a tube from a can of silicon-based cable lubricant into a little hole, and give the nozzle a squeeze. The can's pressure forces the lubricant through the cable. Apply the lubricant in short bursts until the bottom end of the cable begins to bubble or drip. A well-placed rag can catch the drips before they make a mess of the engine.

Before you reassemble each cable, be sure to apply a dab of grease to all the places the cable might rub. The fittings at the cable ends need grease, and any exposed sections of the cable should receive a protective coating too. A small paintbrush will help you grease parts in tight places.

Don't forget the choke cable or the speedometer cable. Lubricate the choke cable like all the others. Mechanical speedometer cables (a dying breed on sportbikes) should be unhooked from the speedometer. Pull out the inner cable and pack the cable top with molybdenum grease. Slide the cable back into place. Any time the front wheel is removed, pack some moly grease into the drive mechanism.

Now go over your bike and lubricate every part that moves. Unscrew the handlebar lever pivots and brush on some grease. Apply a couple drops of oil to the side stand pivot. Give the rider and passenger pegs a quick squirt of WD-40 or oil. Remove the shifter pivot and clean any grit out of the works. Apply grease to the pivot, but be sure to keep the pivot's threads clean and dry. Some manufacturers recommend a drop of nonpermanent thread-locking agent, such as a Loctite compound, on the threads to make sure the pivot bolt doesn't back out after reassembly. Be sure to torque it to the proper spec. Follow the same precautions for the brake pedal.

Although you'll want to perform most of these chores before a ride, save lubing the chain until the end of a ride when the chain is hot—the lube soaks in better that way. Before you lube the chain, spray a clean rag with WD-40 and wipe all of the dirt and grit from the chain. If your chain is really grungy, Motorex makes a chain cleaner that will strip the mung without harming the O-rings. It even smells nice.

A cable luber forces the lubricant through the cable, making sure the entire length of the cable is protected. Do not use chain lube on cables.

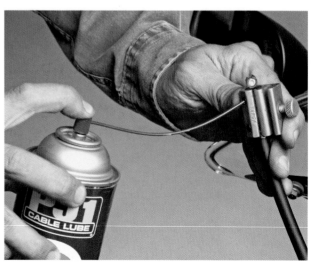

Do *not* succumb to the temptation of using the engine to rotate the chain while you wipe it. The many mechanics missing fingers or parts of fingers can attest to the foolishness of this technique.

Once you've cleaned the chain, apply a coat of quality chain lube to the space between the links where the O-rings reside, spraying from the inside run of the chain to allow centrifugal force to push it through to the other side. (Motorex makes handy small chain lube containers that make it easy to get the spray where you want it. The little containers are then refilled with a large can—very clever.) Don't worry if you spray on too much chain lube. After the lube has had a chance to set, but before you ride your bike again, take another clean rag dampened with WD-40 and wipe off the excess lube before it has a chance to get flung onto your clean wheels. Lubricate your chain every 400 miles or so, but any time your bike is ridden in the rain or is exposed to salt spray from the ocean, you should lube the chain as soon as possible. Take care of your chain, and it will take care of you.

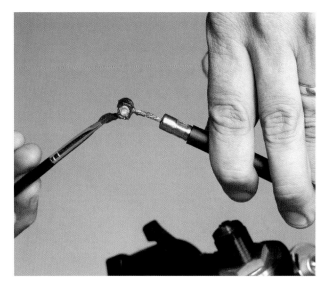

Apply a protective coat of grease to all exposed sections of cables. Don't forget to lube the fittings, so they will move freely within their mounts.

Before lubing pivot points, wipe them clean of any dirt or grit. Keep the threads clean and dry. Retorque the fasteners to the proper spec to keep them from vibrating loose.

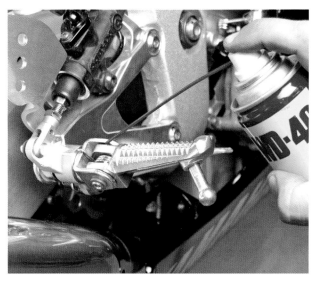

All moving parts, such as peg pivots and side stands, will benefit from a shot of WD-40 or a few drops of oil to keep them working freely. If you're particularly fastidious, you can disassemble the parts and grease them.

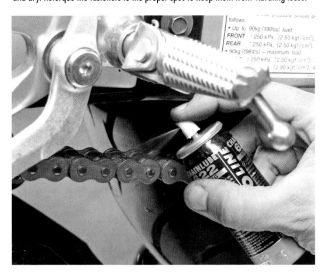

Lubricate the chain when it is warm, but then let it sit until it cools off and the lube sets. To help keep your wheels clean, wipe off the excess lube before your next ride.

PROJECT 8
Oil Change

 Time: 1 hour

 Tools: Oil filter wrench, oil catch pan, wrench for drain plug, miscellaneous tools to remove lower fairing, contact cleaner, rags for cleanup, rear stand (optional), wrench or socket, torque wrench

 Talent: ▮

 Cost: $

 Parts Required: Oil filter, drain plug gasket, five quarts oil

 Tip: Be earth-friendly. Find your local oil recycle center at www.1800CLEANUP.org.

 PERFORMANCE GAIN: You may not feel it, but your engine will: Fresh oil means less friction for better engine operation and power.

The topic of motor oil for motorcycles can stir up some heated arguments. Some riders insist that the pricier, motorcycle-specific oil is nothing more than a way to extort money out of the riding public. These nonbelievers claim that three generations of their riding families (or a riding buddy's family) have used whatever lubricant was on sale down at the local Economart without any mechanical problems. Well, oils have changed more in the last 10 years than they did in the previous 50, so what may have worked before doesn't necessarily apply to the current, highly tuned sportbikes. Use motorcycle oil.

Why don't we want to use automotive oil in motorcycles? First, and most importantly, motorcycle engines share the oil with their transmissions and the clutch (unless you're lucky enough to have a sexy-sounding dry clutch). The shearing forces applied by the transmission and clutch will wear out cheap automobile oil much faster than motorcycle oil. Also, the newer "low-friction" or "energy-conserving" automobile oils use friction modifiers that may have a negative effect on your clutch's ability to engage properly. Several motorcycle manufacturers have even gone so far as to recommend that you not use the SJ-labeled auto oils. Additionally, motorcycle oils usually have higher concentrations of detergents and other compounds that would damage automotive catalytic converters. (As catalysts become more common on bikes, this

feature of motorcycle oil may change.) In short, motorcycle oils are designed for the specific conditions that bike engines exert on them.

The next choice is whether to run petroleum-based or synthetic oils in your engine. Although the lines between the two categories have blurred as dinosaur juice, man-made oils, and additives have all been blended into different types of products, synthetic oils offer some clear advantages. First, synthetics offer more consistent viscosity across a range of temperatures. They thin out less when hot and thicken less when they cool. Second, synthetics transfer heat better than petroleum-based lubricants, so your engine should run cooler. Finally, synthetic oils offer lower volatility and better oxidation stability. This means if your bike overheats for some reason, a synthetic oil stands a better chance of not cooking away, leaving the metal of engine parts vulnerable.

When it comes to actually changing the oil, two schools of thought reign: The first, and more common, states that the engine should be warmed up to operating temperature prior to draining. Mixing up all the crud that settles out of the oil mixture when the bike cools helps flush it out easier. The other camp stresses that if the engine hasn't been operated in more than 24 hours, the contaminants are waiting in the oil pan. Why not just drain the gunk without redistributing it throughout the labyrinth of oil passages? Regardless of which route you follow, make sure you can loosen the oil filter before you heat up the engine and/or drain the oil. You don't want to burn your knuckles on the header struggling to turn the filter or be forced to run that nice, clean oil through a dirty filter. If you can't loosen it by hand, you need to invest in a filter wrench. Channel locks can work, in a pinch.

Novice mechanics shouldn't worry about violating a new bike's warranty. Just save your receipts and keep a record of the date and mileage of each change. Take your time and follow these steps.

Park your bike on a level surface. If you only have the side stand to support your bike, putting it in gear to keep it from rolling off the stand would be a smart move. If you've got a rear stand, this would be the time to use it. Before removing the lower bodywork, slip an absorbent work mat under the bike to prevent any sloppiness from staining your garage floor and to keep your lowers scratch free. Be sure to disconnect all hidden fasteners and turn-signal connectors that may be working behind the plastic.

Wear latex gloves during the messy part of the oil change. Used motor oil is a known carcinogen, and despite claims to the contrary, women do *not* dig greasy fingernails. Locate the drain plug on the bottom of the oil pan and carefully loosen it. If the plug gives you trouble, brace the bike so it doesn't roll off the stand before you give the wrench a yank or resort to a breaker bar. Drain the oil into a container suitable to transport to your local oil recycling center. Pouring old oil into the ground is irresponsible, illegal, and just plain bad juju and will force your descendants to drink funny-tasting water. Unless your catch pan is large enough to catch both the oil from the drain and the filter at the same time, wait until the bike's oil pan is empty before removing the filter. Remove the oil filter with a filter wrench, or by hand if it's loose enough. If your metal band-style wrench is too large to grip the small diameter of your bike's spin-on filter, try the old trick of folding up a rag under the wrench. (K&N makes a nifty filter that has a 17-mm nut welded to the top to make removal a snap. It even has holes for safety wire.) Don't forget to pour out the remaining oil from the filter into the catch pan.

Using your finger, wipe a film of fresh oil on the filter's O-ring. Wipe down the gasket's contact surface on the engine and make sure there is no grit anywhere that might break the O-ring's seal prior to screwing the filter into place. Follow the filter manufacturer's specifications for tightening the filter. Use a new drain plug washer if necessary, and torque it to the factory specification. Don't rely on your torque elbow and risk the embarrassment—and expense—of stripped threads. Fill the engine with the amount and type of oil recommended in the owner's manual. Before starting the engine, wipe down all the engine's oily surfaces. If you're in a well-vented area, give it a quick squirt of contact cleaner. This way oil leaks will be easier to spot after the engine has been run for a short while.

Now it's time to take the bike back out of gear and start it up. When you first start your engine, don't be alarmed if the oil light stays on a little longer than usual. The filter needs to fill with oil. Some fussy riders crank the starter and kill the engine when it fires, repeating the process until the oil light shuts off, in an effort to avoid running the engine while dry. Others crank the engine with the kill switch off until the light disappears. Once the engine reaches operating temperature, shut it down and wait a minute or so before checking the oil level. You may need to add or subtract oil as necessary, since the filter holds a few ounces of oil. Put the bodywork back on and you're done. Now, go for a ride.

The R6 provides the perfect location for using a filter wrench. The compact packaging on sportbikes often leaves little room for removing a filter by hand.

You can't remove a drain plug without getting oil on your hand. Be smart and wear a latex glove, which is cheap, disposable, and doesn't leave your hand filthy and raw.

Lube the filter's O-ring with fresh oil to help it get a good seal with the engine. Make sure the contact surface is clean too. Yes, this mechanic forgot to put on gloves for the photo.

PROJECT 9

Chain Adjustment

Time: 20 minutes

Tools: Assorted wrenches, socket for rear axle, torque wrench, tape measure, rubber mallet, rags for cleanup, rear stand (optional), string, an assistant

Talent: ▮

Cost: None

Parts Required: New cotter pin

Tip: Make sure the chain is properly aligned or you can prematurely wear out both the chain and the sprockets.

PERFORMANCE GAIN: Less driveline lash when modulating the throttle.

Pity the motorcycle drive chain—the component with the weighty responsibility of delivering all those horses to the rear wheel often takes the most abuse and neglect of any part of the bike. Not only does it suffer from the peak loads of wheelies and sudden acceleration but it also feels the pain of every botched downshift. Even in the best of situations, the chain is subjected to constant strain. So how do many motorcyclists reward this hardworking part? By ignoring it.

Walk around at any motorcycle gathering and count the bikes with limp, sagging chains. Most likely, the worst examples also are bone dry with rust and/or crud built up on them. Since you've cleaned and lubed your chain in Project 8, you're ahead of the game. Now you need to make sure that the chain's slack is within specifications. If you lube your chain regularly, you will probably not need to adjust it every time you return from a ride, but as a chain nears its end of its life, you will need to adjust the slack more and more frequently.

Although a rear stand is not required to adjust your chain, it will make the process much easier. When your chain is cold, measure the slack halfway between the sprockets by moving the chain up and down. Press down on the chain slightly to make sure it is at its lowest point. To get an accurate reading, hold a tape measure in front of the chain and look across the top of the links. Adjust your line of sight until the tops of both sides of the chain line up—your eyes will be perpendicular to the chain, and parallel with the top of the links. Then move the tape measure so that one of the inch

markings aligns with the top of the chain. Now, press the chain up until it is tight. Bring your vision up to align with the top of the chain again, and note the measurement. A little arithmetic will tell you if you need to make any adjustments. Since chains don't wear evenly, check the slack measurement in a couple of places. If you need to adjust the chain, set the chain tension to accommodate the tightest point. Also, if the chain is dramatically tighter in one place, consider replacing it.

Before you get down to the nitty-gritty of adjusting the chain, take a look at the chain and sprockets. The most common causes of premature chain wear are an out-of-alignment rear wheel or worn sprockets. Look closely at the sprockets. Are the sides of the teeth worn? If so, expect to find a matching wear pattern on the inside of the chain. Do the teeth of the sprockets look like cresting waves? Why don't you ride down to your local shop and buy a new chain and sprocket set? You'll just be wasting your time adjusting an old, worn-out one.

For bikes with locknuts on their chain adjusters, hold the adjuster in place with a wrench while loosening the locknut. Loosen the axle nut just enough to enable the chain adjusters to move it. If the axle nut is loosened too much, you can accidentally knock the rear wheel out of alignment. For now, assume that your wheel is properly aligned, and make the same adjustments to both chain adjusters. With the exception of eccentric adjusters, you can only move the axle *away* from the countershaft sprocket via the adjusters. So, don't get carried away or you'll have to start all over from scratch. Small adjustments of a quarter turn (or less if your chain is only slightly loose) are the safest bet. Measure the slack after every change. When the chain is within factory specifications (usually around 1.2–1.5 inches), tighten the axle nut to keep it from slipping. If you go too far and the chain becomes too tight, loosen the chain adjusters two full turns and use a rubber mallet or dead-blow hammer to knock the rear wheel forward against the adjusters and begin again.

When the chain has the proper amount of slack, torque the axle nut. Next, tighten each adjuster about one-eighth turn against the axle. Hold the adjuster in position and set the locknuts.

The last step in any chain adjustment is making sure the rear wheel is properly aligned. Don't trust the stamped marks on your bike's swingarm, unless you've verified they are correct by checking the rear wheel alignment several times. A variety of methods of checking the wheel's alignment are available through the aftermarket, but the least expensive and, possibly, the easiest is the "string method."

Take a piece of string a little more than twice the length of the bike, find the center and wrap it once around the forward edge of the front tire just below the front discs. Take each end of the string down opposite sides of the bike. Lie down on your stomach, pulling the strings taut so that they both lightly touch the leading edge of the rear tire. Since the rear wheel is wider

Check the chain's slack at the midpoint between the sprockets. Measure in several places to find the chain's tightest section.

Once you've adjusted your chain a few times, you'll get the feel for when it is loose, but the only way to be certain is to use a tape measure.

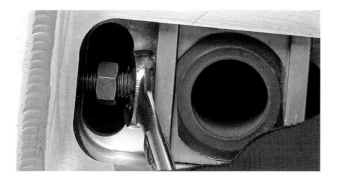

Remember to turn the adjusters the same amounts on both sides of the bike to keep the wheel in alignment.

Chain adjusters come in many shapes and sizes (above/below). The eccentric adjuster is found on many bikes, particularly those with a single-sided swingarm.

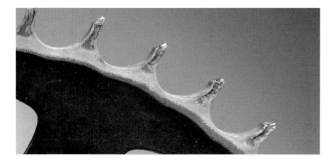

Surf's up! When a sprocket's teeth begin to look like waves, it should be replaced or it will wear out your chain.

If you can pull the chain away to expose half of the sprocket's tooth, it is ready for replacement.

than the front, the strings will leave a slight gap as it passes the rear edge of the front tire. Your assistant should make sure that the front wheel is straight by checking the gap on both sides. Now, keeping your hands steady with the string only lightly touching the rear tire, compare the gaps between the strings and the rear edge of the rear tire. If they are not equivalent, the adjuster on the side that has the smaller gap will need to be tightened slightly. Finally, measure the slack one last time. You'd be surprised how often something tightens up. Don't forget to put a new cotter pin through the axle nut if it requires one.

If you don't have an assistant, a simpler but less precise method for checking rear wheel alignment is to spin the rear wheel a few times and watch that the sprocket stays aligned in the center of the chain. If it rubs against one side or the other, the wheel is out of alignment. Get someone to help you perform the "string method."

When you've got your rear wheel all lined up, take the bike out and "break in" the new chain. Well, *somebody* has to.

Using a string to check wheel alignment may seem like a lot of work, but a crooked rear wheel will trash an expensive chain and sprockets, and it could affect the bike's handling.

Chain and Sprocket Replacement

 Time: 2 hours

 Tools: Sockets, big half-inch socket to fit countershaft nut, big socket for axle nut, ratchet, air-powered impact driver or breaker bar, torque wrench (ft-lbs), wrenches, locking pliers, flathead screwdrivers, punch, chain cleaner or WD-40, contact cleaner, blue Loctite, rags, rotary tool and cutting wheel, chain breaker (or hack saw), chain rivet tool, section of pipe or 2x4 lumber, assistant to work the brake pedal

 Talent:

 Cost: S-SS

 Parts Required: Countershaft and rear sprockets, O-ring chain with rivet master link, countershaft nut lockwasher

 Tip: Loosen the countershaft sprocket before removing old chain.

PERFORMANCE GAIN: The ability to tune your power delivery based on your preferences or a particular track.

Changing a motorcycle chain is a relatively easy job for even the most inexperienced mechanic. Basically, you need little more than a hacksaw, a pair of Vise-Grip locking pliers, and a correctly sized chain. Many beginning mechanics installed their first replacement chain in this manner. However, let's look a little further into the process to consider how to do it properly.

First, you should inspect the sprockets. A worn sprocket will take its crooked teeth and chow down on your shiny new chain. So, look closely at the sprockets. Are the sides of the teeth worn? If so, expect to find a matching wear pattern on the inside of the chain. Do the teeth of the sprockets look like cresting waves? Are teeth—gasp—missing? If you answered yes to any of these questions, you definitely need new sprockets. At the very least, you'll probably want to change the rear sprocket with every new chain. The soft aluminum tends to wear more quickly than the OE steel sprockets. However, if your aluminum sprocket is hard anodized, it should withstand a couple of chain replacements.

Once you've determined you need both chain and sprockets, you have a few decisions in front of you. First, are you going to keep the stock gearing? Like hand and foot control positions, the gearing that comes with your bike is a compromise designed to give you the best performance over a wide range of possible uses for your bike. People doing top speed runs on dry lake beds and stunters who live for wheelies have little in common when it comes to gearing needs. The rest of us fall somewhere in between. Still, you can shift your peak power relative to your speed by tweaking the number of teeth on your sprockets. For example, if you install a front (countershaft) sprocket with fewer teeth, you will gain in acceleration at the expense of top speed. The same is true of adding teeth to the rear. As a rule of thumb, every tooth removed from the countershaft sprocket is the equivalent of adding two to the rear.

Why would you want to do this? Racers use the gearing to tune their engine speed for the exit of key corners. With the exception of some super-high-speed tracks, the launch out of the corner is vastly more important than the top speed of the bike. So, if you reduce the number of teeth on the front or add them to the rear, what can you expect? Acceleration around town will be quicker. Your bike may feel snappier when you roll on the throttle, but there's no free lunch. Since you'll be running the engine at higher rpm for all speeds, your gas mileage will drop. On the superslab, you will notice that the engine feels busier. If you're still unsure about what to do, ask other riders who do the same sort of riding you do if they've changed their gearing.

Once you've decided on your gearing, you need to choose the chain and sprocket pitch. Although 525 series chains are becoming increasingly popular, most stock sportbikes use 530 chains and sprockets. Since 530 chains are heavier and more durable than those with lower numbers, the reason the OEMs choose them as standard parts for your bike should be obvious. However, lots of performance-minded folks switch to 520 rolling gear when chain-replacement time rolls around. The parts are lighter, which lessens rotating mass and the associated power loss. Also, the parts are usually a little cheaper. The downside of this modification is that the chains aren't as strong and wear out quicker. If you're trying to wring out that last bit of power from your bike, this penalty won't seem so great.

To remove the countershaft sprocket nut, you'll need to bend the lockwasher flat.

With the engine in first gear and the rear wheel secured (note pipe through wheel), use a breaker bar to free the countershaft sprocket nut. An impact wrench makes this job a snap.

To make it easier to press out the roller pin, grind off the top of the rivet with a rotary tool and cutting wheel.

When changing the chain and sprockets, if you think the first step would be removing the chain, you'd be wrong. You need to free up the countershaft sprocket while you still have a way to lock it down. Countershaft sprockets are usually secured one of three ways: a pair of bolts securing a plate to the sprocket, a big clip that slips into a groove in the countershaft itself, or a really big nut. For the pair of bolts, simply put the engine in gear, press on the brake pedal, and unbolt them. Follow the first two steps for the clip, but slip it off with a flathead screwdriver instead. The really big nut provides the biggest challenge. Using a punch or big flathead screwdriver (thank goodness for Craftsman's lifetime replacement warranty), bend the tabs on the lockwasher that have been folded against the flats of the nut.

Since the nut was torqued to at least 65 ft-lbs and may have thread lock on it, you'll need to secure the rear wheel before you attempt to break the nut free. Slip a piece of pipe or 2x4 through the rear wheel just above the swingarm. Now, when you muscle the nut free, the wood will keep the wheel, chain, and sprocket from moving. Be prepared to sweat a little. Of course, you could resort to the lazy man's method of pulling the trigger on a (pneumatic) impact driver—no sweating involved.

Once the countershaft sprocket is broken loose you can begin removing the chain. Clip-style master links are easy—too easy—to remove. Slip the clip free with a flathead screwdriver. Next, walk the removable plate off the pins by alternately prying the ends with your screwdriver. Eventually, the plate will pop free. With endless chains or riveted master links, if you don't have a chain breaker, a hacksaw will do the trick. If you have a chain breaker, you may or may not (depending on the strength of the breaker and the size of the chain) need to grind off the head of the roller pin. If you are removing a riveted master link so that you can reuse the chain in the future (common when gearing change at a track requires a longer chain), you'll want to grind off both pins. Usually, the

This Motion Pro tool will make your life much easier. The pin sticking out of the bolt is the breaking tip. The bolt head closest to the tool body tightens the alignment bolt to the chain. The bolt head furthest away from the body pushes the breaking tip through the chain, removing the roller pin.

midpoint between the two sprockets will be the most unobstructed place to break the chain.

Motion Pro's Chain Cutter & Riveting Tool is about the best one around, though the company also sells less expensive units. Install the correct-size breaking tip in the tool, making sure that the tip is withdrawn at least 2 mm inside the alignment bolt. Center the pin in the tool and tighten down the alignment bolt with a 14-mm wrench to hold the tool in position. Using the 14-mm wrench, crank the extraction bolt so that it pushes the breaker tip and the roller pin out of the bottom of the tool. When the pin falls free, back the extraction bolt out until the tip is back inside the alignment bolt. Loosen the alignment bolt until the chain falls free. Repeat if necessary for a master link. If you're using the same-size sprockets, lay the old chain down beside the new one to mark the length. Now, pop the pin out of the new chain to cut it to the correct number of links. For different sprocket sizes, you'll measure the chain to length once the sprockets are mounted.

Before you install the new chain, you'll need to replace the sprockets. To remove the rear wheel, first loosen the chain adjusters three full turns and snug up the locknuts to hold them in place. Remove the axle nut and axle. Lay the wheel down sprocket up. (For more detailed instructions on wheel removal, see Project 24.) Using a socket, remove the nuts from the studs securing the sprocket in a crisscross pattern. Slide the old sprocket free. If the stud threads are greasy, clean them with contact cleaner. (If you've been neglectful in your wheel cleaning because the sprocket was in the way, now would be a good time to take care of any mung sullying your wheel.) Place the new sprocket on the studs. If you're unsure of the orientation, the number of teeth on the sprocket is usually stamped on the side facing out. Screw the nuts down finger tight. Set your torque wrench to half of the value specified in your factory service manual and tighten the nuts in a crisscrossing pattern. Once all nuts are torqued halfway, set the full torque value on your wrench and tighten the nuts again. If you tighten the nuts down to their full-torque setting in one step, you run the risk of stripping the threads. Remount the wheel and loosely fasten the axle nut.

Since you've already loosened the countershaft sprocket, you should be able to spin the nut free. *Before* you pull the sprocket off, take a look at it and any spacers positioning it on the countershaft. You'll notice immediately if the OE sprocket has noise-reducing rubber on the sprocket. Don't worry if your replacement doesn't have this—most aftermarket sprockets don't. While you have the sprocket off the countershaft, take a quick look at the seal with the engine case. You shouldn't see any leakage. Take advantage of the easy access you have with the sprocket removed to clean all the encrusted chain goop

Torque the sprocket nuts in two steps. For the first step, torque the nuts to half of the final specs, the second to the full, factory-specified torque. Tighten the nuts in a crisscross pattern.

If you're changing to different sprocket sizes from your previous setup, measure the proper chain length by wrapping it around both sprockets. Mark the pin where you have to bend the chain as it meets the other end—that's the pin you will remove to set the chain length

from the surrounding area. Clean the countershaft, paying particular attention to the threads for the nut, with contact cleaner. Once the contact cleaner is dry, slide the sprocket onto the shaft. Don't worry about the nut(s) yet. You'll torque it down once the chain is installed. Clip-type sprockets can have the clip pushed into place with a big screwdriver.

Wrap the new chain around both sprockets. If the chain has not been cut to length, turn the chain adjusters in equal amounts until the middle of the adjustment range is indicated on the swingarm. Snug up the axle nut to keep the axle from moving. Pull the chain taut and fold the chain over where it meets the other end. You goal is to mark the rivet that needs to be removed so you can slip the master link into position. Remove the rivet as described earlier.

Master links used to come in two varieties: clip-type and rivet-type. If your chain came with a clip-type link, either return it for one with a rivet master link or go buy one for the chain. Clipping-type master links have a nasty habit of tossing their clips and sometimes the entire link—despite the fact that the clips are a pain to install. A thrown chain can cause Very Bad Things to happen.

When removing a master link from its packaging, make sure you don't wipe any grease off the pins or O-rings. If your chain includes a tube of grease, apply a hefty amount to the pins, O-rings, and plates. Many times when you cut a chain to length, the O-rings will stay mounted on the inner links. If so, remove them. Install the O-rings included with the master link on the pins. Push the pins of the master link through the chain from the back. When you're happy with its position, check and install the O-rings on the front of the chain and press the outer plate on with your fingers. You won't get very far, though.

Assemble the chain-rivet tool with its press plates. The plate with the two holes for the pins should be on the alignment

bolt side. Using a 14-mm wrench, tighten the bolt until the plate is seated. If your rivet tool doesn't have press plates, you can "walk" the plate into position by clamping down a pair of Vise-Grip pliers on alternating ends of the plate. Tighten the pliers' adjuster a little between each step. Whichever technique you use, your goal is to have the outer side plates on the master link the same distance from the inner plates as on the adjoining, permanently riveted links. Proper alignment will make sure that the grease stays in the roller when the chain gets hot, but without the master link being so tight that it binds the chain.

Properly riveting the roller pins is vital to keeping your chain together. Use the right tool for the job, and you'll have no worries. Place the chain tool's anvil behind the pin you'll be riveting. Line the pin up in the tool and tighten the alignment bolt. Push the riveter onto the pin with the tool's push bolt. Tighten the bolt down very tightly until it flares the end of the pin, preventing the plate from sliding out on the pin. Repeat on the other pin.

The countershaft sprocket nut needs to be torqued down to prevent it from backing out at speed. Install any washers required. Use a new lockwasher. Add a few drops of blue Loctite on the countershaft threads and the nut. Secure the countershaft by stopping the rear wheel as you did for the nut removal step. Torque the bolt to factory specification. This R6 required 65 ft-lbs, while other bikes may require as much as 90 ft-lbs. All that remains now is adjusting the chain as described in Project 9. Be sure to double-check the chain slack after 100 miles or so. As the chain breaks in, it will lengthen. And breaking in the chain is the funnest part.

Tighten the rivet tool until it distorts the roller pin. The goal is to make it impossible for the outer plate to be able to back away from the inner plate.

Even though you used Loctite compound on the threads, a new locking washer is required to assure that the countershaft nut doesn't spin free. Make sure the washer is bent so that it is firmly against the entire side (not just one point) of the nut. Note the rivet on the master link too.

Spark Plug Check and Replacement

PROJECT 11

 Time: 1 hour

 Tools: Sockets, screwdrivers, plug wrench, torque wrench, wire gap gauge, rags, anti-seize compound, compressed air, brass brush, magnet to retrieve plug, rear stand

 Talent: ♦

 Cost: $

 Parts Required: Spark plugs

 Tip: Blow off the top of the engine with compressed air to keep abrasives out of the cylinders.

 PERFORMANCE GAIN: Smoother-running engine.

Spark plugs live a hard life: high pressure, extreme temperatures, and constant explosions. Should we be surprised that the OEMs expect us to check the conditions of our bike's plugs at every service? If you look at your manual, you'll find that should be just about every 4,000 miles. Fortunately, the plugs don't often need replacing, just a quick brush-off and back into the chamber of horrors they go. Still, you shouldn't let spark plugs' hardiness lull you into a false sense of security. Few things can wreak havoc on your engine's performance like a fouled plug.

Although you often read about race tuners reading plugs on bikes fresh off the track, we're not trying to squeeze that last 1/10 horsepower that could mean the difference between standing on top of the podium or somewhere else—yet. Right now we're concerned with making sure your bike is running as it's designed to—the modifications come in later sections. Your bike's engine should be cold when you check the plugs.

Place your bike on a rear stand and remove any necessary bodywork, the seat, tank, and air box. While you're at it, you can clean the air filter (Project 64). Your bike may require a few tricks to gain access to the plugs, so check your factory service manual first. While the air box is off the throttle bodies, they're vulnerable to dirt, so cover them with clean rags or paper towels. Once you have access to the plugs, blow the top of the head off with compressed air. Now, remove the plug wire or coil stick from one plug at a time. Although it sounds obvious, you don't want to risk mixing up the plugs and their wiring—Bad Things could happen.

Don't just jump in and remove the plug once it's exposed. Even though a cap has been covering the spark plug well, you should give it a quick blast with compressed air. You'd be surprised how frequently sand or pebbles pop out, and you sure don't want them in your engine. Once you've given it a shot of clean air, now you can safely remove the plug. The tight quarters around the engine's head may require some patience to remove the plug. If you've unscrewed the plug completely and can't get a grip on it to pull it out, try using a magnet to retrieve the wayward part.

Reading Your Plugs

Photos courtesy of Denso Sales California, Inc.

So, you've taken a plug out of its cubby hole, and you're wondering what to do with it. Impress your friends and neighbors by emulating famous race tuners: Closely examine the plug to see what it tells you about the state of your engine. Of course, you'll need some sort of comparison. The photos below will provide examples of what to look for. Remember, these are, for the most part, extreme examples meant to clearly illustrate the various plug conditions. Your plugs, unless they have a perfect tan, will probably have subtler symptoms.

 You want all of your plugs to look as pretty as this one. Note the nice, even gray or tan on the insulator. The electrode exhibits only slight erosion.

 Carbon fouling shows up as dry, soft black soot on the insulator and electrode. Although usually caused by a too-rich fuel mixture, other potential problems are shorting ignition leads and too cold a plug temperature. A badly carbon-fouled plug can lead to difficult starting, misfiring, and uneven acceleration

This plug has been subjected to severe overheating, as illustrated by the extremely white insulator and small black specks. If you look closely, you will see more electrode erosion than on a normal plug. When a plug overheats, the engine will experience a loss of power under heavy loads, like high-speed, high-rpm running. An overly advanced ignition, too-hot plug temperature, or poor engine cooling could be the culprit. Improperly torqued plugs can also overheat.

 Oil fouling is characterized by black, gooey deposits on the insulator and electrode. Have you noticed that your bike was difficult to start and that the engine missed frequently at speed? The oil came from somewhere, and the likely culprits are worn piston rings or valve guides.

Space is tight. If you must remove two or more plug wires at once, wrap them with tape and number them unless the factory was kind enough to do it for you.

Look closely at the electrode and insulator, which should be a light tan or gray color. Check the sidebar "Reading Your Plugs" for tips on what other colors mean. Using a brass brush, clean the plug of any deposits. Next, measure the gap with a wire thickness gauge. The flat spade gauges don't give accurate readings unless held perfectly square to the gap. Don't even bother taking the round ramped gauges out. They're worthless. If the gap is too narrow or too wide, use the gapping tool usually attached to a set of wire gauges to carefully bend the side electrode outward. When you're using force to bend the electrode, a little effort goes a long way.

When the gap is correct, wipe the threads on a clean rag, then apply a little antiseize to them. Carefully, insert the plug into the plug hole. If you can get your fingers down into the plug well, rotate the plug counterclockwise until you feel the threads drop into sync. Then, using only your fingers, rotate it clockwise to engage the threads. You can do this with the plug socket, but your feel is much more limited. Cross-threading a spark plug (or any fastener, for that matter) can be a time-consuming and expensive pain. Screw in the plug finger tight, and then snug it down with a torque wrench. This step is vitally important, since some plug failures are associated with incorrectly torqued plugs.

Before reassembling your entire bike, start the engine to make sure all of the cylinders are firing correctly. (Fuel-injected bikes may need a gas test tank to maintain proper fuel pressure.) If anything sounds amiss, check all plug connections and also make sure all of the wires are connected to the correct cylinders. When everything sounds right, button up your bike and go ride another 4,000 miles.

The best way to check a plug's gap is with a wire tool. This eliminates the requirement that the tool be held perpendicular to the electrode.

Despite the manufacturers' best efforts, sand and pebbles work their way into remarkable places. Blow off the cylinder head before removing the plug caps, and blow out the plug wells too.

Use a brass brush to clean the electrode and insulator. Be sure to clean the plug again with compressed air before you reinstall it.

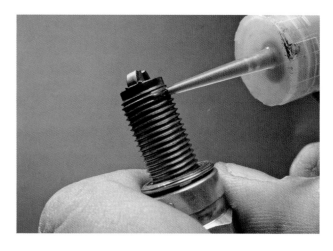

Spark plugs can sometime be ornery when you try to remove them because of cold welding between the aluminum of the head and the steel of the plug. Anti-seize helps to remedy the problem.

PROJECT 12

Headlight/Turn-Signal Replacement and Adjustment

 Time: 30 minutes

 Tools: Screwdrivers, possibly sockets, continuity tester, tape measure, dielectric grease, a willing assistant

 Talent: ▮

 Cost: $

 Parts Required: Headlight or turn-signal bulb(s)

 Tip: Adjusting your headlight for the load you're carrying will enable you to actually see where you're going after dark.

 PERFORMANCE GAIN: You will make yourself more visible to other road users.

A motorcycle's headlight does more than simply allow you to see where you're going at night. The Motorcycle Safety Foundation recommends that riders use the high beam during daylight riding. This simple action can make you much more conspicuous both in the crowded visual environment of the city and out on the open road. For this reason, motorcycles manufactured for U.S. use since the mid-1970s are required to automatically turn on the headlight when the engine is running. Although many sportbikes now have two headlights, checking the high and low beams on both should be part of your daily preride check. Anyone who has felt the sudden, shocking blindness of a filament failure at night (as I did on Interstate 35 in Minnesota) can attest to the relief of flipping on the other beam.

If you discover that your headlight isn't working, what should you do? If both filaments are unresponsive, begin by checking that the bulb is properly seated in its plug. To get to the back of the headlight, some bikes may require that you remove quite a bit of bodywork. Others only ask that you peel off the detachable rubber dust seal. To check the bulb, you don't have to completely remove it unless you are conducting a visual inspection. A bulb that appears to be completely normal may have an internal problem, so a continuity tester will tell you the true status of the bulb.

Inspect the bulb's connectors for signs of moisture or corrosion. The tabs sticking out of the side of this headlight bulb key it into the proper position in the housing.

Note how the tester's probe is being held against the side of this turn-signal bulb. This is where it makes the negative contact with the socket. The buttons on the bottom are the positive contacts for the filaments. If the bulb is OK, clean the contacts before reinstalling it.

Instead, remove the plug to expose the prongs on the back of the bulb. Using a continuity tester, press one electrode onto two of the prongs extending from the back of the bulb. Now, touch the other probe to one of the remaining prongs. Repeat with the two other possible pairings. If you don't get continuity on at least two pairs of the prongs, the bulb is bad. If you get continuity on both filaments, you may have a blown headlight fuse or a short somewhere in the electrical system.

Installing a new headlight is pretty straightforward. Be sure to replace a blown bulb with a similar type. The bulbs are keyed so that they will only fit in the housing in the proper

Turn-signal bulbs either pop out easily or they take some elbow grease. If you find yourself exerting more than minimal effort, use a rag or a pair of gloves to protect yourself from accidental bulb breakage. If the socket is corroded, a dab of dielectric grease will prevent the parts from sticking in the future.

Make small adjustments to the headlight. Sometimes the results are subtle, other times they're not.

orientation. An old wives' tale says that getting your fingerprints on halogen bulbs will cause them to fail prematurely. While that my have been true in the past, there is absolutely no merit to this statement. That being said, good mechanical hygiene stipulates that you wipe off the bulb before locking it in position. Before slipping the plug onto the bulb, check it for signs of moisture or corrosion in the plug. If the plug is damp, give it a quick spray with silicone drying spray. WD-40 will also work, but its lubricating properties can capture dirt. Check to make sure the light works before completely assembling the housing. Make sure the rubber cover is snugly in place over the headlight housing.

The process of checking a dual-filament bulb, like a front turn signal or brake light bulb, is almost identical to the headlight. Remove the bulb from the turn-signal stalk. If you have trouble removing the bulb, use a rag or gloves to get a safer grip on the glass. Bulbs that have corroded into position may break before you're able to remove them. If this happens, a little WD-40 and needle-nose pliers will help.

Hold one probe of the continuity tester on the outside metal edge of the bulb. Now, check the continuity on each of the two little buttons on the bottom of the bulb. Again, don't trust a visual inspection unless it shows an obviously blown filament. Before you screw the cover back on, check to be sure the new bulb works.

Many riders never consider the load a bike carries and its effect on the headlight aim. Yes, the headlight angle is set at the factory, but it is set based on some average—the age-old

compromise. What if you're heavier than average or you've changed your bike's ride height? What about the fact that you've just strapped 65 pounds of gear to your bike for the annual pilgrimage to Daytona? You owe it to yourself and those traveling in the opposite direction to make sure your headlight is properly adjusted.

Your owner's manual will show you where the adjusters are and how to take the measurements. To accurately gauge your headlight's adjustment, make sure your bike has the same load and suspension settings under which it will be operating. You will need an assistant to do the measuring while you and your pillion/luggage are on the bike. For maximum accuracy, have another assistant hold the bike in position. Otherwise, just make sure your feet are only balancing the bike, not supporting any of your weight. Motorcycles in the United States should have their headlight height measured at a distance of 25 feet. While shining the headlight on a wall, have your assistant measure from the center of the headlight beam to the ground while the bike is loaded. The brightest spot of the high beam on the wall should be two inches below the measured height of the headlight center. Of course, seeing this will be easier at dusk or after dark. Using a screwdriver or the headlight's adjuster knobs, center the beam on the appropriate spot. Adjust the second bulb on bikes with two headlights to match the first. If you notice that either beam aims to one side instead of straight ahead, adjust this too. Single headlights should also point straight ahead.

Now you can take that long moonlit ride for which you've been longing.

You should adjust the headlight based on the standard of a 2-inch drop in 25 feet. Remember: Load affects the headlight alignment, so set the height based on what you plan to carry.

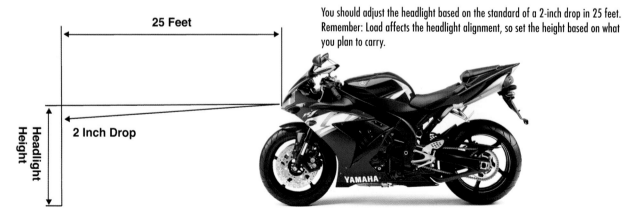

25 Feet

2 Inch Drop

Headlight Height

Chassis Fastener Retorque

Time: 1–2 hours

Tools: Sockets, 18-inch breaker bar, torque wrenches (foot and inch pounds), adapters for any special fasteners, shop manual, thread lock

Talent:

Cost: None

Parts Required: None

Tip: If a fastener that requires a thread-locking agent turns when you retorque it, remove the fastener, reapply the thread lock, and torque to spec.

PERFORMANCE GAIN: A tight, responsive machine.

News flash: Motorcycle fasteners are under a variety of stresses. First, the engine vibrates, even if most of it never reaches the rider. Then every bump, small and large, gets absorbed by the suspension and chassis. Heat cycles expand and contract parts—often at different rates. Finally, a hurried or negligent mechanic can forget to tighten or improperly torque a fastener. With all that you have at stake every time you ride, periodically torquing your bike's important nuts and bolts is a wise investment of your time. Also (dare I mention it again?), getting intimate with your bike will help you spot little problems before they turn into expensive repairs.

So, where do you start? The owner's manual and factory service manual will list the maintenance interval. Typically, the usual mileage interval is around 7,500 miles, or once a year for low-mileage bikes. In places where winter puts your riding on hold, going over the chassis with your torque wrenches can be an important type of PMS (Parked Motorcycle Syndrome) reliever while the snow slowly melts from your lawn. For those of us with year-round riding seasons, twice a year is a good rule of thumb—unless you ride the wheels off your bike. Then, stick to the 7,500-mile recommendation.

Give yourself plenty of time to complete the task. Don't rush yourself. If you're suffering from PMS, that would defeat the purpose, no? Begin by removing any bodywork that will interfere with access to the fasteners you plan to torque. Next,

go over the list of fasteners in your service manual. Often, important torque figures are listed in a general information section, but mixed in with the values for all sorts of parts, like engine internals, that you won't need to bother with during this project. Highlight the values of the chassis, suspension, and brake components you plan on checking so you don't forget anything. Those parts that require thread-locking fluid—any that turn when you apply the factory-specified force—must be removed, coated with thread lock, and retorqued. All other fasteners will simply be torqued down to spec.

Thorough folks will, no doubt, notice that many bolts aren't listed specifically in factory service manuals. If you look closely, you'll find a table entitled something like "General Torque Specifications." These numbers will cover all bolts from clutch covers to hydraulic reservoirs to bodywork brackets. The bolt measurements are for the diameter of the threads, not the head, so the size of the socket does *not* determine the torque. You can look to the next size down from the socket size (i.e., a 10-mm socket/head will have 8-mm threads), but checking with a ruler or caliper is a better idea. A caveat: This approximation only applies to hex heads, and not Allen heads, button caps, or other configurations.

When torquing bolts, the specification is, unless otherwise stated, for clean, dry threads. Using anti-seize or some other lubricant lowers the coefficient of friction between the two metals, increasing the lateral, pulling force required to create the rotational force your wrench is applying. All that gobbledygook means is that you can strip expensive parts if you're not careful. So, clean and dry dirty, oily fasteners before torquing them down. Also, when torquing items like sprockets, don't just dive into the specified torque. In a crisscross or "star" pattern, tighten all the nuts to half or two-thirds of the final value. Then, following the same pattern, torque them to the specification. This can help prevent annoying stripped threads. After all this, you are now "one" with your motorcycle, and ready for your next adventure in the twisties.

General Fastener Torque Table

Thread diameter (in mm)	Newton-meters	foot-pounds
5	3.4–4.9	30–43 (inch-pounds)
6	5.9–7.8	52–69 (inch-pounds)
8	5.9–7.8	10–13
10	25–34	19–25
12	44–61	33–45
14	73–98	54–72
16	115–155	83–115
18	165–225	125–165
20	225–325	165–240

These general torque figures were culled from a variety of service manuals. For the gospel according to your specific bike, consult the factory service manual.

Some of the fasteners will pass all the way through the frame. It is sometimes difficult to hold the wrench on both sides of the bike. Slipping a ratchet on the bolt side of the bike and watching it for movement as you torque down the nut will tell you if contorting yourself to hold the bolt steady is really necessary.

Some bikes will have pinch bolts on the motor mounts. These need to be loosened before the engine mount bolts are retorqued.

Exhaust manifold nuts are notorious for vibrating loose, particularly if you've had to remove the system (or you have installed an aftermarket system). Space will be tight, so use extenders to get to the little buggers. Unfortunately, universal joints will alter the torque value, so use them sparingly.

Winterizing a Motorcycle

 Time: 2 hours

 Tools: Front and rear stands, intelligent battery charger, plug wrench, oil filter wrench, sockets, torque wrench

 Talent: ▮

 Cost: $–$$

 Parts Required: Fuel stabilizer, fogging oil for cylinders, covers for intakes and exhaust openings, oil and filter, S100 Corrosion Protectant, bike cover, coolant, fresh plugs (for next season)

 Tip: Winter is a great time to undertake a bunch of the other projects in this book, as well.

 PERFORMANCE GAIN: You'll be riding while folks who don't winterize will be waiting for their bikes to get out of the shop.

Contrary to popular belief, denial—not laziness—is the real reason many motorcycles don't get winterized. The problem, you see, is that their doting owners don't want to admit that the riding season is over, so these machines sit neglected. How do I know this? Well, I just uncorked the carbs on my race bike—after nine months of disuse. Every month, I planned to get back on the track, but obligations, such as this book in your hands, kept getting in the way. Remember, unintentional neglect is neglect just the same. So, be honest with yourself about how long your bike might sit unused.

The sad truth about motorcycles is that they need special treatment if they're going to sit for just a few weeks. The gas in the carbs and the chemicals storing electricity in the battery are the first to suffer, and both of those are important for getting your bike back under way.

This project is organized so that the longer your bike will be stored, the further you should delve into the preparation for it.

Carburetors

Carburetors have many small parts with tiny orifices that clog easily and resist cleaning. Gasoline is made up of many compounds, some of which are quite volatile (for easy starting and less pollution). Unfortunately, this means the vast majority of gasoline's components will evaporate, given enough time, leaving behind varnish—otherwise known as sticky goo—in places that you definitely don't want sticky goo. To prevent buildup of this stuff, any time you are going to let your bike sit more than a week or so, you should drain the float bowls. Otherwise, the potential consequence is a time-consuming and/or expensive repair.

The best way to drain the float bowls is to attach a hose to the nipple at the bottom of each float bowl. Then loosen the drain screw and let the fuel pour into a clean container. Examine the contents for water, rust, or any other contaminants. (If you find any, you've got a nice winter project.) Unfortunately, the confined quarters on most sportbikes make this a time-consuming process in which several parts, like the tank, need to be removed. So, you might not find this method practical for intermittent storage.

The second-best way to drain the carburetors is to close the petcock with the engine running (which you should do any time you're parking your bike for more than a day, to avoid the possibility of fuel overflowing from your carbs and hydraulically locking the cylinders). Once the engine has run dry, the carbs are safe against fouling from evaporation. Remember, though, you haven't cleared the float bowls of other forms of contamination, and you should drain the carbs properly at least once a year.

While owners of fuel-injected bikes don't have to worry, carburetors can gum up over the winter if they aren't drained. Periodic float-bowl draining also removes any garbage that collects there.

A smart charger keeps your battery in good health. You can't expect a battery to work after several months of neglect, particularly if stored at a low temperature.

Battery

Batteries don't store electricity. Instead, batteries store the chemicals necessary to produce electricity. If left unused, batteries will naturally discharge. Both high and low temperatures will accelerate this loss of charge, and if it's allowed to continue, the battery will reach a deeply discharged state that can dramatically shorten its life. Add a constant drain from an alarm system, and your bike's battery can be stone dead in only two weeks.

Although battery technology continues to improve, producing ever more compact and powerful packages, the only way to maintain a motorcycle battery is to charge it periodically. Fortunately, "smart" charger technology has advanced to the point that buying one can pay for itself in a year or two of ownership. You don't even need to remove the battery from your bike. Just plug it in and forget about it. A fused cable tucked safely out of sight will work fine. However, if your bike will be stored in a subfreezing environment, you should let the battery spend the winter in a less stressful locale.

Intelligent chargers constantly monitor the state of a battery, and when the voltage drops, the charging feature kicks in. Once the voltage rises up to the proper level, the charger enters "float" mode, where a neutral charge keeps the voltage from dropping. The difference between these chargers and the trickle chargers that can be bought for less than $10 is the float mode. Trickle chargers just keep trickling away regardless of the battery's condition, which can do as much damage as not charging the battery at all.

Although a smart charger, like a Battery Minder or Battery Tender, or Yuasa charger, costs considerably less than a new battery, some folks still want to use a trickle charger. If you're that type of person, plug it into a light timer that is set to run for about 15–20 minutes a day. Also, any nonsealed battery should be topped off with distilled water every month or so, if necessary.

Gas Tank

Sealed containers such as gas tanks form microclimates in the atmosphere they happen to contain. If you're going to park your bike for more than a week, completely fill the tank. Otherwise, as the temperature rises and falls, any moisture in the air will condense on the bare metal inside the tank and can cause rust.

If you're storing your bike for the winter, you have two choices for how to prepare the tank. Both methods of tank winterization require that you begin by draining the tank. This is a good maintenance procedure, anyway, since any crud or moisture that has collected during the riding season will be carried out with the fuel. The easiest option is to then pour a fuel stabilizer, like Sta-Bil, into the tank and then fill it completely with fresh gas. Honda recommends the full-tank method for all its fuel-injected bikes, and other manufacturers will most likely agree. The alternative for people who can't or don't want to store their bike with a full tank is to pour a few ounces of heavy oil—50W at a minimum—into the empty tank. Close the tank and spend a few minutes rotating it until the oil has coated the tank internals and washed away any fuel remnants. Pour the remainder into your oil-recycling container. Next spring, empty out the oil that collected in the bottom of the tank before filling it with fresh gas. Always store your bike with the petcock turned off to prevent any accidental leakage.

Engine

The internal combustion engine is a toxic environment. The oil that is the lifeblood of the engine must suffer through high temperatures and extreme pressures—all the while carrying away the by-products of those thousands of explosions per minute. Once the engine stops running, those contaminants settle out of the oil and can sink their teeth into unprotected metal. However, a quick oil change prior to parking your bike for the winter will pay big dividends in the longevity department. Once the oil has been changed, ride your bike for a couple of miles to make sure the new oil has thoroughly flushed out any remaining contaminants.

Although many sportbike cylinder walls are now coated with alloys rather than lined with iron, you'll still want to protect them from moisture contained in the air trapped in the chambers. Some people prefer to remove the spark plugs and squirt some 50W oil into the spark plug holes. Crank the engine over a few times to coat things before reinstalling the plugs. Another method is to spray fogging oil into the throttle bodies with the engine running, which may give the cylinders a more thorough protective coating. Fogging oil can be found at many auto parts stores.

If your bike will be stored in an unheated garage that may see temperatures below freezing, you'll want to check to see that the antifreeze is up to snuff. If you have any doubt, replacing coolant is much cheaper than replacing an engine block. (Don't forget to dispose of the antifreeze properly.) Riders who take their bikes to track days should keep in mind that, if they swapped the glycol coolant for Water Wetter, their cooling systems will freeze at 32 degrees. Completely draining the system will prevent this. Just be sure to stick a big note on the triple clamp or speedometer, warning that the radiator is empty.

Tires

Bike and tire manufacturers generally agree that it's preferable to store a bike on stands, to prevent the tires from sitting on the same spot for several months. When storing on stands, reduce the tire pressure by 20 percent. If this is not an option, fill the tires up to their maximum recommended pressure and check the pressure every month. Periodically rotating the tires so that the bike's weight rests on different portions of the tread is also helpful. Finally, since ozone ages rubber, store your bike away from electric motors, such as refrigerators.

Chassis and Finish

Preparing your bike for hibernation is a good time to perform some of the annual maintenance listed in this book. Brake and clutch hydraulic fluid replacement and chassis lubrication is highly recommended. Pay particular attention to the cables and the chain. They will benefit from a protective layer of grease or other lubricant. Similarly, washing and waxing your bike prior to storage will help protect the finish. Apply a heavy coat of wax and don't buff it off until spring. Some people even go as far as waxing the inside of the bodywork and the frame. You can also spray the engine and other bare metal parts with S100 Corrosion Protectant. Finally, cover the bike to protect it from dust and grit—and salt from cars that may share the space. If your bike is stored indoors, make sure you use a breathable cover like the ones sold by Aerostich and Roadgear. Bikes stored out in the elements need a hardy cover like those from Dowco, or you can use a motorcycle storage system that seals your bike inside a climate-controlled container.

Fuel stored for long periods can stratify into its components unless a fuel stabilizer is used. Be sure the tank is completely full, or the moisture in the air trapped in the tank can cause it to rust. Cylinder walls, like the inside of gas tanks, need to be protected from moisture or they may rust. Spraying fogging oil into the cylinders can prevent this.

This soft Roadgear cover will protect your bike from dust and will keep the light from fading your paint. Elevating the tires off the ground keeps them from developing flat spots on the tread.

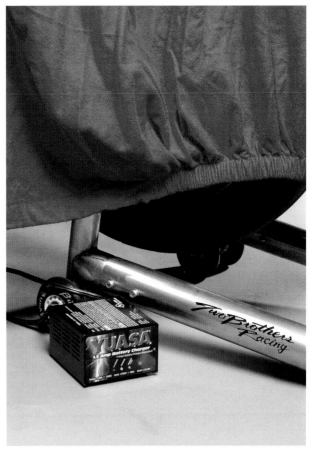

SECTION TWO

BRAKES

From all the attention focused on motorcycle engines, you'd think that gasoline fuels the most powerful system on a bike. You'd be wrong, though. Another liquid—hydraulic fluid—carries that honor. Brakes can scrub off speed faster than an engine can increase it. In other words, brakes decelerate you more quickly than the engine can accelerate you. Consequently, maintaining your bike's brake system is paramount to extracting maximum performance from it. Don't forget that the brakes can also get you out of a lot of trouble—if you know what you're doing. And upgrades to individual components or the entire brake system can help you get more stopping capability and better feel from the binders.

PROJECT 15

Brake Pad Change

Time: 1 hour

Tools: Wrenches; sockets; flathead screwdriver; Allen keys; torque wrench; front stand; rear stand; rags; 60- or 80-grit sandpaper; toothbrush or other small cleaning brush; a thin piece of wood; brake/contact cleaner; organic cleaner like Simple Green; waterproof, high-temperature grease

Talent:

Cost: $

Parts Required: Brake pads

Tip: Since you have the calipers off, clean the pistons to spot problems early and ensure proper brake operation.

PERFORMANCE GAIN: Better stopping power.

COMPLEMENTARY MODIFICATIONS: Change brake fluid and rebuild caliper.

Brakes perform the most important job on a motorcycle. Consequently, you should pay special attention to the condition of your bike's pads. Yes, you could run them to the absolute limits of their service, but you'd be gambling that you won't want to use your brakes multiple times in a series of corners or won't need maximum braking power. That kind of defeats the purpose of owning a sportbike, right? So, plan on replacing your pads when a minimum of 2 mm of the pad material remains. (Even with 2 mm of pad material left, your braking power could be compromised with heavy use, such as at a track day.)

The directions for this project will be based on changing front brake pads, but the steps will be the same for the rear. Begin by placing your bike on a rear stand. Although a front stand isn't required, it makes the process much easier. Some calipers may allow you to remove the pads while they're still mounted on the bike, but since we're also going to clean the calipers, begin by removing the calipers from their hangers.

You may need to pry the pads apart with a large flathead screwdriver before you can slip the pads out. Some calipers secure the pads with a retaining pin and spring clip that you will need to remove first.

Slip the used pads out, but before you set them aside, inspect them closely. Did they wear evenly? If one pad is thinner than the other, take a look at the pistons to see if they may be sticking. Another symptom of a dragging caliper piston is having one end of the pad more worn than the other. These signal the need for a caliper rebuild.

After you have the pads out, don't just toss in another set and be done with it. You need to clean the caliper components and the disc's swept surface. Cleaning the caliper removes the obvious stuff like brake dust, but it also plays an important role in preventing the need for rebuilds. Most brake fluids absorb moisture through the piston seals into the sealed environment of the hydraulic system. And that's not all. That moisture combines with the brake dust and grit and whatever else happens to be wedged into the calipers, forming a kind of shellac that bonds to the surface of the pistons and keeps them from sliding smoothly through the rubber seals.

Since your goal is to clean the caliper and its pistons, exposing more of the pistons' surface would be a good idea. Impatient mechanics may choose to squeeze the brake lever slightly to push the pistons out of their bores. However, squeeze too much, and a piston will pop out of the caliper, creating a huge mess. Smart folks slip a thin piece of wood in between the pistons to prevent the dreaded "piston pop." Be sure to leave enough room for a toothbrush to clean the pistons.

Some mechanics rely on contact cleaner to flush the contaminants out of the calipers. Others arm themselves with Simple Green or other organic cleaners to cut through the mung. Who's right? According to the brake manufacturers, petroleum-based cleaners, like contact cleaner, swell the rubber O-rings that seal the calipers. You should only use organic cleansers to flush out the calipers. You have been warned.

Using the toothbrush and organic cleaner, carefully rub the shellac off the pistons. The side in the top of the caliper is the hardest to reach and may require some dexterity to get to. If you see any signs of brake fluid leaking, go buy the caliper rebuild kit. You should pay attention to the surface of the pistons. If you see rust or pitting, prepare for a rebuild. Once the calipers are clean, blow them dry with compressed air to keep any of the solvents from being forced into the brake fluid as you slide the pistons back into the caliper.

While the pistons are extended out in their cleaning position, you won't be able to install the new brake pads. Press the pistons back into the caliper one or two at a time. Hold the other pistons while you do so to keep them from popping out. If the pistons refuse to press fully into their bores, check the master cylinder's reservoir. Since the fluid in the caliper is displaced back into the reservoir, fluid that was added as the level dropped in the reservoir may hydraulically lock the system if it completely fills the reservoir. Siphon some fluid out and continue to press the caliper pistons into place.

To finish your caliper cleansing, on single-action calipers (those with pistons all on one side), pull back the rubber cover protecting the pins upon which the caliper slides back and forth. Using the same organic cleaners, remove the old, tired grease and check for any notches or unseemly wear to the pins. Lube the clean pins with waterproof, high-temperature grease and slide them into position under their protective covers.

Before you install the new pads, you need to prepare the disc's swept surface. Brake pads leave traces of material in the pores of the rotor's surface. If you're changing pad compounds, removing this material is vital if you want the new pads to bed in properly. However, you still want to remove any buildup of pad material on the disc face, using a piece of 60- or 80-grit sandpaper, even if you're replacing the old pads with ones of the same compound. With your bike on a front stand, simply press the sandpaper against the disc and spin the wheel a few times. Repeat the process on the other side of the disc. Remember: You're not trying to score the disk, just remove the buildup. Finish the disc prep by spraying them with brake cleaner and wiping them down with a clean rag.

Now you can replace the pads. Pay special attention to placing the factory antisqueal plates or springs in the proper position. Check the other caliper if you can't remember how the pieces go together. If the pads are not held in place with a pin, pay special attention to the way they fit in the caliper and verify that they haven't shifted once you've remounted the caliper to its bracket. Torque the fasteners to the proper specification. Also, pump up the brake lever as soon as you finish remounting the caliper. This way you won't experience the unfortunate surprise of having the lever come all the way back to the grip as you try to stop at the bottom of the hill at the end of your block.

After you've mounted your new pads, you need to break them in to receive the maximum stopping power they have to offer. If you go out and immediately hammer them repeatedly, you run the risk of glazing the surface of the pads and vastly reducing their coefficient of friction and performance. Read the "Brake Pad Break-In" sidebar for the best way to assure that your brakes give you the best they can.

If your caliper uses a screw-type retaining pin, be sure to loosen it before removing the caliper from the fork.

Choosing the Right Brake Pad Compound

When choosing new brake pads for your sexy sportbike, you're faced with many, many options. If you don't have the time or desire to research what pads will give you the best stopping power in the conditions in which you ride, simply buy the OE replacement items. Bike manufacturers spend a lot of time developing pad compounds for their sporting machinery, and you can't go wrong with their pads.

Many riders think that they need the absolutely grippiest pads available. Well, you don't. You want pads that deliver consistent stopping power throughout the range of speeds you're traveling—not necessarily a light switch–like transition from little grip to maximum grip. Consequently, "race" compounds may not be ideal for streeting purposes. Do your homework or talk to the manufacturer first, as some race pads need to build up heat to work, and you probably don't want to learn this little tidbit when your neighbor's dog decides to intercept you a half-block after you leave your driveway.

Most pad manufacturers do a good job of describing the type of riding their compounds are designed for. Just be honest with yourself about what type of riding you do when deciding.

If you're buying aftermarket pads, and your bike's original pads were sintered (which would include all current models), you should only use sintered compounds on your discs. What makes sintered pads better than the old organic compounds? Generally, sintered pads combine consistent grip with disc-friendly abrasives. Also, sintered pads should work better in the wet because of their more porous construction. Rather than using chunks of metal in some kind of organic binder, sintered pads have all of their components bonded together under heat and pressure. Different characteristics can be blended into the pads just by varying the material ratios. Finally, some organic pads would suffer from glazing if the manufacturer's break-in procedures weren't followed exactly.

Once you've freed the caliper from its mount, you may want to pry the pads apart with a screwdriver. Then they'll slip out of the center as shown here.

With the organic cleaner of your choice, spray the surface of the piston to loosen the mung. Don't be stingy — soak the caliper. Placing a pan under the caliper will help you catch the mess.

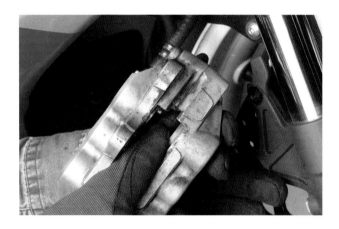

After the caliper's interior is clean, press the pistons back into their bores. Otherwise, you won't be able to slip the new, thicker pads into place.

Cleaning any pad residue off the disc with sandpaper will speed the bedding in of your new binders. This step is vital if you've changed pad compounds.

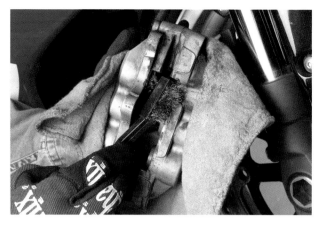

Use a soft-bristled brush to help remove the dust buildup. A brass brush, like the one shown, can be particularly helpful with tough deposits.

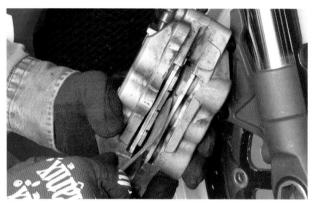

If you can't get the pistons back into their bores far enough to allow the disc to slide between the pads, you can use a pry bar to gently open up more space. Be careful not to mar the pads' surfaces.

Brake Pad Break-In

When you put new pads on your bike, don't rush out and try maximum braking on them right away. The surfaces of neither the pads nor the discs are really as smooth as they look. In fact, they're made up of lots of hills and valleys — up close, they look more like a saw blade. The break-in procedure wears down the pad so that the hills and valleys match each other, giving the maximum surface-area contact. Get too aggressive too soon, and the hills melt and glaze over, lowering the coefficient of friction for the pads and reducing braking performance.

When installing your new pads, you cleaned the disc with brake cleaner, right? Oil, grease, or brake fluid can ruin pads. Begin pad break-in by riding in a parking lot and lightly applying the brake, bringing the bike slowly to a stop. Do this a few times with slightly more pressure each time. Now, go for a ride. Just as when you have new tires and know not to immediately throw your bike into corners, allow yourself some extra room for braking around town. Begin to vary your braking pressure. Be firmer on one stop than the next. Allow for some cooling between applications (i.e., no banzai canyon runs, diving into the corners hard on the brakes at every entrance). If you're in the twisties, give the pads a couple corners' rest before using them hard again.

There is no magic number for how long it takes to break in a set of pads. If you vary the pressure and don't build it up too quickly, a short ride may be enough. However, if you're ever in doubt about how to break in a set of pads, simply look at the instructions that came with them — the manufacturers know.

Hydraulic Fluid Change

BRAKES

 Time: 45 minutes

 Tools: Wrenches, sockets, front and rear stands, rags, torque wrench (inch-pounds), Teflon tape, brake bleeding tool (optional), clear hose, glass jar for brake fluid, rags

 Talent:

 Cost: $

 Parts Required: Brake fluid

 Tip: Only use fresh fluid from unopened containers, and never mix fluid brands.

 PERFORMANCE GAIN: Better lever feel, no nasty surprises.

COMPLEMENTARY MODIFICATIONS: Add braided steel brake lines.

Maybe this weekend, when you pulled that big-whammy, late-braking maneuver, your brake lever came all the way back to the grip, giving you what racers, with their gift for understatement, call a "moment." Or maybe you just checked your brake (or hydraulic clutch) fluid and noticed that it has turned dark or cloudy. Or you could just be following your bike's maintenance schedule (good for you!) and the time has come to freshen your hydraulic fluid. However you came to this point, you should know that fresh hydraulic fluid is vital for proper performance.

Most hydraulic fluids have a taste for water and will gradually suck moisture past the rubber seals in your calipers. Also, if you use your brakes really hard, the heat can cook the fluid. If your fluid is contaminated with water, heavy brake use will raise the temperature to the point where the water will boil (at a significantly lower level than pure fluid would), leading to brake fade and the dread-inducing lever-to-the-grip experience.

Street riders should swap out hydraulic fluid at least once a season. Some people claim you should do this as part of the winterizing process, so that the moisture-free fluid sits in your bike all winter. Having never had problems develop while my

bike was in storage, I prefer to flush the fluid at the beginning of the season so that I get the benefit of fresh fluid in the spring. Those whose priority is maximum braking performance will most likely want to follow this schedule too.

The tools required for this project are minimal, but you can buy some specialized tools if you like—you *know* you want to. The Mityvac bleeding system (from Lockhart Phillips) is perfect for bone-dry systems—such as when you've installed stainless-steel lines. If the system is already primed, an old jar and clear hose will work just fine. The fluid you add to your system should come from an unopened container. Remember the hydraulic fluid's thirst for water. Although DOT 5 fluids are silicon-based and therefore don't absorb moisture, some riders don't like the feel at the lever as much. Most OEMs still recommend DOT 4 fluid. Also, make sure you buy a name-brand fluid. Buy more fluid than you think you need. (If you're having trouble with bubbles in your lines, the best cure is to run lots of fluid through the system to sweep them out.) Finally, never mix brands of brake fluids. If you need to top off the reservoir and don't know what type or brand of fluid is already in the system, flush the entire system to avoid any problems of interaction between the different formulations, even though—in theory—all DOT 4 (and DOT 5.1) fluids should play well together.

Begin with your bike on its stands. Since brake fluid damages paint and some powder coats, remove any vulnerable bodywork or cover it with rags. A preparatory step required for those using vacuum bleeders, and optional but recommended for all others, is to wrap the threads of the calipers' bleeder valves with Teflon tape. Vacuum bleeders create so much suction that they will draw air into the system past the bleeder valves' threads, making it impossible to tell when all air has been removed from the system. Teflon tape fills the minuscule gaps between the threads when the valve is not completely closed and is a worthwhile step for all calipers. One warning, though: Don't just remove the valve with the caliper mounted to the bike. Since the master cylinder is higher than the caliper, fluid will leak out all over the place. Raise the caliper equal to or above the reservoir to keep the mess to a minimum. Of course, if your lines are empty—as when you've just added stainless-steel ones—this is not a problem.

Rear calipers have their own idiosyncrasies to consider. Since the brake line travels horizontally from the master cylinder to the caliper, air bubbles get trapped in the line more easily. To assist the bubbles in their travels, unmount the caliper and hold it higher than the master cylinder, allowing the bubbles' tendency to rise to keep them moving as you run the new fluid through the system. If you're pumping the pedal, make sure you place a spacer between the brake pads to keep the piston from popping out of the caliper.

When using a vacuum bleeder, begin the bleeding by sucking the excess fluid out of the master cylinder. Then wipe

When wrapping the bleed screw's threads with Teflon tape, make sure you wind it so that screwing in the valve tightens the tape. Also, be careful not to cover the bleed holes.

This Mityvac is a handy tool for bleeding hydraulic systems—particularly bone-dry ones. Be prepared to empty the catch container at least once when freshening fluid. Since you'll be working by the caliper instead of the master cylinder, don't forget to keep an eye on the fluid level in the reservoir.

any visible grit out of the reservoir. If you're not using a vacuum bleeder, don't worry about running the old fluid through the system—unless you see dirt or other visible impurities. Don't add fresh fluid to the reservoir until most of the old fluid has been pumped out of it into the system itself.

Swapping the fluid in the system is pretty easy. Put a box-end wrench on the caliper's bleeder valve, then press a length of clear hose over the nipple. This must have a snug fit. The other end should empty into a container that is capable of standing on its own. (Glass containers, while breakable, are usually heavy enough to stay put, unlike plastic bottles or aluminum cans.) Slipping the hose through a hole in the screw-on cap is ideal. Don't forget to leave a breather hole, or the built-up pressure could pump the fluid out of the hose when disconnected from the nipple, creating another mess.

Pump the lever a few times and hold the last squeeze. Using the wrench, open the bleed valve until the pressure forces fluid into the hose. Hold the lever until you've closed the valve. Repeat this process several times until you have a couple inches of fluid in the hose directly above the bleeder. Now, open the valve slightly—only until you can just squeeze fluid out with the lever and no more. Continue to squeeze and release the lever until you see the fresh—usually clearer—fluid emerge from the bleeder. A short pause between every squeeze and release will make sure that any bubbles expelled from the system don't get sucked back in when you release the lever. Pay special attention to the reservoir while you are pumping the fluid through the system. If you let it run low, you'll get air in the system and have to start the bleeding process from scratch. If you started with empty lines, plan on running several more ounces of fluid through the system after you stop seeing bubbles to make sure that none remain.

When you're sure that the hydraulic system is free of old fluid and/or bubbles, slowly squeeze the lever as you

Keeping a big arch in the line will keep bubbles from being drawn back into the caliper. Don't be stingy with your fresh fluid. Keep pumping it through the system after you think you're done. Some bubbles are tenacious.

tighten the bleeder valve. Pump the lever several times and hold. Open the bleed valve to release the fluid. Do this several times. You'd be surprised how often one last bubble pops out during these final, high-pressure bleeds. If one does, run a few more ounces of fluid through the system. You will be rewarded with firmer lever feel. Torque the bleed valve to the recommended spec and finish by topping off the reservoir. Don't forget the other caliper! Make sure that the rubber diaphragm on the master cylinder is clean before placing it on top of the hydraulic fluid and tightening down the reservoir cover. Wipe away any traces of the brake fluid before it has a chance to damage any painted surfaces. Finally, as with all waste fluids from your bike, be a good citizen and recycle the old stuff.

Those of you with vacuum bleeders shouldn't feel left out. All of the steps are the same, except that the fluid will be sucked from the bottom end of the system instead of forced from the master cylinder. The same cautions apply, though. Accidentally let the reservoir go dry, and you'll need to start over.

Any discussion of hydraulic system bleeding usually includes a debate about which method is better: the master cylinder push-through or the vacuum tool suck-through. While many mechanics will subscribe to either one or the other, I've found a combination of the two works best. When bleeding dry lines, nothing gets them primed quicker than a vacuum bleeder. However, when swapping fluid, I prefer the pump-through method. So, when installing new lines, I use both methods. First, draw the fluid through with a suction tool, followed by the final flushing of air with the master cylinder method. Regardless of which technique you incorporate, the goal is to fill the system completely with fresh hydraulic fluid and no air bubbles. You'll be glad you took the time to do this the next time you grab a handful of brake.

When topping off the reservoir, don't fill beyond the full mark. Be sure to clean the diaphragm that floats on top of the fluid before installing it. Always use name-brand hydraulic fluid.

PROJECT 17

Caliper Rebuild

 Time: 2–3 hours

 Tools: Wrenches, sockets, front and rear stands, rags, torque wrenches (inch-pounds and foot-pounds), Teflon tape, brake bleeding tool (optional), clear hose, glass jar for brake fluid, compressed air, pick, Scotch-Brite, Crafts-man soft jaws plier covers, latex gloves

 Talent:

 Cost: <$–$$

 Parts Required: Piston seals, dust covers, pistons, and calipers as required. Crush washers.

 Tip: Make sure you keep your fingers clear when pressing out the pistons.

 PERFORMANCE GAIN: Brakes that don't drag

COMPLEMENTARY MODIFICATIONS: Rebuild master cylinder, replace pads, upgrade brake lines.

Remember back at the beginning of this section when you looked for uneven wear on brake pads as a sign of sticky brakes? Well, even if no pistons in the calipers are sticking, you should consider rebuilding a caliper if you can't remove the brake dust deposits from a piston with solvent and a brush. Proper functioning of the brake system depends on pistons that move easily within their bores.

Calipers, no matter how many pistons they have, are broken into two categories: single-action and dual-action. Single-action calipers have pistons that only press from one side of the disc and are most common in rear brakes. Dual-action calipers squeeze the disc with pistons from both sides. Rebuilding these two kinds of binders follows exactly the same steps—you just do more on dual-action units.

The rebuild starts with pressing the pistons out of the calipers. The recommended method is to drain the system and carefully blow the pistons out with compressed air. If you don't have compressed air, you can use the hydraulic fluid and lever to achieve the same result. Unfortunately, this technique is so messy that most people only try it once. Be sure to place a container to catch the fluid under the caliper. Follow the

same procedures for restraining the pistons described below. And don't forget latex gloves to protect your skin from the hydraulic fluid.

Begin the rebuild by draining the system and removing the caliper. To avoid a mess, wrap the line's fitting with a rag and tape it in place. Remove the pads, springs, clips, piston insulators, and any other hardware around the caliper's pistons. It's easiest to remove pistons from single-action calipers. For a one-piston, single-action caliper, place a rag between the piston and the bracket for the second brake pad. Carefully blow compressed air into the hole for the banjo fitting. Keep the air pressure low and your fingers clear of the piston! If the caliper has more than one piston, you will want to place a piece of wood, as well as the rag, into the caliper. This will keep one piston from popping out and leaving the other deeply recessed in its bore.

Similarly, one-piece, dual-action calipers should have their pistons blown out with a piece of wood in between the sets of pistons. The goal here is to have the wood thin enough to allow the pistons to fully extend, but not pop free. Two-piece, dual-action calipers can sometimes be unbolted, giving you better access to one set of pistons at a time. (Check your service manual before attempting this. Some manufacturers recommend against it.) Since you'd have to fashion a means of controlling the pistons as you blow them out of their bores, I'd recommend treating the calipers like one-piece units until you have the pistons extended.

If you're lucky, you'll be able to pull the pistons free of their bores with your fingers. If not, use a set of "soft jaws" on a pair of locking pliers. These plastic covers will keep the metal of the pliers from touching the piston and scratching its surface while still giving you a remarkably strong grip on it. After the pistons are removed, use a pick to gently pry out the dust covers and inner seals. Be careful not to scratch the piston bores—although this is less vital than with the pistons. Thoroughly clean the interior and exterior of the calipers and pistons with brake cleaner or other solvent. If the parts are particularly dirty, soak them for a few hours in parts cleaner. Remove any traces of the solvent and blow the parts dry, making sure that all fluid passages are clear.

Inspect the pistons. If you find any rust or pitting, polish the surface with Scotch-Brite until it is perfectly smooth. If the corrosion is too great, replace the piston. Similarly, buff away any pitting in the piston bores, and replace the caliper if you can't make the interior look like new. Spray the parts with brake cleaner and blow them dry again.

Although you don't need to replace the O-ring piston seals unless they're damaged, why would you go through all this trouble and not replace them? Install fresh seals and the dust seals by applying a coating of fresh brake fluid and slipping them into place. (Note: The dust seal is closest to the bore's opening.) To avoid damaging the seals, don't use any tools to install them—just your fingers. Apply a coat of brake fluid to the pistons and slide them all the way into their chambers. If you disassembled the caliper halves, install new O-rings and torque them together to factory specs.

Install any antirattle springs, clips, and other parts you removed from the caliper. On single-action calipers, apply a coating of high-temperature, water-resistant grease to the caliper holder shafts and the holder holes. If the boot and dust cover for the shaft is cracked, you should replace it. This is also a good time to wrap the caliper bleed-valve threads with Teflon tape to make bleeding the system easier. (See the preceding project.) Install fresh pads and bolt the caliper into place. Torque the banjo fitting and its fresh crush washers into place. Bleed the lines, break in the new pads, and you're done.

Be careful not to damage the piston bore as you remove the seals.

A piece of wood can keep the pistons from popping completely out of dual-action calipers. Again, apply the pressure slowly to keep the pistons from banging against the board.

If a piston is stuck, try removing it with soft jaws and a set of locking pliers. Also, try rotating it in the bore as you attempt to pull it out.

Remove any corrosion with Scotch-Brite. If you can't restore the piston to a polished surface, replace it.

PROJECT 18

Rebuilding the Master Cylinder

 Time: 2 hours

 Tools: Wrenches, sockets, front and rear stands, rags, torque wrench (inch-pounds), Teflon tape, brake bleeding tool (optional), clear hose, glass jar for brake fluid, compressed air, pick, Scotch-Brite, circlip pliers

 Talent: 👤👤👤

 Cost: $

 Parts Required: Dust cover, master cylinder, or piston as required, crush washers

 Tip: Be extremely careful when clearing the bleed holes, because they're delicate.

 PERFORMANCE GAIN: Brakes that work properly.

COMPLEMENTARY MODIFICATIONS: Rebuild calipers, replace pads, upgrade to stainless-steel brake lines.

Calipers aren't the only part of the brake system that will need to be rebuilt occasionally. The master cylinder, which powers the entire hydraulic system, needs attention from time to time. If it has a problem, you won't get full performance from your brakes. The most common issue is a piston with a worn primary or secondary cup, which allows hydraulic fluid to flow past the seal, resulting in low power or leaking at the brake lever. The master cylinder also has several tiny orifices that, if they clog, can prevent proper operation of the brakes. If you have gone through the trouble of rebuilding the calipers, you should spend the extra time to clean and inspect the master cylinder.

Drain the system and disconnect the brake line. On units with a remote reservoir, remove the hose connecting the reservoir to the master cylinder and unbolt it from its mounting bracket. Remove the brake lever or pedal, and brake switch wires. Take the master cylinder off of the clip-on or the footpeg hanger/frame for the remainder of the steps. Using a pick, carefully remove the dust cover and inspect it for cracks or punctures. If you find any, replace it. Look inside the piston bore for any signs of brake fluid leakage. If you see any, the piston needs to be replaced. Remove the circlip that holds the piston in its bore. The piston should slide out far enough for you to remove it by hand. Do not attempt to remove either the primary or secondary cups from the piston, as you will damage them. For rear-brake master cylinders, follow the same steps.

With the piston removed, give the master cylinder a thorough flush with an organic cleaner. (The rubber parts on the piston require special treatment and should only be cleaned with brake fluid or isopropyl alcohol.) Make sure all solvents are rinsed away with brake cleaner from the master cylinder internals. Blow it dry with compressed air. Closely inspect the piston bore. If you find any corrosion, rust pitting, or scratches, replace the master cylinder and the piston (which may have had its cups damaged by the abrasive corrosion). Make sure the supply and relief ports between the reservoir and the piston bore are clear. A piece of grit blocking the relief port can cause your brakes to drag, reducing pad and disc life. Blow the ports clear with compressed air. If you can't clear the port with air, carefully use a piece of safety wire, but beware, as damaging the port will affect the function of your brakes.

A tight seal is necessary for maximum braking power. So, give the piston a once-over, or even a twice-over. If either cup is worn, rotted, or swollen, replace the entire piston assembly. If the piston has any visible rust or corrosion, replace it. Finally, check the return spring for any kinks or corrosion and replace if necessary.

Before reassembling your master cylinder, coat the interior of the piston bore with brake fluid. Coat the piston cups with fluid. Make sure the return spring has the correct orientation before inserting the piston. Press the piston in as you reinstall the circlip. Don't forget to make sure that the dust cover is properly installed, sealing the piston from the outside environment. Remount the brake lever, and be sure to lube the pivot with grease and torque the pivot bolt's locknut. Bolt the master cylinder to the clip-on or frame. Attach the brake line with a fresh set of crush washers and torque the banjo bolt to spec. Reconnect the reservoir and bleed the system.

Once you have the dust cover out of the way, press the piston in slightly and remove the circlip.

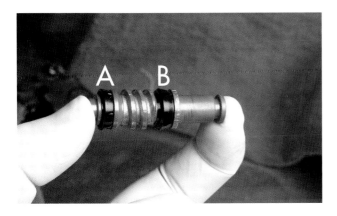

Inspect the primary (A) and secondary (B) cups for any signs of swelling or wear. The piston should be free of corrosion.

Visually inspect the supply (A) and relief (B) ports in the master cylinder. If compressed air won't clear them, carefully use a piece of safety wire.

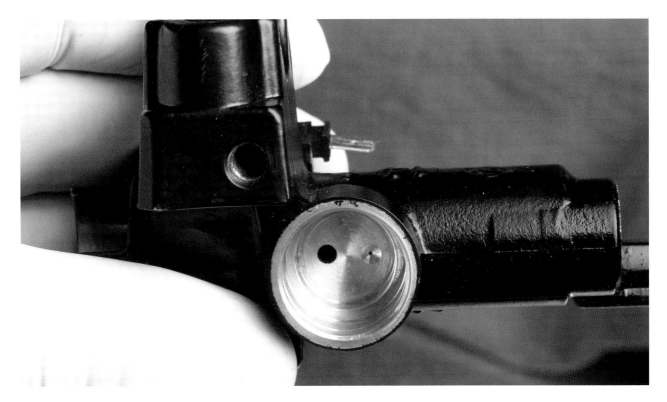

The same ports reside in master cylinders with remote reservoirs, but the space is much tighter.

PROJECT 19

Stainless-Steel Brake Line Installation

 Time: 1–2 hours

 Tools: Wrenches, sockets, front and rear stands (optional), rags, torque wrench (inch-pounds), Teflon tape, brake bleeding tool (optional), clear hose, glass jar for brake fluid

 Talent: ▮▮

 Cost: $–$$

 Parts Required: Brake lines, brake fluid

Tip: If you've modified your bike by raising or lowering the bars or extending the swingarm, order a custom-length kit.

 PERFORMANCE GAIN: A firmer squeeze at the lever and better feedback.

COMPLEMENTARY MODIFICATIONS: Replace brake pads, rebuild the caliper and master cylinder.

Although you can't see OE brake lines expand when you squeeze the lever the way you could in the Bad Old Days, fitting a set of braided, stainless steel brake lines to your sportbike can have a dramatic effect on your bike's stopping power. The initial onset of braking will be much quicker, since stainless lines don't expand at all. And since the lines are sheathed in metal (usually with a protective plastic outer coating), you don't have to worry about stainless lines cracking from age and exposure to the sun. Also, the Teflon interior is less prone to becoming brittle than rubber. So, a trip to the aftermarket will give you better braking and longer-lasting lines, to boot. Oh, yeah—they look cool.

Most of the major line manufacturers, like Goodridge, have premeasured kits available for almost every sportbike manufactured in the last 10 years. So, you shouldn't have any problem finding one for your ride. However, if you've modified your bike by raising or lowering the bars or extending the swingarm, you'll probably want to have a custom-length kit special-ordered for you. Some manufacturers offer build-'em-yourself kits, in which you cut the lines and attach the fittings.

While these kits are great for custom applications, be forewarned that you need to order each individual part, right down to the angle of the bend on the banjo fitting.

Before you begin installation, check to make sure that all of the lines in your kit are the correct length. Nothing will make you crazier than having a line end up an inch short, while your bike sits idle with the entire system disassembled. You're then stuck with no ride until you get the correct part, or reassembling lines you want to take off anyway. The simplest way to check the length of the lines is by zip-tying them to the existing lines. Although this takes a couple of extra minutes, you can tell right away if the lines will have the proper amount of slack in them. Having your brake lines go taut before the fork is fully extended would be a Very Bad Thing.

Even in the best-case scenario, changing hydraulic lines is messy. Since brake fluid can damage paint and other shiny stuff on your bike, you should remove or cover any vulnerable painted surfaces. You will also want to get the system as empty of fluid as possible before removing the lines. A vacuum bleeder is ideal for this. Begin by sucking the extra fluid out of the reservoir. Then attach the hose to a caliper's bleeder valve. Give the bleeder a couple of pumps to build up the suction, and crack the valve until fluid starts to be drawn into the catch tank. Keep pumping until the system is dry. Do this for both front calipers.

Unscrew or unclasp all of the fasteners holding the hydraulic line in place. Using a ratchet, remove the banjo bolt from the caliper. To keep the fluid leakage to a minimum, wrap the banjo with a rag and secure it with a zip-tie or piece of tape. Remove the master cylinder banjo and feed the line out of the chassis. Now, feed the new line into place, following the exact same route as the stock line. Usually, aftermarket front brake kits will use two lines from the master cylinder instead of a T-junction further down the line. Be sure you run the correct line to each caliper. (One is usually longer than the other.)

Always replace the crush washers when the banjo bolts have been removed. The soft copper (for steel banjos) or aluminum (for aluminum banjos) is designed to conform to any irregularities on the fitting or mounting surface. A washer should be used on both sides of the banjo. If two banjos are being bolted together (as on the front brake master cylinder), be sure to use a crush washer between the two banjos, as well. Screw the banjo bolts in finger tight and check your hose routing before you torque things down. You don't want any sharp bends or kinks in the lines. If things don't line up right, you may have the banjos at the wrong mounting point. Hydraulic line manufacturers spend a lot of time making sure that the fittings have the same bend as the OE lines they replace—if something doesn't look right, it probably isn't.

Once you've torqued banjo bolts down, make sure you attach the lines to the chassis at all the original points. Sometimes you'll need to use zip-ties to hold the thinner, stainless lines to the OE clips. Although most stainless lines are sold in protective sheaths, bare, braided stainless-steel lines can cut through metal like a hacksaw. If your lines are uncoated, make sure you wrap the lines with tape or spiral wrap specifically designed for the purpose at all potential points of contact with the chassis. Then, follow the bleeding instructions in Project 16.

Sure, they look great—but just wait until you feel the difference. (Don't grab too hard the first time.)

Sucking the fluid out of the reservoir will speed up the task of draining the system. Place the cap back on the system—but don't screw it down—to keep dust out of it while you're changing the lines.

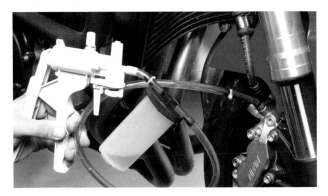

Using a vacuum bleeder is much more effective at draining the brake system than trying to pump it dry with the master cylinder.

The OE system only used a single line at the master cylinder, so the second aftermarket line needs to be held in place while the banjo is torqued. Note the three copper crush washers used to seal the system.

Quickly attaching the new line to the stocker will tell you if it is the right length. This will also help you to prepare for any idiosyncrasies of your bike's brake line routing.

Notice the gentle curve of the stainless line as it leaves the caliper. If it had the wrong bend in the banjo fitting, the line could kink.

59

Aftermarket Disc Installation

 Time: 1 hour

 Tools: Wrenches, sockets, Allen key sockets, front and rear stands, torque wrench, thread lock, hammer, eye protection, impact wrench (optional)

 Talent:

 Cost: $–$$$

 Parts Required: Aftermarket disc, new pads

 Tip: : Rap the bolts a couple of times to free the thread lock.

 PERFORMANCE GAIN: More stopping power and no pumping at the lever.

COMPLEMENTARY MODIFICATIONS: Add aftermarket calipers.

Although brake pad technology has advanced to the point that the compounds providing quick stops don't necessarily mean you're wearing your discs out, you may find that you want to replace your discs. The good news is that aftermarket discs are usually lighter and grippier than OE steel. The bad news is that none of the discs come cheap. Also, if you only need to replace one front disc and have decided to turn to the aftermarket, you'll need to replace both. So, consider that when you make your decision.

What you get for your money is pretty impressive, though. Almost all front discs are now floating models, meaning the swept area of the disc is loosely mounted on a carrier. This space between the two pieces allows the disc to expand without warping in high-temperature situations. Also, since the swept area and the carrier now have unrelated jobs, their composition can vary more widely. For example, high-carbon stainless steel is fairly common for the abrasive surface. Cast iron is also used here. You won't find carbon-fiber swept areas on street bikes, since it requires heat to work properly. Recently, wave-patterned discs have entered the fray. Aside from the obvious lessening of unsprung weight, the manufacturers say that the wave shape lets a disc expand under heavy use without deforming. Laser cutting of the disc

is now a common practice, assuring a smooth surface on the swept area. The carrier can vary from ordinary (and heavy) steel to aluminum or featherweight carbon fiber.

Installing new discs has few pitfalls. You begin by placing your bike on front and rear stands. Next, unmount and hang the calipers by something other than their hoses. Remove the front wheel. While you may be tempted to lay the wheel on its side so you can remove the discs, be careful not to support the wheel with the disc. Instead, place an old tire under the wheel.

People sometimes run into trouble on what seems like the easiest step. The manufacturers often use thread lock on the bolts securing the disc, and these bolts usually incorporate Allen (hex) heads. So if you're not using an impact wrench to loosen the bolts, insert an Allen socket and extender into the bolt and give it a couple of good raps with a hammer. Don't forget eye protection. The loosened thread lock should allow the bolts to spin out easily. For stubborn bolts, use a bit of heat on the area around the bolt—just enough with a propane torch to melt the thread lock. While you've got the disc off, you might want to clean the parts of the wheel that are hard to get to otherwise.

On dual-disc front wheels (which means almost all of them), place the wheel on a spare tire to keep from pressing on the bottom disc while you wrench on the top one. Once all the bolts have been loosened, a speed wrench makes quick work of removing them.

Some discs are listed as being for either the left or the right side of the wheel so that they rotate the correct way against the pads. Read the instructions for the discs. Also, some will have the rotational direction marked on the disc or carrier. This is vitally important. Place the new disc in position, put thread lock on the bolt threads, and screw them into place so that they are finger tight. Next, torque them down in a crisscross pattern to assure that the disc mounts evenly. Before moving on to the next disc, take a rag moistened with contact cleaner and wipe down the swept surface of the disc. Frequently, discs will be shipped with a coating of protective oil. You want to be certain that this is completely removed or it will contaminate the new pads and dramatically reduce your braking power. If the disc has a particularly heavy coat of oil, you can wash and blow-dry the disc before you mount it.

Now remount the wheel and calipers. Don't forget to break in your new pads and discs properly for maximum stopping power.

Some discs were designed with a particular rotational direction in mind. Inspect the disc closely for an arrow that indicates the proper wheel rotation. (If you're unsure, check the arrow on the tire and match that.)

Make sure you wipe off the protective oil coating on the disc before remounting the wheel. In fact you should always wipe the discs before you position the calipers. It's far too easy to leave grease or some other contamination on the swept surface while you're wrenching. Be sure to wear gloves when using contact cleaner.

PROJECT 21

Checking Disc Runout and Thickness

 Time: 30 minutes

 Tools: Micrometer, dial gauge, front and rear stands, calculator

 Talent:

 Cost: None–$$$

 Parts Required: Replacement disc, if needed

 Tip: Consider replacing discs that are within, but near the limits of, the factory tolerances.

 PERFORMANCE GAIN: Smooth brake application without fade.

COMPLEMENTARY MODIFICATIONS: Replace discs with aftermarket items.

Make sure you've chosen the thinnest point of the disc for your measurement.

The last time you changed your brake pads you may have noticed that the swept surface of the rotor was beginning to look like an old vinyl record—a progression of peaks and valleys, some of which are quite deep. Or maybe you've noticed the telltale pulsing in your lever during light application of the brake that is often a sign of a warped disc. It's time to see if your disc is still within specifications for thickness or excessive runout (warping).

Since motorcycle brakes essentially convert movement into heat via the friction of the pads against the discs, the parts will wear out. Most frequently, we replace only the pads, but if you use your brakes hard or mount particularly abrasive pad compounds, the discs will wear noticeably. Grooves and an overall thinning of the rotor is usually the reason for swapping discs, but on occasion, intense abuse—read: track use—may cause the discs to overheat and warp, giving a pulse at the lever. Warped rotors brake very inefficiently, since on each rotation the pistons are being pushed back into the caliper by the high point, while at the other end of the system, you're pushing the pistons back out of the caliper with the lever. A warped disc will also take away much of the "feel" you have at the lever as the wheel approaches lockup and increase the potential for nasty surprises.

As with most projects, the best source for the specifications you'll be verifying is your factory repair manual. However, in

the case of disc thickness, you can usually find the minimum stamped somewhere on the disc or its carrier. Armed with this information and a micrometer, you can ascertain your rotor's health in a matter of seconds. Select the portion of the swept area that looks the thinnest and measure the thickness with your micrometer. (Unfortunately, you can't use a dial or vernier caliper for this measurement.) If your micrometer measures in inches, get out your calculator and convert the number you measured into millimeters. In case you forgot, there are 25.4 mm per inch. To convert from inches to millimeters, multiply the measurement by 25.4. If the number is larger than the number stamped on the disc, you're still in business.

Checking for runout requires a little more setup. Place your bike on front and rear stands to allow you to freely rotate the wheel. Solidly mount a dial gauge so that the piston rests against the disc on its outer side, facing away from the side of the disc, not the outer edge. Slowly rotate the wheel and note the high point and low point for the disc's runout. If this number exceeds the manufacturer's recommendation, you'll want to replace the disc. (If the front disc is part of a dual-disc system, you'll want to replace both.) For those riders who are too cheap to buy a dial gauge (inexpensive gauges can be found online), you can bend an old wire coat hanger into a pointer and tape it solidly to a fork leg. Now find the high point in the disc runout, and set the wire so that it just touches the disc. Rotate to the low point and measure the gap. The wire must be completely stable or you'll be wasting your time. Also, due to the potential margin of error, if your numbers are close to the maximum, borrow a dial indicator to be certain.

When it comes to braking feel, the less runout the better. If your disc is near the limits, consider investing in a new one.

PROJECT 22

Installing an Aftermarket Brake System

 Time: 2 hours

 Tools: Wrenches, sockets, front and rear stands, torque wrench, thread lock, Teflon tape

 Talent:

 Cost: : $$$$$ (Big bucks)

 Parts Required: Aftermarket discs, calipers, brake lines, pads, and brake fluid. Brake light switch, if needed.

 Tip: A complete aftermarket brake system gives you maximum flexibility for setting up your controls.

 PERFORMANCE GAIN: More stopping power, better feel, and envious looks from your friends.

This eight-piston caliper saves a bunch of weight over the stock unit, reducing the front wheel's unsprung weight. The braking power is also improved tremendously.

Here's the grandaddy of brake modifications! Aftermarket brake systems don't need the compromises of an OE system. Instead, system performance, weight, and feel are the motivating factors—you can get exactly what you want. While most calipers on stock sportbikes feature four pistons, you can order aftermarket kits with six or more pistons. Why do you want these? More pistons will press on a larger portion of the disc, multiplying the effective force transferred from your fingers to the pads. Similarly, aftermarket discs are often larger in diameter than the OE ones. By clamping on the disc farther from the center of the wheel, the brakes generate more friction because more material of the disc passes the pads on each revolution of the wheel—which is very good, since friction is what slows you down. Also, the larger disc will exert more leverage over the wheel.

The master cylinder's skinny mounting bracket makes easy work of locating the lever where you want it. Adjusting the lever height is simple too.

For such a pricey modification, installation is pretty straightforward. If you've changed the brake fluid, lines, or pads, you've done about half of the work before! Swapping the stock brake system for an aftermarket one is a two-part process. First, remove the old system. Second, mount the new one. Well, duh.

Begin with your bike on front and rear stands. Remove the front wheel and swap the rotors, following the instructions in Project 20. Drain the system as described in Project 19. An empty system is much easier to disassemble. Take note of the path taken by the lines before removing the stock system. You'll also want to clean all the parts before you pack them away for storage.

The beauty of an aftermarket master cylinder is that you should have complete freedom to adjust the lever position to suit your needs. Mount the master cylinder and the reservoir to the clip-on. Next, reinstall the front wheel on the fork before mounting up the beefy new calipers. Now, run the braided lines along the same route as the stock lines. If the new master cylinder doesn't have a brake light switch, you can buy a clever banjo bolt switch from Four Strokes Only (www.fourstrokesonly.com), which will mount just like any other banjo bolt—only with a wire to connect for your brake light.

Once the whole kit is torqued into place, just bleed the system as outlined in Project 16. Finish by bedding in the pads according to the manufacturer's instructions. Then go show off your trick new parts and improved street cred.

SECTION THREE

WHEELS AND TIRES

What can be said about tires? They're black, round, and keep the wheels from touching the ground, right? Actually, they are your critical link to the asphalt when you're riding your sportbike. Motorcycle and tire manufacturers spend more time studying how tires interact with the road than any of us can imagine. The amazing increase in sporting machinery's capabilities owes as much to tire advances as it does to suspension and engine improvement. When it comes to wheels, lighter is always better, but wheels also play an important role in how your bike steers and even how stable it is in a straight line. Read on to learn how to keep those hoops rolling straight and true.

Flat Fix

 Time: 30 minutes

 Tools: Tire pressure gauge

 Talent:

 Cost: <$

 Parts Required: Progressive Suspension tire repair kit, extra CO2 cartridges

 Tip: Check your kit every couple of months — vulcanizing glue has a habit of hardening all by itself.

 PERFORMANCE GAIN: None, other than that you can finish the ride you started.

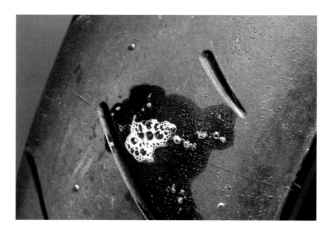

The most effective means to find a leak out on the road is to look for impressions or debris in the tire and administer a liberal application of saliva.

WHEELS AND TIRES

Guess what? You don't even need a garage to do this project—many riders learn it on the side of the road. Practicing at home first (experimenting with a bald tire before you swap it for a fresh one) will make the experience on the road that much less painful.

Being stranded on the side of the road by a flat tire is one of the worst feelings a motorcyclist can encounter. Unfortunately, flat tires seem to occur at the most inconvenient place and time, like on a remote section of road, 150 miles from home, with no cell service to call a friend. Since bikes don't carry spare tires, we're usually at the mercy of luck—or our planning. Carrying a tire repair kit with CO_2 cartridges can help turn getting back to civilization into a mere inconvenience rather than a daylong event.

When you suspect you have a leaking tire, before you attempt to assess the damage, make sure you're well away from the side of the road. Even if you're in a remote area and only one car may pass every half hour, drivers (who have important things to do like eating, putting on makeup, or changing CDs) may suffer from inattention, or worse, target fixation, and clip you or your bike if you're too close to the road. So be smart and plan your "work area."

Begin by checking your tire for visual damage. If you find a nail, don't pull it out right away. Instead, rub some spit on it where it enters the tread to see if it bubbles. If it doesn't, leave it for now. You may have a leak somewhere else. (If you find a leak somewhere else, go back and pull the nail and check that you don't have two leaks.) Keep looking for your leak. A generous application of saliva to any holes you suspect in the rubber will reveal the culprit.

Once you've found the hole, free it of any debris. Open your flat-fix kit and assemble the pieces, but don't puncture the CO_2 yet. Coat the metal portion of the plug tool with vulcanizing cement. Insert the tool into the hole. (You may have to push fairly hard.) Now rotate the tool back and forth in order to clean out the hole, coat it with cement, and give it a uniform shape.

Remove the plug from its protective casing and place it snugly on the tip of the tool. When you unwrap the film protecting the sealing portion of the plug, be sure not to handle the sticky section, as doing so may weaken the plug's seal. Coat the plug with the vulcanizing cement. Push the plug firmly into the puncture. You want the sticky ring around the plug to be solidly pressed into the tire's carcass with the plug's adhesive strip in the center. Remove the tool. Some of the plug should remain on the outside of the tread. Just prior to inflating the tire, cut the excess rubber from the plug, leaving about an eighth of an inch protruding from the tire.

Although the vulcanizing cement will dry fairly quickly, you should wait at least 15 minutes (longer in temperatures below 60 degrees) before you pressurize the tire with the CO_2. The Moto-Pump tire inflator in the flat fix kit must be used in an upright position. Screw the flexible adapter hose to the inflator until tight. Unscrew the inflator and drop a fresh CO_2 cartridge into the chamber. Screw the cap onto the inflator until it makes contact with the cartridge. Lift the lever into the outermost locked position. (Holding a finger under it will keep it from being accidentally pressed.) Quickly, screw the base of the Moto-Pump to puncture and then seal the CO_2 cartridge. Thread the adapter hose onto the tire's valve stem. Gradually squeeze the lever to initiate the flow of the CO_2 into the tire. You will most likely need to inject more than one cartridge into the tire to get it up to a decent pressure. Stop at the first gas station you find to check for further leaking and set your tire to the correct pressure.

Just because your tire will hold air doesn't mean that you can ride the way you normally would. A plug is a temporary fix until you can get to a shop and have either an internal plug installed or your tire replaced. Progressive Suspension recommends not exceeding 45 miles per hour with a plug in your tire. If you decide to ignore that advice, don't ride any faster than you're willing to tumble down the pavement. As long as I've taken on a fatherly tone, don't waste your money having a permanent plug put into your tire. If you're into performance riding (and why else would you be reading this book?), the risks inherent in plugged tires at speed are too great to ignore, and you should replace the tire instead. If that approach doesn't persuade you, consider the cost of replacing body parts—both motorcycle and human—before you wick up the pace on a plugged tire.

Rotating the plug tool inside the tire performs two services: It reams the puncture a uniform shape and coats the surface with cement.

Don't skimp when applying vulcanizing cement to the plug. You want to be sure that the entire surface is covered.

Trim the excess plug, leaving an eighth of an inch above the tread.

While keeping the CO2 cartridge upright, inflate the tire to a workable pressure. You will probably need more than one cartridge.

Removing Wheels

 Time: 15 minutes–1 hour

 Tools: Various sockets, various Allen sockets, open end wrenches, torque wrench, breaker bar, front and rear stands, tape measure, grease, rags

 Talent:

 Cost: None

 Parts Required: Cotter pin

 Tip: Plan ahead for when you need to remove the front wheel by buying or building the correct-size hex key.

 PERFORMANCE GAIN: None, but with practice you'll soon be faster at this than all your buddies.

You won't be able to complete most of the projects in this section if you don't know how to remove your bike's wheels. While the process seems complicated the first time you do it, with a little practice you'll be able to cut down the time it takes dramatically, and you'll think nothing of pulling the rear wheel to swap out the sprocket with less than a half hour before the next track session.

Front Wheel

You'll want to begin with the bike on the rear stand only. Since the axle nut is torqued on pretty tight, loosen it with a breaker bar while the front tire still rests on the ground. To prepare to loosen the axle, loosen the axle clamp bolts at the bottom of the fork leg. The trick to easing the dismounting of the front wheel is to loosen only the bolts that pinch the axle and not the nut. While the correct pinch bolts are usually on the right side, a quick glance at your owner's manual or service manual will confirm this.

If you're lucky, your bike will have an axle with a separate nut. However, in recent years, manufacturers have been installing axles with increasingly large hex heads. Now, just try to find a half-inch socket with an Allen key that large. Some run as large as 24 mm! Some aftermarket companies have started selling adapters that fit these axles, and you can sometimes get a spark plug socket to do the trick. Simply insert an extender inside the socket and use the external hex on the socket. Of course, you need the right size, but you can

take your dial caliper to your local tool store to find one. Using a breaker bar, loosen the axle about one turn. On virtually all bikes, you'll have to remove the calipers first. Even on those that don't require it, remounting the wheel will be much easier if you do. So, remove the calipers and support them with something other than the brake lines. Now, you can use the front stand to support the bike. Spin the axle free and remove the wheel.

If you weren't able to find a tool to fit the axle, all is not lost. Another trick for removing ornery front axles (like those on Kawasakis) is to keep the pinch bolts on the axle locked, loosen the pinch bolts on the nut, and, using a smaller hex key, loosen the nut. Once your have the nut out, lift the front end, loosen the axle pinch bolts, and pull it free.

Installing the front wheel is the reverse of removal—with a couple of additional steps. Wipe the axle clean and apply a thin coat of high-temperature grease to it. Before you torque the axle, you'll want to snug it up and take the bike off the front stand. Pump the brakes up, squeeze the brake lever, and bounce the front end a few times to make sure that the wheel is centered in the fork. Torque the axle and the pinch bolts to factory specifications.

Rear Wheel

Depending on what type of swingarm you have on your bike, removing the wheel is either ridiculously easy or just plain easy. For single-sided swingarms (VFR750/800, for example), remove the big, honkin' nut or nuts securing the wheel, then pull the wheel free. You may need to move the exhaust can, though. Standard swingarms require just a little more work. Some swingers don't mind if the chain adjusters are left the way they are. Others won't let you pull the axle free without some work—and you can just forget about getting the axle back in. So, first try removing the wheel without changing the chain adjusters. If you find that you do have to loosen them, give the adjusters three full turns of slack and retighten the locknuts. Once you get the wheel back on the bike, tighten the adjusters those three turns.

So, you've removed the cotter pin and spun the axle nut off the axle. While holding the wheel in position (to take the strain off the axle as you slide it free), remove the axle. Now, push the wheel forward to create some slack in the chain. Remove the chain from the sprocket and hang it on the swingarm. The wheel can now be lowered out of the swingarm. You may have to support the rear caliper to pull the wheel free.

When you're ready to put the wheel back in the swingarm, begin by spreading the brake pads with a flathead screwdriver. Next, clean and grease the axle. Carefully slide the wheel into the swingarm and lift it up in the forward position it was in when you removed the chain. You may need to try a couple of different angles to get the disc in the caliper. Once the disc is in the caliper and the chain is on the sprocket,

Loosen the axle pinch bolts before you attempt to remove the axle.

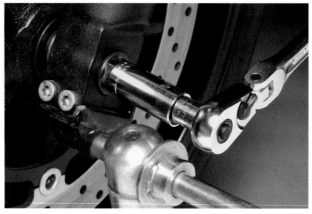

Big axle heads require special tools. If you can't find an Allen key big enough, you may be able to use a spark plug socket to free up the axle.

After you've slid the axle free of the swingarm, move the wheel forward and remove the chain from the sprocket.

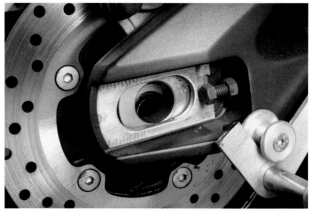

With the hub hanging on the axle, lift the opposite side of the wheel until the holes line up. Then push the axle home.

pull the wheel backward until the hole in the hub lines up with the hole in the swingarm. (Having the axle hanging in the swingarm eases the next step.) Slide the axle into the hub far enough to support the wheel. Move to the opposite side of the bike, where you can see through the swingarm to the hub. Lift the wheel until the hole lines up with the swingarm. Tap the axle through using your hand or a dead-blow hammer.

Snug down the axle nut. If you had to loosen the chain adjusters, reset them. If you haven't adjusted your chain in a while, now is a good time. Verify that the marks on the chain adjusters match up on both sides before torquing down the axle nut. Verify that everything is in place and the wheel turns freely. Pump up the rear brake lever to make sure the pads aren't dragging. Finally, add a fresh cotter pin to the axle nut if your bike requires one.

Tightening the axle nuts to the proper torque specification is vital for your safety. Cranking them down too tight can compress bearing spacers and lead to bearing failure. Leaving them too loose can let them spin free, with disastrous results.

Choosing the Right Tire

Time: As much as you want

Tools: None

Talent:

Cost: None

Parts Required: None

Tip: Race tires don't belong on the street. Really.

PERFORMANCE GAIN: Choose wisely, and you can maximize traction, performance, and mileage.

Many of the projects in this book involve bringing race technology to bear on street bikes to improve performance. For the most part, you can expect these modifications to improve the way your bike handles—even if it introduces compromises in other areas. However, one area where you should leave the racing parts to the track is tires. Running race rubber on the street offers no benefit. All you do is spend more money for tires that don't work as well as their more domesticated counterparts. You can even compromise your safety. Stick with the street tires.

No one can argue that motorcycles have gotten more specialized since the early 1980s. Gone are the days of the Universal Japanese Motorcycle, the blank slate upon which you applied the aftermarket to turn it into the type of bike you wanted. Off-the-rack sportbikes can perform feats only factory racers could conceive of just 10 years ago. Specialization has given us the sportbike niche that we love. And if bikes have narrowed their focus, tires have become laser beams directed at very specific activities. Race tires and street tires are two beneficiaries of these advances.

Race tires are designed to give maximum grip for an extremely limited time. To make things even more specific, they are formulated to work at temperatures only achievable at track speeds. Below those temperatures, they can be downright scary. While top riders with expert feel can tell when they've got fresh race skins and when they have tires that have been through one heat cycle, the vast majority of us lack the sensitivity to extract every last bit of these tires' capabilities.

Within the category of "race tires," many subsets exist. Qualifying tires won't survive two full laps at speed. Dual-compound tires put a harder, more durable rubber on sections of the tire that get abused at certain tracks. Intermediates look like cut slicks for transitional track conditions, while rains are for the weather that their name implies.

Street tires are segmented by the bikes for which they're designed: sport, sport touring, touring, cruiser, and dual purpose. So in many ways, your choice of tires has been simplified, rather than made more complicated, by the stratification of motorcycles. Sportbikes need sport tires. If you're the kind of rider who commutes, travels, and runs the twisties on the weekend, you'll be fine with the OE tires for your bike. Some bike manufacturers even use two brands of OE tires, giving you a choice.

The tire companies are now tuning their tires for different levels of sport riding. Suppose you're the type of rider who only canyon scratches or attends track days: The premium model sport tires are what you'll want to run. According to Jeff Johnson from Metzeler/Pirelli, the Diablo tires were designed for riders who spend about 30 percent of their time on the track and 70 percent on the street. The Diablo Corsa is for someone who spends 70 percent of the time at the track and 30 percent on the street—rubber compounds have gotten that specific. The best sources of information about particular tire applications are the manufacturers themselves. They know that if they're designing tires for specific riders, they need to let them know what the differences are.

So, instead of worrying about which tire is stickier, concentrate on things like the tire profile. Are you the kind of rider who likes to slam your bike on its side and rail through corners at maximum lean? A more triangular profile, with quicker steering and a larger contact patch at full lean, will be more suited to you. If you're the kind of rider who trail brakes into turns, hanging at the outside, waiting to see where the pavement goes before committing to your final line, you should look at rounder profiles that have a larger contact patch for braking while upright and allow for easier adjustment of lines midcorner.

Similarly, you should look into what riders and tire manufacturers recommend for the type of riding conditions you're likely to face. If most of your favorite roads are bumpy, you'll be looking for a tire with a softer carcass to allow the tread to flex over the bumps. If rain is a regular part of your locale, pay special attention to a tire's silica content for wet pavement grip. Also, while the big, blocky tread of some hyper-sport tires looks sexy, you can end up doing the two-wheel two-step with them in the wet. Some tires have a reputation for taking a long time to warm up in cooler temperatures, so consider what season it is when you're buying new rubber. Finally, only use tires that are designed to fit on your rims' width. Putting bigger tires on your rim may not give you the bigger contact patch you desire. Since the carcass will be squeezed smaller to fit, the carefully designed profile will be erased. To find out all this important information, ask the advice of your local shops, or call or e-mail the tire manufacturers. They will be happy to help you.

Did I mention? Don't waste your money or risk your bike by running race tires on the street.

Yes, tires are all black and round, but there is much more to them than that. This collection features a slick, a DOT-legal race tire, a street-legal sport tire, an intermediate rain tire, and a full rain tire. Only one of these belongs on the street.

Tire Pressure

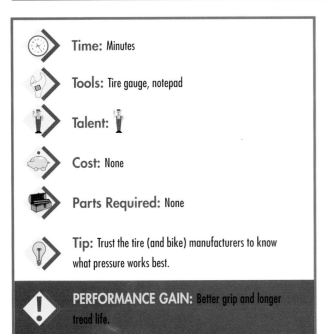

Time: Minutes

Tools: Tire gauge, notepad

Talent:

Cost: None

Parts Required: None

Tip: Trust the tire (and bike) manufacturers to know what pressure works best.

PERFORMANCE GAIN: Better grip and longer tread life.

Tire pressure plays an important role on your motorcycle. First, the tire is an important part of the suspension. Air pressure can stiffen or soften the ride qualities in undesirable ways. Perhaps the most important effect tire pressure has for sport riders is controlling the size of the contact patch and, by extension, the life of the tire.

As a tire rolls down the road, it goes from being almost perfectly round to flat where it engages the tarmac. This flat oval of rubber constitutes the contact patch. To form this flat spot that moves around the tire with each revolution, the carcass actually bends in two directions. It begins by bowing out slightly before it bends back on itself under the force of the road. This bowing and bending back and forth creates heat inside the tire. Tire manufacturers use this heat buildup to their advantage by designing rubber compounds that reach their peak effectiveness at a particular temperature. Air pressure helps the tire develop and maintain that temperature.

Just because one tire gauge is more expensive than the other doesn't mean that it is more accurate. The budget Roadgear digital gauge on the left has been spot on since its package was opened. The dial gauge on the right has been consistently reading two pounds low since it was new. Compare your gauge to one of the tire vendors' at your local track to see how yours stacks up.

You may have heard stories about the obsession with tire pressure at the track. However, this type of tuning plays less of a role with today's radials than it did back when bias-ply tires were the norm. According to Metzeler/Pirelli's Jeff Johnson, "Pressure rise is no longer a valid way to check for tire temperature. Instead, understand what the motorcycle is doing underneath you, then ride to the capabilities of that bike at that time."

If checking pressure isn't a good way to tell if your tires are running up to temperature, why do some manufacturers recommend lower pressures on the track? The lower pressure allows for a larger contact patch and therefore more grip in the corners. A word of caution: They shouldn't be so low that they allow the carcass to deform and cause handling problems. Also, if the pressure is too low, the tires could overheat and have the extra traction slip away. Trackside tire vendors (they *know* what they're talking about) constantly watch what tires are winning and what pressures are working the best so that they can recommend the best options and keep their customers happy.

Street riders need to remember that racers are willing to sacrifice straight-line stability for increased grip. The truth about street riding is that, regardless of how talented the rider is, most street bikes spend a high percentage of their time straight up. A side benefit of using the proper pressure is that the front tire will feel more precise and turn in quicker—a good thing during point and shoot sessions. If you run your tire pressures too low, you can easily overheat your tires, simply riding in a straight line. Remember, the lower pressure is to ensure a large contact patch, which is created by the carcass flex. The same process happens when you're not cornering too. Take your sportbike out on an extended interstate ride with too little air, and all that flexing of the tire can cook the life right out of it.

Tire manufacturers spend a lot of time determining the pressures that will provide the best compromise of performance and tire wear on the street. While some manufacturers recommend running the same pressures listed in the owner's manual for the bike's OE tires, a significant number have proprietary pressures that should be run on particular tire/bike combinations. Be sure to ask your dealer or check the tire manufacturer's product literature or website for specific numbers—these numbers do change as information is gathered about current-model bikes. Johnson sums up his feelings about tire pressure: "Trust all of the tire manufacturers to build a quality product and follow their pressure recommendations." And check the pressure before every ride!

Remember, the tire manufacturers want you to be satisfied with your tires so that you'll buy more from them, so they have everything to gain by telling you what pressures will work best for their product. Representatives for these companies always stress that between 75 and 80 percent of the tire warranty claims are caused by underinflation. When the cost of today's premium rubber is considered, investing in a good tire gauge—and using it religixously—is cheap insurance.

Tire Change

WHEELS AND TIRES

 Time: 2 hours

 Tools: Front and rear stands, bead breaker, rim protectors, tire irons, valve stem tool, milk crate or oil drum, spray container with soapy water, tire pressure gauge, compressed air, gloves (or Band-Aids)

 Talent: ▌▌▌

 Cost: $–$$$

 Parts Required: Front and rear tires

 Tip: Use a dedicated bead breaker and ignore the people who say wood blocks and C-clamps work just as well.

 PERFORMANCE GAIN: Superior traction, particularly in wet or dusty conditions.

COMPLEMENTARY MODIFICATIONS: Replace rubber valve stem with metal one, check wheel runout.

Why would anyone want to change their own tires? Isn't it hard work that usually involves at least one bleeding knuckle? Don't the tools cost a small fortune when you consider that shops only charge about 20 bucks for the service? Well, some riders don't live within 5 miles of a bike shop. Racers who can't afford multiple sets of wheels may need to change from slicks to DOT tires for different classes. And some folks, well, they've always got to do things their own way.

The good news is that, overworked sweat glands aside, changing tires is relatively easy—once you have the right tools. Rider Wearhouse (www.aerostich.com) offers a complete Tire Changing Set containing everything you need, or you can piece your own kit together, filling the gaps in your current tool selection. Still, the first time you attempt it, you may swear up and down that you'll never do it again.

Begin with your bike on front and rear stands. If you're changing tire brands or models and are concerned about adjusting ride height to compensate for the new tire profile, read Project 30 before moving on to the next step. Once you've removed a wheel, unscrew the valve core with a valve stem tool. After the tire has finished its lengthy sigh, place your wheel on your milk crate or oil drum. (Although milk crates are easier to come by, oil drums put your wheel at a more comfortable working height.) Whatever support you use, you want to make sure the wheel is not resting on a brake disc while you're working on the bead. Discs bend all too easily and are quite expensive.

Slip the bead breaker through the center of the wheel. If you're worried about scratching the wheel, wrap the support beam of the bead breaker with a rag. Working carefully will also help avoid scratches. Breaking the bead requires some force. Expect to exert some effort to break the "interference fit"—engineering-speak meaning "hell-for-tight"—between the bead and the rim. Complicating matters is the stiffness designed into the bead. Strap on your biggest muscles and press down on the bead breaker until the bead slides to the center of the rim. You'll know the bead has let go when it stops resisting.

The rim center has a depression to allow the rest of the bead to loosen. Using the section of tire bead already in the wheel center, work the bead loose by pressing your way around the tire with your hands. If the bead resists, do your best Bruce Lee yell as you push on the tire. Once the entire bead is in the depression, flip the wheel and break the bead on the other side.

Your next chore will be lifting the bead over the lip of the rim. Lubrication makes this job infinitely easier, but don't use anything that you can't wipe away or air-dry. So, leave the WD-40 and silicone lubricants on the shelf. A spray bottle of diluted dish detergent works just fine. Spray the outer edge of the bead and the rim with enough fluid to cover the surface. Next, you're going to wedge a tire iron between your shiny rim and the rubber. If you're worried about marring your rim's finish, using rim protectors or wrapping duct tape around the tire iron can help—but nothing can prevent rim damage if you pull an Incredible Hulk routine while operating the irons. Slip the edge of the tire iron under the bead, and using the rim as the fulcrum, carefully lever the bead over the lip. With your second—and possibly third—hand, make sure the rest of the bead (on both sides of the wheel) is still in the center rim depression.

Taking your second tire iron, lift the bead over the rim a couple of inches from the first iron. Moving an inch or two at a time, work your way around the rim until the bead pops off the wheel. Don't get impatient while levering the bead, though; you can easily scratch the paint off the rim. Turn the wheel over, and you should be able to push the second bead off the rim by hand. If you have trouble, give the bead an assist with one of the tire irons.

Wipe off the excess lube from the wheel before mounting the new tire. (This would also be a great time to install a metal valve stem, as shown in the following project.) Check to make sure you place the tire on the wheel in the correct orientation for rotation. The tire will have an arrow indicating the correct direction. If your front discs are directional, they should have arrows too. You can figure out the rear yourself, right? Spray the first bead you'll slip onto the rim and line up the painted spot (the lightest point on the tire) with the valve stem.

Although you should be able to get the first bead over the rim most of the way by hand, the tire iron will work in a pinch. Now, lube the other bead, and, while keeping the first bead in the rim's center depression, work the second bead over the lip. Finish off with the tire irons, keeping the beads opposite the iron in the wheel's center depression.

Screw the valve stem valve core back into place. If you have control over the maximum air pressure for the air supply, set it to no more than 60 psi to keep from accidentally over-inflating the tire while trying to seat the beads. You should hear each bead pop into place as you inflate the tire. Watch your fingers! Using an accurate air gauge, set the tire pressure. Before moving on to balancing the wheel, give the tire a once-over, paying particular attention to the beads. Sometimes the bead will seat with a slight kink, as evidenced by a bump in the tire's mold line. If you notice this problem, deflate the tire and try reseating the bead. If that doesn't work, deflate the tire, break the bead in that spot, apply some more soapy lubricant, and reinflate.

Don't forget to balance your wheels before riding (Project 29). And remember, new tires—though they feel sticky to the touch—are extremely slippery for the first few miles, so no funny business, OK?

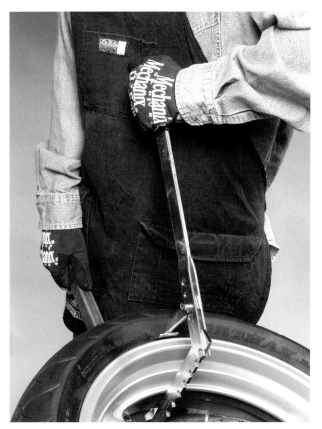

Be sure to set your bead breaker so that it will not scrape the rim as you press the bead toward the center of the wheel.

Remove the valve core from the valve stem and let the tire deflate.

Working your way around the tire, press the bead into the center depression in the wheel. Flip the wheel and repeat.

Before you attempt to lift the bead over the rim, spray down the bead with a diluted dish detergent solution.

Work deliberately with the tire irons. Your discs, knuckles, and rim paint will be much happier.

Make sure the rotational direction of the tire is correct. Otherwise, Bad Things could happen.

When mounting the new tire, you should be able to press most of the bead over the lip by hand. On the second bead, keeping the first one in the rim's center depression will help.

Valve Stem Replacement

 Time: 30 minutes

 Tools: Valve stem tool, open end wrenches, pliers, contact cleaner or organic cleaner, nonhardening silicone sealer

 Talent:

 Cost: $

 Parts Required: Metal valve stems

 Tip: Angled valve stems can ease tire inflation in certain setups.

 PERFORMANCE GAIN: Tires that don't lose pressure at ultrahigh speeds.

To assure consistent airtightness, a dab of nonhardening silicone sealant should be applied to the sealing surface of the valve stem.

Ponder, for a moment, the lowly valve stem. It's such a little part for such an important job. Without the valve stem, how would we adjust tire pressure or even keep the air in the tire?

Now, consider how the valve actually works inside the stem. The air chuck presses the valve down toward the tire to allow air to flow. Let your mind wander a bit further to what happens to your wheel as you travel at the hypersonic velocities of which your sportbike is capable. The centrifugal forces want to fling the wheel components toward the outside of the wheel. Remember which way the valve is pressed to let air out of your tire? Well, now you may notice a little problem. The forces of high-speed riding could, conceivably, force the valve into releasing pressure (in a snowballing progression as the pressure drops). Not exactly on your list of desired activities, right?

Metal valve stem assemblies usually sport a metal cap with a rubber O-ring to help seal the valve closed, thus preventing the above mishap. Also, metal valve stems are less vulnerable to dry rot and chemicals than the rubber ones mounted on many stock bikes. (This reason alone is enough to warrant swapping stems.)

Removing the rubber valve stem couldn't be easier. Just pull it off with a pair of pliers.

Before you buy just any old metal valve stem, you have the opportunity to select an angled one to ease your tire pressure check and inflation. Look at the valve's location relative to the disc(s) and/or sprocket. Sometimes, the right angle can radically change your quality of life. Or not.

With the tires off your wheels, begin by simply pulling the rubber valve stem out of the wheel or cutting. Clean the mounting surface with contact cleaner or your favorite nontoxic cleaner. After drying the wheel's orifice, check for proper fit of the new valve stem, particularly angled ones. Once you're satisfied with the location, remove the stem and apply nonhardening silicone to the inner surface of the stem where it will contact the inside of the wheel. Similarly, apply a small amount to the gasket that will be held in place by the exterior washer and nut. Insert the stem and rotate it into position. Snug the nut down finger tight. Use an open end wrench to finish the tightening—but not so tight as to distort the delicate threads on the stem.

Wipe off the excess sealant, and you're ready to mount your tires. Once the tires are inflated, spread a soapy water solution around the base of the valve stem to make sure that the seal is airtight. Now, you can break the sound barrier without worrying about your valve stems letting you down.

An angled valve stem can make the job of checking air pressure infinitely easier.

Wheel Balancing

Time: 15 minutes

Tools: : Tire-balancing tool, dykes, contact cleaner or organic cleaner, colored duct tape (to match your wheels), chalk

Talent: ♟

Cost: None (if you've got the tools)—$$

Parts Required: Wheel weights

Tip: Cover the weights with duct tape to make them stay put.

PERFORMANCE GAIN: Smooth running at any speed.

Anyone who has witnessed a washing machine walking its way across the basement floor can understand how important balancing the load on rotating objects can be. Some people mistakenly think that, because modern wheels have gotten so much lighter and better balanced, they don't need to balance wheels when fresh tires are installed. This is wrong. Even the smallest difference in weight is amplified many, many times as the wheel rotates. Also, your tires will wear more evenly and your bike will be more stable with balanced tires.

Most mechanics—with the exception of the persnickety—assume that the heaviest part of a wheel is the location of the valve stem. And they'd almost always be right. However, "almost always" isn't good enough for some fastidious souls, so they can follow these instructions to find—and mark—the heaviest part of the wheel *before* mounting the tire. The rest of us will get along just fine assuming the valve stem marks the location.

While these instructions assume you're using a balancing stand, you can fashion your own and use your bike's axle or a similarly sized rod. However, you need to make sure that the rod is free to turn on its own in the stand, since the wheel's bearings have enough internal friction to prevent an accurate reading of the wheel's balance. The stand used here (provided by Rider Wearhouse, www.aerostich.com) solidly holds the wheel on a rod via a pair of coned, self-centering inserts. (Note: If you're using coned inserts, remove any spacers from the wheel before inserting the rod and cones.) The rod then rotates on two pairs of wheels.

Finding a wheel's heaviest point is easy. Place the rod on the balancing stand and give the wheel a slight spin. When the wheel stops, the heaviest section of the wheel will settle to the bottom. Although experienced wheel balancers can gauge how much weight to add to the wheel by the speed with which the wheel drops to the heavy point (go to the track and watch the tire vendors sometime), we can usually begin with two quarter-ounce weights. Remove a small portion of the stickum's protective cover (or use some tape) and attach the weights to the opposite edge of the rim directly at the top of the wheel.

Turn the wheel a quarter turn so the weight is level with the axle. If you're close to the right amount of weight, the wheel should not turn when you let go. If you need to add more weight, the lead you attached will return to the top of the wheel. You can probably guess that if the weights end up on the bottom, it means you need to remove some. You can trim the weights down to size with a pair of dykes. When the wheel doesn't move when you stop it at random places, it's balanced.

Mark the tire with chalk where the weights are mounted. Pull the weights free and clean the spot with contact cleaner. Remove the rest of the protective backing on the weights and apply them as close to the rim's centerline as possible. For more than half an ounce of weights, split the weight up to either side of the wheel. If you find that you need more than an ounce of weights, check to be sure that the tire is properly mounted. (You did remember to remove the old weights, didn't you?)

Before you remove the wheel from the balancer, give it one last check. Cover the weights with a piece of duct tape that extends at least an inch beyond the lead. If you don't want to look like a geek, make sure the tape is the same color as the wheels. However, gray duct tape is still better than no tape at all, and mankind almost unanimously agrees that duct tape is one of technology's greatest achievements.

Since you have to remove the weights to clean the wheel, mark the tire with chalk so you can affix the weights to the right place. Note how the weight is temporarily placed on the edge of the rim to make it easier to move during the balancing process.

The discs on the balancing tool allow the rod supporting your motorcycle wheel to rotate freely, giving a more accurate measure. Once the wheel stops moving, you're ready to temporarily attach the weights to the top of the rim.

Since even the best stickum can fail, cover the weights with duct tape to keep everything in place for the life of the tire.

Checking Tire Diameter for Ride Height Adjustment

WHEELS AND TIRES

Time: 20 minutes

Tools: Thin metal tape measure or cloth tape, balancing stand (optional), note pad, calculator

Talent: 👤

Cost: None (if you've got the tools)—$$

Parts Required: None

Tip: For the most accurate number, make sure the tape measure stays on the center of the tire.

PERFORMANCE GAIN: Consistent chassis attitude and handling

If you've set your bike's ride height to tune its handling, you don't want to just toss new tires on it willy-nilly. Changing brands or models of tires—even those marked as the same size—will usually change the outer diameter of the complete wheel assembly. Those of you who stayed awake during geometry class know that if the circumference of a circle increases or decreases, the radius does too. In the case of motorcycles, the radius is the distance from the axle to the ground. Having the front radius increase while the rear decreases could turn your razor-sharp canyon weapon to a slow-steering dump truck. So, how do we keep this from happening?

Although you can measure your tires' circumference while the wheels are still mounted on the bike by using a little clever measuring tape technique, the best time to measure the circumference is when the wheel is on the balancing stand. Wrap a metric measuring tape around the wheel, making sure that the tape stays in the center of the carcass. (A thin tape, like Race Tech's Sag Master, is ideal, since it bends much easier than wide tapes do.) To get your baseline measurement, measure the properly inflated tire before you replace it. Then remeasure after you've mounted and inflated the new tire.

So, what do you do with the numbers? Some of us may remember that the circumference of a circle is equal to two times pi times the radius, or $c = 2\pi r$. Since we measured the circumference and need to calculate the radius, the equation we need is: $r = c/2\pi$. Now we only need to get out our calculators

and substitute the measurement for c and 3.1416 for π. You can shorten the equation by subtracting the new measurement from the baseline measurement to calculate the ride height change in one step with:

$$\text{Ride height adjustment} = \frac{(c_{old} - c_{new})}{2\pi}$$

If the number is positive (the old circumference is greater than the new), the ride height must be raised by the calculated amount to make up for the shorter tire. If the number is negative, the ride height must be lowered by this amount.

Suppose your old front tire measured 184.2 centimeters (72.5 inches) and your new tire was 188.0 centimeters (74 inches). Your front ride height needs to be adjusted -0.6 centimeters or -1.5 inches. So, you would lower the triple clamp 6 mm down the fork. Get it?

This method works great for bikes with adjustable front and rear ride heights. However, most stock bikes don't have rear ride height adjusters. In this situation the front ride height is adjusted to maintain chassis attitude. To maintain the proper chassis attitude, the equation needs to include the rear ride height and be modified to:

$$\text{Front ride height adjustment} = \frac{(F_{old} - F_{new}) + (R_{new} - R_{old})}{2\pi}$$

where R is the rear wheel circumference and F is the front. (As in the first equation, a positive number means you increase the ride height by sliding the triple clamp up the fork.) Unfortunately, the overall height of the bike can't be maintained, because the rear stays at the same height. So, you'll get a bike that should handle the same with either slightly more or less ground clearance.

Now you can go out riding on your new tires, secure in the fact that the chassis is set in the same attitude as it was before the change. You may, however, notice handling changes that have nothing to do with suspension or chassis setup. Different tires have different profiles and will respond differently to steering inputs. That's half the fun of trying new tires.

With the bike on its stands, you can measure the circumference of the tires if you're careful.

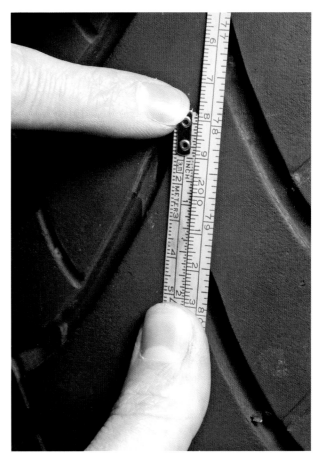

Since you'll have your wheels on the balancer after the tire change, why not measure the tires there, both before and after the rubber swap?

Wheel Runout Check

WHEELS AND TIRES

 Time: 2 hours

 Tools: Dial indicator, balancing stand

 Talent: ＊＊＊

Cost: None

 Parts Required: None

Tip: Verify that excess runout is not caused by bearing problems before suspecting a damaged wheel.

PERFORMANCE GAIN: Elimination of wobble and/or front-wheel vagueness.

COMPLEMENTARY MODIFICATIONS: Mount new tires and rebalance the wheels.

If you're experiencing a wobble or speed-related vibration on your bike and you're certain that your wheels are balanced, you may have a wheel or tire that is out of round. Checking for these problems is a process of elimination. By ruling out the possible causes one by one, you eventually arrive at the most likely culprit.

Using stands, raise the wheels off the ground. Gently spin the wheel while feeling for roughness or binding. If the brake pads touching the discs prevent you from getting an accurate feel for the roughness, temporarily remove the calipers. Failing wheel bearings can exhibit a gritty feeling, like sand in the bearing, or you may notice a stiff spot in the rotation. If you find any of these symptoms, replace the bearings as shown in the following project.

Next, perform a close visual inspection of the wheels for any small cracks, dents, bends, or warpage. If you find any cracks—even a hairline crack—in the wheel, replace it. You'd hate to have it fail at speed. Dents are another story. While your factory manual will tell you to replace the wheel, many riders have had luck with repairing dents. (See Project 33.) If you don't see any signs of dents, try spinning the wheel a little faster in a quick initial check for warp. Also look at the tires at this point; one of those could be out of round.

If you still haven't found anything, you'll want to check the wheels with a dial indicator for warpage. Support the wheel by its axle in a wheel balancer or similar device. Using a dial indicator, measure the radial (in and out) runout and the axial (side-to-side) runout against the service limits listed in your factory manual. Take your time when measuring the runout, because service limits on a wheel are typically less than 1 mm. Rotate the wheel slowly until you find the lowest point. Now, find the highest point. A quick bit of subtraction will tell you if your rim exceeds the specs.

You may wonder why the wheel should be mounted to the axle instead of the cones on a wheel balancer. That's because the bearings still haven't been completely ruled out in our hunt for the problem. Using the self-centering cones on a balancer could mask bearing issues. If you measured runout beyond the factory specifications, your next step will be to closely examine the wheel. If the warpage is localized to one section of the wheel, you can probably assume that it received an impact. If the entire wheel seems crooked with no visible signs of damage, the bearings could be worn. Try replacing the bearings to see if the problem goes away.

Once you've replaced the bearings, determine the wheel's runout again. If it is still beyond the service limits, you need to decide whether you are going to replace the wheel, try to repair it yourself, or send it to someone to straighten it. Again, your factory service manual will tell you that the wheel should be replaced, since there is a slight increase in risk associated with straightening a wheel.

Once you've determined that your wheels are OK, reinstall the tires, balance, and remount the wheels. If you didn't find a problem with the wheel and since it's hard to tell if a tire is out of round, consider mounting new tires to see if this helps remedy your wobble or vibration problem.

The dial indicator is set to measure the axial (side-to-side) runout.

Measuring the radial runout is a little more difficult. Have the dial indicator follow the inside edge of the rim's lip.

Wheel Bearing Replacement

 Time: 2 hours

 Tools: Circlip pliers, drift or bar stock, propane torch, flathead screwdriver, socket matching outer diameter of bearing, hammer

 Talent: 🔧🔧🔧

 Cost: $

 Parts Required: : Bearings, grease seals, circlips (if used on your wheel)

 Tip: Stubborn bearings can be removed with the proper application of some heat.

 PERFORMANCE GAIN: Less drag from bearing friction, especially if you use ceramic bearings.

Wheel bearings make their impending demise known in a variety of ways. Unless you're troubleshooting a problem such as a wobble, the first indication you may get that a bearing is in trouble will most likely come through your ears. Bearings rumble and groan as they get tired. You may also feel the rumble through the grips or pegs. If you notice these signs, immediately replace the bearings or limit your riding until you do. However, performing a quick bearing check each time you change your tires can prevent the need for such drastic measures.

To inspect wheel bearings you need the wheel off the bike—which is what makes tire change time such a convenient opportunity. Look over the bearings and dust/grease seals closely. Are the seals cracked or torn? If so, water could have gotten in and damaged the bearing. Do you see any evidence of seal leakage? If you do, the bearing is shot. However, don't confuse the grease rubbed around the lip of the grease seal with bearing leakage.

Next, insert your finger into the bearing and spin it. Is it noisy? Does it have rough spots and not spin smoothly? Also, rotate the bearing slowly with your finger. Does the movement feel gritty, as if sand were inside? Answering yes to any of these questions means that new bearings are in your future.

Always replace bearings as a set—even if only one side of the wheel is bad. Also, you should buy new grease seals when you replace the bearings. The additional expense is worth it to prevent premature bearing failure. Similarly, if your wheels

have circlips outboard of the bearings to hold them in position, replace them too.

Crazy stories about removing wheel bearings abound. My personal favorite involves baking your wheel in a 400-degree oven and then dropping it onto a wooden frame to

Bearings

A wheel bearing's sole purpose in life is to bridge the gap between the rotating wheel and the stationary axle. Traditionally, wheel bearings have been conc-structed of steel balls captured inside two steel races. They are then packed with grease and (usually) sealed against the elements. So, bearings, by design, are a source of frictional drag as the wheel turns. Decreasing this drag would free up horsepower for use propelling you forward.

Worldwide Bearings has essentially reinvented the wheel bearing by pro-ducing bearings with ceramic balls. These bearings offer 40 percent less friction and 60 percent less rotating mass while outlasting standard bearings by as much as three to five times! What do these numbers translate into? The drag race versions typically increase trap speed at the end of the quarter-mile 4 to 6 miles per hour. The fully streetable version (packed with grease instead of a light oil) gives a 2-mile per hour increase and will outlast the OE bearings.

Road racers are just starting to catch on to ceramic bearings, but all the big names in motorcycle drag racing—including Larry McBride (top fuel record holder)—use them. So, if you're looking for the ultimate in performance, you should consider ceramic bearings.

"surprise" the bearings into falling out. On the other end of the spectrum, bike manufacturers will sell you expensive, special bearing-remover tools designed specifically for their bearings. In the real world, most mechanics get by with a drift (which is really just a piece of metal bar stock cut to length for hammering), a flathead screwdriver, and a hammer. Careful mechanics will label and remove brake discs before attempting a bearing swap. Why risk bending these delicate items? Another note of caution: From the moment you take that first whack at the bearing race, the bearing is junk. Never reuse bearings.

Begin by placing the new bearings in the freezer a couple of hours before you plan on needing them. Next, place a piece of wood, or similarly forgiving surface, under the hub. Insert the drift or bar stock into the opposite side of the hub from the bearing you want to press out. If you can't catch the lip of the inner race because of the internal spacer, you may find that a flathead screwdriver will help get the bearing started. With the drift on the inner race, give the bearing a whack or two until it moves slightly. Now switch to the other side of the bearing and repeat. Essentially, you are walking the bearing out of the hub.

If the bearing is stubborn and refuses to move or stops partway out, you may need to apply a little heat to the situation. Using a propane torch, heat the hub around the bearing. Don't use a superhot flame that may burn or bubble the wheel's powder coat, but you want to get the hub hot enough that a drop of water (or spit) will sizzle on it. Return to the hammer and drift to liberate the intransigent bearing. Remove the inner spacer and the second bearing.

When installing new bearings, you can use a bearing driver set or a socket that has the same outer diameter as the outer race. If you're unable to find a suitable socket, you can always use the old bearing. The key is to never tap directly on the new bearing itself. Note that it won't sit as high out of the wheel (as in the photo) if the bearing is deeply recessed in the hub. To ease seating the bearing in the hub, we're going to play with expansion and contraction of solid objects. The new bearing should be plenty cold and just a bit smaller after its stint in the freezer. Before you remove it from its nest among the frozen foods, heat the hub to the aforementioned sizzle mode. Don't waste any time transferring the bearing from the freezer to the hot hub. With the difference in temperature, you should only need a couple of whacks to bottom the bearing in the hole. Do not exert *any* pressure on the inner race, just the outer one. If a circlip is used to secure the bearing, install it before moving on to the next bearing.

With one side of the hub complete, drop the internal spacer into place before sparking up the torch to begin the hub expansion. Install the second bearing the same way as the first. Don't forget about the bearing inside the sprocket carrier. Once the bearings are in position, let the hub cool to room temperature before placing the grease seals in place. Make sure they are flush with the outer edge of the bearing hole. Finally, lube the lips of the grease seal with high-temperature grease. The revitalized wheels are now good to go.

Some hubs have circlips outboard of the bearings that must be removed before you can proceed.

This screwdriver's curved blade is perfect for catching the edge of the bearing's inner race. Once there is a gap between the bearing and the spacer in the hub, switch to the drift.

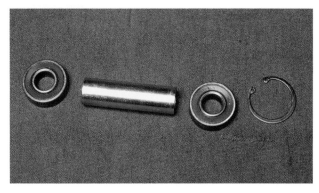

Lay the parts out in order to simplify reassembly. Take particular note of the orientation of the bearings. Some are only sealed on one side.

Using a socket or the old bearing, make sure the new bearing has bottomed out in its hole.

Lube the lips of the grease seal before re-mountinng the wheel. Note how the seal is flush with the end of the hub.

PROJECT 33

Wheel Straightening

 Time: Minutes to hours

 Tools: Leather mallet, dead-blow hammer, dial indicator, hydraulic press, wheel mounting jigs

 Talent: 👤👤👤👤

 Cost: $–$$

 Parts Required: None

 Tip: The wheel starts out as junk — there is no harm in trying.

 PERFORMANCE GAIN: Round wheels track the road better.

The beatings will continue until your attitude improves: A leather mallet straightens things out quickly.

OK, so you may have been following that car too closely to react when the 2x4 emerged from underneath it. Or perhaps you were riding in the rain and hit a pothole that was filled with water. Either way, your bike's rims aren't so round anymore. Never fear, sometimes you can smooth your wheel's new hump yourself. If you can't, you can find mechanics who specialize in this kind of work. Many a club racer has spent an evening (or two) with a nonmarring hammer working out the little ripple they made in a wheel during an off-track excursion. For a truly twisted rim—say, from a curb—you need to consult a professional.

An afternoon trip to a wheel shop allows us a glimpse of a craft that should appeal to the Luddite in all of us. As a technician puts it, "I simply massage wheels until they cooperate—or break." The tools he utilizes for his brand of massage therapy are a dial gauge, a grease pencil, a Porto-Power hydraulic press, a really big leather mallet (the spawn of an illicit union

between a sledge hammer and a marproof hammer, no doubt), and some beefy mounting bracketry.

In a process that is more art than science, he mounts the tweaked wheel to his workbench and checks for the out-of-round sections with a dial gauge. After marking the high and low points with his cryptic code, the hydraulic press flexes the rim in the right direction. Problems with the faces of the rim are handled with a whack or three from the leather mallet. The wheel abuse continues—with occasional pauses to flip the rim—until the runout is less than 0.025 inch. A quick check of your factory service manual should reveal that this runout lies right on the edge of the service limits!

Some people might worry about how he treats wheels, but never fear—remember that they start out as junk anyway. If the wheel expires while strapped to his table, many shops charge nothing. In this technician's experience, Honda wheels fracture more often than others. Similarly, magnesium wheels, which lack the flexibility of aluminum ones, also tend to go to pieces under the strain of straightening. However, with the cost of a new CBR600RR wheel in the neighborhood of $500, paying for the shipping of a bent wheel to your local shop is a worthwhile investment. However, if your wheel has already been straightened once, don't waste your time. Most mechanics won't touch it as previously straightened wheels are prone to failing, both on the bench and back out on the road, if they survive the second repair.

Tough cases get a visit from Mr. Hydraulic Press.

The dial gauge illustrates how badly twisted this wheel is. Once the magic had been worked, the runout was only 0.015 inch.

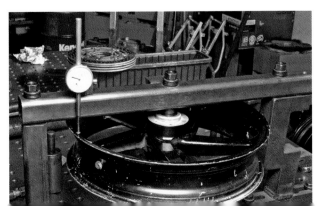

Wheel Widening

 Time: A week or more

 Tools: Enormous lathe, giant calipers, TIG (tungsten inert gas) welder

 Talent: ♦♦♦♦

 Cost: $$$$

 Parts Required: Donor rims

 Tip: Wider wheels will allow you to run current rubber on a less-than-current sportbike.

 PERFORMANCE GAIN: Better grip, impressed friends, more dates

COMPLEMENTARY MODIFICATIONS:

Replace bearings.

Owners of older sportbikes lead difficult lives. Like most sport riders, they're fascinated by technology. They can usually quote the specifications of the latest-and-greatest sporting machinery, but they also live in the real world where bikes must be bought over time. By the time they've paid for their rides, they've formed a bond with them. After all, the motor's been breathed on, they've added aftermarket pipes and carbs, the suspension's been upgraded. The only thing missing is current tire technology. Unfortunately, older rims can be too narrow for the new rubber. Still, for those folks who know that the only thing between them and a second honeymoon with their bike is the ability to mount those sticky, sexy tires, there is some hope.

Since aftermarket hoops can cost the same as a nice down payment on a new bike, many folks will rule them out right away. Thrifty riders, road racers, and drag racers have long enjoyed the benefit of wider wheels without coughing up the big bucks for replacement items. Weld-up wheels (widened stock wheels) offer many advantages over aftermarket wheels. First, the modifications are usually cheaper than buying new wheels. Second, the other stock components that have to interact with the wheels are guaranteed to work since the only part of the wheel being modified is the rim. Finally, many aftermarket wheels require the sacrifice of the cush drive to the sticky rubber gods—and potentially lead to clutch and transmission problems.

When it comes to weld-up wheels, Kosman Specialties is the leader in what is essentially a field of one. Widening wheels is a labor-intensive operation that requires in-depth knowledge of machining, welding, and, most importantly, motorcycle wheels. Cut too far into some wheels, such as those with hollow rims, and you've crafted an expensive, hard-to-replace piece of junk.

Measure First

Sending your wheels off to Kosman for widening irrevocably changes them, so a little research is in order prior to pulling them off your bike. After all, you don't want to find out that you've got clearance problems after the wheels have been widened. So, decide on the sizes of the tires you want to run. You will need to know the rim width on which they are designed to be mounted and the final width of the tire when mounted and inflated. Next, measure the width of the tires currently residing on your wheels. Finally, measure the clearance between the widest part of the tire and the next-closest parts of the bike. On the rear, the swingarm on the right and the chain on the left are usually the points of contact. In the front, the fork itself or the mounts for the fender will be the first points of interference. (You can always raise the fender if it gets in the way.)

Now, do the math. Find out how much broader the new tire is by subtracting the measured width of the current tire from the manufacturer's width of the new tire. Divide the result in half and compare the number to the clearances measured on the current tire. If the calculated number is less than both measurements, you've got room for the tire. Make sure there is at least an eighth-inch to spare.

Don't pull the wheels off just yet. If the new tires are significantly larger in diameter, the room *above* the current tire (measured from the axle when the suspension is fully compressed) should also be checked and compared to the

Since motorcycle wheels aren't necessarily centered in the swingarm, measure the clearance between the widest point on the tire and the narrowest point. It must clear on both sides.

The stock flanges are machined off the wheel, leaving only the center. If the machinist miscalculates, even only slightly, the rim is junk.

radius calculated from the new tire's outer diameter ($r=$circumference/2pi). Remember, there should be enough room for the diameter of the tire to grow at speed. Now, start wrenching.

Slimming Down and Widening Up

When wheels arrive at Kosman, they are checked for straightness. Some wheels may have a ding in a flange that can be machined off, but Kosman doesn't straighten bent wheels. (If you think your wheels might be bent, turn to the preceding project.) In order to widen a rim, the customer's rim needs to have its flanges removed so that the flanges from a donor rim can be grafted on. A machinist mounts the wheel to a lathe, and, using a parting tool, cuts off the stock flange. Next, the cut is cleaned up and machined with an interface to accept the donor flange. According to Kosman, the shape of the interface is crucial to the construction and long-term integrity of the weld-up wheel. The new flanges receive a mirror image of the rim—only with enough difference in size to create an interference fit that will hold the flange to the rim once

they're pressed together. The machinist's final step is to press the flanges onto the rim and check for runout.

The welder tack welds the seams together to keep the seams in line as he welds his way around the wheel. Once the flanges have been affixed to the rim, the seams of the flanges are welded on both the inside and outside of the wheel. When the welding is complete, the wheels are again checked for runout before they are packaged for shipping.

Weld-up wheels require no more special treatment than the stockers. Painting or powder coating poses no problem. However, some riders may be tempted to grind down the visible weld on the inside of the rim to keep things pretty. Don't. The weld is integral to holding things together. Besides, those in the know will see the welds as a sign of a cool modification. Contrary to popular myth, weld-ups don't add "lots" of weight to stock rims, but they will be a little heavier, than stock. So, if you want to go wide with your old, faithful bike, consider weld-up wheels before plopping down the big bucks for custom wheels.

To make a strong wheel, the seams—both inside and out—get welded together. Don't try to make the wheels pretty by grinding away the outer weld.

Aftermarket Wheel Installation

 Time: 2 hours

 Tools: Wrenches, sockets, front and rear stands, rags, torque wrench, measuring tape, Loctite

 Talent:

 Cost: $$$$$

 Parts Required: Aftermarket wheels

 Tip: Check spacers and disc attachment points to be sure they match *before* you mount the tires.

 PERFORMANCE GAIN: Faster acceleration and braking, quicker turning, better suspension compliance.

COMPLEMENTARY MODIFICATIONS: Install aftermarket brake system.

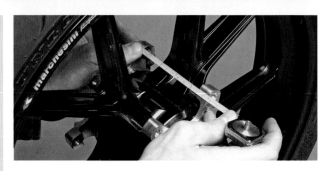

Measuring the distance between the brake mounts will help you make sure that your new wheel is correctly set up for your model sportbike.

In its most basic sense, installing a set of aftermarket wheels is not much different from remounting the stock rims after a tire change or brake disc swap—except for the extra money and the massive street cred. Seriously, though, mounting up a set of sexy forged magnesium wheels, like the Marchesini set provided for this project by TAW Vehicle Concepts, gets you far more than a big credit-card bill. According to TAW, lighter wheels are the biggest bang for the buck of all motorcycle modifications.

The theory behind this claim is straightforward: In motorcycle performance, weight is everything. First, even though the OEMs have wised up and started producing some exceptionally light wheels, any reduction in unsprung weight (weight not supported by the suspension) makes it easier for your suspenders to help the tires track across pavement irregularities. So, even saving a couple of pounds here is a big deal. Replace wheels from a bike more than a couple of years old, and you can save as much as 10 pounds.

Next, consider the weight of the wheel in regard to acceleration. As Kevin Cameron says in *Sportbike Performance Handbook*, "A pound saved in a wheel rim . . . is worth two pounds anywhere else on the machine. A wheel has to be accelerated twice; once in a straight-line, and also in the second sense of rotating around its own center." Since wheels rotate, generating gyroscopic forces, a lighter wheel will turn in quicker and accept steering inputs more readily. Riders who

like flicking their bikes into turns will love the effect lighter wheels will have on steering.

When taking delivery of aftermarket wheels, be sure to measure a few dimensions before mounting them up. If it doesn't fit, you'd hate to have to send it back and pay for restocking—especially if you scratched it. While you don't have to measure to aerospace tolerances, try to be as accurate as possible. Measure the distance between the mounting surface of the disc carriers or disc and sprocket mounts. Also, measure the distance to the outside of both wheel spacers when they are fully seated in the hub. Compare these numbers to those of your stock hoops. A millimeter or two difference is probably your margin of error if you're using a tape measure. If you get a discrepancy of any more than that, remeasure both sets of wheels. Since wheel manufacturers sell the same wheels for multiple bike models and ship them with spacer kits, receiving a wheel with the wrong kit is not uncommon. Call the seller if you have any questions about the dimensions.

One tradeoff with superlight magnesium is that it is more brittle than aluminum, and may be more prone to damage if you crash—or if you're not careful when mounting the tires. Be extra careful. The only other caution about mounting aftermarket wheels for the first time is to double-check that you have the spacers on the correct side of the wheel. While this is usually only an issue with the rear wheel, you could mount the wheel off center and run into problems like the caliper resting against the disc when you torque the axle nut.

OK, now quit polishing those beautiful new hoops and get out there and try 'em.

If you get a strange reading when measuring the hub, make sure that the spacers are bottomed out in the holes and are sitting straight.

Installing Oversized Wheels

 Time: 5 hours

 Tools: : Enormous lathe, giant calipers, large machine-shop hardware

 Talent: ♟♟♟♟

 Cost: SS–SSSS

 Parts Required: Aftermarket wheels

 Tip: If you can't afford aftermarket items, this is a less expensive way to mount wider wheels to your bike while keeping the weight down.

 PERFORMANCE GAIN: Better grip from the cool new rubber you can mount.

If you look around the club racing scene, you'll see a lot of clever modifications designed to get more rubber on the ground on older, narrower-wheeled bikes. Often these bikes sport wheels from more modern bikes. With some of these mods, the new wheels are actually lighter than the stockers, offering the same benefits of lightweight aftermarket hoops—for significantly less money. If you buy parts at salvage yards, you can expect to pay about half of the list price of the new wheel. Buying them online can save you even more money. Do some price comparisons to see if this approach can be cheaper than widening your stock wheels.

As you read over this project, two thoughts will probably occur to you. The first will be the acknowledgment that you won't be able to do this yourself—unless you're a machinist by trade. (Kosman Specialties performed the installation shown here.) The second will probably be to wonder why this project is in the wheel section, when most of the work is to get the brakes to fit. Well, the answer is simple: The owner of this Buell found these magnesium wheels on eBay and had to have them. Since the steps would be the same when using the stock brakes on this wheel, why not upgrade? So, the mounting of the new wheels precipitated the addition of the aftermarket brakes being installed on the wheel.

When undertaking a project such as this, you need to keep several dimensions in mind at once. First, the space between the fork legs or inside the swingarm remains constant, and spacers must be machined to hold the wheels in those spaces. Second, if possible, the distance between the discs (or disc and sprocket) needs to remain the same, making it possible to use the stock mounting points and the OE brake system. In the case of this example, the discs' relationship to each other could not be maintained on the front wheel because of the hub's design.

If you plan on running your OE brakes, you need to make sure to maintain the distance between the discs on the new wheel. Some wheels' spokes are thicker than others. Make sure your calipers will clear the spokes when grasping the discs.

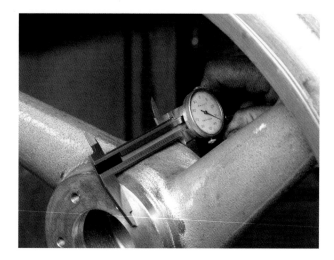

Measuring the hub's thickness will determine the size of the spacers needed to mount the discs.

The initial step is measuring the distance between the discs. After that, the new hub is measured. The difference between the two hubs is divided by two to determine what size spacer is required for each disc on this hub. If you're lucky, you'll simply be able to machine off some of the hub and then bolt the disc to the existing holes. If not, you need to create a spacer for the disc. However, for maximum disc stability, the spacer needs to be bolted to the hub and then drilled and tapped so that the disc can bolt to both the hub and the spacer. Otherwise, the spacer can allow movement between the disc and hub.

With the discs mounted to the wheel, the next step is machining spacers to hold the wheel between the fork legs. Knowing the distance between the fork legs and the thickness of the hub makes the initial calculation of the axle spacers easy. The wheel is slipped into the fork on the axle and the numbers are tested with calipers set to the calculated thickness. If everything checks out, the spacers are machined and tested.

Once the wheel is solidly located in the fork and bolted up, the final mounting of the calipers begins. In this case, since the new hub was thinner than the stocker, washers were simply added to the caliper bracket until the binders and rotors developed a productive relationship. Since this bracket is one that Kosman sells for Buells, all that needed to be done was to use the new thickness for the hanger in the CAD file and have it cut by their expensive, high-tech machines. Your machinist may need to cut the new bracket by hand from a fresh chunk of billet.

Although grafting a foreign wheel to your sportbike may seem like a lot of work, it will pay many of the dividends that aftermarket wheels do. You can run current-spec rubber on the new rims. If they are lighter, you will also gain quicker acceleration and steering. If this seems hard to believe, just ask all those racers who have Frankensteined their bike's wheels.

The hubs have been machined to accept countersunk bolts. Now the holes for the disc are drilled and tapped. This way the disc will be solidly bolted to both the spacer and the wheel.

The calculated size of the axle spacers is verified and adjusted, if necessary.

SECTION FOUR

SUSPENSION

Back in the Bad Old Days, riders thought the only way to improve a motorcycle's performance was to increase the horsepower output. While this approach to performance gave us some particularly exciting racing, as the likes of Eddie Lawson and Wayne Rainey slid their wobbling-but-snarling beasts around the track, both the motorcycle manufacturers and the aftermarket companies realized that all that power wasn't doing any good, because it couldn't be put to the pavement. The results of that effort can be seen on the showroom floor of any motorcycle dealership in the country, where off-the-rack sportbikes come equipped with handling capabilities the pros could only dream of back then. The fact that the average street rider and the average club racer have suspension adjustments and technology that were only available to the factory teams a mere 10 years ago is a mixed blessing. Proper suspension setup is key for fast riding. But approach suspension tuning in a willy-nilly fashion, and you'll have an ill-handling beast in no time. If you follow an orderly path, you'll not only improve your bike's handling, in the process you'll also become a more perceptive rider.

Measure and Set Sag

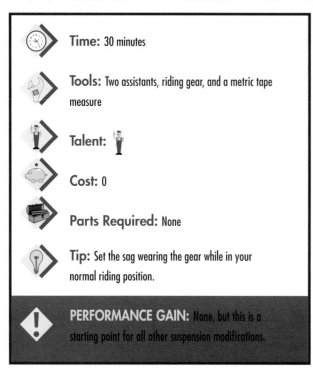

Time: 30 minutes

Tools: Two assistants, riding gear, and a metric tape measure

Talent: ☗

Cost: 0

Parts Required: None

Tip: Set the sag wearing the gear while in your normal riding position.

! PERFORMANCE GAIN: None, but this is a starting point for all other suspension modifications.

The measurement's the same, whether the fork is upside down or right side up. Starting at the wiper, measure to a fixed spot like the bottom of the triple clamp or axle clamp.

Riders eager to learn about their suspension often jump headlong into adjusting the damping rates on their bikes and frequently end up confused and stuck with a poorly handling mess. Before you decide to move beyond your bike's factory suspension settings, you must do two things. First, make sure that all the components of the system are in good working condition. Fix any leaks and perform any other maintenance chores before making modifications. If you don't, you'll likely have to start from scratch when you finish the maintenance in the near future. The second thing, which in reality is the first step toward setting your suspension to your riding style, is to set your bike's sag by adjusting the suspension's preload.

Proper sag is important for two reasons. First, a suspension unit needs a certain amount of room within its travel to work properly. If you have too little sag, your bike will be prone to "topping out" the suspension as it extends to its limit. Similarly, too much sag could allow you to experience the unpleasant jolt of "bottoming out." Second, once your sag is set, you will be able to ascertain whether or not your suspenders' spring rate is correct for your weight and size.

Your bike's sag is broken into two categories: "static sag," the distance your bike compresses its suspension from fully extended when you and your riding gear are aboard, and "free sag," the distance your bike settles from full extension under its own weight. Using the algebra you suffered through in high school and an equation popularized by

Race Tech founder Paul Thede, you'll be able to determine whether you need to increase or decrease your preload to reach the magic combination.

In order to measure the static sag, you'll need two assistants. A metric tape measure will also make the calculations easier than an SAE one. Before you mount the bike, you'll want to measure the suspension when it's completely topped out. For the fork, lift on the grips until the front wheel begins to come off the ground. On traditional forks, measure from the stanchion wiper to the bottom of the triple clamp. Measure from the wiper to the top of the axle clamp on inverted forks. We will name this number L1 and write down the measurement.

Now it's time to do it while you're on the bike. Have one of your assistants hold the bike from the rear while you get into your riding position. Your other assistant should push down on the fork and let it slowly rise up until it stops. The new measurement will be called L2. The front end should now be lifted and allowed to settle slowly down until it stops, forming measurement L3. Exactly in the middle of

For the rear suspension, you need to measure to a spot directly above the axle.

measurements L2 and L3 is the point the fork would want to live in a frictionless system. So, the average between the measurements would be (L2+L3)/2.

Armed with this information, you can determine the static sag by subtracting the average measurement calculated above from L1, or to write it out as an equation: static sag = L1-(L2+L3)/2. (Aren't you glad you stayed awake in class that day?) Now that you've got this number, what does it mean? For street riding, suspension gurus generally agree that between 30 and 35 mm (1.2–1.5 inches) is optimum sag. If you're track-bound, a stiffer 25 to 30 mm (1.0–1.2 inches) is preferred. If you have too much sag, you'll need to increase the fork's preload. Conversely, if you have too little, back off on the preload a bit. (Look to the next project for the lowdown on preload adjustment.) The jockey-sized and big-boned members of the audience may be wondering if they should fiddle with these figures to account for their mass. In a word, no. The static sag figures are an accepted constant. Measuring the bike's free sag will reveal if any alterations need to be made for rider size.

Once you have the front suspension dialed in, repeat the process with the rear suspension. The key to getting accurate measurements out back is to pick a solid point on the frame or bodywork directly above the axle. If you don't measure straight up from the axle, you may get inaccurate numbers.

Now that the static sag is set, the rear free sag means something. Measure the amount the bike sags under its own weight. If you want to be really anal, you can use the equation above, but a single quick measurement will tell you if your spring rate is in the right zip code. The free sag should be between 0 and 5 mm. Simply lifting the weight of your bike to see if it moves up slightly before topping out the suspension will give you an idea of how much free sag it has. While this may not seem to make sense, if your suspension has no free sag, your spring rate is too soft. The soft rate forced you to use too much preload to get the desired sag. If you have a bunch of free sag, your spring is too stiff. Look ahead to Project 41 to learn how to install new springs.

You've successfully set your sag. Now, what else can you do to tweak your suspension?

Adjusting Preload

SUSPENSION

 Time: 30 minutes

 Tools: Open end wrench or socket, shock preload adjusting tool or long screwdriver and hammer, hacksaw or pipe/tubing cutter (for PVC spacers), jack

 Talent:

 Cost: 0

 Parts Required: PVC pipe to cut spacers for bikes without preload adjusters

 Tip: Adjust the preload to suit the load the bike will carry—rider, passenger, gear, etc.

 PERFORMANCE GAIN: With preload adjusted for proper sag, your suspension will be able to its job better

Either a wrench or a socket will work fine on this adjuster. Just be careful not to whack your gas tank.

Springs are pretty simple-minded. The harder you push on them, the harder they push back. Preload adjusters on motorcycles use this relationship to help riders fine-tune their suspension to fit the variety of loads their motorcycles are asked to carry. Riding solo on a twisty road puts an entirely different load on the suspension than riding two-up with soft luggage on the same road. In order for the suspension to have its full range of travel to soak up pavement irregularities, you'll want to take advantage of the front and rear preload adjusters most bikes have. If you invest some time, you can find both the loaded and solo preload settings for your bike, which makes changing them before a ride as simple as turning a few wrenches. Even forks that don't have external adjusters can have their preload altered. It just takes a little more time.

The threaded preload adjusters on forks simply push down on the fork spring when you screw them in. Some fork adjusters have only two flat surfaces, which forces you to use a wrench, while the hexagonal ones will allow you to use a socket. Be careful when turning these adjusters. Their anodized surface mars easily (so don't use pliers) and they live dangerously close to your shiny gas tank. Many forks have lines demarcating different settings. If your bike has only slightly too much front sag, try screwing the adjusters in one line and then remeasuring the sag. Keep cranking the adjuster in or out as you fine-tune the sag. Although many bikes have the rebound damping adjuster located in the center of the

preload adjuster, the damping adjuster will remain unaffected by changes in preload.

If you want to adjust the preload on a fork that doesn't have factory adjusters, you have two choices. First, you might be able to find some trick aftermarket adjusters to mount in the stanchions. If not, you can use the old-fashioned method of cutting preload spacers out of the largest PVC pipe that will fit inside the fork. Although you don't have to take the front end off the ground, removing the pressure from the front suspension will make reassembly easier. When changing spacers without jacking the front end up, only remove the cap from one side of the fork at a time, or the bike will crash down to the bottom of the fork travel.

Begin by loosening the bolt on one side of the top triple clamp to relieve pressure on the cap's threads. Next, remove the fork cap either by unscrewing it with a wrench or by (the increasingly rare method of) pressing down on the cap and removing the circlip. The caps are under pressure from the spring, so be prepared for it to pop out. Remove the stock spacer and measure its length. Since the amount of sag you need to gain/lose is almost a one-to-one ratio to the amount you need to remove/add to the spacer, you can easily approximate the right length with simple arithmetic. While you've got the saw out, cut a couple sets of PVC spacers in quarter-inch increments on either side of your calculated length. File down any rough edges on the PVC and clean the spacers of any grit. Label the spacers with a Sharpie. Slip the new spacer into place with any washers you may have also removed with the stock spacer. If you've increased the preload, expect to work a bit to get the fork cap in place.

Notice how the locking ring has been loosened from the adjusting ring. The black mark will make it easy to keep track of how far the ring has been turned.

While changing the preload doesn't get any easier than using a stepped adjuster, you can't fine-tune the preload the same way you can with a threaded collar.

Changing rear shock preload is fairly easy on all bikes. Most stock shocks will have either a stepped adjuster or threaded, locking-ring adjusters. The stepped adjusters ramp the preload over five or six settings. Using the tool supplied in the factory toolkit, simply lever the collar onto the proper step. The process should take less time than it took to get the tool out from under the scat. Locking-ring adjusters can also be altered with a tool. Motion Pro makes a clawed adjuster that mounts to a 3/8-inch ratchet. Many aftermarket shocks also ship with an adjuster. If you don't have a tool, a long screwdriver and hammer will work in a pinch.

Begin by loosening the locking ring (the one farthest away from the spring). Using a Sharpie or a scribe, mark the adjusting ring so that you can count the number of turns you increased/decreased the preload. The fine-pitched threads move the adjusting ring approximately 1 mm per revolution. When you're roughing in the preload, make adjustments in full-turn increments. Fine-tuning the preload will be done with much smaller increments. Once the preload is set, tighten the lock ring down to keep the adjusting ring from backing out. Don't jamb the lock ring down more than a quarter turn, or you may have trouble loosening it next time you adjust the preload.

A final note about preload: If you take the time to measure the preload required for solo riding and two-up, write the settings down. When you need to change the preload for different riding situations, all you'll have to do is take out the wrenches and make the changes. Not having to lure assistants with free beer to measure the sag will save you time *and* money.

Make sure your cuts on the PVC spacers are square. A miter box or pipe cutter will help with this. Also, cut, clean up, and label three or four spacers to ease the swapping process as you dial in the front end.

If your bike doesn't have fork preload adjusters, the aftermarket may be your salvation.

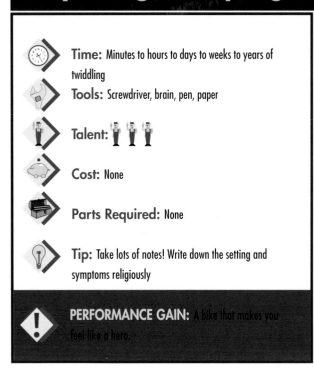

PROJECT 39

Adjusting Damping Settings

Time: Minutes to hours to days to weeks to years of twiddling

Tools: Screwdriver, brain, pen, paper

Talent: ⚉⚉⚉

Cost: None

Parts Required: None

Tip: Take lots of notes! Write down the setting and symptoms religiously

PERFORMANCE GAIN: A bike that makes you feel like a hero.

You'll find the compression-damping adjuster on the bottom of the fork.

SUSPENSION

Modern sportbikes are impressive handling machines. While their ultrarigid chassis and weight distribution have a lot to do with this, the fully adjustable suspensions can take much of the credit too. Although stock suspension components offer quite a bit of adjustability, many after-market units will give you even more flexibility. That's the good news. Unfortunately, the plethora of suspension settings can be a double-edged sword that turns your state-of-the-art machine into a bucking bronco. Although you probably won't cause your bike do anything truly evil through suspension adjustments alone, you will want to keep a record of any changes you make so that you can step back from mistakes—just like the "undo" function on a computer. Don't just dive in and start twiddling mindlessly.

When you initially set up your bike's damping, start with the sag properly set. If you don't, you won't get a good baseline. Also, consider the condition of your suspension components. If it's been a couple of years since the fork oil was freshened or you've got a couple of hard seasons on your shock, do that maintenance first. Similarly, if you've squared off your tires with the daily commute or your last three-day sport tour, spoon some new rubber onto the rims. Trying to tune damping on poorly maintained suspenders or tires is a time-consuming exercise in futility.

Begin by setting your bike's damping adjusters to the factory-specified positions. They probably won't stay there, but the settings should get you in the general area. Damping adjusters measure their settings one of two ways: clicks or

turns. If your bike uses clicks, turn the adjuster all the way in (clockwise) and unscrew the adjuster the correct number of clicks. For turns, do the same thing but count the turns instead of clicks. From here, you'll set your suspension's rebound before you ride and then modify the compression and rebound based on your riding impressions.

To test your fork's rebound damping, stand your bike straight up. Press firmly down on the center of the triple clamp—not the handlebar. Be sure not to hold the brake. The suspension should rebound back to its starting point and not beyond. If it bounces back beyond the original position, you need to increase damping by screwing in the rebound adjuster on top of the fork. Generally, make adjustments in single clicks or half turns. If the fork rises back directly to its original position, press on the triple clamp and time how long it takes to rise back. You want the rebound to take about a second. Adjust the rebound damping until you feel the timing is right. Follow the same procedure in the rear, pressing on the center of the seat. The shock's rebound adjuster is usually on the bottom of the shock body.

Although you can test your suspension settings anywhere, the best way to get an accurate measurement of changes is to repeatedly ride the same section of road. Dial in the front and rear suspension separately. To get a feel for what direction you need to go with your compression damping, ride your test road with the compression set to the factory specs to form a baseline. Next, go a couple of clicks firmer. Did the handling improve or get worse? Now try a couple clicks softer than stock. Which of the three settings do you prefer? Keep experimenting. Take notes. When you're

94

satisfied with the front suspension, continue the process with the rear.

If you're having trouble figuring out what signals your bike is giving you, consult the "Suspension Troubleshooting Symptoms" sidebar. The challenge of setting up your suspension to suit your personal riding style is that some symptoms can be caused by completely opposite problems. For example, if the front of your bike has a vague mushy feeling, you could be suffering from a lack of either compression damping or rebound damping. Looking for other symptoms will help you determine which setting to alter. Careful notes will help you in your detective work. Settings that worked great on your canyon runs may not be firm enough on the track and vice versa. Generally, street pavement is much rougher and necessitates softer compression and rebound damping.

Contrary to the fork adjusters, the shock rebound adjuster is on the bottom of the shock.

Riders are more familiar with the fork rebound adjusters than any others. Perhaps it's because they're in plain sight every time you ride.

You'll find the shock compression adjuster either on the top of the shock or on the reservoir.

Suspension Troubleshooting Symptoms

Here are some basic symptoms of suspension damping problems that you might find affecting your bike. Remember, these are extreme examples; your symptoms may be more subtle. You may also have to find an acceptable compromise on either end of the adjustment spectrum. It all depends on how the bike's handling "feels" to you.

LACK OF REBOUND DAMPING (FORK)
- The fork offers a supremely plush ride, especially when riding straight up. When the pace picks up, however, the feeling of control is lost. The fork feels mushy, and traction "feel" is poor.
- After hitting bumps at speed, the front tire tends to chatter or bounce.
- When flicking the bike into a corner at speed, the front tire begins to chatter and lose traction. This translates into an unstable feel at the clip-ons.
- As speed increases and steering inputs become more aggressive, a lack of control begins to appear. Chassis attitude and pitch become a real problem, with the front end refusing to stabilize after the bike is countersteered hard into a turn.

TOO MUCH REBOUND DAMPING (FORK)
- The ride is quite harsh—just the opposite of the plush feel of too little rebound. Rough pavement makes the fork feel as if it's locking up with stiction and harshness.
- Under hard acceleration exiting bumpy corners, the front end feels as if it wants to "wiggle" or "tankslap." The tire feels as if it isn't staying in contact with the pavement when you're on the gas.
- The harsh, unforgiving ride makes the bike hard to control when riding through dips and rolling bumps at speed. The suspension's reluctance to maintain tire traction through these sections erodes rider confidence.

LACK OF COMPRESSION DAMPING (FORK)
- Front-end dive while on the brakes becomes excessive.
- The rear end of the motorcycle wants to "come around" when using the front brakes aggressively.
- The front suspension "bottoms out" with a solid hit under heavy braking and after hitting bumps.
- The front end has a mushy and semivague feeling—similar to lack of rebound damping.

TOO MUCH COMPRESSION DAMPING (FORK)
- The ride is overly harsh, especially at the point when bumps and ripples are contacted by the front wheel.
- Bumps and ripples are felt directly; the initial "hit" is routed through the chassis instantly, with big bumps bouncing the tire off the pavement.

- The bike's ride height is affected negatively—the front end winds up riding too high in the corners.
- Brake dive is reduced drastically, though the chassis is upset significantly by bumps encountered during braking.

LACK OF REBOUND DAMPING (REAR SHOCK)
- The ride is plush at cruising speeds, but as the pace increases, the chassis begins to wallow and weave through bumpy corners.
- This causes poor traction over bumps under hard acceleration; the rear tire starts to chatter due to a lack of wheel control.
- There is excessive chassis pitch through large bumps and dips at speed, and the rear end rebounds too quickly, upsetting the chassis with a pogo-stick action.

TOO MUCH REBOUND DAMPING (REAR SHOCK)
- This creates an uneven ride. The rear suspension compliance is poor and the "feel" is vague.
- Traction is poor over bumps during hard acceleration (due to lack of suspension compliance).
- The bike wants to run wide in corners since the rear end is "packing down"; this forces a nose-high chassis attitude, which slows down steering.
- The rear end wants to hop and skip when the throttle is chopped during aggressive corner entries.

LACK OF COMPRESSION DAMPING (REAR SHOCK)
- There is too much rear-end "squat" under acceleration; the bike wants to steer wide exiting corners (since the chassis is riding rear low/nose high).
- Hitting bumps at speed causes the rear to bottom out, which upsets the chassis.
- The chassis attitude is affected too much by large dips and G-outs.
- Steering and control become difficult due to excessive suspension movement.

TOO MUCH COMPRESSION DAMPING (REAR SHOCK)
- The ride is harsh, though not quite as bad as too much rebound; the faster you go, the worse it gets, however.
- Harshness hurts rear tire traction over bumps, especially during deceleration. There's little rear-end "squat" under acceleration.
- Medium to large bumps are felt directly through the chassis; when hit at speed, the rear end kicks up.

Reprinted courtesy of *Sport Rider Magazine*—www.sportrider.com.

When you're happy with how your bike's suspenders perform, try one last test to make sure that you have balanced settings. Support the bike without any stands and press firmly on the tank. The front and rear suspension should compress and rebound in unison. If either end compresses or rebounds differently from the other, try altering the settings slightly to get the chassis movement in sync.

As your riding and suspension tuning skills improve with time, don't be surprised to find that your settings need to change too. You may find yourself developing "bumpy" and "smooth" road settings or "canyon" and "commuting" settings. Have fun, and give yourself a pat on the back for being so intimate with your bike.

Adjusting Ride Height

 Time: 1 hour

 Tools: Tape measure, ruler or caliper, wrenches, sockets, torque wrench, screwdrivers, Allen keys, jack or lift, assistant

 Talent:

 Cost: None

 Parts Required: None

 Tip: Lowering a bike can dramatically affect ground clearance, so be careful what you wish for.

! PERFORMANCE GAIN: A bike that steers the way you want it.

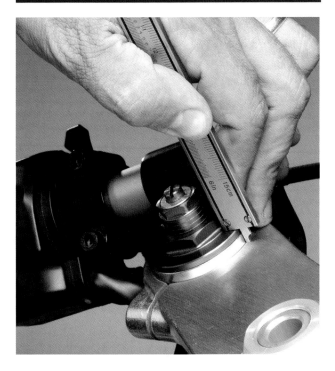

Although you can measure the height of a fork leg above the triple clamp with a ruler, a caliper will lock into position and allow you to accurately compare the height of both fork legs.

In recent years, sportbike suspensions have sprouted adjustments that, in the not-too-distant past, only GP riders could dream about. With all the talk about preload and compression/rebound damping, the average rider often overlooks one adjustment. Adjusting the ride height of your bike can be an important step toward getting it to behave the way you want it to. Changing the ride height can help with speeding up or slowing down steering, altering rear wheel traction, keeping the chassis attitude the same after changing to a different tire profile (see Project 30), or simply lowering the bike for a shorter rider (see sidebar "Lowering Cautions").

SUSPENSION

Lowering Cautions

Anyone with a shorter inseam looking to get better footing while straddling his or her bike needs to be aware of the compromises involved in lowering a bike. First and most importantly, you will decrease your cornering clearance. To put it in plain English, you can no longer lean your bike over as far as its designers intended. If you even only occasionally scraped your footpegs or any other part of your bike while riding, you should avoid lowering your bike. Try reshaping your seat or buying a lower aftermarket seat. Also, consider simply getting more comfortable with only one foot on the ground at a stop. Look at the grid of any AMA National, and you'll see lots of jockey-sized riders in perfect control of their machines with only one foot down.

If you're still with me, the maximum you should ever consider raising the fork tubes in the triple clamp is 15 mm. The increasingly compact sporting packages built today won't allow much more than that. Even then, you should test to make sure that full fork travel doesn't allow the fender or tire to contact the triple clamp or other components, such as the radiator. Since you'll be lowering the front and rear the same amount to maintain chassis attitude, you'll most likely be pretty safe lowering the rear 15 mm, but you should check to make sure that your rear wheel doesn't hit the rear fender when fully compressed.

Lowering your bike any more than the 15 mm will require installation of lowering blocks in the fork as shown in Project 51. You'll also need to shorten the fork springs to deliver the appropriate rate over their new, shorter travel. Also, you won't want to lower the rear of your bike by using longer dog bones than described in that project. Lengthening the tie rods also makes the rear linkage significantly more progressive (i.e., stiffer) and limits your shock's effectiveness. If your shock doesn't have ride-height adjusters, you should consider buying a shorter shock or having a suspension company shorten your shock's shaft. Otherwise you risk significantly compromising the suspension's function.

Other lowering considerations include shortening the side stand. You need to make sure the stand allows the bike to lean over far enough to remain stable and not fall over. Finally, if you do lower your bike, carefully build up to your new maximum lean. Flicking your bike into a corner before you know where the hard parts will drag could have you touching down hard enough to lever a wheel off the ground—and then you'll *really* touch down.

This ZX-6R has a factory spacer already installed. The two washers (right) will allow the shock to be lengthened or shortened in 2-mm increments, which should be more than adequate.

This Penske shock has an integral ride-height adjuster. Just loosen the lower locknut (as shown) and turn the adjuster to lengthen or shorten the shock length. Don't forget to tighten the locknut.

As with any suspension change, little alterations can have big effects on your bike. Take careful notes, beginning with the baseline measurements. After that, make sure you record every change you make. If you ever go in the wrong direction with changes, these notes will make going back to your starting point much easier. To find your baseline rear ride height, measure from the center of the rear axle to a spot on the frame or bodywork directly above the axle with your bike's rear suspension topped out. Write down both the measurement and the point measured to, so you can ensure repeatability. For the fork, measuring a change in ride height is easy. Since the fork tubes extend through the triple clamp on most sportbikes, you simply measure how far they protrude above the triple clamp.

Be clear on what you are seeking with changes to ride height. The factory settings are designed as a compromise to handle most situations a rider is likely to encounter. For example, if you drop the front end to steepen the rake angle and speed up the steering, you may get a bike that turns in quickly but is unstable in a straight line and wants to shake its head over every little road imperfection. You can also experience the same behavior if you raise the rear of the bike to increase ground clearance. The general rules of thumb concerning ride height can be summarized as:

Bike is nose high (front too high or rear too low):
• Chatter or poor grip on front tire exiting corners
• Difficult to steer or change direction
• Motorcycle runs wide (understeers) exiting corners

Bike is nose low (front too low or rear too high):
• Motorcycle unstable at high speeds
• Unstable, tries to swap ends under hard braking
• Lack of grip from rear tire

Since these same symptoms can also represent damping problems, you should consider talking to a suspension expert or having an experienced friend help you when attempting to alter a bike's geometry for the first time.

Typically, you change the front's ride height by sliding the triple clamp up or down on the fork legs. While you can do this with the bodywork on the bike, I usually take it off and use a jack to support the front end when I'm working alone. (At the track, where strong bodies are easier to come by, I can ask people to help lift or lower the bike while I work on the fork.) Use a rear stand to stabilize the bike. Place a jack or lift under the front of the bike and crank it up until the fork is fully extended. This takes the pressure off the fork and makes it easier to slide the legs up and down inside the triple clamp.

Working on one leg at a time, loosen all of the triple clamp pinch bolts except one. Even if you've supported the front of the bike with a jack, prepare for the front to drop when you loosen the final bolt. You can assist a fork tube in slipping through the triple clamp by twisting it slightly. If the triple clamp will not slide down on the fork leg, a retaining clip may be hidden under the top triple clamp. You'll need to raise the clamp and remove the clip before you can lower the triple clamp. When the front has been lowered or raised the proper amount, tighten one bolt and carefully measure the fork height. If you are raising the triple clamp on the

Those of you with nonadjustable shocks have two choices for altering the rear ride height. You can change the length of the shock, or change the suspension tie rods (or dog bones). Both of these options offer compromises. First, changing the length of the dog bones will change the progression rate of the entire rear suspension. If you lengthen the dog bones to drop the bike, the progression rate will increase, giving a stiffer ride. For instructions on how to install dog bones, refer to Project 51. While you can alter the rear ride height by changing the shock's sag, you will compromise its ability do its job.

To keep the progression rate the same on a lowered or raised bike, altering the length of the shock or the shock mount is the preferred way to go. Some bikes, like the ZX-6R shown in the photos, have the top shock mount bolted to the frame with a spacer. You'll need to remove the shock, as shown in Project 47, to gain access to the mounting bracket. Next, take the bracket (or the spacer) to your local hardware store to find washers that fit the mount. By combining washers of varying thicknesses with the stock spacer, you will be able to raise or lower the rear ride height. Keep the changes small. Current rear suspension linkages have a leverage ratio of about 2:1. So, a 2-mm spacer will raise the rear about 4 mm.

After each change—either front or rear—reassemble your bike and ride it to make sure you haven't created handling problems. If you have, set your suspension back to the previous state before the problem cropped up. If you have lowered the bike, remember that you have *decreased* your cornering clearance. If you were touching down toe feelers before, carefully build up to maximum lean so you can find where it is. If you drag hard parts, you can lever (or high-center) one of your wheels off the ground, putting you and your bike in a world of hurt.

A bike lift eases the process of adjusting the front ride height by taking the bike's weight off the front suspension. You can also use the lift to assist in raising or lowering the triple clamp on the fork tubes.

fork, lifting the bike slightly on the jack may help. Don't raise the triple clamp on the fork so high that the fork cap is below the clamp's top surface. If you get to this point, move to the back of the bike and lower the rear. Some bikes with inverted forks have registration marks on the top of the tube to assist in setting the height, but you should still double-check the height with a ruler or caliper. When you're certain of the height, retorque all of the pinch bolts and move on to the second fork leg.

Altering a bike's rear ride height can be a bit more complicated than the front. If you've already installed a spiffy aftermarket shock with an integral ride-height adjuster, simply loosen the locknut and crank the adjuster up or down until the desired height is reached. However, make sure that you don't alter the height beyond the shock manufacturer's recommended range. You don't want the shock's piston rod to fail, do you?

Although dragging bodywork is relatively benign, beware: Hard parts usually aren't far away. To increase the ride height without altering the chassis attitude, the front and rear of this bike needed to be raised an equal amount to eke out some more clearance on a tight and bumpy track.

Installing Fork Springs

Time: 1 hour

Tools: Wrenches and/or sockets, torque wrench, circlip pliers or jewelers screwdrivers (for non-screw-on caps), press (for non-screw-on caps), claw-type pickup tool to grab cartridge piston rod (optional), saw with miter box or pipe cutter, rags, jack or front stand

Talent: ▌▌▌

Cost: None

Parts Required: Fork springs, PVC tubing

Tip: Installing progressive-rate springs with the tightly wound section up will make the heavier end part of the sprung weight of the chassis as opposed to the unsprung weight of the wheel. On the track, this is a Good Thing.

PERFORMANCE GAIN: Proper relationship between sag and preload.

COMPLEMENTARY MODIFICATIONS: Change fork oil.

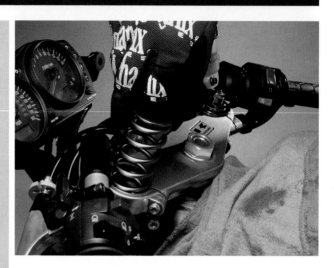

To keep your bike clean, slowly pull the spring out of the fork leg. Turning it counterclockwise can also help leave the oil in the fork.

So, you set your sag only to find that your spring rate was wrong. Or perhaps your stock springs are starting to sack out after a couple of years of riding. Either way, you're looking at installing a new set of fork springs.

With traditional forks, whether damping rod or cartridge units, swapping springs is so easy to that, if you've changed the fork oil or added Cartridge Emulators, you've done the work before. Inverted forks require special tools and techniques for the swap (see Project 45), but the process is still pretty easy.

Begin with your bike on a rear stand. Remove the lower bodywork to make room for a jack or a lift. A jack isn't required—you can support the front of your bike with a couple of tie-downs thrown over a garage rafter. However, the job is much easier with solid support under the chassis. If you don't support the front end, the bike will drop on the fork as you remove the cap of each tube, leaving you no recourse but to lift the front end when you want to put the cap back on.

Start by lifting the front end with the jack or lift until just before the tire leaves the ground. On bikes with adjustable preload, back the adjusters all the way out. Loosen the bolt(s) securing the top triple clamp. Bikes with screw-on caps only need to have the caps unscrewed with a wrench or deep socket. Caps secured with a circlip or retaining ring must be pressed in to take the pressure off the circlip. Two tools can make this much easier. Some automotive part pullers will hook over the triple clamp and press in the cap via a thumbscrew. A woodworker's corner clamp can achieve the same result for much less money (usually around $5). Press down on the cap just enough to take the strain off the circlip. Using a jewelers screwdriver or pick, remove the circlip, and slowly ease the cap out with the press. You will want to hold a rag over the cap, as it may jump out from the force of the spring.

Damping-rod forks are the easiest to swap springs on, but only slightly more so than cartridge units. Once the cap is removed, pull out the spacer and any washers and lift out the spring. Turning the spring counterclockwise as you lift it out helps to free it of excess oil, but you'll still want to wipe it off and place it on a clean rag. Folks with cartridge forks need to go through one additional step to free the spring and spacers: You will need to disconnect the fork cap from the piston rod by loosening the locknut securing it to the cap with a wrench on the nut and socket on the preload adjuster. Then simply unscrew the cap from the rod and remove the spacer and spring.

Although you may be tempted to drop your new springs into place, don't—unless you want to wipe up the fork oil that splashes out. If you are using progressive rate springs that are wound more tightly at one end than the other, some manuals will recommend placing the spring with the tightly wound end down. Why? According to the folks at Progressive Suspension,

Progressively wound springs can be identified by the tighter wind at one end. This helps the spring to function at one rate fully extended and a stiffer one as it compresses.

the direction of the spring wind makes no mechanical difference, though sometimes orienting the spring this way will lessen the spring noise. Racers, on the other hand, recommend keeping the tightly wound section up to make it part of the bike's sprung weight (the part of the bike supported by the suspension) instead of the unsprung weight on the wheel that must track over pavement irregularities.

If you need to make your own preload spacer to fit this spring, use the largest PVC pipe that will fit inside the fork leg. You will need to cut the spacer perpendicular to the tubing. A miter box or pipe cutter will help, but isn't necessary. Those with nonadjustable forks will want to make a variety of spacers in quarter-inch increments on either side of the spring

Although you can remove a circlip fork cap by pressing down on the cap with a screwdriver while simultaneously removing the circlip, this cheap woodworking clamp makes the job much easier.

These precut and labeled spacers will speed setting your bike's preload if you don't have adjustable forks.

manufacturer's recommendation to aid in the setting of sag. Use a knife and a bit of sandpaper to deburr the spacers. Wipe both the interior and the exterior of the spacers clean before installing them. Don't forget to write their length on them with a Sharpie, so you don't have to measure them each time you change them. Make sure that the preload spacer is the length specified by the spring manufacturer before placing it, and any necessary washers, into the fork leg. Reassemble the freshened fork in the reverse of the way you disassembled it.

You have a choice of two methods for setting the rebound damping adjuster for assembly. First, refer to your factory service manual to set the rebound damping adjuster before assembly. For example, the ZX-6R shown in the photo on the previous page required 25 mm between the bottom of the damping adjuster and the base of the preload adjuster. If you fail to set the adjuster correctly, you will not be able to adjust the fork's damping over its full range of settings. Proper measurement is critical, since any incorrect setting will limit the adjustment range. When reconnecting the piston rod to the fork cap, be sure you have the service manual's recommended minimum length of threads showing above the locknut. If not, you could pull out the rod as you torque the locknut or limit your adjustment range. Every inverted fork has its idiosyncrasies, so read the factory assembly instructions carefully.

Your second rebound assembly option is to use a rule of thumb that trackside mechanics have found quite useful. Screw the rebound adjuster all the way into the cap and back it out one-half turn (two clicks). Make sure the cartridge rod's locknut is down at the base of the threads. Next, spin the fork cap onto the rod until it bottoms out on the rod, and back it out one-half turn. While holding the cap in position on the rod, tighten the locknut up to the cap. Once the nut is torqued properly, you should have the full range of rebound-damping adjustment via the screw adjuster.

To finish up your fork, make sure you torque the fork caps, and don't forget the pinch bolts on the triple clamp. Once you've reset your sag, you should feel a noticeable improvement in your suspension.

PROJECT 42

Changing Fork Oil

 Time: 1–2 hours

 Tools: Wrenches, sockets, torque wrench, screwdrivers, Allen keys, metric tape measure, jack, circlip pliers or jewelers screwdrivers (for non-screw-on caps), press (for non-screw-on caps), caliper or ruler, Ratio Rite or another graduated container, spring compression tool (for inverted forks)

 Talent:

 Cost: $

 Parts Required: Fork oil

 Tip: Overfill the fork slightly if you are using a suction-type tool to set oil height.

 PERFORMANCE GAIN: Consistent damping from year to year.

After you remove the front wheel, unbolt the fender. You may need to squeeze the sides slightly to remove it. Beware, the plastic scratches very easily.

Fork oil must be one of the most neglected components on any motorcycle. Unless an owner follows the recommended maintenance interval to the letter or has a quality shop perform maintenance, fork oil may go years without being refreshed. I've seen oil come out of forks that looked as if it had been in there since the well-used machine was set up at the factory. Fork oil, like motor oil, loses viscosity over time. If ignored, the fork will cease to perform properly, and internal components, like the slider bushings, will begin to wear. So, even if you're not planning to upgrade your front suspension, be sure to replace your fork's slippery stuff ever two years or 15,000 miles, or at the interval your factory service manual recommends.

Like most fork projects, changing the fork oil begins by removing the fork from the chassis. Follow the directions for supporting the front end outlined in the previous project. Caps secured with circlips should be removed while the fork leg is on the bike. Screw-on caps should only be loosened, but not removed, before the leg is removed from the triple clamp. Make sure you remember your compression and rebound settings for reassembly.

Loosen the bolts on the lower triple clamp and slide the fork free. Screw caps should be removed with a socket or wrench. Holding the fork cap is good advice—even for those with screw-type caps. As you reach the last thread, the cap will tend to fly off. If you're not holding on to it, you could be injured, or worse, the cap could get dinged up.

Damping-rod forks are the easiest to prepare for changing oil, but not by much. Once the cap is removed, pull out the spacer and any washers and lift out the spring. Turning the spring counterclockwise as you lift it out helps to free it of excess oil, but you'll still want to wipe it off and place it on a clean rag. Folks with cartridge forks need to go through one additional step to free the spring and spacers: You will need to disconnect the fork cap from the cartridge piston rod by loosening the locknut securing it to the cap with a wrench on the nut and socket on the cap or preload adjuster. Inverted forks require special tools to remove the fork cap. Refer to Project 45 for disassembly instructions.

Empty the oil into a suitable container for transport to a recycling center. To make sure that all the old, dirty oil is expelled from the fork, you'll need to pump the slider up and

Whenever you do any work that requires removing the calipers, don't leave them hanging by the brake lines.

After you loosen the top triple clamp bolt, but before you release the lower ones, be sure to loosen the fork cap a turn or two. Removing the cap when the fork leg is off the bike will be much easier.

down a minimum of 10 times. Cartridge forks (both standard and inverted) require that the piston rod be pumped to expel the oil. If you can't grip the locknut on the end of the rod while pumping it, you may need to buy the screw-on factory part intended for this job.

Cartridge forks need to have the fork piston rod disconnected from the cap before the preload spacer and spring can be removed. Take note of the order of the washers and spacers for reassembly. Laying the parts down in order on a clean rag is the easiest method for maintaining the proper sequence.

If you don't have a fork oil level tool, measure out the factory-specified amount of oil before pouring it into the fork leg. Add an ounce of extra oil if you plan on using a suction-type tool.

Measure out the amount of oil recommended by your factory service manual before adding it to the fork. If you plan on using a fork oil level tool, add between half an ounce and an ounce of extra oil. If you're using the old pour-it-in-and-pour-it-out method, stick with the manufacturer's recommended amount. Pour the oil into the fork and fill the system by pumping the fork and piston rod a minimum of 10 times. Keep pumping until you no longer hear air being expelled.

The fork oil height should be measured with the fork fully compressed and no spring installed. You can measure the oil height with a simple dipstick fashioned out of a coat hanger (as I did for many years), or, if you plan on changing your fork oil more than once, buy one of the fork oil level tools sold by Race Tech or Progressive Suspension. You'll be glad you did. These tools feature a metal tube with an adjuster on the end that you measure to the appropriate oil height and lock in place. Then, when you place the end of the tool on the fork, it sucks out all the excess oil and stops at the specified height. If you're using the dipstick method, you'll measure the height, add a little (or subtract a little), and remeasure until you reach the proper level.

Don't worry about torquing fork caps into the fork tubes until the unit is reinstalled in the triple clamp with the lower clamp bolts torqued to spec. Before you tighten the triple clamp bolts, however, make sure that the fork tube is in the triple clamp at exactly the same height as the other one. A caliper will help with this, but you can use a metal ruler.

When the completed fork leg is torqued back into position, return the preload and damping to your preferred settings. (You did write them down, didn't you?) Stop to think about how much fun you're going to have when you're out riding next time. Now you're ready to move on the other one.

With the fork leg perpendicular to the ground and the slider completely compressed, place the fork oil tool against the top of the fork and draw out any excess oil. Drain the tool and repeat to be certain the oil is at the correct height. If no oil is drawn into the tool on the first attempt, add an ounce of oil.

Tuning Fork Performance with Oil Height

 Time: From a half hour to weeks of experimentation

 Tools: Wrenches and/or sockets, torque wrench, zip-ties, fork oil height tool or syringe with tubing, circlip pliers or jewelers screwdrivers (for non-screw-on caps), press (for non-screw-on caps), claw-type pickup tool to grab cartridge piston rod (optional), rear stand, metric tape measure, oil recycling container

 Talent:

 Cost: $

 Parts Required: Fork oil

 Tip: Use a zip-tie around your fork to make sure you are achieving full travel.

 PERFORMANCE GAIN: Suspension function that can only come from fine-tuning.

SUSPENSION

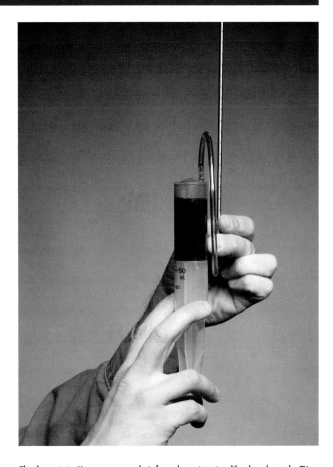

The doctor is in: You want to expel air from the syringe just like they do on the TV hospital shows. Don't squirt oil into the air though

Get out your way-back machine and take a gander at the fork caps from 10 to 15 years ago. What are those funny things on top that look like the valve stems on your wheel? Why on earth would you want to put air in a fork? Well, fortunately, fork technology has advanced beyond the need for air preload in forks, but these caps do point out the fact that air plays an important role in how your fork operates.

Think about it. Your fork works as a sealed environment. Once the cap is in place, the air above the oil has nowhere to go. So, what happens as a fork—any fork: damping rod, cartridge, or inverted—is compressed? The stanchion (inner fork tube) slides into the slider, effectively lessening the volume of the fork. Since oil doesn't compress very easily, the air inside the system squeezes into the smaller space. The smaller the space, the harder the air will resist. When compressed like this, the air acts as a spring with a progressive rate that gets stiffer the further it is compressed. If the fork has too much oil in it (or conversely, too little air), the resistance may build to the point that the air pressure alone may stop the fork from compressing, as if it had bottomed out, but without the benefit of using the entire mechanical travel that the fork can deliver.

Imagine you're entering a corner, hard on the brakes, when the fork decides to stop moving. What happens if you encounter even a little bump on the pavement? Yep, the tire will bounce, causing chatter or a loss of traction. You may end up shopping for new bodywork. Is the importance of oil height beginning to dawn on you?

As we all know, factory settings are designed for an "average" rider of "average" weight in "average" conditions. Most likely, you don't fit one of those averages. So, we want to adjust the fork oil height so that the spring force from the air comes into play just before the fork bottoms out. This way, you're softening the blow of bottoming with the progressive compression ratio of the air.

Begin with the oil height at the factory-specified level. If you don't know how to do this, read the preceding project. For adjustments of this order, you need a controlled environment, like a track, to run multiple sessions on the same tarmac. Wrap

105

Keep track of the registration marks on the syringe as you add or remove oil from the fork. Take careful notes or you'll never be able to duplicate your final settings.

a zip-tie around the fork leg and go for a ride. Ideally, you want to use all but a few millimeters of the fork's travel. Now, back in the pit, measure how far the fork compressed. Your factory service manual will tell you how much travel the fork has, but really detail-oriented mechanics will measure the travel with the fork off the bike and no spring in place.

If the fork isn't anywhere near bottoming, consider two options: First, maybe you're not braking hard enough. Second, the oil height is too high and needs to be lowered. If the fork is bottoming and you have the proper sag settings and spring rate installed, you'll need to add oil. Remember, the oil level only affects the last little bit of fork travel.

The proper way to change the oil level is to remove the fork from the bike, take out the spring, and use a fork oil height tool. Unfortunately, you probably won't have a team of mechanics working with you, but fortunately, you can cheat a bit. All you need is the measurement of the internal diameter of the fork leg (inside the fork, not at the cap, which may be larger), some geometry, and a calculator.

When adjusting oil height, you want to make changes 5 mm at a time. With a few calculations, you can make changes to the volume to alter height. A 1-mm slice of oil inside a fork tube is really just a cylinder of oil. Going back to high school geometry, cylindrical volume (V) is:

$$V = pi * r^2 * h/1000$$

where pi is 3.142, r^2 is the radius (or half the internal diameter of the fork) squared, and h is the height. So, to calculate the volume you need to remove or add to change the fork height. Enter your numbers for the radius and the height, and you'll get the number of milliliters you need to change for the change in height. One problem needs to be addressed, though. The number you calculated is accurate only for changing the oil height with no spring installed and ignoring the volume of the cartridge rod. Some riders like to divide the number by two to account for the rod and spring. Decide which method you want to follow and stick with it for all your oil height adjustments.

Armed with this information, you now know how to proceed. Record all addition or subtractions so that you can set the proper height next time you change the fork oil.

Put your bike on a rear stand, remove the fork caps, and let it settle down on the fork. Extra hands to keep it from dropping when you release the caps would be helpful. Call on these same helpers when you want to bolt the caps back on. It is much easier to alter the oil height on bikes with standard forks, because the caps and damping-rod pistons are easily removed with the fork on the bike. However, if you find a tube thin enough to slip between the spring and the stanchion, you can save a few steps. Similarly, on inverted forks you can avoid disassembling (since you can't remove the fork cap without a special tool) and removing oil the traditional way with this method. To add oil, you can squirt it down the side of the preload spacer.

Accuracy and repeatability are important, so you'll need to prime the syringe and tubing you use to add or remove oil. (You'll want to be able to reset the oil height after the next fork oil change, right?) To prime the syringe and tubing, simply stick the tube into a can of fresh fork oil and draw in about half a syringe of oil. Now, upend the syringe so that the air rises to the top. Press on the syringe until the bubbles are expelled. You can now dispose of any excess oil in the syringe back into the oil container. If you are adding oil, carefully measure the amount and squirt it into the fork legs, button them up, and go ride.

To remove oil, you will find that a fork oil tool like the one sold by Progressive Suspension is ideal for this on-bike task. The metal tube at the end of the hose will hang down into the oil and be less prone to pulling out and letting air into the syringe. Any oil that has been drawn out of the fork should be discarded into a recycling container. Take careful notes of every change and the way the fork behaves during the test runs.

As your riding ability or locale changes, you may find that you need to adjust the oil height again. A good memory, and good notes, will help you fine-tune your bike exactly the way you want it.

Installing Cartridge Emulators

 Time: 2-3 hours

 Tools: Wrenches, sockets, screwdrivers, Allen keys, drill or drill press, rotary tool or deburring tool, jack or front stand, hack saw, tape measure, rattle gun (optional), recycling container

 Talent:

 Cost: S

 Parts Required: Race Tech Cartridge Emulators, fork oil, Loctite

 Tip: Cartridge Emulators only affect compression damping. Adjust rebound damping with the oil viscosity.

 PERFORMANCE GAIN: An impressively well-handling motorcycle.

COMPLEMENTARY MODIFICATIONS: Add aftermarket fork springs.

Cartridge forks have been all the rage for a while. By allowing adjustable damping rates for compression and rebound, cartridge forks give riders more control in their search for the ideal suspension setup. Folks with damping-rod forks could usually only adjust the spring preload, change the spring rate, or vary oil height and viscosity and hope things went the way they wanted. (However, some damping-rod forks did allow for rebound adjustment, the Kawasaki ZX-6E being one example.) If the suspension was firm enough, the ride became harsh; if the right level of plushness was found, the bike would wallow, beginning to feel like a mid-1970s

Those who don't have an impact driver will want to loosen the damping-rod bolt on the bottom of the fork before removing the fork cap.

Cadillac. Paul Thede, mechanical engineer and president of Race Tech, Inc., recognized the problems inherent in damping-rod forks and designed the Gold Valve Cartridge Emulator to give damping-rod units the plush yet firm ride offered by cartridge forks.

A fork's actions are affected by three forces: friction, spring resistance, and damping. Since most people don't toss around the big bucks that factory race teams use to put low-friction coatings on fork sliders, the static friction between the stanchion (inner fork tube) and slider remains constant and is not affected by other suspension changes. Springs know only one thing: position—how much they are compressed. The more compression, the more pressure with which the spring pushes back. Damping responds to variations in road surface in a way that is different from, but complementary to, a spring's response. Since small bumps produce different forces on the front wheel than big bumps do, damping responds to the velocity of the fork's compression or rebound.

Traditional damping rods control the velocity of a fork's travel by pumping oil through holes in the damping rod. Since these holes are a fixed size, a compromise needs to be made to accommodate the slower fork movement of rounder road irregularities and the fast movement of square-edged bumps. As with any compromise, neither situation's requirements are completely met. What's needed is a way to make the fork firmer during low-speed compression and softer during high-speed compression.

By separating the low-speed and high-speed damping portions of a fork's duties, cartridge forks address the compromise inherent in the less sophisticated damping rods. Using shims to restrict the oil flow when the slider is compressing slowly, the bike has a firm ride that doesn't feel mushy and is less prone to squatting or wallowing in corners. When the tire encounters a large or sharp-edged bump, the shims flex to allow larger volumes of oil to move by quickly, giving a plush ride that doesn't hammer the rider's kidneys.

SUSPENSION

107

Be careful when removing the fork cap. The more spring preload it's under, the more forcefully it'll come out to greet you.

Deburr both the inside and outside of the new holes in the damping rod. You don't want to risk having any metal shavings get into the fork oil and damage sensitive components.

For years, riders with bikes using damping-rod forks could only watch from the sidelines as this suspension advance reverberated through the sportbike world. Fortunately, Thede's deceptively simple invention, the Gold Valve Cartridge Emulator, gives a conventional damping-rod fork a cartridgelike ride by providing tunable compression damping. Only 14 mm thick, the Cartridge Emulator sits atop the damping rod and conducts its business through a flapper valve (called the emulator plate) and a spring. The emulator plate has a small hole to control the low-speed compression damping, and the high-speed compression damping is tuned by varying the emulator spring's preload. Crank in more preload with an Allen key, and more pressure is required to lift the emulator plate, resulting in a firmer ride. With the compression damping control separate from the damping rod, the rebound damping can be controlled through oil viscosity. Simple, huh?

To install the emulators, support your bike with the front end off the ground. Remove the calipers and use a piece of wire or zip-ties to hang them from the bike, taking the strain off the brake lines. Remove the wheel, fender, and fork brace. Using a wrench, loosen screw-on-type fork caps a turn. Fork caps secured with circlips will be taken care of once the fork is off the bike. Loosen the top triple clamp pinch bolt. Next, be sure to hold on to the fork leg as you loosen the lower pinch bolt. The stanchion should slide out of the triple clamp.

Those without impact drivers should invert the fork and place an Allen key into the bolt securing the damping rod on

A drill press will simplify the task of opening up the holes in the damping rod, but if you have a steady grip, don't hesitate to use a hand drill. Drill all the way through both sides of the damping rod to speed the process.

the bottom of the fork. Rap on the Allen key two or three times to shock the threads. Now, loosen the bolt a bit. Don't remove it yet.

Although not absolutely necessary, a vise to hold the fork tube will make most of the remaining steps easier, but be sure not to overtighten the vise, which can distort the tube. Use soft jaws or a couple of pieces of wood between the tube and the vise. Remove the fork cap by either unscrewing it or pushing it down and removing the circlip. Lift out the spring. Drain the fork oil by inverting the fork over a suitable container and pumping the tubes until no more oil comes out. Remove the Allen bolt holding the damping rod in the bottom of the lower fork tube. If the damping rod spins inside the fork, preventing its removal, try the time-honored method of inserting a wooden broom handle or dowel to hold the damper rod in place. An impact driver may help too. Once the bolt is removed, the damper rod should fall out of the inverted fork. Don't lose the brass washer under the damping-rod bolt. Often it will stick to the fork but fall out later when you're not looking.

Before proceeding any further, check to see that the Cartridge Emulator fits on the large end of the damping rod, completely covering the opening. Make sure the inner diameter of the fork spring is at least 4 mm larger than the emulator plate. If your fork uses a flattop-style damping rod, you will need a special adapter (which should be included with the Cartridge Emulator kit, with rare exceptions) to hold the emulator in position.

The Cartridge Emulator requires an unrestricted oil flow in order to work its magic. To meet the necessary minimum flow-through, the damping rods need at least 6 (3 sets of 2) 5/16-inch compression holes. Since most forks' damping rods are more restrictive than the Cartridge Emulator, the existing compression holes need to be enlarged to the correct size and extra holes drilled, if necessary. Make sure the new holes are drilled perpendicular to, and at least 10 mm center to center from, the adjacent holes to keep from weakening the damping rod. Mark the damping rod and make an indentation with a punch to keep the bit from walking as you start to drill. Continue drilling through both sides of the damping rod. Chamfer and deburr the new holes, leaving a smooth surface on both the inside and the outside of the rod. Do not enlarge or make any modifications to the rebound holes.

On the bottom, the new holes will allow free flow of oil to the emulator. On the top, a stock damping rod shows how big a change we made.

Start reassembling the fork by sliding the thoroughly cleaned damping rod back into the inner fork tube. Install and torque the Allen bolt in the bottom of the fork tube. Again, the old wooden dowel trick will help hold the rod in place. If the Cartridge Emulator is being installed in a fork with a preload spacer, the spacer will need to be shortened 12 to 14 mm, depending on the model of the emulator, to maintain the correct preload.

Before placing the emulator into the stanchion, set the preload on the valve spring. Loosen the jam nut on the bottom of the emulator, and, using an Allen key, loosen the bolt until the spring is completely free. Tighten the bolt until it just touches the spring. Now, count in the turns of preload you put on the spring. Two full turns is the standard starting point for street riders, while four turns should be used for racing conditions or very heavy riders. Apply blue Loctite to the threads before tightening down the jam nut.

Pour the fork oil into the stanchion and pump until no more bubbles appear in the oil. (If you're unsure what viscosity to use, Race Tech's instructions feature a handy table of suggestions.) Install the emulator with the spring up. Set the oil level with the emulator installed and the fork completely compressed. Do not set oil level with the fork spring installed. (See Project 42.)

Replace the fork cap. Pump the fork a few times to check for binding caused by an improperly seated emulator. Reinstall the fork on your bike and go have some fun. Crank through some corners, try hitting some bumps, and feel the difference a couple of hours just made.

Start with the recommended preload on the Cartridge Emulator. Install them, and make changes to the preload depending on how you want to modify the performance.

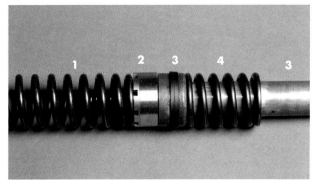

The lay of the land: 1. fork spring, 2. Cartridge Emulator, 3. damping rod, 4. top-out spring.

Adjusting Cartridge Emulator Damping

Although Cartridge Emulators mimic the function of cartridge forks, they can't match the ease of adjustment that cartridges offer. To adjust a Cartridge Emulator, you will need to remove it from the fork. Don't sweat it—the more you do this, the easier and quicker it gets. Since you will most likely be doing this at the track, the help you need to support the bike while you replace the fork caps will be close at hand.

When you have the cap off and the spring removed, you need to lift the emulator out of the fork. While magnetic tools can accomplish this, they tend to grab the stanchion as you try to lift the emulator out. A claw tool works much better. Clean and dry the emulator to make it easier to handle. Loosen the locknut on the base of the emulator. Now, adjust the emulator's preload in quarter-turn to half-turn increments, depending on how big an adjustment you feel you need. As you get closer to your final setting, make the adjustments in quarter turns. If you want more compression damping, add to the preload, and for less compression damping, lessen the preload.

Adjusting the rebound damping is an entirely different ball of wax, but pays off big when you take the time. Remember how you only drilled the compression orifices in the damping rod when you installed the emulator? Well, the rebound circuit now operates separately from the compression. Since the holes will stay the same size in the damping rod, varying the viscosity of the oil will change the rebound damping. Of course, you will need to dump the current oil to change the viscosity. If you want more rebound damping, put in heavier oil, and vice versa.

If you discover that neither 10W nor 20W will work and no 15W is around, mix the two oils 50/50 to approximate 15W. You can further tune the rebound by varying the ratios.

Just remember to set the oil height correctly after each change.

Although time-consuming, these adjustments are well worth the effort.

Installing Cartridge Fork Valves

 Time: 2-3 hours

 Tools: Wrenches, sockets, screwdrivers, Allen keys, foot-pound and inch-pound torque wrenches, jewelers screwdrivers or pick, bench grinder, jack or front stand, rear stand, oil recycling container, Ratio Rite or another graduated container, blue Loctite 242

 Talent:

 Cost: $$–$$$

 Parts Required: Gold valves or aftermarket valving shims, fork oil

 Tip: This project requires meticulous attention to detail, particularly when stacking the shims.

 PERFORMANCE GAIN: Better control over your fork's performance, better grip, better handling.

COMPLEMENTARY MODIFICATIONS: Add aftermarket fork springs.

The locknut securing the fork cap to the cartridge piston rod is hiding behind the preload spacer. You'll need to compress the spring with a special tool to gain access to the nut.

The introduction of cartridge forks for the sportbikes that you and I ride was nothing short of revolutionary. First seen on GP bikes and factory-supported superbikes, cartridge forks allowed both the compression and rebound damping to be adjusted separately and enabled the tuning of high-and low-speed damping, as well. Before, with the old standard damping-rod forks, with which damping was controlled by the size of holes in the damping rods, an alteration that improved the high-speed damping might make low-speed damping problematic—or vice versa. The adjustability that has trickled down to street riders in the OE suspensions is a vast improvement over the Bad Old Days. However, damping adjusters can only make changes over a fixed range. What is the "average" rider to do when the riding environment, or his or her riding style, requires that the fork go beyond the OE supported range?

The aftermarket has stepped in with solutions in the form of the Race Tech Gold Valve valving kits, as well as those from other suspension companies. These kits will allow you to adjust the damping characteristics of your cartridge fork well beyond the factory settings. Although the technology of adjusting suspension settings is based on a relatively simple idea of bending thin washers (or shims) of varying thickness to respond to different levels of fork oil pressure, the knowledge base required to group the shims into meaningful sets presents a steep learning curve. Fortunately, you're also benefiting from the R&D time of these suspension companies when you buy their shim kits, as they will recommend a shim stack based on your weight and the type of riding you do. Now *that's* value.

Upgrading your cartridge fork's valving does not involve completely disassembling the fork, but you do completely disassemble the delicate parts of the cartridge. If you're uncomfortable with measuring small parts, meticulous cleaning, and assembling delicate items, perhaps you should ship your fork off to your favorite suspension company for a tune-up. Those adventuresome souls who prefer to perform the work themselves should proceed with a vigilant eye for detail.

Remove the fork from your bike and mount it in a vise. Owners of traditional cartridge forks should disassemble the

With the spring compressed, use two wrenches to loosen the locknut. Then spin the cap off the piston rod.

cap and damping piston rod as described in Project 42. Inverted forks, which require additional steps and tools, will be discussed in a moment, but all of the cartridge disassembly, valving, and shim information applies to both styles of fork.

Once the fork is mounted in the vise, back the preload adjuster all the way out. Using a socket or large wrench, unscrew the fork cap from the fork leg. You should now completely compress the fork to give maximum access to the cartridge. Using a cartridge fork tool (available as a factory service part from your bike's manufacturer, or from an aftermarket company such as Race Tech), compress the fork spring to reveal the locknut securing the cartridge to the cap. Using a pair of wrenches, loosen the locknut and spin the cap off the cartridge piston rod. Put the fork oil in a container for recycling.

To remove the cartridge from both a standard or inverted fork, you need another cartridge tool to hold the fork internals in place while the bolt securing it to the bottom of the assembly is removed. Although sometimes you don't need this tool to disassemble the fork, don't cheap out or you may find yourself with a partially assembled fork, after business hours, the night before your big track day. After the bolt is removed, the cartridge should simply lift out of the fork by the piston rod. Completely clean and dry the cartridge before attempting to disassemble it.

The compression valve is located on the bottom of the cartridge. Typically, the valve on some models screws to the bottom of the cartridge body, usually requiring only a pair of wrenches and elbow grease to remove it. Others have punch marks 15 mm from the bottom of the assembly. These marks will need to be drilled out with a 3/16-inch drill bit. Do not drill any deeper than is required to penetrate the cartridge tube. A piece of electrical tape wrapped around the bit can tell you when you've drilled far enough. Once the holes have been drilled, push the compression valve holder into the cartridge body approximately 5 mm to gain access to the wire clip securing the valve. Use a small screwdriver or pick to remove the clip, and the valve should slide free. Be sure to deburr the holes on the interior of the cartridge tube so that the O-ring doesn't get damaged after reassembly.

Screw-on type compression valves can be downright ornery at times, thanks to the thread lock used on them. If you have trouble with one of these, try a couple of taps with a hammer on the tube directly outside the threads (*not* above, which could damage the tube). More stubborn valve assemblies might even require that the cartridge tube be heated with a blowtorch.

When disassembling the valve stack, remove the parts and lay them out in order on a clean rag. Otherwise, you'll never be able to remember the exact order all these tiny

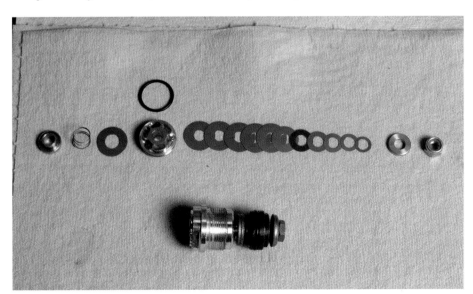

A Race Tech Gold Valve and its shim stack laid out in order, with a stock valve assembly below it. Your work space should be this organized if you want to avoid problems when revalving your fork.

Your freshened valve will look something like this when it's ready to go back into the cartridge.

parts, some of which you may need for reassembly. If the valve stacks are secured by an Allen bolt, remove it to free the shims. Some valves utilize a nut to hold the shims. In this case, the threads above the nut must be ground flat to the surface of the nut to allow it to spin free. Be very careful when doing this, and don't forget to deburr the threads after removing the nut.

Slide the original base plate (one or more thick washers) onto the shaft. Assemble the shim stack according to the manufacturer's directions, and slide them onto the compression valve, smallest shim first. If you're installing a Gold Valve kit, place the Gold Valve on the shaft with the recess in the piston facing up toward the mounting nut or bolt. Place the Gold Valve's check valve sleeve, check valve plate, check valve spring, and spring cup on the shaft. Make sure the spring cup

faces down and straddles the "step" in the shaft at the base of the threads, if there is one. You may need to add shims to the shaft below the base plate to raise the stack height and help the cup straddle the step. If you're reinstalling the stock valve, make sure you place it in the correct orientation and mount a fresh O-ring. Mount the shims in the same order as stated for the Gold Valve. Apply blue Loctite 242 to the threads and screw the nut or Allen bolt into position. Torque the fastener to 30 in-lb and no more. If you exceed this value, you will damage the threads and render the valve worthless.

Hold the valve up to a bright light to make sure all of the shims are flat with no bends or buckles. If things don't seem right, disassemble and clean the parts. Assemble and check them again. Once you are satisfied with the valve, set it aside and follow the same process on the rebound valve located on the end of the cartridge piston rod.

Once the new valving has taken up residence on the compression and rebound circuits, reassemble the cartridge. For cartridges in which the compression valve screws solidly onto the tube, apply Loctite 242 and torque the valve to manufacturer's specs. On cartridges in which the valve must be recessed in the tube a certain distance for full use of the damping adjusters, follow the directions in the factory service manual. For all cartridges, follow the directions in the service manual on how many clicks (or turns) or millimeters to unscrew the damping adjuster from the maximum setting (screwed all the way in).

Reassemble the forks in the reverse of the order in which you disassembled them, being sure to follow all the manufacturer's torque values. Set the oil height to the manufacturer's spec (or the one you decided on in Project 43). Remount the fork on your bike and check to make sure the sag setting is still accurate. Finally, set the compression damping to 1 1/4 turns out, and the rebound damping to 1 turn out (or the setting recommended by your suspension-valving vendor).

Remember, if, after all this work, you still don't have quite the valving you want, you now have the tools to make more adjustments through shims. Ask your suspension vendor how to make the settings stiffer or softer from this setting based on what you feel you need. Sometimes, the fun is in the experimentation!

Replacing Fork Seals

A jewelers screwdriver is a good tool for getting under the dust seal. Be careful not to scratch the stanchion or damage the wiper.

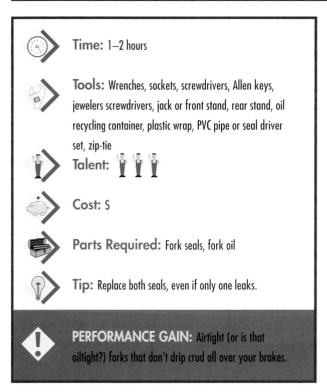

Time: 1–2 hours

Tools: Wrenches, sockets, screwdrivers, Allen keys, jewelers screwdrivers, jack or front stand, rear stand, oil recycling container, plastic wrap, PVC pipe or seal driver set, zip-tie

Talent: ▮ ▮ ▮

Cost: $

Parts Required: Fork seals, fork oil

Tip: Replace both seals, even if only one leaks.

PERFORMANCE GAIN: Airtight (or is that oiltight?) forks that don't drip crud all over your brakes.

SUSPENSION

Fork oil seals lead a hard life. Just riding down the road exerts extreme pressure on the front suspension. Add to that wheelies that get dropped from several feet up (you know who you are) or potholes, and you can see what a high-stress job they have. Sometimes they just wear out and begin to weep. Perhaps, even though you've been a good caretaker, you noticed a teardrop of oil on the top of the slider during your preride check. You'll need to replace the seal and should minimize your riding until you do. If you're not careful, the oil could drip onto the caliper or disc and render that brake useless.

Even if you only need to replace one seal, replace them in pairs to keep them on the same schedule. The parts are only about $13 for the pair, so don't cheap out. Owners of traditional forks should follow the directions in Project 42 until you have the fork legs off the bike and the springs removed. Some inverted forks require complete disassembly, while others (such as Ohlins units) will slip apart once the cap and the cartridge have been separated. If you have inverted forks, begin with the cartridge removal described in the preceding project, then, if the inner tube slides out, you'll need to pry out the oil seal with a large screwdriver or tire iron. If the inner tube doesn't slide out, you'll need to pull the fork apart the way you would with a conventional unit.

Those with traditional forks now stand at a fork in the road. (Sorry about the pun.) To the left is the traditional means of replacing the fork seal: Drain the fork, remove the

damping rod or cartridge bolt from the bottom of the slider, remove the damping rod/cartridge, remove the stanchion wiper, pry out the retaining ring, and, returning to your prehistoric roots, muscle the stanchion out of the slider. The advantage of this method is that you can check the fork bushing for signs of wear. So, if you suspect bushing wear, follow this path. The disadvantage is that lots of extra steps and sweat are involved. (I've always felt that if I'm sweating while working on a bike, I'm doing something wrong.)

On the other side, the road less traveled—my personal favorite—all you'll need is some extremely cheap, fresh motor oil, a catch pan, a jack, a piece of wood, and a car or truck. Once the wiper and retaining ring have been removed from the slider, fully extend the stanchion and completely fill the fork with motor oil. If possible, make sure there is no air in the system. Reinstall the fork cap. You now have a closed system with nowhere for the oil to go. Lay the fork on top of the catch pan with one end against your garage-door frame. If the cap has a damping adjuster, drill a hole in a small piece of wood to keep the adjuster from being damaged as you press out the oil seal. Now park your car with its front wheel parallel to the door frame. Place a board across the car wheel and wedge your jack between the fork and the board. Slowly extend the jack. With nowhere for the oil to go, the fork seal will push out. As soon as the seal slides out far enough that you can pry it the rest of the way with a

113

The oil seal retaining ring is pretty easy to get at with a jewelers screwdriver or pick.

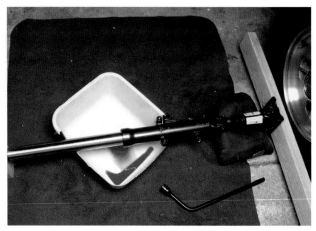

Once the truck was in the right position, pressing out the seal took less than five minutes, saving several steps in the process.

screwdriver, stop compressing the fork, or things could get messy. See, four-wheeled vehicles *are* good for something!

Remove the fork cap and drain the oil into a recycling container. Pump the fork several times and drain again, the way you did when changing the fork oil. Before you slide the old seal off the stanchion, note its orientation. While most fork seals look similar, their orientation can vary from model to model of motorcycle. Closely inspect the stanchion for any dings from stones. Minor ones can be cleaned up with a gentle rub of fine grit wet/dry 400-grit followed by 600-grit sandpaper. Use a little WD-40 as lubricant and wrap a rag around the top of the slider to keep any grit out of the fork. Wash the stanchion with contact cleaner and a rag. If you find a major ding, take the fork to your local bike shop to have a pro look at it.

Moisten the inner surface of the new seal with fresh fork oil. Carefully slip it over the top of the stanchion and slide it down to the slider. Some mechanics will protect the seal from

damage by placing a piece of plastic wrap (from your kitchen) over the top of the stanchion. If you have a fancy seal driver set, simply drive the seal into the slider. If you're cheap (like me), take the old seal, cut out the inner surface, and place it upside down over the new seal. If you're lucky, you can find a piece of PVC pipe that matches the outer diameter of the fork seal perfectly. If not, take a hacksaw and cut out about six sections, evenly spaced around the PVC. Clean up all the grit and place it over the stanchion. Wrap a beefy wire-tie around the pipe and tighten it until the PVC fingers exactly match the diameter of the fork seal. Now, gently tap the top of the PVC until the fork seal is completely seated. Remove the old seal and verify that the new seal is deep enough to allow the retaining ring to snap into place in its groove.

After installing the retaining ring, slip the dust seal back over the stanchion. Add fresh fork oil, set the oil height, and move on to the next fork leg. Once the bike is back together, you can go do more wheelies.

Tap the seal into place. You don't need to brutalize it—be gentle. This seal driver may not be pretty, but it cost $3 for 10 feet of PVC. Actual seal driving tools cost significantly more.

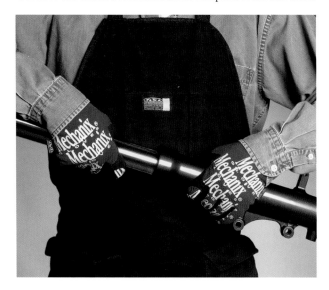

If you have issues to work out, you can remove the stanchion by pressing it in and jerking it out. Repeat until it pops free. If this method doesn't work, mount the slider in a vise and put your weight into tugging the stanchion.

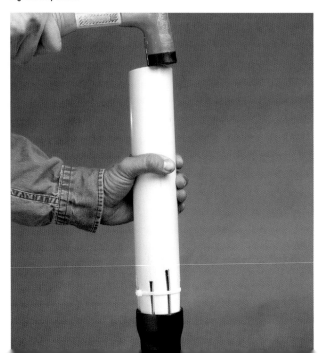

Installing an Aftermarket Shock

 Time: 1 hour

 Tools: Wrenches, sockets, torque wrench, socket extenders and/or universal joint, bottle jack, rear stand, zip-tie, an optional assistant

 Talent:

 Cost: $$$–$$$$

 Parts Required: Aftermarket shock, optional cover for reservoir line

 Tip: Make sure the new reservoir doesn't interfere with either the rider or the motorcycle's moving parts.

 PERFORMANCE GAIN: Better control of your bike's rear suspension, better grip, better handling.

COMPLEMENTARY MODIFICATIONS: Lube suspension linkage.

Although you can use a lift to support your bike, a bottle jack makes fine-tuning the suspension height to line up bolt holes on the new shock as easy as a few turns on the jack's adjuster. If you're concerned about the jack shifting while the shock is removed, put your bike in gear.

Stock sportbike shocks are pretty good. They usually feature adjustments for preload, compression damping, and rebound damping. Some even have provisions for ride height adjustment. Still, these off-the-rack shocks simply can't compare to a purpose-built aftermarket unit that's been set up to your weight and riding-style specifications. Of course, you'd expect an improvement in the suspension performance an aftermarket shocks provides since they are usually quite pricey. Even if you're not adding an aftermarket piece, this project will be helpful to those who need to remove their shock to send it off for revalving or a simple rebuild.

Begin by putting your bike on a rear stand. Next, you'll want to secure the front end so that it doesn't roll away while you're elbow deep in the bowels of your bike. While some people perform this modification with the front wheel snugged up against a wall, I've found that a zip-tie around the front brake lever works just fine for a simple shock swap.

If your bike will be sitting without a shock while it's out for freshening, you should consider finding a way to secure your bike. Regardless of how long you expect the project to take, don't lie under your bike until you're certain that it is safely supported. Remove the lower bodywork to give yourself unfettered access to the area around the linkage. Since the shock supports the back of the motorcycle even when it's on the rear stand, you need to fashion a way to maintain the chassis in the proper position. A bottle jack resting on the top of the rear wheel will do the trick. Center the jack on the tire and raise the jack until it takes the weight off the suspension. Although the plastic fender can easily support this weight, you may want to use a small piece of wood to spread out the load. Try to locate the jack so that it presses up on one of the subframe's metal crosspieces.

Now, you can start disassembling the linkage. Begin with the base of the shock. If you have an assistant, you should both work on opposite sides of the same bolt. Space is tight and the torque values are reasonably high on the bolts. If you're working alone, be prepared to exert yourself a little as you break the locknut and bolt free. Before you yank out the bolt, though, check to see how easily it slides free. Try adjusting the height of the jack until the bolt just slips out. You'll have a much easier time with reassembly if you take the time to do this.

Look closely at the bolts securing the tie rods (or dog bones). On many bikes, you will have difficulty removing the bolts for either the top or bottom end of the rods. Determine which bolt is easiest to remove, and lower the linkage out of the way. Remove the bolt securing the top of the shock to its mount and carefully lower the shock out past the swingarm.

Measure the length of the stock shock from shock mount to shock mount and make sure the aftermarket piece is the correct length. If not, use the shock's ride height adjuster to alter the length. If the shock is not adjustable, contact the manufacturer to determine what the problem is.

115

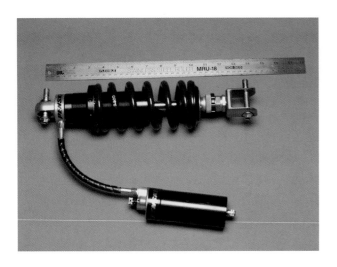

Make sure that the new shock is the same length as the stock unit. Inserting the bolts into the eyelet and clevis will make measuring easier.

The reservoir on this Penske shock fits perfectly on the subframe. Note how the excess clamp length and the adjusters are tucked slightly behind the reservoir to keep them from interfering with the rider.

Carefully place the shock into position inside the swingarm. Some shocks are easier to slip into place from above the swingarm than from below. Place the top mounting bolt through the shock's eyelet and let it hang in place. If your new shock has a remote reservoir, you need to find a place to mount it. If the shock's instructions don't have a recommended position, find a place that you can securely mount the reservoir so that it does not interfere with the rear wheel travel or with the rider's leg or foot. Using the supplied rubber spacers and hose clamps, loosely mount the reservoir and check that the shock's braided stainless-steel line doesn't abrade the frame or any other part of the bike. You can buy line covers that wrap around the line like a spring at your local bike shop. Once you are certain about the reservoir position, tighten the hose clamps.

Reassemble the suspension linkage in the reverse order of your disassembly. A light coat of grease on the bolts' shafts

(while keeping the threads clean) will help them slip into place and prevent corrosion. You may find that you have to rotate the shock shaft slightly to help the shaft eyelet, or clevis, slide over the linkage. Also, if you have trouble lining up the bolt holes, adjust the length of the bottle jack supporting the rear of the bike. Proper torquing of the bolts is essential for keeping everything where it belongs. This ZX-6R required 25 ft-lbs for the shock mounts and 43 ft-lbs for the tie-rod bolts. Most bikes will require similar numbers.

Once you have the bodywork buttoned up and the jack removed from the rear wheel, ignore the irresistible urge to jump on the bike, go for a ride, and then twiddle with the damping adjusters. First, you need to set the sag and damping to the shock manufacturer's recommendations. Once you have this last step completed, then go play with your new toy.

Getting a shock into position can be a puzzle. Because of the positioning of its reservoir, this Fox shock needed to be lowered into the swingarm from above, rather than fed up from below.

PROJECT 48

PROJECT 48

Lubing Swingarm Pivot and Suspension Linkage

 Time: 1 hour

 Tools: Wrenches, sockets, torque wrench, socket extenders and/or universal joint, pick, bike lift, parts cleaner, small brush, suspension grease, compressed air or hair dryer, ratchet straps

 Talent:

 Cost: 0

 Parts Required: None

 Tip: You may need to remove the exhaust system first to remove the bolts securing the linkage.

 PERFORMANCE GAIN: A rear suspension that moves with a minimum of "stiction."

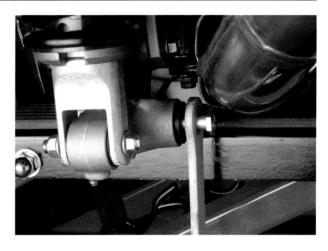

Compactness gives sportbikes their incredible ground clearance. Unfortunately, this means you have to remove unrelated components to get access to the parts you want to work on. This ZX-6R needed to have its stock exhaust removed to allow the bolts securing the suspension linkage to be removed. So you won't have a future interference problem, insert the bolts from the other side when you reassemble the bike to make the next service easier.

You can't avoid friction. No matter how hard you try, you're stuck with it. However, you can do everything possible to reduce it. Friction in your bike's rear suspension will keep it from performing up to its maximum capability. When you minimize the amount of friction in the suspension linkage, the maximum amount of the forces exerted by the pavement to the rear wheel are transferred to the shock, which is designed to control the rate of the rear end's movement. Friction—or stiction, as it can be considered in this case—will control your rear wheel's movement with much less finesse than the expensive shock on your bike.

Regular lubrication of the rear suspension linkage will help keep the movements of the rear wheel as fluid as possible. First, the lubricant makes things slide easier. Second, as with most maintenance, you'll have the opportunity to find failing parts before they adversely affect other parts. Lubing the linkage doesn't take very long. Motorcyclists who live in parts of the world with a real winter could find this an ideal task for staying acquainted with their bikes during the off-season. If you have a full-year riding season, just follow the recommended service interval for lubing the linkage.

Although you may be tempted to support the rear of the bike the way you did in the previous project, you should plan on using a bike lift or a jack under the engine. You will be removing the swingarm and consequently can't use the bottle-jack-on-top-of-the-rear-tire trick. Begin by removing the lower bodywork and inspecting the linkage. If you aren't able to extract the bolts (particularly where the linkage meets the frame) because of the exhaust system, take the exhaust off the bike before you have it on the lift. Although you won't be lifting the bike far off the ground, secure it to the lift with ratchet straps. You may also want to fabricate some wooden wedges to help steady your bike on the lift. Once the bike is secure on the lift, remove the rear wheel.

While you don't necessarily have to completely remove the shock, in many cases you do gain better access to the linkage with the shock removed. Begin removing the linkage at the base of the shock. Be prepared for the swingarm to drop a bit as the bolt slides out. Once the swingarm is free of the suspension parts, remove the swingarm pivot. Some swingarms are secured with a long bolt going through the pivot, as with this ZX-6R. Others utilize a bolt with a recessed hex head similar to those found on the front axles of most current sportbikes. You may also need a special tool to remove a jam nut.

After removing the pivot, slide the swingarm out of the frame. Push the sleeve out of the swingarm and clean it. Inspect the polished or pressed-on portion of the sleeve for

These marks on the swingarm pivot are normal and are not a sign of trouble, as long as they are just polished marks and not divots.

rust or wear. Needle bearings will typically leave small polished marks on the sleeve. These are perfectly normal. However, if they have progressed to indentations you can feel with your fingernail, the sleeve and its associated bearings will need to be replaced as a set. The same goes for the smaller sleeves on the linkage and tie-rod attachment points on the swingarm. Clean and inspect them in the same manner.

Replacing Linkage Bearings

Linkage plain bearings and needle bearings (just bearings, for simplicity) are press-fit into their respective homes. Smaller bearings can be pressed out by holding them with a simple vise you may already have. All you need to do is find the right-sized socket — one that exactly fits the internal diameter of the part is ideal. The purpose of the socket is to press evenly on the side of the bearing. Using a vise or clamp, slowly press the bearing out of the part.

Before you attempt to press the new bearing into place, lube both it and the opening in which it goes with a light oil. Needle bearings require special care. If you press unevenly or try to tap the bearing with a hammer to get it into place, you could damage the needles. Work slowly and carefully with the press to start the bearing. While you want to make sure that plain bearings are square with the part, they are less susceptible to distortion.

For larger bearings, like swingarm pivots, you may need to buy the special tool to remove and install the bearing. In this case, paying your local shop to replace the bearings may be a more cost-effective way to swap out a worn bearing.

For most linkage bearings, you don't need to invest in a special tool to press them out. Simply find a socket of the right size and crank them out with a clamp.

This sleeve is in dire need of replacement. Rust, rather than wear, resulted in the demise of this part. Don't be tempted to polish it up with Scotch-Brite and wait another year.

Plain bearings can be wiped clean and inspected like sleeves. Most will have a Teflon-like lining. Look for any signs of tearing of the surface. Often wear will first appear as loose strands of the surface material. If the bike has been neglected, rust may be visible through a hole in the surface material. If you spot any problems, replace the sleeve and bearing as a set.

Needle bearings offer much lower friction than plain bearings, but you pay a price for that slippiness. Cleaning and

A general solvent will make quick work of most of the old grease. Brushes help you reach the tight places. Wear solvent gloves and work in a well-ventilated area.

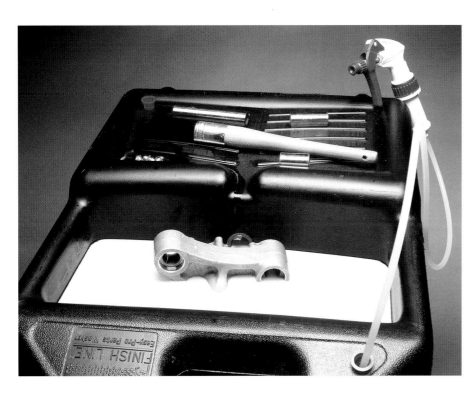

repacking needle bearings requires additional work to do right. (Note: The ball joints that some shocks use should be cleaned and lubed in the same manner as needle bearings.) Begin by wiping out the excess grease with paper towels. Next, move to a well-ventilated area and soak the parts in a general purpose degreaser. Work outside and wear chemical gloves, because this stuff is pretty toxic. Also, some needle bearings have plastic components. Double-check with the manufacturer to be certain that the degreaser won't damage the bearing. Using a brush, wipe out the grease that is loosened. Repeat this process until the grease is gone.

You could move on to the washing and drying step, but for an extra bit of cleaning, wash the bearings with soap and water then rinse thoroughly. For a final cleaning, use an organic parts cleaner such as those offered by Finish Line. This will remove any remaining grease and root out the solvent too. Wash the parts a final time with soap and water. Be sure to rinse the parts thoroughly. Once the parts are clean, don't let them sit to air-dry overnight. Rust will form almost immediately. Use compressed air or a hair dryer to quickly get rid of any remaining moisture. Before you repack the bearings with grease, check the needles for signs of damage, rust, or wear. If you find anything wrong, replace the needle bearings and sleeves as a set.

Repacking the needle bearings is messy fun. Using high-quality suspension grease, cover the bearings and press the grease into the spaces with your finger. If you have a hard time reaching some sections, use a paintbrush to apply the grease. Take your time to make sure you have fully filled the space inside the bearings. You want everything "packed" with the protective grease to prevent rust and mechanical wear. Some suspensions have zerk fittings that allow you to inject grease into the space behind the needles. Using a grease gun that you filled with suspension grease (don't use the cheap automotive stuff that comes in the prepackaged cartridges), pump the

gun until you see grease beginning to ooze out of the needle bearings.

When reassembling the linkage and swingarm, make sure you coat the sleeves with grease before slipping them back into place. Clean the grease seals and press them into position. Wipe away any excess grease that oozed onto the outside of the linkage—it will only catch dirt. Reinstall the swingarm and torque it to specifications. Don't forget to thread the endless chain into position before installing the swingarm. Remount and torque the linkage in the reverse order it was disassembled. Once the bike is completely assembled, bounce the rear suspension and notice how fluidly it operates. Go on a bumpy ride and see if you can tell the difference.

After you dry the parts with compressed air or a hair dryer, immediately repack the bearings and insert the sleeves. The parts will rust if you wait for any length of time before protecting them with the grease.

119

Changing Shock Spring

SUSPENSION

Time: 30 minutes

Tools: Wrenches, sockets, torque wrench, socket extenders and/or universal joint, pick, preload adjustment tool or long screwdriver and hammer, dead-blow hammer, bottle jack, rear stand, metric tape measure, shock spring compressor

Talent:

Cost: $–$$

Parts Required: Shock spring

Tip: Write the spring rate on both springs for future reference.

PERFORMANCE GAIN: Full use of the shock travel without sacrificing proper sag.

COMPLEMENTARY MODIFICATIONS: Lube suspension linkage, rebuild shock.

Using a pick, slide the circlip off the shock body. Notice the corrosion that can make it difficult to slide the retaining ring out of the way to expose the circlip.

So, you dutifully set your bike's sag as outlined in Project 37. As you were following the directions, you realized that your shock's spring has the wrong rate. Fortunately for you, the fix is quite simple. All you need is a little research with your favorite aftermarket suspension company and some basic tools. In as little as a half hour your can upgrade your bike's rear suspenders.

For this project you'll begin and end with the instructions for removing/installing your shock described in Project 47, so read that first. This page will still be here when you get back.

Before you go any further, clean the shock of all the grit and mung it may have collected. Working on a clean part is more enjoyable, and easier too. Now, place your shock in a vise. Using a preload adjustment tool, loosen the locking ring on the preload adjuster. (See below for ramped adjusters.) Once loosened, it should just spin off. If you don't have the specialized tool, use a screwdriver and a hammer. Then loosen the actual adjuster completely.

If you didn't already have the shock upside down in the vise, orient it that way now. Press down on the retaining ring

that is (now) above the spring. If it won't budge, tap on it with a dead-blow hammer. If it's still stubborn, give it a spritz of WD-40 or another penetrating lubricant and let it sit for a few minutes while the lube works its way into the corrosion. Now, tap the ring down. You should see a circlip once the retaining ring has been moved. Remove the circlip and slide off the retaining ring. Remember which way the retaining ring faces, if applicable. Slide the spring off the shock body.

To release the spring on shocks that can't have preload completely removed (such as those with ramped adjusters), you need to use a spring compressor. You'll still want to back the preload as far off as possible. Although you can compress the spring and remove the C-collar that secures it, having an assistant compress the spring while you do the work makes the job easier. Mount the shock upside down in the spring compressor (and in a vise). Press down on the tool until the spring no longer touches its base plate. You may need to tap the plate and the C-ring with a hammer to free it up. Be careful when releasing the pressure on the spring compressor.

With the new spring in place, lock the retaining ring in position with the circlip. Did you take the time to clean the parts of any corrosion?

Since you'll still need to set the sag once the shock is back on the bike, make the process easier by setting the spring length to the manufacturer's specifications.

While you've got the shock vulnerable, take a look at the shaft. Does it have any pockmarks or dings? Is the seal leaking? If you notice any problems with the shock, now would be a great time to order the parts or send your shock off for a rebuild. Why ride with a shock that's not in tip-top shape? After all, you spent good money to buy a sportbike because you want cutting-edge performance, right?

Place the new spring on the shock. If your suspension manufacturer recommends a specific orientation, heed that advice and take care to install the spring right side up. Reinstall the retaining ring over the spring. Make sure it's in the proper position. You'd be amazed how many people accidentally put the retaining ring on upside down and then can't understand why they have trouble getting the shock back together. Slip the circlip back into position and check to be sure that the retaining ring will return to its proper position over the circlip. If you're using a spring compressor, slip the spring and its base plate onto the shock before bolting it into the compressor. Have your assistant press the spring down until you can slip the C-collar in place.

While you hold the spring up against the retaining ring, rethread the adjuster ring back onto the shock's threads and spin it up to the spring. Tighten up the adjuster until the spring is compressed to the manufacturer's recommended length. Thread the lock ring in place, but don't tighten it yet.

Once you get the shock back on your bike, you'll need to set the sag again.

With your new spring installed, go remount the shock on your bike. Now reset your sag, then bask in the glow of a major modification that took only minutes to complete.

For shocks that can't have their preload completely removed, you need a spring compressor tool. Have an assistant operate the tool while you work on the shock.

121

PROJECT 50

Shock Rebuild and Gold Valve Installation

 Time: 2 hours

 Tools: Calipers or a metric ruler, torque wrench, chisel, hammer, dead-blow hammer, bench grinder, numbered drill set, drill, valve core removal tool, permanent thread lock, safety glasses, latex or similar gloves. Special tools: high-pressure nitrogen with high-pressure gauge and air chuck, end cap tool (Ohlins and White Power), metric micrometer (if you're measuring shims to build your own stack)

 Talent:

 Cost: $$–$$$

 Parts Required: Gold Valve Kit or other shock rebuild kit, shock fluid (Race Tech Ultra Slick US-1 Light [for KYB, Yamaha, and White Power] or US-2 Medium [for Showa and Ohlins]), permanent thread lock

 Tip: If you don't have nitrogen, you can take the shock to a suspension specialist to have it charged.

 PERFORMANCE GAIN: A shock that performs better than new, better grip, better handling.

COMPLEMENTARY MODIFICATIONS:
Replace stock spring, lube suspension linkage.

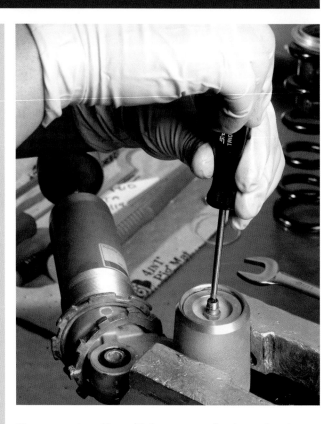

Wear eye protection and be careful when you remove the valve stem from the reservoir. The nitrogen is under 200 psi of pressure.

Saying that a motorcycle shock feels every little ripple in the pavement isn't hyperbole, it's fact. Add a stressful working environment, including such fun things as flying stones, grit, water, heat, and cold, and you should be pretty impressed with the performance and stamina that shocks deliver. Unfortunately, like all mechanical things, shocks wear out and require maintenance. Long before your shock begins to deliver pogo-stick damping or starts to leak fluid, it should be rebuilt. Since your shock's performance starts degrading from the first time you ride your bike, the timing of your shock rebuild depends on how you use your bike.

Jim Lindemann, the force behind Lindemann Engineering, says, "A shock starts degrading from day one, just very gradually.

Hot racers should plan on rebuilding the shock every three months." The folks at Race Tech concur, stating that freshening it up every 35–50 hours of use will maintain optimal 10/10 performance. Where does that leave fast street riders? Both Lindemann and Race Tech contend that the shock fluid needs to be replaced every year—just like the fork oil. Of course, this offers a prime opportunity to upgrade the valving too.

Disassembly

Before you do anything, if you haven't written down the compression and rebound settings for your shock, record them in the number of clicks or turns (depending on the shock) it takes to move the adjuster (usually clockwise) into the stiffest-setting mode. Also note the length of the spring if you have it set to the correct sag. (If you're not changing the spring rate, this will make getting your shock properly set up after reassembly much easier.) Remove the shock from your bike as shown in Project 47. Now, follow Project 49 to remove the spring. Clean the shock—and yourself—thoroughly. You don't want any crud on your hands as you work on the delicate internals. If your factory service manual describes how to disassemble the shock, note the differences compared to these instructions.

Using a deep socket, press down on the reservoir cap until the circlip is exposed. Removing the circlip is a two-second affair.

Since you'll be working with compressed gas, shock fluid, solvents, and a bench grinder in this project, wear proper eye protection throughout the process. Begin by clamping your shock in a vise with the reservoir positioned to access the nitrogen valve and the reservoir cap. Next, set both the

Although you could buy this special tool from Race Tech, a screw-on bicycle pump would work just as well.

If you use a screwdriver or a piece of bar stock, it would compress the seal head, potentially damaging the shaft or seal if something goes awry. Pop for the Race Tech Seal Head Tool for this step.

compression and rebound damping adjusters to their softest settings, which will allow the oil to flow through the system more easily as you recharge the shock. If your shock doesn't have a reservoir, release the nitrogen and skip ahead to the shock body disassembly. When you release the nitrogen pressure with a valve stem remover, be sure you are wearing safety glasses and the opening is pointing away from you. If your bike has a sheet metal cap covering the valve, drill a 1/4-inch hole in the cover. Be careful! The cover is very thin, and you don't want to damage the cap below the cover. Insert a screwdriver into the hole and pry off the cover.

To remove the reservoir cap, you need to compress the bladder behind the cap to gain access to a circlip. A deep socket and a couple of gentle taps from a dead-blow hammer will suffice. Use a pick to remove the circlip. To aid removal of the cap and its attached bladder, Race Tech sells a nifty tool that screws onto the valve nipple, but a bicycle pump with a screw-on valve adapter will do the trick. Or you can cover the cap with a rag and use compressed air to push the cap out, but don't overdo it and risk damaging the bladder. Drain any oil in the reservoir into a recycling container.

Remount the shock in the vise to give access to the shock's end cap (where the piston exits the shock body). Some end caps require a special tool to unscrew it. If you are unsure if yours does, contact the manufacturer before you embark on this project. Press-on-type caps can be removed with a hammer and sharp chisel. Using a hammer, tap the cap on the seam with the shock body. Move around the shock as you tap the cap off evenly.

Once the cover has been removed, depress the seal head with a Race Tech Seal Head Tool. You may have to tap the tool lightly with the dead-blow hammer. Remove the circlip as you did with the reservoir cap. Now, gently tap the shaft eyelet away from the shock body to remove the shaft assembly. Since some oil will leak out during this process, you'll want to have a pan below the shock to catch the excess oil. Remove the shock body from the vise, and pour the old fluid into a recycling container. Clean the shock body with solvent and blow-dry with compressed air. Clean and dry the shaft assembly too.

If you look closely at the nut topping the shock shaft, you'll see the peen marks securing the nut. Note the damping pin sticking out of the center of the shaft.

The nut is now ready to be removed. Notice that enough of the flats were left to allow a wrench to get a bite. Also, see how the pin was left untouched.

Now comes the dangerous part. You need to grind off the top of the shaft nut and part of the shaft threads to remove the peening that secures the nut. Caution: If you do this incorrectly and damage the damping adjuster that sticks out of the shaft, you will have to replace the shock. You have been warned. On a Showa shock, the best way to grind the nut is to hold the shaft with the nut and threads at a 45-degree angle to the bench grinder. Keep rotating the shaft to make the nut cone-shaped. Stop frequently to check your progress. Be sure to leave enough of the nut's flats to allow a wrench to get a bite on

it. Also, you must leave enough of a lip at the inner diameter of the shaft to hold the damping adjuster in. Some KYB shocks can be ground off flat at the peening, but the cautions about the damping adjuster still apply. Proceed with great care.

Place the shaft eyelet in the vise and remove the nut securing the valving stack. Lay the used parts—in order and in the correct orientation—on a clean rag, so you don't have to do it from memory later. Clean all parts with solvent and blow-dry. Don't forget the inside of the shaft, where proper oil flow is essential. As you clean all the parts, inspect them

Wear eye protection so you can closely watch how you grind off the nut and the peen marks. Beware! If you accidentally grind the damping adjuster pin, the shock is junk.

To replace the shaft seal, remove and examine the top-out bumper, the washer behind the bumper, if there is one, and the seal. Carefully insert a new seal.

Although Race Tech recommends using its bullet tool to protect the new shaft seal from the shaft's threads and lip, you can achieve the same result by wrapping those sharp edges with a turn or two of electrical tape. Apply a generous amount of grease to the seal before sliding it over the tape.

The bleed jet is the small hole drilled inside the plug at about the 12 o'clock position. Not all shocks will need the plug drilled. Mount the Gold Valve on the shaft with the plug facing down toward the compression shims and head seal.

for wear. If the grease seal, O-rings, or top-out bumper are worn, replace them. Grease the seal and reassemble the seal head. Don't forget the cover! Now reinstall the base plate and any washers it requires.

Revalving

Consult your replacement valving instructions for the proper order of the shims. Or you can let the pros do it for you: If you are installing a Race Tech Gold Valve kit, you can base your valving on your bike, weight, and riding style by entering your product code on their website (www.racetech.com). The shim stacks are installed in the following order (from the base plate up to the shaft threads): high-speed compression, low-speed compression, the piston, low-speed rebound, high-speed rebound. Slip the high-speed compression shims, smallest shim to largest, on the shaft, followed by the low-speed shims in the same relative order. Some shocks will not require a low-speed shim stack.

You'll want to reface the piston flats (even a new Gold Valve) with 320-grit sandpaper on a known flat surface, like glass. Rub the flats against the sandpaper in a figure eight pattern and blow the part clean with compressed air. Install the new O-ring(s) and slide the piston onto the shaft in the proper orientation. This is extremely important! Gold Valve users will need to install the brass plug into the piston. Use red (permanent) locking compound, and if the instructions specify, drill the appropriately sized hole, converting the plug into a bleed jet. Not all shocks will require this, but if yours does, be sure to deburr and clean the jet prior to installation. Now, install the low-speed rebound stack with the larger shims against the piston, followed by the high-speed stack, again with the larger shims downward. Remember, not all shocks will require a low-speed stack.

The players are: 1. nut; 2. rebound base plate; 3. washer spacer; 4. high-speed rebound stack (no low-speed on this shock); 5. Gold Valve; 6. high-speed compression stack (no low-speed on this shock); 7. shim spacers; 8. compression backing plate.

Before you install the nut and torque it down, you need to make a crucial inspection. The top shim must be below the lip on the shaft at the bottom of the threads. Next, make sure that the lip does not show above the rebound base plate. If the lip shows, you need to add a spacer to the top of the shim stack. In the case of the GSXR shock in our photos, the stock base plate (gray) was backed with a Race Tech spacer (gold). You could also add shims to the top of the shim stack, but below the base plate. However, the shims must all be larger than the base plate or the valving will be affected.

Install a new nut using permanent locking agent and torque it to 25–30 ft-lbs. Carefully inspect the shim stacks. They should be flat against each other with no distortions. If you find any irregularities, disassemble the shim stacks, checking for dirt or burrs on the parts. Reassemble and verify again. Now, you're ready to start slipping things back together.

Reassembly

If the shock body has been sitting around for a while, blow out all parts with compressed air. Clamp the shock in a vise with the reservoir facing up and fill it about halfway with shock fluid of the proper weight. Reinstall the filler valve in the cap assembly and insert it, bladder first, into the reservoir, pressing it down so that the cap is below the circlip ring. If excess fluid was not displaced from the reservoir, remove the bladder and add more fluid. Reinsert the cap and secure it with the circlip. Fill the bladder with 40 psi of air to force the fluid through the compression adjuster valve. (Don't worry, you'll be filling it with nitrogen later.) A rag in the shock body will keep the fluid from pouring out of the shock.

Mount the shock in the vise with the shock body up. Fill the shock body about four-fifths of the way with fluid. Wrap the piston ring around the piston as you slide the valving assembly into the shock body. Bleed air from the system by pumping the shock quickly on the compression stroke and

To assure that no air is left in the system, you should have enough shock fluid in the reservoir to overflow as the bladder and cap are pressed into place.

126

Bleed the shock body by compressing the shock quickly and letting it rebound slowly. When no more bubbles are present, top off the fluid.

pulling it out slowly on the rebound. The quick movement opens the shim stacks to allow air bubbles to pass while the slow rebound keeps the stack closed. Continue this pumping until no more bubbles float up to the surface.

Once you've finished bleeding the fluid, if your shock has a bladder reservoir, extend the shock as completely as you can without lifting the valving assembly out of the oil. If it breaks the surface, rebleed the shock. Top the shock off with more oil, and slide the seal head down the shaft until it begins to displace oil. Using the seal head tool, continue pressing the seal head into the fluid until the O-ring passes below the shock opening, sealing the shock body. Keep pressure on the seal head and press down on the reservoir valve, allowing the pressurized air to escape. The seal head will depress easily. When the seal head drops below the circlip groove, install the circlip and pour out the excess fluid. Shocks with piston reservoirs need to have the piston set to the correct height. Consult the service manual for these units, as the piston height varies, and an incorrect setting could potentially damage the shock.

Once the circlip is in place, charge the system with nitrogen to just 20 psi to seat the seal head on the circlip. Inspect the shock for leaks and to be sure that the seal head and reservoir caps have seated properly. Double-check the piston height again in piston reservoirs. Press the seal head cover into place. Tap it with a dead-blow hammer, if necessary. Screw-on covers need to be tightened down with the special tool. If everything looks good, now charge the system up to 200 psi with nitrogen. Give the shock a couple of test bounces. The shaft should rebound to its fully extended position. If it doesn't, something's wrong. Disassemble the shock, locate the problem, and reassemble.

Now all you need to do is mount the spring, reinstall the shock, check the sag, and reset the damping. Take your bike for a test ride first. You may find that your old damping settings need to be adjusted to suit the freshened shock.

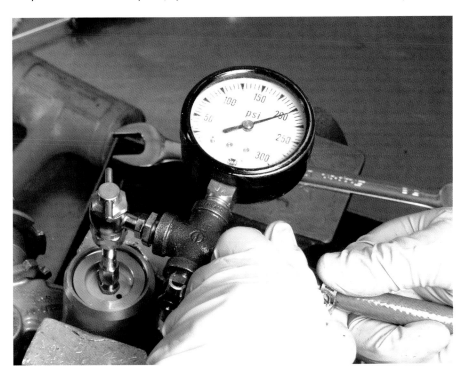

If you don't have the specialized tools to regulate the nitrogen pressure in the shock, you should take it to a suspension shop to have the shock charged.

PROJECT 51

Lowering for Drag Racing

 Time: 1–3 hours

 Tools: Wrenches, sockets, torque wrench, socket extenders and/or universal joint, pick, preload adjustment tool or long screwdriver and hammer, dead-blow hammer, bottle jack, rear stand, metric tape measure, rattle gun (optional), cartridge fork tool

 Talent:

 Cost: $$–$$$

 Parts Required: Lowering blocks or tie-down straps, lowering tie rods

 Tip: These modifications limit suspension effectiveness and ground clearance for normal riding.

 PERFORMANCE GAIN: Less shifting of weight on those aggressive launches.

A tie-down strap is the quickest, most versatile way to lower the front of your sportbike for drag racing. Crank it down to race; loosen it to commute.

If straight-line blasts do more for you than maximum lean angles, you are probably considering lowering your bike. Drag racing puts a set of demands on motorcycle suspensions that are entirely different from any other activity. The one goal of drag racing is to get all the horsepower to the ground without looping the bike. To that end, lowering a bike for the strip is a time-honored means to achieving that goal. With the center of gravity (CG) closer to the ground, the weight shift under acceleration is minimized, as is the leverage that could lift the front wheel off the ground.

Front Suspension

Since you can't just drop the triple clamp down on the fork without running into clearance problems between the tire or fender and the chassis, you've got two choices for lowering the front end. Tie-down straps simplify temporarily dropping the front for street races or Friday Night Grudge Matches at the local drag strip. Those looking for a more permanent solution insert lowering blocks into the fork. Although tie-down straps are an easy modification—particularly for novice mechanics—if you're truly getting into drag racing, you'll need to install the lowering blocks.

To mount lowering straps to your sportbike, securely support your bike with a rear stand. Remove the top bolt securing one of the front calipers and insert it through the bottom plate of the tie-down strap. Hold the plate so that the strap will pull evenly on it, parallel to the fork leg, and torque the bolt to factory spec. You may need to remove the reflector from some bikes to mount the plate. Also, some builders stress that you should buy a longer bolt to make up for the additional space taken up by the plate. This way, you know the bolt's threads have a solid bite in the caliper.

Next, thread the strap up over the top triple clamp and back down to the other caliper. Make sure that the strap has no twists in it. Also check that the strap doesn't interfere with or pinch any hoses or cables. Attach the second plate to the caliper the same way you did the first. When the time comes to lower the bike, back the preload out all the way and pull on the strap. If you can't get the front end as low as you want, bounce the front end while you have an assistant tug on the strap. Once you have the front at the correct height, crank the preload all the way in to hold the fork in position.

Make sure the tie-down strap doesn't interfere with any of the nearby cables or hoses. If the strap prevents full lock-to-lock steering, reroute it. Finally, secure the excess strap to keep it from flapping around when you ride.

To drop the front of a bike with a lowering kit, you need to disassemble the fork. The block provides a mechanical stop that keeps the fork from fully extending. For damping-rod forks, a spacer is inserted between the stanchion and the slider, keeping the stanchion from being able to extend fully out of the slider. Installing a lowering kit in a damping-rod fork is no more complicated than changing an oil seal. In cartridge forks, however, the spacer is inserted into the cartridge, and it requires considerably more mechanical experience. If you're adventurous, and you're trying this for the first time, modify one fork leg at a time so that you have an assembled, functional one for comparison.

Begin by disassembling the fork and removing the compression valve as described in Project 45. Once you have the valve separate from the cartridge body, you will need to remove the locknut from the piston rod and slide it free of the

cap. Slip the lowering block over the piston rod. Before you reassemble the cartridge, make sure that all the parts are clean and free of grit. When you reassemble the fork, use 20-weight oil to help minimize suspension movement. You will also need to shorten the preload spacer the same length as the lowering block. If you don't, you won't be able to get the fork cap back on. Depending on the type of kit you installed, your fork should now be 2 to 3 inches shorter than stock.

This partially assembled cartridge shows all the players. These Schnitz Racing lowering blocks drop the ZX-6R 2 inches. A 3-inch version is also available.

Damping for Drag Racing

Damping chores in drag racing are divided into the differing duties of the front and rear suspension. The sole purpose of the front suspension is to have something to point toward the timing lights. Otherwise, it should be dead weight until the throttle is cut and the brakes are applied. Lowering the bike's CG is designed to minimize the rearward weight shift when you launch the bike, and to keep the bike from looping when the rear tire hooks up. The fork's movement plays a vital role in this. By cranking down on the preload, running heavy fork oil, and setting the damping at maximum for both compression and rebound, the front of the bike turns into one solid unit. In order to wheelie, the rear wheel must lift the entire front at once. On the other hand, if the fork has any suspension travel, the chassis can rotate as the rear tire hooks up, giving the mass of the bike momentum as it tops out the fork. If this momentum is sufficient, the front tire will lift. Lifting the entire front end at once requires much more force.

Contrary to what many riders believe, you want to maintain the tunability of the rear suspension. Different tracks have different surfaces. One may be glass-smooth and allow for a stiff suspension, while another may require some adjustments to cope with midtrack bumps. Run your shock too stiff, and those bumps could get your tire airborne, resulting in wheelspin and slower times. So, while you may want to firm things up, don't completely lock them down the way you did with the front end.

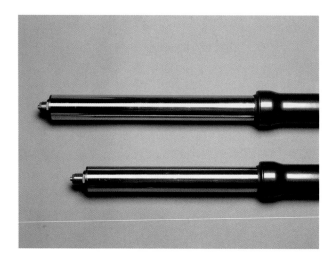

These fork legs are identical except for the Schnitz lowering block in the shorter one. By lowering the fork internally, as opposed to dropping the triple clamp down on the stanchions, you prevent clearance problems between the tire and chassis.

Rear Suspension

Lowering the back of your bike is a simple operation if you choose to go the tie-rod route. Although some companies offer adjustable tie rods, you can't beat the quick adjustability of dog bones that have premeasured lengths. In a little more than a half hour, you can switch your bike from a slammed street racer to a fully suspended canyon carver.

Begin with your bike on a rear stand with the slack of the suspension taken up with a bottle jack. Simply remove the bolts securing the tie rods the way you did in Project 48.

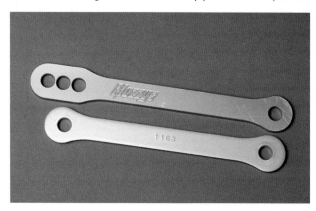

The gold Muzzys tie rod allows you to run your bike at the stock height or lowered by either 1 or 2 inches.

Lower the bike onto its suspension until the desired hole lines up with the linkage. The top hole will give stock ride height while the bottom hole makes it 2 inches lower.

Hopefully, you've already flipped the bolts so that they don't interfere with the exhaust system. If not, plan on this taking a little extra time. Once the OE tie rods are free, loosely mount the top of the new tie rods to the swingarm. Tighten the top bolts so that the tie rod will stay in position by the linkage as you lower the jack. Unfortunately, not all bottle jacks will compress far enough to allow the suspension to be lowered 1 to 2 inches. In the event that you have this problem, you can either enlist a couple of strong, trustworthy friends, or use a tie-down secured to a rafter in your garage to lower the bike to the point that the dog-bone holes line up with the linkage. Insert the bolt and torque everything back to specification.

Now, you're ready for the strip.

SECTION FIVE

CHASSIS

Motorcycle chassis technology has steadily advanced over the years. Your average, off-the-rack middleweight contains technology that only a few short years ago was unobtainable by anyone not in the GP paddock. Today, chassis modifications of the cut-and-weld type are few and far between. Instead, we now rely on the aftermarket to help mold our sportbikes into the vision we have for them—drag racer, road racer, or street bike.

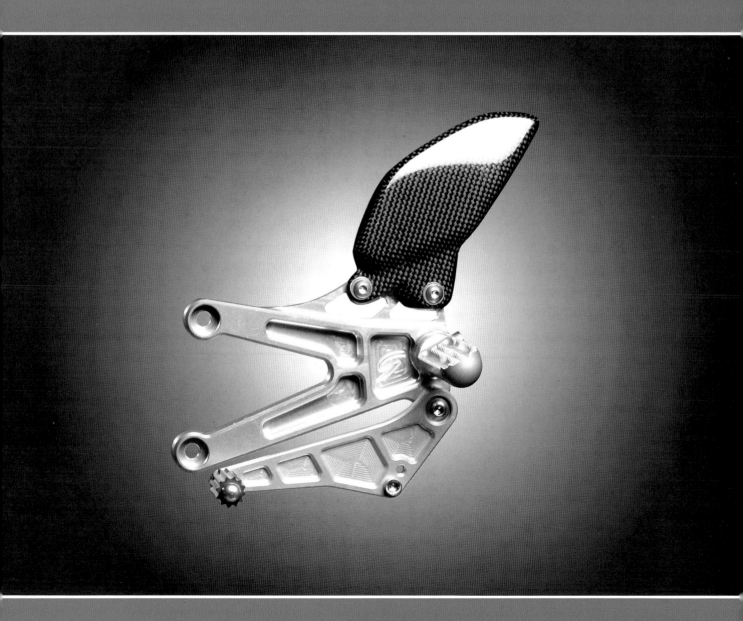

Steering Head Maintenance and Adjustment

CHASSIS

Time: 2-plus hours, depending on what maintenance is required

Tools: Wrenches and sockets, large socket, steering nut wrench, torque wrench, rear stand, bike jack, rubber mallet or dead-blow hammer, drift, blow torch, bearing grease, bearing race puller, safety glasses

Talent: 👤👤👤

Cost: $

Parts Required: Replacement bearings

Tip: All parts that could exert any force on the front end (brake lines and cables) should be removed before checking the steering head bearing.

PERFORMANCE GAIN: Seamless response to steering input.

Every time you turn your sportbike, you require the steering stem to move inside the steering head. As time passes, portions of the bearing races can get dents from the bearings' balls or tapered roller bearings transferring loads from the fork to the frame. The result is steering that wants to self-center the bearings to those familiar grooves. Oddly, although accurate steering requires that the steering head bearings be in good condition, they are routinely overlooked by all but the most meticulous riders. Talk to high-caliber race teams and you'll find that they place such a high priority on how the bike steers that they will check and adjust the steering head bearings before every race weekend.

While street riders may scoff at that type of maintenance schedule, they should be forewarned that if they don't make a point of checking their steering head bearings every 10,000 miles, or at least once a season, they may suffer from a couple of handling maladies. First, they may notice that their bike will shake its head under normal deceleration under hard braking or if their hands are removed from the grips. Also, as the steering head binds and requires increasing effort to overcome the internal friction, riders may find themselves weaving at low speeds as they oversteer. (This symptom is similar to having a steering damper set too tight.) According to Chuck Graves, race team owner, gifted tuner, and longtime fast guy at Willow

Springs, overtight head bearings will also affect turn-in on the brakes at corner entrances—and give the bike the tendency to oversteer. One last sign of bad bearings is that riders may actually feel a clunk in the grips as the steering stem shifts in the steering head.

For an accurate check of the steering head bearings, the bike needs to be on a rear stand with the front wheel off the ground. To check for loose or damaged bearings, grasp the base of the fork legs and move it back and forth (front to back). If you feel any movement or the telltale clunk and your steering stem is properly torqued, your bike needs new bearings. For the subtler, but no less important, tests, all components that could impart a force on the fork should be removed. So the brake lines, throttle cables, and clutch cables need to go away.

With the fork stripped of all but the clip-ons and wheel, begin testing the bearings by turning the bar full-lock to one side. When the bar is turned approximately 15 degrees back toward center and released, the fork should fall back to the stop, barely bounce, and settle down. If the bearing is too tight, it won't reach the stop. A loose bearing results in a couple of bounces on the stop. This is called the fallback test.

The next test is to lightly hold the front wheel between your fingers and move it back and forth across the center of the travel. You should feel no notchiness or restriction of movement, which would signal worn spots on the bearing races. Finally, turn the fork just a couple of degrees off center and release it. The fork should not move. If it tries to self-center, the bearings are worn.

Now that you're armed with information about the bearings' condition, you know what you need to do. If the bearings are fine, and you are on a regular maintenance interval (as in checking the bearings before a race weekend), bolt the front end back together, and you're good to go. If you're doing your 10,000-mile or annual maintenance, and if the bearings passed every test, disassemble the triple clamp, lube the bearings, and retorque your front end. If your bike failed any of the tests, it's time to replace the bearings.

Remove the wheel and the fork legs. Remove the top triple clamp. The steering stem is usually secured by a nut and a locking nut. You may also find spacers and lockwashers. When you unscrew the stem nut, be prepared for the bottom clamp to drop out of the frame. Clean all of the bearing parts with solvent and blow-dry with compressed air. Examine the rubber dust seals for cracks or tears and replace them, if necessary.

If you're replacing the bearings, you'll want to take the steering stem to a machine shop to remove the bottom race. While you can remove the bottom race by tapping the space between the race and the bottom clamp with a chisel, you shouldn't do this. One misplaced whack, and you could ruin the stem. Take the stem to a machine shop that has a guillotine bearing puller and/or a big hydraulic press. Flip ahead to the next project to see how to replace the bottom race with a press.

Here one of the mechanics for the Graves Motorsports race team tests the steering head bearing on Damon Buckmaster's Formula Xtreme bike. Note how he lightly holds the wheel with his left hand before letting the fork drop for the bounce test.

Removing the races from the steering head will appeal to your destructive side. Reach through the steering head with a metal drift and locate the back of the lower bearing race. With a ball-peen hammer, walk the race out of the frame by hammering on alternating sides of the race. (Some mechanics like to heat the steering head with a blow torch, but it only seems to make a noticeable difference on race installation, not removal.) To remove the top bearing race, repeat the process with the drift reaching from the bottom of the neck. Be cautious, though. You're hammering up and don't want to dislodge the bike from its supports.

When installing new bearings, you can use a bearing-driver set or a socket that has the same outer diameter as the outer edge of the race. If you're unable to find a suitable socket, you can always flip the old race upside down and use it as the driver. To ease locating the races in the steering head, we're going to utilize temperature to expand and contract solid objects. Place the new races in the freezer for a couple of hours. Before you remove each from its bed amongst the frozen peas, heat the neck until it is hot, but not so hot that it discolors. Quickly place the race in the neck and drive it into position. With the difference in temperature, you should only need a couple of whacks to bottom the race. You may then have to pry the old race out of the neck if you used it to drive the new one home.

Let the steering head and races return to ambient temperature and smear a light covering of suspension grease over the races. Also, cover the race on the steering stem with grease. Don't glop the grease onto the races or you run the risk of keeping the bearings from seating completely on assembly. Instead, just cover each race's surface. Packing the bearing (next) will play the primary role in keeping everything lubed up.

To pack the bearings—whether ball or tapered rollers—you want to push grease into them until it oozes out the other side of the carrier. When the bearings lift out of the races, as with steering head ball bearings, the job is easy. Just put a healthy dollop of grease in the palm of your hand and press the bearing into it, forcing the grease into the gaps between the carrier and the balls. You'll do the same for the removable tapered roller bearing used at the top of the steering stem. For tapered roller bearings affixed to the stem, press the grease into the rollers until you see it start to ooze out of the top of the roller cage.

Before torquing the steering stem, you must have the fork legs and wheel properly reinstalled and torqued. Also, the front wheel should be raised off the ground. Remount the steering stem to the frame and finger-tighten the stem nut. Mount the fork legs and make sure they are aligned so that the axle will slide easily from one leg into the other. Torque the triple clamp pinch bolts. Mount the front wheel and torque the axle down. You're now ready to perform the stem bearing adjustment.

If your steering head uses ball bearings, the job is pretty simple. Using a steering nut wrench or one of the cool steering nut sockets sold by Komoto Draggin Racing, torque the steering nut down to the factory-specified initial tightening specification to set the bearings in the races. This number will be quite a bit higher than the final torque setting. (For example, the R6 factory service manual specifies 38 ft-lbs.) Once you set the seating torque, turn the fork back and forth a few times to distribute the grease.

Here the mechanic demonstrates how to knock the lower race out of the steering head.

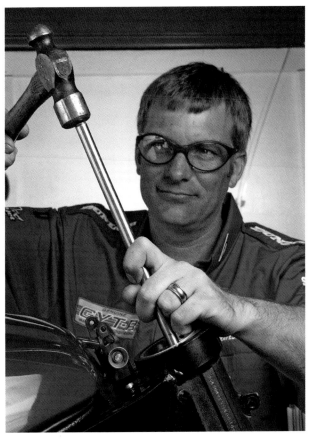

133

Generally, the final torque for ball bearings will be 10 ft-lbs. Set it and you're done. Still, you should check your factory service manual for any differences. For example, the 2000 ZX-6R manual specifies setting the torque to 11 ft-lbs and then backing the nut off slightly until the fork moves "lightly." Install the stem locknut (making sure the stem nut doesn't turn as you lock it down). Install the top triple clamp, torque it down, and recheck with the fallback test to make sure that you haven't affected the steering.

Tapered roller bearings are much more finicky, and you'll have to adjust them by hand. Tighten the stem nut down to set the bearings, then loosen them back up. Now begin tightening the nut. After each adjustment, give the fork the fallback test you used at the beginning of this project. Once the fork passes the test, carefully lock down the stem nut with the locknut. Different bikes use different locking methods, so consult your factory manual. (For example, some bikes use a locknut clamping down directly on the stem nut, while others, such as Yamaha, have a rubber spacer between the nut and the locknut.)

But wait—you're not done checking the stem nut torque yet. After you mount the top triple clamp and torque it down, you'll need to retest by the fall-back method. When you torque down the stem nut, the pressure is on the top of the stem threads. Torquing the top clamp into place shifts the stress on the threads to the bottom which actually increases the force on the tapered roller bearings. So, if the fork now fails the fall back test, remove the top clamp, loosen the stem nut 1/16th of a turn, reassemble, and repeat the test. Once it passes the test with the top clamp in place, your tapered roller bearings will operate optimally, and your bike will steer factory-smooth or better.

Note how he presses the grease from the inside of the bearing so that he can see when it begins to ooze out of the spaces between the balls and the carrier.

Using a stem nut tool and a torque wrench, seat the bearings and then loosen them up before setting the final torque. Some mechanics prefer to line the torque wrench up with the tool, while others set it at 90 degrees to the tool.

This steering nut tool sold by Komoto Draggin Racing (inset) takes some of the guesswork out of torquing the stem nut. You simply place it over the nut and torque it down like any other fastener. It's worth every penny to those who practice regular steering maintenance.

Installing Aftermarket Top Triple Clamp

 Time: 2–3 hours

 Tools: The usual suspects — wrenches and sockets, large socket, steering nut wrench, torque wrench, rear stand, bike jack, rubber mallet or dead-blow hammer, drift, blow torch, red thread lock, bearing grease, drill press, hydraulic press

 Talent:

 Cost: $$$$$

 Parts Required: Aftermarket triple clamps

 Tip: Do your research before plunking down your cash. Ask around at your local track to see what the fast guys are running.

 PERFORMANCE GAIN: Better handling.

Try as they might, the OEMs don't always get the chassis settings right in first-generation (or, sometimes, second-generation) motorcycles. The big race teams are generally the only ones with enough know-how and resources to develop alternatives to the original part. Fortunately for the rest of us, these teams are generally affiliated with aftermarket companies that will capitalize on the development of these parts by selling replicas to performance-minded enthusiasts and budding

Tracing the wires and unhooking the ignition switch connectors is the easy part. Passing them through the frame can test your patience.

racers. Sometimes, after a year or so, the OEMs take note of the aftermarket's improvement of their bike and work it into the new model. (This was the case with the triple-clamp offset on the 2002 R1, which mimicked the settings of the Graves Motorsports modification for the 1998–2001 R1.)

So, what should you look for when shopping for an aftermarket triple clamp? First, talk to the manufacturer of the part to see what you should expect from installing the part. Also, look at what people who race your model bike are using. For example, Graves Motorsports sells both adjustable-offset and fixed-offset R1 triple clamps. When asked what triple clamps Graves recommends to customers, the response was that the fixed will be perfect for almost all conditions, both on and off the track, that riders are likely to encounter. The adjustable offsets, useful primarily for their own team's race bikes, are meant only to be varied from the 26-mm offset of the fixed units for tuning out a specific problem encountered at a specific track. The simple truth is that, while we may dream big, most of us will never be capable of riding at the level where we will need to vary the offset from what race teams have found to be the hot setup. The upside is that the fixed offset units are a good bit cheaper than the adjustable ones.

Installing a Graves R1 triple clamp is fairly easy if you have the right tools. Begin by removing the tank and the bodywork, including the headlight/instrument cluster assembly. Trace the ignition wiring back to where it connects to the wiring harness. (This would also be a good time to note the routing of the cables and wiring.) Although unhooking the connectors is easy, getting them to slip through the minimal space by the frame and radiator can be challenging. If loosening and dropping the radiator slightly doesn't work for you, remove the wires from the connector. (Note the location of the wires in the connector before disassembly.)

Remove the stem nut with a 36-mm socket (on this R1) and loosen the pinch bolts on the fork legs. A tap with a dead-blow hammer will help to remove the top triple clamp and ignition switch assembly. Note the two nuts securing the stem in the steering head. A washer with two tabs keeps the nuts from loosening, while a rubber spacer separates the two nuts.

In order to move the ignition switch to the Graves top triple clamp, you need to drill out the two breakaway bolts securing the assembly to the stock clamp. Since these bolts are hardened, attempting to use a hand drill is fraught with risk. Make sure you center-punch the bolts to keep the bit from walking if you are going to attempt to use a hand drill. A better method is to mount the top clamp on a drill press. This will prevent the bit from walking and will lead to a cleaner bolt hole. Whichever drill you use, begin by drilling a small guide hole. Follow with a bit that is wide enough to drill out the cap all the way to the threads. You don't need to drill any deeper than necessary to reach the threads. When the bolt cap pops off the bolt, stop drilling. After you have removed both bolt caps, simply pull the ignition switch assembly free of the triple clamp. Using Loctite and the bolts and spacers included with the new top triple clamp, mount the switch.

Making sure that the bike is supported on a jack, remove the front wheel, clip-ons, and fork legs. Next, loosen and remove the two nuts securing the steering stem. Slide the lower triple clamp free of the frame. Clean the races until they are free of grease.

The Graves lower triple clamp needs to have a bearing race installed in it. You can either buy a spare from your local Yamaha shop (the "easy" way), or, if the race on the stock stem is in good condition, you can press the race off the stem with a hydraulic press (the "fun" way). To free up the race, you will actually press the steering stem partially out of the lower clamp. Begin by heating the lower clamp with a blowtorch. Support the clamp with a socket or some other sturdy object that has a center hole large enough for the stem to slide partway inside. Do not just place the lower triple clamp on the press and try to push out the stem. Since the center of the clamp is raised, the clamp will flex, potentially ruining both the clamp and the stem. Press on the stem until it sinks far enough into the clamp to move the narrower portion of the stem to the race. Now the race will simply slide off by hand.

When pressing the race onto the Graves stem, make sure the lower clamp is supported in the center, as it was with the stock clamp. Slide the race over the stem until it reaches the wider portion of the stem. Using a hardened piece of metal tubing of a diameter just large enough to clear the stem and rest on the inner edge of the race—and not the bearing itself—press the race down until it snugs up against the lower clamp.

Once the race is installed on the stem, the rest of the installation is the same as lubing the steering head, as described in the previous project. But wait—rerouting the ignition wires back through the frame is even tougher than removing them. Be patient, and you will prevail.

Once you've put everything back together, turn a few laps and see if your new triple clamp doesn't shave a little off your lap times.

Note how the new clamp is supported by a socket directly under the steering stem to prevent the clamp from bending. The aluminum tubing pressing the race into place is exactly the same diameter as the inside lip of the race.

After you drill a small pilot hole in the retaining bolt, drill the cap off the bolt with a bit that is the same size as the bolt. Only drill until the bit reaches the bolt threads.

The washer on top of the stem nuts makes sure nothing loosens up. The top nut is a locknut. The rubber spacer gives the locknut something to compress, and the bottom nut is what actually holds the stem in place.

If you don't have access to a hydraulic press, find a machine shop to remove the lower race for you.

The Graves triple clamp gives those who notice a hint at the R1's new handling abilities.

Installing an Aftermarket Top Triple Clamp

 Time: 1 hour

 Tools: Wrenches, sockets (including a really big one for the steering nut), Allen sockets, ratchets, torque wrench, rubber mallet or dead-blow hammer, rear stand, caliper or metal ruler, drill press

 Talent:

 Cost: $$$

 Parts Required: Aftermarket top triple clamp

 Tip: To maintain current ride height, keep the lower triple-clamp pinch bolts torqued down.

 PERFORMANCE GAIN: The ability to adjust chassis attitude or lower the front end ride height for more aggressive drag-racing launches—your choice.

COMPLEMENTARY MODIFICATIONS: Install lowering links, check and retorque steering stem bearing.

As bikes have gotten more capable, they've included more adjustments for the rider. So, when the design of a stock component limits the adjustments that riders might otherwise have at their disposal, you can bet that the aftermarket will step in with an alternative. For example, the Hayabusa's top triple-clamp cover/clip-on mount does not allow for the front end to be lowered by dropping the triple clamp on the fork legs. With a bike that is so obviously suited to the drag strip, this oversight on Suzuki's part seems almost *negligent*. Don't fret, though. Companies like Trac Dynamics have filled this void with a bolt-on replacement for the top triple clamp.

Since only the top triple clamp will be replaced, you won't have to remove the entire front end. In fact, you want to keep the bottom triple clamp locked in position so that you can measure the relationship of the fork legs to the new top clamp when they're at the original baseline front-end height.

Begin with the bike supported on a rear stand. Cover the tank and nearby bodywork with rags to prevent chips or dents. If the clip-ons are an integral part of the top clamp, remove them and let them hang with their wires safely out of the way. Next, loosen the pinch bolts. Remove the triple-clamp nut.

Begin by removing the clip-ons and letting them dangle safely out of the way.

Since the bike is supported by the front wheel, you may need to tap the bottom of the triple clamp to allow it to slide free of the fork legs and steering stem. Follow the instructions for drilling out the ignition switch bolt in the preceeding project.

Install the ignition switch assembly with red Loctite on the new threads. Slip the aftermarket triple clamp over the fork legs and slide it down until it reaches the steering stem. If you're lucky (or have the bike on a jack that is taking the weight off the front wheel), the clamp will slide right into place. If the clamp won't slide into place because the weight of the bike on the front wheel is tweaking the fork legs slightly rearward, try pressing down and forward on the triple clamp. Of course you'll need a helper keeping the bike from rolling while you do this. Usually, a couple of light bounces on the front end will slip the clamp onto the steering stem. Tap the clamp into place with a dead-blow hammer on either side of the steering stem. Torque the steering stem nut down onto the triple clamp. Hook up the ignition switch to the wiring harness. Install, adjust, and torque down the clip-ons. If you're going to lower the front end, go back to Project 40 before you torque the pinch bolts. Now, go try out your new drag bike setup.

Carefully remove the OE top clamp. Protect your tank and bodywork with rags.

137

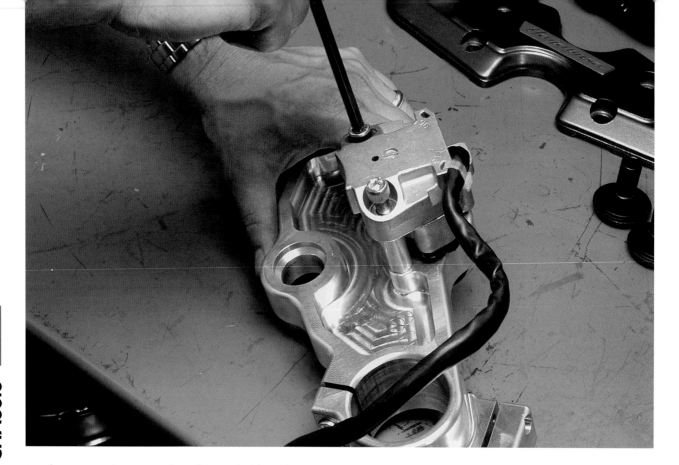

Don't forget to Loctite the ignition switch. You don't want the bolts to vibrate out, and you certainly don't want to make it easy for someone to steal your bike.

Although it may not look like it, the ride height on this Hayabusa has been lowered by 1 inch—with more available—thanks to this Trac Dynamics triple clamp.

Installing Superbike Bars

 Time: 2.5 hours

 Tools: Wrenches, sockets, big socket for triple clamp, torque wrench, screwdrivers, front and rear stand, drill or rotary tool, vise, punch

 Talent:

 Cost: $$$$

 Parts Required: Superbike bar kit, brake fluid

 Tip: If you plan to drill the bar so that the registration pins hold the controls in position, roughly assemble the bar and controls so that you get everything in position before drilling the bar.

 PERFORMANCE GAIN: More streetable riding position, more leverage on bar, better platform for stunt riding.

Before you drill any holes in the handlebar, you'll want to loosely mount the controls and switch gear to the bar and position it so that it doesn't interfere with turning. Don't hook up the hoses and cables until you're ready for the final installation. The work will be much easier. Don't ask me how I know . . .

Remember back in the 1980s when superbike racing meant wide handlebars, flexible chassis, and big black marks on the pavement as the rear tires spun and slid exiting corners? If you are too young to remember those days, go rent a video or two. The rest of us can count on our fading memories to fill in the blanks. While the rest of the world was coming to grips with the newfound power of racing machinery, American racers bred on dirt tracking were tearing up the pavement all over the planet. They were used to steering with wheelspin and liked wide bars for the extra leverage they afforded.

Today's racing machinery is much stiffer and the steering more precise. Riding positions have gotten progressively more compact as aerodynamics has begun to play an increasing role on the track. While the bikes are much easier to control at speed, many more . . . uh . . . seasoned riders find the bent-over riding position somewhat less desirable for everyday sporting duty. Handlebar risers have helped move clip-ons a bit skyward, but none of them have the cool retro factor of superbike bars. Ironically, two contradictory demographics—aging sport riders and streetfighter customizers—have prompted aftermarket companies like Spiegler Brake Systems USA to branch out into the superbike bar market.

You'll start this project by removing the top triple clamp and ignition switch as described in Project 54. However, instead of dangling the controls out of the cockpit, you'll remove them completely, since you'll need to swap out the brake lines, the clutch cable, and possibly the throttle cables anyway. Disconnect them, but leave the lines in place so you can remember their routing. Since you will be working with brake fluid, cautious mechanics will remove the gas tank to prevent the possibility of having the paint eaten by the hydraulic fluid. Once you have all those parts removed, mount the top triple clamp, a.k.a. the fork bridge. Torque the pinch bolts and triple-clamp nut. Now you begin the real assembly by attaching the handlebar risers to the fork bridge. Of course, you'll torque the bolts to the proper spec for their thread diameter. Place the handlebar so it is centered in the risers. Tighten the top clamps just enough to hold the bar in place while you adjust it.

Now, play with the adjustment. Temporarily remount the controls on the bar so that you can find the proper position for both the bar and the controls. Sit on the bike and first set the bar in the most comfortable position for you. Adjust the orientation of the controls so that they are where your hands would naturally fall. Now, turn the bar lock to lock to make sure that nothing contacts either the fairing or the tank. If you can't turn the bar all the way in both directions, reposition the handlebar and controls until you can.

Now, you need to make a decision. Are you going to drill the bar so that the registration pins on the factory controls lock into place on the bar, or are you going to grind the pins out of the controls? Both routes offer distinct advantages. Getting the holes so that the switch gear is in exactly the right position by both grips requires careful measuring. On the

Careful measurement and drilling produced these professional-looking holes for the registration pins.

other hand, you can tweak the pin-free parts to your heart's content, but be prepared for them to rotate periodically. While this may not be a problem with the switches, you do want the throttle assembly to stay put!

If you opt to drill, measure each hole's distance from the bar end. Mark the pin location on the outside of the housing, temporarily mount the assembly on the line, and adjust it to the correct position. Using the mark on the housing and the prior measurement on the bar, you will know where the registration pin belongs. Drill a pilot hole and then follow with a hole just large enough for the pin to fit. For those who decide to grind off the pin, reassemble the housings tightly. If they rotate on the bar during use, wrap some electrical tape around the bar and then tighten down the housing screws.

To torque the handlebar in the risers, alternate between the front bolts and the rear ones until the bar is at the proper torque with the top bar clamp base parallel with the bottom clamp. After you mount the levers, and switch gear and grips, you need to get the controls to work. The Spiegler superbike handlebar kit includes all of the longer cables and hoses you need. Install the braided steel lines as described in Project 19. Route any new cables in the same path as the stock ones. However, if you are going to reuse any of the OE cables, you may need to resort to trial and error. (You may also need to be creative with the switch wiring.) You must be able to turn the bar lock to lock without the idle speed changing or the clutch cable binding. Do not ride your bike until you are certain turning the bar does not affect the controls.

Now, go for a ride and enjoy a more comfortable riding position. Oh, and enjoy the nice new view of your elbows you have in the mirrors. Perhaps you'll want to fashion some mirror-mount risers too.

When you're finished with the installation, your R1 could look like this. Adding the spiffy bar-end weights (also sold by Spiegler) completes the package, don't you think? Note the zip-tie holding the brake reservoir in place.

PROJECT 56

Installing Clip-Ons

 Time: 2 hours

 Tools: Wrenches, sockets (including a really big one for the triple-clamp nut), Allen sockets, torque wrench, rear stand, hammer, drift, punch, drill, 3-mm drill bit, ruler, duct tape, Loctite

 Talent:

 Cost: $$

 Parts Required: Aftermarket clip-ons

 Tip: Always check that the new clip-on position does not limit lock-to-lock turning.

 PERFORMANCE GAIN: More comfort and better control of steering inputs.

COMPLEMENTARY MODIFICATIONS: Install aftermarket triple clamp or top clamp.

Despite their best efforts, the engineers in charge of ergonomics at the OEMs don't always get it right for you. How could they? We're all shaped differently. So, if you find yourself wishing your bike's grips were just a little bit lower, or maybe tweaked out at a different angle, you'll end up taking a trip to the aftermarket for a set of clip-ons.

Stock clip-ons are generally attached to two locations on your bike. First, they grip the fork leg, but (you may have to look closely on some bikes) they're also attached to the top triple clamp (probably to keep the lawyers happy). What this means is that you're locked into the height and angle that the factory determined was best for all riders. Well, motorcycling is a sport of individuals. Consequently, you'll find more companies than you can count selling clip-ons. Graves Motorsports provided the clip-ons shown here.

Racers prefer aftermarket units because the bar itself is usually separate from the clamp, making the replacement of bent tubing easy and inexpensive. (Racers wreck a lot of handlebars.) Riders who want complete control over the position of their controls like clip-ons because they are infinitely adjustable.

Installing aftermarket clip-ons is a relatively painless operation. With the bike on the stand, remove the controls and grips from the stock bars. If the mounts attach to the top of the triple clamp, loosen and remove them. If not, you'll need to remove the top clamp to be able to lift the clip-on free. Unless your fork protrudes far enough above the triple clamp to mount the new clip-ons, you'll be removing the top clamp anyway.

Slide the mount onto the fork leg with the bar on the forward edge. Tighten the bolts finger tight to hold the clip-on in position. Adjust the clip-on until it is in the approximate height and orientation you desire. Now, loosely mount the controls to the bars. Position the controls to your liking and snug up the bolts and screws. Turn the bar from lock to lock to make sure that neither the grips nor the controls contact the fairing. You should have at least 1 inch of space between the grip and the gas tank so that you don't risk pinching your thumb during U-turns. The extra space also lessens the chance you getting your thumb trapped in a crash.

Once you have the controls positioned correctly, torque the clip-on mounts and triple clamp to factory spec. Finally, you will need to decide (as was outlined in Project 55) whether you want to drill holes for the switch housings' registration pins. If not, you'll need to grind the pins out of the housing. Take a gander at the preceding project to see what path is best for you.

After you've finished mounting the controls and switch gear, give all the fasteners a final check of torque. You don't want the bars to push forward under braking, would you? Go give your bike a try and see what all the clip-on fuss is about.

The stock handlebar mounts are usually secured to both the fork and the triple clamp. The purpose is to prevent the bars from being able to rotate on the fork legs while riding.

CHASSIS

Finger-tighten the clip-on mount in its approximate location before reassembling the top triple clamp.

Allow at least 1 inch clearance between the grip and the gas tank. You'll be glad you did the first time you snap the fork to one side to make a U-turn.

Installing Steering Damper

 Time: 1–2 hours

 Tools: Wrenches, sockets (including a really big one for the triple-clamp nut), Allen sockets, torque wrench, rear stand, hammer, drift, punch, drill, ruler, duct tape, electrical tape, Loctite

 Talent:

 Cost: $$$$

 Parts Required: Steering damper

 Tip: Start with the damper at full loose and tighten in steps until the head shake goes away.

 PERFORMANCE GAIN: End head shake exiting bumpy corners hard on the gas.

Nothing comes free of charge. Today's sportbikes have had their handling tuned to a razor-sharp edge. We now own bikes that turn with the precision of factory racers. However, that flickability comes at the expense of stability. Get on the gas hard enough to lighten the front wheel exiting a corner, and you'll feel the bike start to shake its head. The steep rake of the fork conspires with the road surface to make the clip-ons wag back and forth. This wagging is your bike simply saying that if you want complete control over where it's going, you need to slow down a bit so the front tire can sort things out. In a racing situation, this is unacceptable. Backing off means letting people pass.

Enter the steering damper. Dampers were developed to minimize the high-speed bar oscillations associated with head shake. When set up correctly, a steering damper works its magic by limiting handlebar movement to a certain velocity. The slower, human-controlled movement remains unaffected, and presto! You're back in the game.

While the reason racers use steering dampers is pretty clear, street riders can also benefit from the additional degree of control offered by a damper. First, pavement irregularities contribute to head shake, and public roads are usually bumpier than carefully groomed racetracks. Second, runoff room is at more of a premium on the street. Run wide and you'll end up in a ditch or oncoming traffic—both Very Bad

Things. Finally, street riders have less experience at handling a misbehaving motorcycle. Often, the first reaction to a violent head shake is to chop the throttle. Unfortunately, all this does is load up the front end, potentially leading to further loss of control and a crash. The proper way to react to head shake is to *carefully* roll off the throttle until the problem stops. After all this, the bike is probably not pointed in the right direction, and you'll need to steer it back on to your intended path of travel—and quickly. By preventing head shake in the first place, a steering damper is a worthwhile investment for the aggressive street rider.

Steering dampers used to hang on the sides of bikes in an extremely vulnerable position—one that could destroy the unit in even a low-speed tipover. The current trend, though, is to mount the damper between the tank and the triple clamp. The Matris damper provided here by Two Brothers Racing serves as a prime example.

As with most projects, begin with your bike securely supported by a rear stand. Cover the tank with a rag to prevent scratches. Remove the triple-clamp nut with a big honkin' socket. Remove the washer that resides below the nut. While not all steering dampers require this, the Matris damper needs holes drilled in the triple clamp for registration pins to hold the wiper arm bracket in position.

Before you start drilling, you need to make sure that the wiper arm bracket is perpendicular to the line drawn, and centered between the fork legs' centers. Although you can probably eyeball this, use a ruler if you're unsure of the positioning. While holding the bracket in place, tape it securely with duct tape. Double-check to be sure that it is still in the correct position before you carefully insert a punch through the registration pinhole in the bracket. Give the punch a couple of good taps with the hammer before moving to the other hole. Check the alignment of the bracket one last time before you remove the tape.

You should have two good marks on the triple clamp for your drill bit to bite into. Take your 3-mm drill bit and wrap a piece of tape around it 8.5 mm from the tip. This will keep you from drilling too far into the clamp. If you don't stop at the right depth, the pins will sit too far into the clamp to hold the bracket in place. When the holes are drilled to the correct depth, the pins will sit flush with the top of the wiper bracket.

Next, mount the other bracket to the gas-tank mount. Some bikes have more than one bolt for this job. Once this bracket is secure, install the wiper arm bracket and torque the new triple-clamp nut into place. Since the nut has been powder-coated to match the triple clamp, give it a couple of turns of electrical tape before you place a socket over it to torque it down to 76 ft-lbs. That way it'll stay shiny. If, as with this R1, the nut bottoms out on the stem before securing the wiper arm, simply place the OE washer on top of the bracket and crank down the nut.

CHASSIS

Make sure that the wiper arm bracket is centered on the triple clamp. Duct tape will hold it steady while you mark the clamp with a punch.

Don't trust yourself to stop drilling at the right depth. Measure 8.5 mm on the bit and mark it with tape.

Torque the gas-tank arm down to 7 ft-lbs. Note how the registration pin is flush to the wiper arm bracket's surface.

Protect the pretty anodized nut from marring with some electrical tape. Note the rubber O-ring on the bottom of the bracket.

Make sure the recessed portion of the Heim joint faces up before bolting the damping arm to the tank bracket.

The steering damper mounts neatly in this relatively protected location. The adjuster knob on the left can easily be tweaked out on the road.

Place the rubber O-ring on the wiper arm's nipple. Now, bolt down the steering damper body bracket. Use blue Loctite and torque the bolt to 7 ft-lbs. Slide the damper body into the bracket, leaving it loose for now. The Heim joint at the end of the damping rod has one recessed side. Place the bolt through the joint from the recessed side so that the offset will be pressed against the tank bracket. Again, Loctite and torque the bolt. Turn the bars from lock to lock. If the steering damper binds at any point, slide the damper body in its bracket until the bars turn completely in both directions. Torque the damper body pinch bolts to 4 ft-lbs. Double-check that the damper doesn't hit the tank or hinder handlebar movement.

Now, for the fun part. Start with the damper set on its loosest setting. Go ride to see if it helps your head shake problem. If not, tighten the adjuster a bit more. Be careful, though, and don't adjust it too much, too quickly. A steering damper that is set too tightly will cause you to weave at low speeds, because the effort required to turn against the damper requires too much force for steering inputs, and then you overcompensate in the other direction—really. You can try it for fun, I guess, but set the damping back to the correct position when you're finished horsing around.

Installing Extended Swingarm

 Time: 2 hours

 Tools: Wrenches, sockets, torque wrench, front and rear stand, bike jack, hammer, drift, blowtorch, red thread lock, bearing grease, chain cutter/rivet tool

 Talent: ⚏⚏

 Cost: $$$$$

 Parts Required: Aftermarket swingarm, swingarm bearings (if required), longer rear brake line, longer chain

 Tip: Set your wheelbase length first, then fit your chain to that swingarm position.

 PERFORMANCE GAIN: Better traction for launches.

COMPLEMENTARY MODIFICATIONS: Install lowering links, lower front end.

The biggest challenge when drag racing big-horsepower motorcycles is getting the power to the ground. Either the rear wheel spins up or you loft the front. Lowering the bike to keep the center of gravity as close to the ground as possible only goes so far. A longer swingarm may be just the ticket for your quarter-mile dreams. Aftermarket companies such as Trac Dynamics sell swingarms in lengths varying from stock to 14 inches over.

Swapping out the OE swinger for a 6-inch stretched version is a fairly easy endeavor. Since you'll be taking off the rear suspension, you'll need a jack or bike lift to support the rear of the bike after you remove the rear stand. A tie-down (or two) attached to the back end and thrown over a rafter will act as a safety net. Remove the rear wheel. Removing the canister(s) and S-bend(s) of the exhaust system may not be necessary, but the job is much easier with them out of the way. Remove the chain. Drain and remove the rear brake line and caliper. Now, focus your attention on the shock and linkage. Unbolt the bottom of the shock from the rocker. Remove the bolt securing the bottom of the tie rods. Rest the back of the swingarm on the floor while you extricate the pivot shaft from the frame.

Although Trac Dynamics' swingarm ships with its own bearings, you'll need to remove at least one of the OE bearings to access the crush tube inside the pivot. Remember, from the moment you take that first whack at the bearing race, the bearing is junk. Never reuse bearings. So, buy new ones if your new swingarm doesn't come with them. While you can go Neanderthal on the old bearing, heating the bearing's sleeve with a propane torch makes the job of tapping out the bearing much easier. Once the sleeve is heated, most mechanics get by with a drift, a flathead screwdriver, and a hammer—all without breaking a sweat. You'll also need to press the linkage bearings into place (as shown in Project 48), giving the tie rods a pivot point.

Take the swingarm and slide it into the frame. Loosely assemble all of the bolts for the swingarm pivot, tie rods, and linkage. Torque the bolts to spec. Set the chain adjusters to hold the axle blocks in the appropriate position. Before you mount the wheel, you'll probably have to trim or remove the rear fender. Now, mount the wheel.

Since the new swingarm is significantly longer, you'll need to custom-cut your chain. Wrap the chain around the sprockets and mark where the end meets the rest of the chain. If you are planning to race in a class that has a maximum wheelbase, set the wheel in position for that length and then cut the chain one link shorter than the chain measures out. Street riders can simply cut the chain at the most convenient link. Don't forget to install a longer brake line and bleed it thoroughly before you go practice your launches.

Once you've installed the bearings, the new swingarm pops in the same way the old one came out. Now would be a good time to add lowering links.

CHASSIS

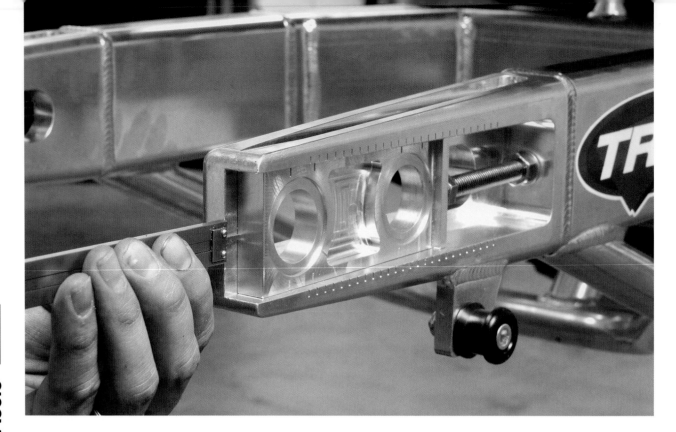

To ease rear wheel alignment, measure and place the axle blocks before you mount the wheel. Note the clever design of the blocks: The front hole is for the first half of the 6-inch adjustment range, while the rear hole moves the wheel way back.

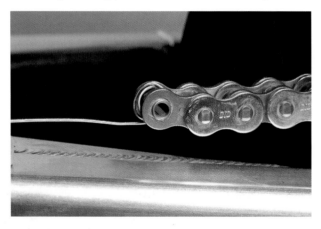

For bikes like the Hayabusa, removing the countershaft cover can be a real pain. By using a piece of welding wire, you can simply pull the new chain around the countershaft sprocket.

If you plan on using an air shifter, Trac Dynamics offers the option of having an air tank built right into the swingarm.

Here's what a Hayabusa looks like with the extended swingarm set to 3 inches over stock and lowered 4 inches.

146

Swingarm Pivot Bearing Replacement

 Time: 2 hours

 Tools: Wrenches, sockets, torque wrench, screwdrivers, pliers, circlip pliers, bike lift or jack, hammer, drift, bearing driver, propane torch, red Loctite, vise

 Talent: ▐▐

 Cost: $

 Parts Required: Replacement bearings

 Tip: Heating the bearing sleeve makes driving the bearings out much easier..

 PERFORMANCE GAIN: Less stiction in swingarm movement, better suspension performance.

Heating the outside of the swingarm around the bearing will ease its removal.

CHASSIS

Perhaps the most overlooked item on motorcycles is the lowly swingarm pivot. Well, if you've spent money and time upgrading and dialing in your suspension, don't you think it's a good idea to take as much of the fluid-movement-sapping stiction out of the swingarm travel? Bikes that have been ridden in wet weather or near the ocean are particularly susceptible to having corrosion damage any bearing—not just the swingarm bearings.

How do you know when the swingarm bearings need replacing? Well, if you lubricate your bearings on a regular basis, check them before you regrease them. What to look for at those times are wear marks or rust on the pivot shaft. If you see any divots on the shaft, you can bet the bearings aren't happy about it either.

You'll need to strip off your bike's lowers if you're planning on using a jack under the engine. Also, be careful where you place the jack; exhaust pipe walls get thinner and thinner in an effort to save weight. You don't want to crush them. Follow the directions for removing the swingarm that were outlined in the preceding project.

Once you have the swingarm free, place it in a vise to hold it steady while you work on it. Remove the collars, pivot, and dust seals with a screwdriver and replace any ripped or torn seals. If a circlip is present, remove it. Heat the swingarm outside of the bearing, but not so hot as to cause it to discolor. Using a drift, reach through from the opposite side of the

swingarm and place the edge on the seam between the crush tube and the bearing. If you can't catch the lip of the inner race because of the internal spacer, you may find that a flathead screwdriver will help get the bearing started. With the drift on the inner race, give the bearing a whack or two until it moves slightly. Now switch to the other side of the bearing and repeat. Essentially, you are walking the bearing out of the hub. When the bearing pops out, set the crush tube aside for later. Flip the swingarm in the vise and tap out the remaining bearing. Remember, after you've rapped a bearing with a drift just once, the bearing is junk.

Opinions vary on how best to drive a bearing into place. Some people freeze the bearing for several hours and then heat the part on which it will be installed. Others lubricate

Tap on alternating sides of the bearing to walk it out of the swingarm.

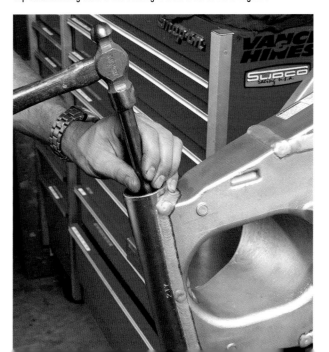

the outside edge of the bearing with assembly lube to ease the insertion. The mechanic from Trac Dynamics featured in the photos here uses red Loctite. He feels that the Loctite helps lubricate the two metal surfaces when wet and makes the bearing stay in position better when it dries. You choose your preferred method.

If you have a bearing driver set, use it to install the bearings. Otherwise, find a socket that has the exact outer diameter as the outside edge of the bearing. If you're unable to find a suitable socket, you can always use the old bearing. The key is to never tap directly on the new bearing itself. Tap the bearing until it is seated in the pivot flush with the outer edge (or the edge below the circlip housing). Slip the crush tube into the pivot and install the other bearing. Don't forget to reinstall any circlips you removed.

When replacing bearings, consult your factory service manual for proper bearing orientation. Some bearings need to be placed in certain ways. For example, on a ZX-6R the ball bearings need to be oriented with the manufacturer's markings pointing out, but needle bearings require that the markings face in. Getting oriented before you tap the bearings in will save you time and money.

Once the bearings are installed, you'll need to pack them with grease. This serves two purposes. It helps the metal parts move against each other, and it keeps out corrosive moisture. Using healthy dollops on your finger, mash the grease into the spaces of the rollers. Keep doing this as you work your way around the bearing, until it is completely filled. Wipe a thin layer of grease to the pivot sleeve and slide it into the pivot. Apply a bit of grease to the grease seals and press them onto the swingarm. Finally, place the collars into the seals. The swingarm is now ready to be mounted back in the frame.

This mechanic prefers to use red Loctite as the lubricant between the bearing and the swingarm.

Packing needle bearings completely full of grease takes patience, but it will keep corrosion away.

Installing Rearsets

 Time: 1 hour

 Tools: Wrenches, sockets, Allen sockets, torque wrench, screwdrivers, rear stand, needle nose pliers, zip-ties

 Talent:

 Cost: $$$$

 Parts Required: Aftermarket rearsets, hydraulic brake-light switch

 Tip: Loosen all of the fasteners you can reach before removing the components from the bike.

PERFORMANCE GAIN: Better ground clearance and, depending on the rearsets, GP-style shifting.

Most sportbikers remember moments where they achieved new plateaus in their riding ability. For many, dragging a knee for the first time makes the list. But what about dragging pegs? If you're not already hanging off, learn that trick before you start thinking about rearsets. However, if you are already draping yourself off the bike like a pro and you're still touching pegs down, your next best option is to create more ground clearance by moving them higher.

Tons of companies offer rearsets for varying prices. Before ordering, consider the following: Are they adjustable?

Some people want to get their feet as high as possible. Others just want a little flexibility in where they rest their feet. You do pay a premium for adjustability, though. Do the rearsets use street or GP (press down for upshifting) linkage? Some riders don't like to switch to a race-shift pattern—even on race bikes (even notables like Kevin Schwantze and Mat Mladin). Others want even their street bikes to use this shift pattern. Make sure you know what you really want before buying the race-oriented version. Can you easily replace crash-damaged portions of the rearsets? The pegs usually take the brunt of the damage in a crash, though other parts get twisted too.

The Graves Motorsports rearsets used in this project were developed by riders with last names like Buckmaster, Gobert, and Hacking, and, according to the company, the riders prefer these to the more expensive, fully adjustable model. Since they were developed for racing, the rearsets reverse the shift pattern. Installing them is basically an easy bolt-on operation with one exception. The right bracket has no accommodations for mounting the OE brake-light switch. So, you will be faced with fabricating a mount for the original switch or buying a hydraulic brake-light switch. The hydraulic switch imported by Four Strokes Only would add some time to the rearset installation by requiring brake line bleeding. Creating a switch mount for the stock piece could be a black hole that takes too much time away from riding. You get to decide.

Before you remove the stock peg mounting brackets, make sure that all parts you need to remove from them have their bolts loosened. Often the factory uses thread locker on the fasteners, and these are much easier to break free if still mounted to the bike. Also, be sure to disconnect any parts that are staying on the bike from the peg or pedal assemblies to which they're attached. For example: Before removing the brake-side peg, loosen or remove the bolts securing the master

The stock rearsets have been removed, leaving the master cylinder dangling. The brake-light switch can be unplugged, since there is no way to mount it.

The master cylinder actually lives between the heel guard and the rearset's mounting bracket. Since the master cylinder has been relocated, make sure that none of its hoses are kinked.

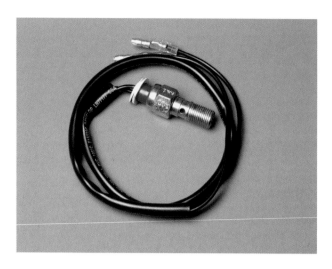

This nifty brake-light switch from Four Strokes Only replaces the banjo bolt on the master cylinder and hooks into the stock brake-light connector.

cylinder, if it's attached to the parts you're removing. Pull the cotter pin and the pin holding the master cylinder's clevis to the brake pedal. Then remove the stock rearset. Some bikes will need to have bodywork or other parts removed or modified to allow access to the shift linkage. For example, this R6 needed to have the coolant expansion tank moved out using spacers included with the rearsets.

Assemble the new rearsets before mounting them on your bike. Don't forget to lube all pivot points, even if they were preassembled by the manufacturer. All bolts should be secured with blue Loctite unless the part will need to be adjusted while on the bike. If that is the case, Loctite the fastener once the component is adjusted. Note that some parts of the rearsets can't be assembled until on the bike. The Graves rearsets feature cool carbon-fiber heel guards, but the right-hand guard gets mounted with the same bolts that secure the brake master cylinder.

When installing the right-side rearset you may find that you have to maneuver the master cylinder into position before you mount the bracket. Screw the bolts in finger tight. You'll Loctite and torque them when everything is adjusted. Attach the clevis to the brake pedal before bolting down the master cylinder. Then go back and set the brake pedal height with the adjuster on the master cylinder's piston. Then you can torque the rearset bracket to the frame.

On the left side, you might need to hold the rearset by hand until you have the shift rod connected to both ends of the linkage. Then you can mount the rearset. Adjust the shifter to the proper height and tighten the shift-rod locknuts. Torque down the rearset. Since foot controls are critically important after your first ride, you should recheck them for tightness. The folks at Graves suggest retorquing all of the fasteners after an hour of track time or riding.

Yamaha's through-the-frame shift-rod location can't be used with most rearsets. The Graves rod tucks out of the way next to the frame.

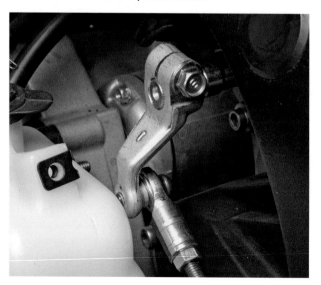

In order for the shift rod to clear the frame, the shifter knuckle must be flipped backward. The factory Heim joint is replaced by a Graves unit. Note how tight the space is between the coolant tank, which, although it has been moved outward with spacers, still fits inside the stock bodywork.

Safety Wiring

Time: 1–2 hours or more, depending on how many parts you're wiring

Tools: Wrenches, sockets, torque wrench, screwdrivers, front and rear stand, drill, safety-wire pliers, needle nose pliers, wire cutters, vise, punch, drilling jig (optional), tapping fluid

Talent:

Cost: S

Parts Required: Many, many 1/16-inch drill bits, .025-inch or .032-inch safety wire

Tip: When wiring several fasteners together, make sure that if one tries to work its way loose, it tightens the others.

PERFORMANCE GAIN: A track-legal bike that won't fall apart.

So you're going to start club racing, or maybe you're just prepping your bike for a track day. Either way, you'll need to safety-wire at least a few of the key fasteners. Racers use safety wire for two main reasons. First, safety wire provides positive locking on fasteners, preventing them from backing out by fixing them to each other or an immobile object. Second, safety-wired fasteners allow mechanics and scrutineers (tech inspectors) to visually determine that key components have been tightened. By simply glancing at various parts, the inspector can be sure that they won't back out—even if they were torqued incorrectly.

What parts do you need to wire? That depends on the organization you're riding with. Your best bet is to contact it for a list. However, here is the rule regarding safety wire from the Willow Springs Motorcycle Club (WSMC) rule book: "All plugs and fittings with oil or water behind them (this can include oil galley plugs) must be securely fastened and safety wired. Yellow 3M weather-strip cement or RTV silicone sealant may be used in cases where it is impractical to drill fasteners." Many clubs also require some kind of positive securing of axle nuts, caliper bolts, and sprocket nuts/bolts. Save yourself some time by making sure you know what you need to wire before you start taking your bike apart.

To safety-wire your bike, all you really need are the tools to remove the fasteners to be drilled, a vise in which to hold

them, a drill, safety-wire pliers, safety wire, and lots of drill bits. Also, having plenty of time to do the work without rushing will help prevent mistakes. Consider it "quality time" with your best friend.

When it comes to drilling nuts and bolts for safety wire, two methods are commonly employed. The best approach is to invest in a drilling jig, a device that holds the heads at the right angle and provides a guide hole for the drill bit. Of course, you can follow the time-honored (and broken-bit filled) tradition of putting the bolt in a vise, center-punching one of the flats, and drilling the hole manually. After starting the hole perpendicular to the flat, the drill needs to be progressively angled so that the hole ultimately exits from the adjacent flat. Get a little too energetic with the change in angle and . . . snap! (You'll get really good at switching bits quickly.) Trying to drill fasteners when they are on the bike is a recipe for disaster. Take the time to remove the parts. Regardless of which drilling method you employ, make sure you have plenty of 1/16-inch bits on hand, and always wear eye protection.

With some fasteners, it makes more sense to drill all the way through rather than from flat to flat. Oil drain plugs are a prime example. Drilling one hole all the way through the plug (or two at right angles to each other) makes wiring the plug after an oil change much easier. The wire is simply run through a hole and twisted to the appropriate length for the distance to a hole drilled in one of the case's flanges. Similarly, if your racing organization requires the radiator cap to be wired, drill both sides of the cap and secure it to a nearby object.

Since all fasteners that come in contact with fluid should be wired, every banjo bolt—on the brake system or the engine's lubrication system—needs to be safety-wired. The simplest way is to wire a banjo bolt to the line itself. In cases of oil lines on the engine, simply find a convenient place to secure the wire to the engine or frame. Oil galley plugs offer their own challenge. If they can be easily removed, mark them with a center punch so that the wire will line up easily in the correct pull-to-tighten manner. As noted above, some organizations will allow an application of silicone sealant or weather-stripping to suffice in places where wiring is not practical. Always double-check fasteners for tightness prior to wiring them. When in doubt, retorque it.

Selecting the right length of safety wire will make the job much easier. Make it too long, and the wire wraps around the pliers, getting tangled. Cut it too short, and you'll have to start from scratch. A good rule of thumb is to measure the distance between the components you want to wire and cut the wire to three times that length. Proper safety-wire technique dictates that the bolt be wired so that if it starts to back out, the twisted wire prevents it from doing so. Novices often forget this simple fact. Next, begin the wire twist at the approximate distance between mounting points. Avoid clamping the pliers

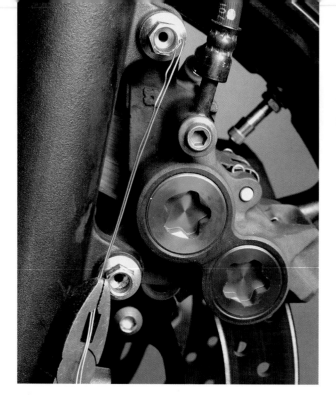

You'll want to wire the caliper bolts and axle pinch bolts together, making sure that if one pulls on the other, it will tighten it. Loop the wire through one fastener and measure to the next.

onto crossed wires. You create a weak point when you crush the wires together. And make sure you don't overwind the safety wire. Seven to nine twists per inch will provide optimum performance. Increasing the tightness of the wind could actually weaken the wire braid. Once the completed braid is cut, be sure to bend the end back on itself. Otherwise, you'll experience the joy of punctured fingertips and bloody tools. Also, when installing or removing safety wire, be sure to pick up all wire bits that drop to the ground. Sticky race tires have a knack for picking up small metal objects. A flat tire at speed could be bad news. Now, your bike is ready for the keen eyes of the scrutineers.

If either fastener tries to loosen, what does it do to the other? You'd be surprised how often people do this incorrectly. Note the bent end of the wire tucked out of the way.

Since you can't drill a hole in an oil filter to safety-wire it, a hose clamp will provide a mounting point for the wire. Tighten the clamp to the filter and wire the screw on the clamp to an anchor on either the frame or the engine.

The two most common methods of clamping hoses are: Route the wire braid through the slot in the clamp screw (left), thus preventing it from backing out, or loop the wire through the hose clamp on either side of the screw (right). Although this latter method may be more secure (the clamp may be held in place even if it breaks), be careful that the wire doesn't slip off of the clamp onto the hose. Otherwise, you may damage the hose as you tighten the wire.

Use 3M Weather Stripping to secure bolts on bikes that have recessed Allen bolts that can't be wired.

Sometimes, despite your best efforts, you forget to drill a part that the tech inspector notices. These star-shaped washers get crimped around the bolt's flats and can save your bacon

You'll find lots of uses for safety wire. Wrapping it tightly around aftermarket grips will keep them from turning. Tuck the sharp end down into the grip material.

CARBURETION, EFI, EXHAUST, IGNITION, AND ENGINE

The engine is the heart of a sportbike. The way you treat it, from the time you first press the starter button, will determine what kind of power you're able to wring from it. For generations, the first modifications most motorcyclists made to their bikes were installing an aftermarket pipe and changing the jetting. While some forms of tuning no longer deliver the enormous output increases of the past, the technological advance of sportbikes has created new areas to mine for extra power. You'll now find more tuning available, for the average rider with the proper tools, than ever before. Be it maintenance or modification, some of the most challenging projects a home mechanic will perform on a motorcycle are with the engine. So, if you want it to perform its absolute best, you should dive in to this section.

Installing a Full Exhaust System

Time: 1–2 hours

Tools: Wrenches, sockets, universal joint sockets or universal joint socket adapter, 3- to 4-inch extension, Allen keys or Allen sockets, torque wrench, front and rear stand, rubber mallet or dead-blow hammer, spring puller, flashlight, high-temp grease, WD-40, soft cloth or work mat

 Talent:

Cost: $$$$

Parts Required: Aftermarket exhaust system, exhaust manifold gaskets

Tip: Tighten fasteners from front to back to ensure you aren't pinching the system cockeyed against the chassis.

PERFORMANCE GAIN: Increased power in portions of rpm range.

COMPLEMENTARY MODIFICATIONS: Install jet kit or retune EFI for optimal power.

Not too many years ago, one of the quickest ways to increase the performance of your motorcycle was to pull off the heavy and restrictive stock exhaust system and replace it with a lighter, higher-flowing aftermarket one. Well, there's no free lunch, and the aftermarket units were significantly louder than stock, negating (through the noise-sensitive ill will of the general public) some of their impressive performance gains. Two things have happened in recent years to change this. First, the OE systems have themselves become significantly lighter and capable of flowing almost as much volume as aftermarket systems. Because of the improvement in stock systems, you can no longer count on an instantaneous, double-digit percentage power increase after mounting an aftermarket exhaust. Similarly, replacement exhaust manufacturers have become more socially conscious in their approach to making less noise with their systems while still offering improvements in power delivery.

If weight and back pressure (and, by extension, lower peak horsepower) have traditionally been the shortcomings of the stock systems, many aftermarket kits have had flat spots that were much larger than those on the stock system. However, you do get other benefits, such as more ground clearance, since the OE canisters have gotten progressively larger to allow for high flow while still staying within EPA sound regulations.

Aftermarket exhaust systems fall into two categories: full systems and slip-ons. The full systems replace the entire stock system. High-end exhausts with titanium headers still offer a fair weight savings compared to the new, lighter stock ones. Some headers have various tapers and crossovers to enhance low- and midrange torque while still improving top-end power. On the other hand, some systems offer minimal gains in peak power, choosing instead to shape the power curve for a stronger midrange and a broader horsepower peak. However, one possible disadvantage of aftermarket systems is that they require the removal of the servo-controlled valves that some OE exhausts use for better low-end power.

How do exhaust systems work their magic? The common generalization of internal combustion engines is that they are really nothing more than big air pumps. Like most generalizations, this one has a basis in truth while still being a vast exaggeration/oversimplification, but it serves as a good starting point. If we were only looking for peak horsepower, we would want to remove as much of the restriction inherent in an exhaust system as possible. This way, the engine would be unhindered as it pumped through the maximum volume of atmosphere of which it was capable. While drag racers may live for peak power in a wide-open throttle environment,

Space is tight behind the radiator, even with it tilted forward. Accessing this Allen bolt would be just about impossible if not for the universal joint (hidden by hose) connected to the extender. The top bolt is even tougher to reach.

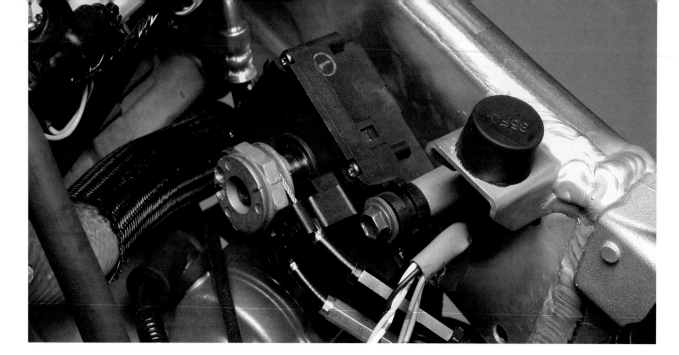

The Suzuki Exhaust Tuning System is controlled by this servo motor. You need to disconnect the cables connecting it to the valve in the S-bend before disassembling the stock pipe. Removing the servo will save you a couple of ounces.

most motorcycles, be they street bikes or race bikes, spend little time at full throttle. Instead, the throttle is almost constantly being adjusted. Not surprisingly, the engine runs over a variety of rpm too.

Straight pipes that allow maximum peak horsepower will suffer at other rpm. So, where's the advantage? Here is where the pump analogy falls apart. The individual pulses of expanding gases flow out of the engine in waves. When they hit expansions or restrictions in the exhaust system, the waves reflect back in both beneficial and harmful ways. You see, the exhaust system can also act as a pump to help draw the spent charge out and the new charge into the cylinder—if the pulses are in sync with the valve openings. However, if the pulses are working against the flow by either preventing the cylinder from filling or causing the air to pass through the car-buretors more than once, a process called multiple carburetion occurs (not a factor for fuel-injected bikes) that makes the charge burn inefficiently. Either way, the result is a flat spot in the power curve. (For more information on this, read Kevin Cameron's excellent *Sportbike Performance Handbook*.)

So, long story short, the design of a pipe will make it operate better at some rpm than others. This is where the exhaust pipe comparisons published in motorcycle magazines (such as those of my former employer, *Sport Rider*) can be useful. If you look at the dyno charts, you'll see where the power is better—or worse—than stock. With an honest assessment of your riding style, you can choose the pipe that gives you power where you need it the most. For most of us, fattening up the midrange and extending the peak horsepower output is ideal. Riders in need of ego augmentation can simply look for the biggest peak numbers.

Finally, no preamble about installing aftermarket pipes would be complete without some comments about noise. First, the use of loud pipes probably has the biggest negative impact on motorcyclists in the eyes of the nonriding public than any other motorcycle activity. While that race baffle may be music to your ears while you squeeze out that extra 3

horsepower you need to get to Taco Bell to meet your riding buddies, you are spreading ill will in every direction. And the junk about loud pipes saving lives is just a bunch of arrogant, self-delusional hoo-ha that is not supported in accident studies. Use common sense and consider street baffles instead of wide-open race units. The good news is that the aftermarket has responded with progressively quieter pipes that still produce good power. Just look at how much muffler sizes have changed since the early 1990s.

The physics of exhaust pulses are such that the only thing that can quietly flow a healthy volume of gases is a large muffler. This puts big twins at a disadvantage. While a 1,000-cc inline-four only pumps out the contents of a 250-cc cylinder on each pulse, a 1,000-cc twin's pulse is twice as large and therefore more difficult to quiet without reducing power output. Consequently, the best-performing exhaust systems for high-displacement twins will have two high-volume (as in large) mufflers.

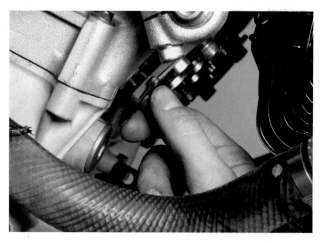

Even with the individual flanges, screw both bolts in finger tight before reaching for your ratchet. You want the bolts to pull in evenly on both sides of the manifold.

Look closely, and you'll see why this type of pipe is called a 4-into-2-into-1 system. Working your way front to back, install the headers into the collector. The springs will hold everything in place.

Installing a Full Exhaust System

Begin by placing your bike on front and rear stands. Next, remove all the lower bodywork. Remove the side panels if they are separate units. A soft cloth or a work mat under the bike will prevent scratching the plastic as you slide it out from under your bike. If your bike has a servo-controlled exhaust valve, disconnect the cables that attach to the header. Unbolt the stock muffler from the passenger peg. If necessary, unbolt the muffler from the collector outlet. You may also find clamps pinching pipe connections. If you have trouble pulling pipe sections apart, try spraying some WD-40 into the seams and letting it soak a bit. Tapping the offending part in the direction you want it to move with a rubber mallet can also help.

Eventually, you'll work your way to the front of the engine. You'll probably need to loosen and tilt the radiator and oil cooler up out of the way to give you access to the exhaust manifold nuts (or bolts). You'll find it helpful to use a socket with a universal joint to reach the fasteners. Loosen, but don't remove, the outermost manifold nut. This will keep the header from falling off while you're unscrewing the rest of the nuts. Once all of the nuts are removed, wiggle the header loose from the studs. Make sure to remove all of the exhaust manifold gaskets. Sometimes they're hard to see. Use a flashlight to check.

Installation of the new system will be the reverse of the removal process. You'll start at the engine and work your way back. Don't tighten any of the fasteners any more than finger tight until you have the entire system installed and adjusted into its final position. Otherwise, you risk torquing the system in a way that places constant forces on it. This could transfer annoying vibrations to the chassis that may lead to premature wear (metal fatigue) and failure of your expensive new exhaust system.

If your new system utilizes manifold flanges that are separate from the header, as on the Yoshimura system in the photos, be sure to install the flanges so that the holes for attaching the header springs are in the proper position. Unlike systems in which the header bolts directly to the engine, you can torque these flanges now, since they won't affect header positioning. Next, slip the headers, one at a time, onto the pipes extending from the flanges. Tap the headers with a rubber mallet to seat them fully. Install the retaining springs to hold the pipes in position.

For one-piece headers, you'll want to secure the manifold gaskets with a dollop of grease. Otherwise, you'll need three or four hands to hold the gaskets in place while jockeying the header and its assorted flanges into position behind the radiator. You probably won't even notice the grease burning off, since new exhaust systems smoke on their first run-in anyway. Screw the nuts or bolts so that they are finger tight evenly across the header tubes.

Many aftermarket exhaust systems will include a spring puller with the other parts. If not, you can create one easily with a piece of coat hanger or safety wire and a combination wrench. Get creative!

Tighten the muffler strap last. Don't forget to wipe the system down completely before you fire it up for the first time. Otherwise, you may get to look at your fingerprints for the rest of your exhaust system's life.

Depending on your exhaust system, you'll either install the S-bend individually or paired with the muffler. A spritz of WD-40 on the portion of the pipe that slips inside of the other will make the parts slide easier. Again, this will burn off without your noticing. Once you have the S-bend and the canister attached to the header, you may need to do some jiggling or rotating of the components to get all of the mounts to line up correctly. You may also need to slide the canister mounting strap to accommodate the location of the pipe hanger or passenger peg. To avoid scratching the surface of the muffler, spread the ends of the strap slightly. Tighten all nuts and bolts finger tight and check the alignment of the system. You don't want the entire exhaust system to have an unnecessary load on it once you tighten the bolts. Install any retaining springs. Beginning with the manifold nuts or bolts and moving rearward, torque the systems fasteners to spec.

Before you reinstall the bodywork or start the engine, wipe down the entire system to take off your grubby fingerprints. Pay special attention to the visible areas of the pipe. Some manufacturers recommend using rubbing alcohol to cut the oil. Even stainless steel will permanently display your fingerprints once it heats up to operating temperature.

Tilt the radiator (and oil cooler) back into position and tighten down all the mounting bolts. When reinstalling the bodywork, make sure that there is adequate clearance between the pipe and the plastic. Some exhaust systems may include insulation to stick to the bodywork. If you find interference problems, double-check the pipe for correct mounting.

Owners of naked bikes or street fighters will want to take some time to season their pipes before taking the bike for a ride, since the headers will be visible. Start your engine and let it idle for a couple of minutes, shut it off, and let the pipe return to ambient temperature. Repeat this process two more times, adding a couple of minutes to the run time. Although all single-walled pipes discolor from heat, performing this process will help to minimize the initial bluing of your headers. Owners of fully faired sporty bikes can follow or ignore these steps. Don't forget that new pipes will smoke for a few minutes, so don't be surprised. Check all of the fasteners, particularly the manifold bolts, after about 50–100 miles and retighten, if necessary.

Now for the fun part: Get out there and try out your new exhaust and additional street cred. To get maximum performance from your new exhaust system, consider rejetting or altering your fuel injection. Your bike may run fine without it, but it will run better with the proper fuel mixture.

Bikes with exhaust control valves like the Suzuki Exhaust Tuning System will need to have their wiring disabled, or the engine may not run correctly, defaulting to a fail-safe, limp home mode. For the GSX-R1000, one wire needs to be pulled from the harness. Cover the exposed pin with electrical tape.

Installing a Slip-on Exhaust System

 Time: 1 hour

 Tools: Wrenches, sockets, torque wrench, rear stand, rubber mallet or dead-blow hammer, spring puller, WD-40, soft cloth or work mat

 Talent:

 Cost: $$$–$$$$

 Parts Required: Aftermarket slip-on system

 Tip: Stuck or ornery components can be benefit from some WD-40.

! PERFORMANCE GAIN: Increase of power in portions of rpm range.

COMPLEMENTARY MODIFICATIONS: Install jet kit or retune EFI (electronic fuel injection).

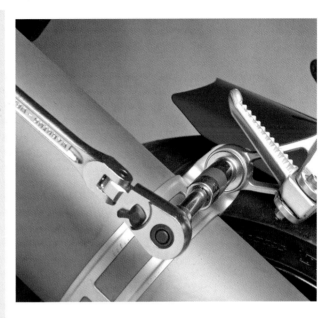

When you remove the stock pieces, loosen the clamp securing the connecting pipe first. Then unbolt the muffler and slide it free.

Slip-on exhaust systems deliver the racy look of an aftermarket system and some of the performance of a replacement system at a significantly lower price than a full aftermarket system. Installation is much simpler for novice mechanics too. One real benefit of a slip-on system is that exhausts that use auxiliary valves to improve low-end power can keep this feature.

Although you could install a slip-on system with your bike on its side stand, use a rear stand to stabilize it. Before you begin wrenching, take a look at the fasteners securing the stock components you will be removing. Some bikes, such as this R1, don't even need the bodywork removed. While some bikes will need a little more work, installing this Two Brothers Racing system only required the removal of two parts. First, the clamp securing the connector pipe to the header was loosened; next, the bolt attaching the muffler to the passenger footpeg bracket. A quick tap with a rubber mallet, and the OE canister and connector pipe slipped free. Once again, stuck components can be benefit from some WD-40.

Mount the S-bend and any necessary clamps, leaving the clamps loose initially. If the manufacturer requires it, squeeze a bead of high-temperature sealant around the exterior of the pipe approximately one-quarter inch below the lip. Slide the canister over the pipe until it is fully seated on the S-bend. Wipe any of the sealant that oozes out of the forward edge of the canister. Wrap the muffler clamp around the canister and

slip it into position. You may need to rotate oblong mufflers on the S-bend or rotate the connector pipe itself to get the clamp's holes to line up with the footpeg bracket. Tighten the muffler clamp bolt finger tight and check all exhaust parts for proper alignment. When you're satisfied that everything is correct, install any springs and tighten the clamps and bolts.

This R1 didn't require the bodywork to be removed. There is just enough space inside the fairing to tighten the pipe clamp.

CARBURETION, EFI, EXHAUST, IGNITION, AND ENGINE

The high-temp sealant will keep exhaust gases from leaking forward out of the muffler and possibly discoloring the pipe.

Wiping all fingerprints and smudges off the system is vital to keeping the dirt from etching itself into the surface of the metal. (Heed the warning in the preceding project.) Also, check to see that cosmetic parts, such as the badge on the canister, have the protective plastic covers removed. You don't want it melting onto the parts when they get hot.

When you start your bike for the first time, don't be surprised to see smoke. WD-40 will burn off, as will any machining oils or volatile components in the muffler packing. After riding for about 50–100 miles, check the fasteners to make sure that they are still tight. Also, consider rejetting or adjusting the EFI to gain maximum benefit from your slip-on system.

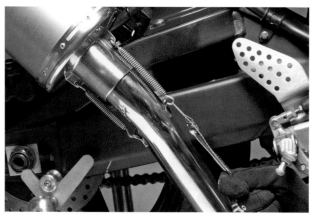

If you don't have a spring puller, you can easily make one out of a combination wrench and some safety wire.

Some systems require that the muffler clamp be secured to the outside of the footpeg bracket. Others need it on the inside. Make sure you follow the instructions, or the pipe may interfere with the swingarm travel.

Cleaning the exterior of the muffler — especially a titanium one — and S-bend is vital before you run the engine. You risk burning the marks into the finish if you don't.

Cleaning/Replacing Air Filter

 Time: 30 minutes or a couple of hours if air-drying a filter

 Tools: Wrenches, sockets, ratchet, No. 2 Phillips screwdriver, rear stand, clean rags, compressed air

 Talent:

 Cost: $

 Parts Required: : OE or aftermarket air filter, air filter cleaner, air filter oil

 Tip: Buying a washable aftermarket filter will pay for itself in a couple of cleanings.

 PERFORMANCE GAIN: Consistent fuel mixture, better airflow.

COMPLEMENTARY MODIFICATIONS: Rejet carbs, synchronize carbs, install velocity stacks.

Not too long ago, a great way to increase your bike's horsepower was to toss the stock air box, install a set of pod filters, and rejet your carbs. Well, all that changed with the advent of Ram-Air, which forces cool, outside air into the air box. The faster you go, the more air forced into the mixers, giving the bike more power. One thing hasn't changed, though. For your engine to operate at peak efficiencies, the air filter needs to be clean to allow maximum airflow. Let your filter get dirty, and you'll experience power loss, reduced gas mileage, and possible plug fouling. Regular—or at least annual—cleaning of your bike's air filter is a simple way to keep it running great.

Gaining access to your bike's air filter has gotten progressively easier since the introduction of Ram-Air. Most sporty bikes, like the GSX-R750 shown here, provide a means of tilting the gas tank out of the way. Many even provide a prop to hold the tank in position. Before you raise the tank, put your bike on a rear stand. Consult your owner's or factory service manual to see if the seat or any bodywork needs to be removed prior to unbolting the tank. If your bike requires that the tank be removed, be sure to turn the petcock to the off position and place a rag below the fuel line you'll be disconnecting. Remove the bolts securing the tank and loosen the bolt on the tank's pivot.

Lift the tank up and insert a prop to hold it securely out of your way. Give the top of the air box a quick blast with compressed air to clear out any dirt that may have accumulated in the screw holes. Remove the Phillips head screws on the air box cover, making sure that you don't drop any into the depths of the engine compartment, never to be seen again. You may find that the screws closest to the tank's pivot can only be accessed with a stubby screwdriver or by tilting the tank so that it is vertical. (If the tank is full, some gas may leak out of the cap or into the charcoal canister—both Bad Things—so hold the tank vertical for as short a time as possible.) Once all of the screws are removed, remove the lid and inspect the air box to determine the path of airflow in from the outside. Carefully remove the air filter, making sure you don't knock any grit into the clean side of the air box. If the top of the air box is going to be off for more than a minute or so, cover the throttle intakes with clean rags or paper towels.

The kinds of air filters used vary by manufacturer. Generally, you will clean foam filters in a solvent. Paper filters can be blown out with compressed air from the back side of the filter. The best idea, though, is to buy an aftermarket filter, such as BMC or K&N. These pleated cotton filters are reusable and should last the life of your motorcycle. The filters are constructed out of cotton that is trapped between two sheets of wire mesh. The manufacturers make sure that the filters will not require rejetting. So, they are true drop-in replacements to the OE versions. While they may cost more to replace, you will save money over the years that you own your bike.

Cleaning a reusable filter is a four-part operation. First, spray or pour on the solvent to cut the oil that is used to trap the dirt and let it soak for a few minutes. Rinse the oil out from the back side (the clean side) of the filter with cold

Unbolt your tank and tilt it up out of the way. Cover the paint with a rag if you're worried about scratches.

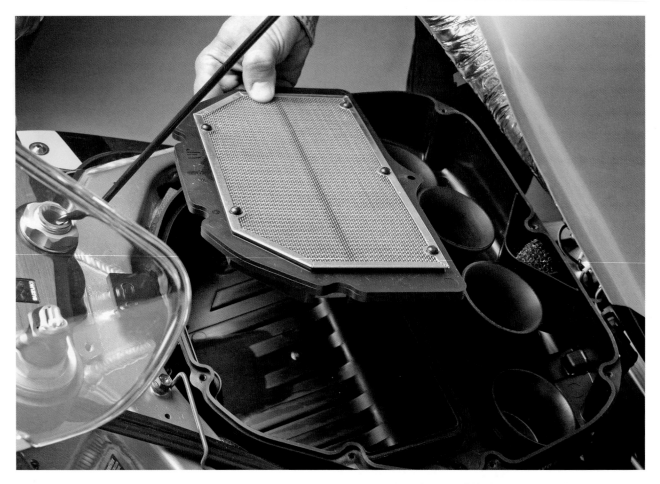

Carefully lift the filter out of the air box. On filters with the dirty side facing down (like this one), keep it away from the throttle intakes. You don't want to dump stuff directly into the engine, do you?

water until the cotton fibers are clean. Dry the filter by placing it in the sun for a few hours or hanging it in your garage overnight. Do not use compressed air or a hair dryer unless you want to shrink the cotton and render the filter useless. When it's dry, you want to coat the cotton with filter oil. (Never use any other kind of oil but filter oil.) If you are using a spray, one pass per pleat will suffice. For squeeze bottles, make one pass per pleat in the bottom of the pleat. Don't saturate the filter. Let it sit for 20 minutes and reoil any white spots on the cotton.

Installing a fresh or cleaned filter is as easy as its removal. However, you should make sure that you have the filter facing the correct direction. For example, paper filters will generally have a screen to support the back of the filter to keep it from flexing or tearing during operation. If your air box has an O-ring to seal the filter access, ascertain that it is in position. After you place the lid on the air box, take a moment to make sure that it is seated properly. Screw the lid in place in an alternating pattern (rather than going around the circumference) to make sure that the pressure is evenly applied. Reinstall the tank, bodywork, and seat, as necessary—and breathe easy.

Oil the filter one pleat at a time. Let it sit for 20 minutes, then reoil any white spots in the cotton.

Installing Velocity Stacks

 Time: 30 minutes

 Tools: Wrenches, sockets, ratchet, No. 2 Phillips screwdriver, rear stand, clean rags

 Talent:

 Cost: $

 Parts Required: Velocity stacks

 Tip: Some velocity stacks will bolt into the air box itself, while others need to attach to the carburetors.

 PERFORMANCE GAIN: More power in portions of the rpm range.

COMPLEMENTARY MODIFICATIONS:
Clean/replace air filter, rejet carbs, synchronize carbs.

Aftermarket velocity stacks come in a variety of shapes, sizes, and materials, as these from Factory Pro Tuning illustrate. They can help you to massage some more power out of your engine without any tradeoffs.

Free horsepower is every gearhead's dream. Well, that will probably remain a fantasy, but how about easy horsepower? On some bikes, bolting a set of velocity stacks in your sportbike's air box will deliver 1–4 horsepower in the top end without rejetting or loss of power in the midrange. On others, you get a fatter midrange with a minimal change up top. It all depends on the airflow characteristics of the air box. Either way, more horsepower is good, right?

Since the velocity stacks reside in the air box, you shouldn't be surprised that you're going to follow the same procedures as replacing your air filter. Remove the tank and any bodywork that will prevent access to the air box. Simple enough. Now, look at the air box and the velocity stacks you're about to install. Do you need to remove the air box to mount them directly on the carburetors, or do they bolt to the air box? To remove the air box, you'll need to remove all the fasteners securing it. Blow out the dirt with compressed air first, then loosen the clamps cinching it to the Ram-Air ducts and the throttle bodies. Unplug any hoses and sensors you find, but remember and mark where they go. Smart mechanics label the various hoses as they are disconnected. The air box should slip off with little effort. If you find yourself struggling, look for a hidden fastener impeding your progress.

Some velocity stack kits ship with different-length pieces for the inner two cylinders on an inline-four. Make sure you've got the sizes sorted or all your money and labor will be wasted. When tightening the screws on the throttle bodies, make sure they are secure, but don't go Neanderthal on them. You don't want to strip the threads. While most velocity stack kits don't require rejetting, in some cases you may need to install new jets. Look at Project 69 to find out how to do this.

Before you reassemble your air box, give the filter a quick cleaning. (See the preceding project.) It would be silly to put a dirty filter back when you're trying to increase airflow. Now all you need to do to make more horsepower is start the engine and twist the throttle. Easy, huh?

Installing velocity stacks inside your air box is a simple modification that even a neophyte mechanic can perform with little trepidation.

CARBURETION, EFI, EXHAUST, IGNITION, AND ENGINE

Installing R1/R6 Slide Stops

 Time: 1 hour

 Tools: Wrenches, sockets, ratchet, Phillips screwdriver, flathead screwdriver, Allen keys, pliers, clean rags

 Talent: ♔♔♔

 Cost: $

 Parts Required: Graves Motorsports Slide Stops

 Tip: This modification requires that you load the Graves fuel maps into a Power Commander.

 PERFORMANCE GAIN: Quicker throttle response.

COMPLEMENTARY MODIFICATIONS: Install velocity stacks.

When fuel injection first made its way onto motorcycles, riders found that the newfangled "carburetion" could be abrupt when they tried to move from deceleration or neutral throttle to positive throttle. When coupled with any driveline lash, the results could be disconcerting midcorner. Some manufacturers added a set of servo-controlled butterflies to help soften the hit of acceleration. However, Yamaha chose to fit vacuum slides to its throttle bodies. After all, this setup worked quite well in constant velocity (CV) carburetors for years. In the on-off-on throttle world of street riding, where you may not know what is just around every corner, the slightly slower throttle response of a CV system is desirable. However, on the track, where precise control of the throttle is paramount, tuners found that the slides in a CV throttle body inhibited optimal control. Graves Motorsports, seeing a need to give racers and track riders the crisp response they desired, developed a clever kit to literally take the slides in the CV system out of the mix.

Begin this project by stripping off all of the hardware covering the throttle bodies. Aside from the usual bodywork, tank, and air box, you'll also need to remove the plastic heat shield on top of the engine. Don't forget to remove the throttle cables. Loosen the Allen bolts securing the throttle bodies to the rubber boots and pull the assembly free. Look for the pressure regulator on the right side of the fuel rail. When you find

something that looks like the product of an unholy union between a flying saucer and a mushroom, you're in the right place. You need to unscrew the Phillips-head screws holding the regulator in place. They're pretty tight, so you'll need to use some force—and care, if you don't want to strip them. Shocking the threads by inserting the screwdriver and rapping on it lightly with a hammer should do the trick.

Once you have the pressure regulator off the throttle assembly, insert the fuel pressure booster from the Graves kit. It will press into place, small end first. You may need to tap it with the handle of a screwdriver to get it to seat completely. The regulator can now be reinstalled. Boosting the fuel pressure in the fuel rail makes it possible to better atomize the fuel as it squirts from the injector nozzles. In order to maintain proper mixture, though, a Power Commander is required to shorten the pulses at the fuel injector. (See Project 73.)

Remove the diaphragm cover as you would when installing a needle in a CV carb. The slide will easily slip free of the throttle body. Take the Graves slide stop and place it over the slide until it reaches the bottom of the diaphragm. Reinstall the slide in the throttle body. The vacuum slide should now stay in the fully open position. If it doesn't, make sure that the stop has been seated against the diaphragm. When reassembling the throttle body, you'll have to monkey a bit to keep the diaphragm's rim seated in the top of the throttle body. Insert the spring before you screw down the diaphragm cover. Repeat this process for the remaining three throttle bodies.

After the bike is buttoned up, you'll need to remap the Power Commander's fuel delivery curve. Don't ride your bike until you've performed this vitally important step! When you go ride you'll discover how snappy the throttle response is. You'll also find that you're more aware of when you roll on the throttle properly—and when you have midcorner miscues.

Hiding under the wiring harness on the right side of the fuel rail is the pressure regulator and its maddeningly tight mounting screws. Shock the threads to avoid stripping the screw.

The pressure booster is the plug with a little hole in it under the rightmost finger. Simply snap it into place.

The slide stop just slides over the slide until it reaches the bottom of the diaphragm. With the stop in place, the slide can't move from the full open position.

Note how far the diaphragm sticks up with the slide stop in place. If you have trouble keeping the diaphragm bead in the groove, you can try using a little grease in the groove to help hold the rubber in place.

PROJECT 67

Installing R1 Ram-Air Box

 Time: 2 hours

 Tools: Wrenches, sockets, ratchet, Phillips screwdriver, flathead screwdriver, Allen keys, mat knife, pliers, clean rags or paper towels

 Talent: ▮▮▮

 Cost: $$$$

 Parts Required: Graves Motorsports Ram-Air Box Kit, Graves Motorsports Velocity Stack Kit, Graves Motorsports Carbon Aluminum Air Director (optional)

 Tip: To get proper performance out of this modification, you need to load the Graves fuel maps into a Power Commander.

 PERFORMANCE GAIN: A truckload of whup-ass between your knees.

COMPLEMENTARY MODIFICATIONS: Clean air filter or replace with aftermarket part, install Graves Motorsports Slide Stop Kit.

You need a fresh blade on your mat knife to cut off the plastic lip on the air box bracket.

A sane person might be satisfied with the power an R1 delivers in stock form. However, most R1 owners won't be happy until they bolt on a full exhaust system and a Power Commander to unleash a few more horses. Still, for those special few for whom too much of everything is just enough, Graves Motorsports offers a Ram-Air box that slips stealthily in place of the stock unit. Although the average gearhead probably won't notice the longer snorkel lurking under the triple clamp of your 2003 or earlier R1, the difference will be obvious to the rider—and those breathing the exhaust fumes.

Begin as you would with any of the throttle body projects. Place your R1 on a stand and strip it down to the air box. Don't forget to note how the various hoses connect to the fuel pump and air box, since you'll be reattaching them when you're done. This would be a good time to make sure the air filter is clean and in good repair, as you'll be installing it in the Graves air box.

Before you slip the sexy new air box into position, you'll need to make some adjustments to the stock parts to accommodate the Ram-Air system. If you look near the steering head you'll notice a plastic lip that helped to hold the stock air box in position. Using a sharp mat knife, cut the offending lip off the brace. Not that folks who make this type of modification really care, but this is the only nonreversible modification involved in this project.

Rotate the vent hose between the number 1 and 2 throttle bodies up and remove the plastic filter and fastening clip. Next, remove the hose from the vacuum slide vent tube on the right side of the throttle bank. Using an 8-mm Allen key or screwdriver, rotate the tube so that it aims up perpendicular to the throttle body. You'll be slipping the hose (but not the plastic filter) back onto it and then placing the Graves air box over it with an interference fit. If you don't have the angle right, the hose will refuse to slide into the air box, or it will leave a gap that will allow pressure loss at speed.

Locate the atmospheric-pressure sensor in the rear section and turn it over in its mounting bracket. In order for the EFI

Make sure the vacuum slide vent tubes are lined up correctly so they fit into the air box base.

166

system to calculate the proper mixture, it needs to be tricked into thinking that the pressure inside the air box is actually ambient pressure. After lubricating the sensor's nipple with a little saliva, attach the nonkink rubber tubing included in the kit and route the hose back to the air box in a way that prevents it from getting pinched. Finally, plug the emissions system hose or, better yet, remove the system and replace it with one of Graves' covers.

Now you're ready to work on the air box. Remove the velocity stacks/air box boots from the stock air box. Install the number 1 and 4 OE boots into the Graves air box from the bottom. The Graves velocity stacks go in the center two holes. Again, they should be slipped in position from the bottom of the air box with the flared end up. Stop when the first groove snaps into place over the air-box base. Install the stock clamps on the Graves boots. Remove the air-temperature sensor from the OE air box and install it in the new one. Be careful not to overtighten the sensor, or you'll be making a trip to your local Yamaha parts department.

Maneuver the air box, snorkel first, into place. Insert the hoses from the vacuum slide vents into the bottom of the air box. Slide the velocity stack boots onto the throttle bodies and secure them with the clamps. Attach the crankcase breather hose to the spout on the back of the air box. Place the air filter into the slot in the air box. Make sure it has the proper orientation. If it doesn't slide into position easily, rub a little grease on the rubber edges of the filter. Apply a little grease to the O-ring on the under side of the air box lid to assist it in maintaining a tight seal. Place the lid onto the air box, making sure that the filter lines up properly with the grooves in the bottom of the lid. The bolt-tightening sequence for the lid is also important for the airtightness of the air box. Begin at the front, screwing the two 5-mm bolts finger tight. On the rear bolts, secure them finger tight before snugging them up with an Allen key. Finally, tighten the front bolts with the Allen key.

Find the nipple next to the air temperature sensor and push the hose connected to the atmospheric sensor onto it. Again, a little lube in the form of saliva will make the hose slide on easier. Connect the wiring for the temperature sensor. Load the Graves fuel maps into the Power Commander, button up the bike, and you're good to go . . . very fast.

The atmospheric-pressure sensor needs to be flipped in order to attach the nonkink hose.

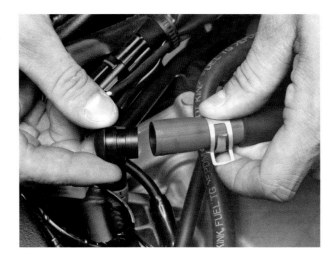

Although removing the air induction system is the more elegant route, you can get away with simply plugging the hose.

Ready for the air filter. Note the vacuum slide vent hose in the right side of the air box.

Note to those who don't like to read directions: A large percentage of technical support calls about the R1 air box are resolved by simply inserting the velocity stacks from the bottom of the air box base. The air-temperature sensor and the nipple for the atmospheric-pressure hose can be seen on the right corner of the air box.

PROJECT 68

Synchronizing Carburetors and EFI Throttle Bodies

 Time: 1 hour

 Tools: Wrenches, sockets, ratchet, No. 2 Phillips screwdriver, rear stand, clean rags, carb balancer, box fan, auxiliary fuel tank

 Talent: ∦ ∦

 Cost: $

 Parts Required: None

 Tip: Make sure all vacuum leaks are plugged, or you will get false readings.

 PERFORMANCE GAIN: Smoother power delivery.

COMPLEMENTARY MODIFICATIONS:
Clean/replace air filter, install aftermarket velocity stacks.

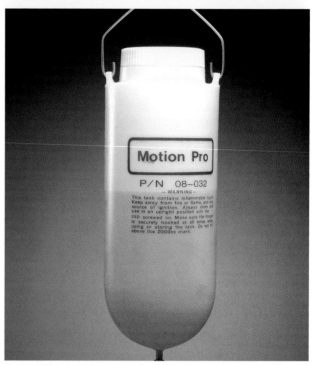

Since you'll be running your engine for a while, you need a supply of gas for your carburetors. Hang the auxiliary tank above the level of the carbs but out of the way for your wrenching.

L ike other mechanical devices, carburetor and EFI linkages periodically need to be adjusted to ensure that, when you roll on the throttle, the same thing happens in every throttle body. Since motorcycles generally have as many carburetors as cylinders, multicylinder engines use linkages to open the butterfly valves as you roll on the throttle. By making sure that all of the butterflies are open the same amount at idle speed, the throttles should allow the same amount of air through at all throttle positions and engine speeds. If carburetors or EFI throttle bodies (hereafter lumped together as carburetors) are out of sync, the cylinders will receive different-sized charges. The symptoms can be as mild as rough idling or an uneven engine sound at partial throttle. Severe cases can cause surging while at any constant throttle setting.

The reward for spending an hour syncing your carbs is a smoother idling, quicker revving engine. The only tools required other than typical home mechanic's sockets and wrenches are a vacuum gauge and an auxiliary fuel tank (for bikes that don't have a fuel pump). While you can spend big bucks on a fancy digital vacuum gauge if you want, you only need one that measures pressure by how far it sucks mercury up a tube. Motion Pro sells two reasonably priced versions of

its carb tuner through distributors and motorcycle dealerships. A purpose-built auxiliary tank supplies fuel to your engine while keeping any gas from dripping on the engine's hot parts. This is also available from Motion Pro.

Since the bike will be running, make sure your work area for this project has good ventilation. Start by placing your bike on a rear stand, and then remove the seat, gas tank (or tilt it up out of the way), and side panels. Be careful when disconnecting the fuel line from the petcock, particularly if the engine is hot. Hold a rag under the open line until all the gas has drained out. To avoid damage to the petcock and possible fuel spillage, place the fuel tank on an old tire to keep it from tipping over. Smart mechanics label the various hoses as they are disconnected from the air box.

Now, take a look at the hoses around the carburetors or throttle bodies. If you're lucky, the manufacturer has preconnected hoses to allow for easy synchronization. Your factory service manual will help you find them. If you don't have those hoses and can't access the nipples on the throttle bodies with the air box in place, disassemble and remove the air box to give unfettered access to the carburetors. If you haven't done so lately, this would be a good time to make sure the air filter is clean and in good repair. Hook the auxiliary tank to the fuel line and hang it so that the tank is higher than

Your bike will have either a capped nipple or a threaded plug. Some manufacturers make your job easier by routing hoses out from under the throttle bodies. You'll need to attach your carb balancer to either the nipple or the hose.

the carburetors. If your bike uses a fuel pump that is built into the gas tank, you will need to find a way to keep the fuel line, return line, wiring harness, and tank mounted to feed the carbs—a tricky operation. (Many—but not all—of the bikes that have their tanks pivot out of the way can also be run with the tank in the tilted position.)

Locate and uncover the ports into the intake tract. You will find either bolt plugs or capped nipples. Your carb balancer should include threaded adapters to fit the ports. While most port threads will be 5-mm, some bikes use 6-mm threads. Once you have the adapters screwed in, attach the hoses to the nipples. Starting at the left cylinder, connect the number 1 hose and move across from left to right making sure to keep the hoses in order. Find a convenient place to hang the carb balancer, so you can see it while the engine is running.

Even water-cooled bikes need to have air moving around them to maintain proper operating temperature. A box fan will work nicely.

Before you start the engine, make sure that the hoses do not interfere with the throttle linkage. Also, make a thorough visual check to see that all possible vacuum leaks have been sealed. When you start the engine, be careful if you need to give it some gas. Blip the throttle too energetically, and you'll get the pleasure (not) of seeing the mercury sucked out of the carb stick into the engine. If you value your brain cells, don't forget to make *sure* you have proper ventilation. While the engine warms up, listen for any vacuum leaks you may have forgotten to seal. After your engine reaches operating temperature, make sure you have a fan blowing across the radiator to help keep your bike from overheating. If you let it get too hot, the carb syncing may not be accurate. Finally, make sure the idle speed is set to factory specs.

Most bikes, be they carbureted or fuel-injected, synchronize the throttle bodies by adjusting the linkage connecting

You want your columns of mercury to look like this when you're finished with your adjustments. Be sure to test the synchronization at cruising rpm to make sure they maintain their relative closeness.

the butterfly valves that control the flow into the engine. However, some fuel-injected bikes simply require that you adjust an air screw in each throttle body to get it to match the one body that doesn't have an air screw. Check your factory service manual. Either way, the carb balancer displays the same information. The vacuum created in the intake tract will draw the mercury up from the reservoir in the bottom of the carb tool. There will always be some variance between the columns, but most manufacturers say that a 1/2- to 1-inch difference of mercury level is fine. However, adjusting the columns of mercury so that they are as close to identical as possible is worth the minimal effort it requires. Twins will have only one screw to adjust the synchronization. Multis require that the process be done in steps—as do EFI systems that use the butterfly valves to synchronize the throttle bodies.

Begin by finding the adjuster screw between the number 1 and 2 cylinders. Turn it until you have the two carb-balancer readings identical. Blip the throttle slightly and let the engine return to idle. Make an adjustment, if necessary. Once you're happy with the results, switch to the adjustment of the number 3 and 4 cylinders. Again, once the two sets of two carburetors are set, find the adjuster screw between the number

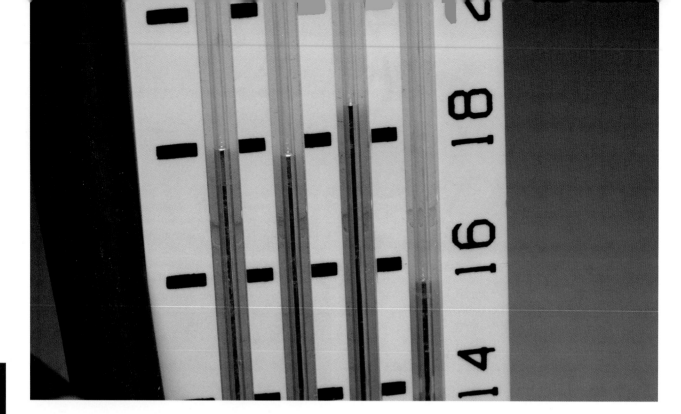

After — and possibly while — adjusting the linkage to improve throttle synchronization, you will need to adjust the idle speed back to factory spec.

3 and 4 cylinders to balance the two pairs of butterfly valves.

Now that the carbs are in sync, raise the rpm to 3,000 and hold it steady. The columns of mercury should settle at a consistent height. If one or more of the columns rises to a lower level than the others, a vacuum leak or some other problem will need to be identified and corrected for your bike to run its best. Common problems are a worn slide that is sticking or something ailing the linkage. Finally, adjust the engine's idle speed back to the factory specs if it changed. Carefully remove the carb tool and reposition all vacuum hoses and plugs. Start the engine again to see if there are air leaks—the idle speed should stay the same. Replace the tank, side panels, and seat, paying special attention to the fuel and vacuum lines connected to the petcock. Your bike's engine should now idle smoother and rev more cleanly.

Throttle bodies 3 and 4 are out of sync with each other. The lines on the scale mark off 2-centimeter increments.

Installing a Jet Kit

 Time: 2 hours

 Tools: Wrenches, sockets, ratchet, Phillips screwdriver, flathead screwdriver, screw gun (optional), Allen keys, float-height tool, pliers, drill, rags

 Talent:

 Cost: $

 Parts Required: Jet kit

 Tip: Installing a jet kit is more than just tossing in a new main jet—take your time and work carefully.

 PERFORMANCE GAIN: A bike that carburets cleanly throughout the entire rev range.

COMPLEMENTARY MODIFICATIONS:
Clean/replace air filter.

Common knowledge dictates that the first hop-up item most riders purchase is an aftermarket pipe. While most aftermarket exhaust manufacturers say rejetting is not required, they generally recommend installing a jet kit for optimum power. However, experienced mechanics will tell you that only about half of the folks who have fitted freer-flowing exhaust systems to their bikes have also installed jet kits. The people who refrained from installing jet kits usually give one or both of the following reasons: "The jet kit was too expensive," or "The pipe improved my bike's power so much, I didn't need a jet kit."

When you open the box to your new jet kit, a few brass jets (one per carburetor) and stainless-steel or titanium needles don't look like much for $60–$100 you just plopped down, but the CD that expensive computer software rides on doesn't look like much, either. Remember, you're not only paying for the machining of the jet kit's little pieces of metal, but also for the development time. Sometimes, a kit may take several weeks of tweaking to reach perfection. (For more information on what it takes to develop a jet kit, read Project 70.)

All riders, not just racers, benefit from having a well-carbureted bike. While an aftermarket pipe may make a bike more powerful, properly jetting a bike's carbs will make an engine not only produce even more power, but also improve the quality of the power is delivered—whether a hot pipe is bolted on or not. Many bikes come from the factory with extremely lean jetting to meet EPA requirements, and sometimes something as simple as raising the needle with a shim can produce a night-and-day difference in your bike's performance. (Kawasaki's ZX-9R is a prime example of such a setup.) When you order a jet kit for your bike, be sure to order the kit based on the current tune of your bike. Don't get a Stage III kit just because you plan to make big changes later on. If you've only got a pipe right now, jet for your bike with the pipe.

Begin by placing the bike on a rear stand and removing the gas tank, air box, and any other crud that keeps you from gaining direct access to your carburetors. Make reassembly easier by labeling all hoses and wire connections. Disconnect the throttle cables from the bell crank. Loosen all of the clamps securing the carburetor mouths to the rubber boots. Gently wiggle the carbs up and down until they pop free of the boots. Don't put them down just yet. Hold the carbs over a suitable container and drain the float bowls. Before you do anything else, place clean rags or paper towels in each intake manifold to keep the nasties out.

Prior to exposing the carbs' innards, you might as well remove the brass plugs covering the idle screws. Most jet kits will include a drill bit and self-tapping screw to remove the plug. If you don't have one, use a 1/8-inch drill bit and any wood or drywall screw you have sitting around. To keep from drilling too deeply past the plug and possibly damaging the idle jet, wrap a piece of tape around it about one-eighth inch above the tip. Don't drill any deeper than the tape. Insert the screw far enough to have a solid grip on the plug with the threads. Using a pair of pliers (locking pliers, if you like), pull the plug free of the carburetor body. Before you go any farther, insert a flathead screwdriver and count the number of turns as you screw the idle jet's needle valve into the carburetor until it touches bottom. Do not tighten the valve against the jet or you may damage both the needle and the jet itself. Write down the number of turns you counted, in case you someday decide to return to stock jetting. Now, unscrew the needle valve the number of turns specified by your jet kit.

Turn the carburetors upside down. Remove the float bowls with either a Phillips screwdriver or an Allen key. (A screw gun really speeds things up.) Clean out any gunk that may have collected in the bottom of the float bowls. Also check to be sure that none of the float bowl gaskets are cracked, dried, or ripped. Replace any that are suspect.

The float bowls get their name from the plastic floats that control the fuel height within the carburetors. When working on the main jet, make sure you don't put any pressure on the floats, or you could bend the tab responsible for the fuel height. While most jet kits don't have you fiddle with the float height, some do. See Project 70 for the lowdown on how to check and set float height.

In order to access the idle jet, you need to remove the EPA-mandated cover. Note how the drill bit is taped to prevent damaging the adjuster screw below the cover.

Turn your attention to the brass main jet located in the center of the carb body. You can identify it by the flathead screwdriver slot in the base of the jet. Make sure your screwdriver fits snugly into the jet or you may mangle it as you attempt to remove it. If the emulsion tube (the brass part into which the main jet is screwed) turns with the jet, hold it in position with an 8-mm wrench. Jet kits without new emulsion tubes simply require that you screw the new jet in place of the old one. If your jet kit includes a new pilot jet, you'll want to replace it the same way you did the main jet. The pilot jet is significantly smaller than the main jet and located near the main jet. Simply unscrew it and replace it with the new one. Before your reinstall the float bowls, make sure that the gasket surfaces are clear of any dirt or grit. One grain of sand can cause a leak that forces you to tunnel back down to the carbs. When screwing the float bowls back onto the carbs, make sure the screws are tight, but not overly tight.

Flip the carbs so that you now have access to the top covers and unscrew the retaining screws/bolts. When you remove a cover, you'll be presented with the top of a diaphragm. Constant velocity (CV) carburetors use the vacuum created as air flows through the carb's throat to lift a slide. The slide itself performs two duties. First, by restricting the size of the throat opening at lower air speeds (usually during lower rpm), the slide keeps the air speed high as it passes over the nozzle (or emulsion tube), thus atomizing the fuel more effectively. Second, it helps to keep the engine from stumbling when you whack the carbs open, since the slides will only rise as quickly as the airflow requires.

Carefully, lift out the slide and examine the rubber diaphragm. If you find any cracks or pinholes, the diaphragm must be replaced. Notice how the needle hangs out of the bottom of the slide. Press up from the tip of the needle to remove it from the slide—but be sure you remember the

order in which parts come out of the slide. You will find a spacer that holds the slide spring in place above the needle. You may also find a small washer below the needle. Carefully set these parts aside for use later.

Since carburetors with factory jetting usually have non-adjustable needles, most jet kits include an adjustable needle with instructions on how to correctly set the needle height. When affixing the circlip to the appropriate slot in the needle, always count from the top slot. If your jet kit instructions specify installing a washer, make sure it is on the needle below the circlip to raise the needle halfway between two circlip notches. If the jet kit requires the slide vacuum hole to be drilled, make sure you deburr the new hole. Slip the new needle and washer (if required) into the slide assembly. Place the spring holder in with its prongs down toward the needle.

When reinstalling the slide, make sure that the needle fits into the top of the emulsion tube. Carefully place the lip of the diaphragm in the groove at the top of the carb body. Any folds or buckles will lessen the vacuum inside the top of the carburetor and prevent proper slide function.

Once you have all of the jets replaced, needles installed, and idle screws adjusted, you need to reinstall the carburetors. A little WD-40 on the carb mouths will ease their reinsertion into the boots. Tighten the clamps to secure the carbs. Reinstall the throttle cables and adjust the throttle free play. When the engine has warmed up, adjust the idle speed to factory specifications. If the jet kit you installed was designed for your bike's exact engine/pipe configuration, you should now go out and enjoy your new power. However, if you've made other modifications to the engine, you may have some debugging to do in order to make it perfect. Book some dyno time to sort things out quickly.

All you need is a large flathead screwdriver to remove the main jet. Just install the new one and snug it into place. Save the old jet, in case you decide to go back to stock setting.

Carefully check the diaphragms on top of the vacuum slides. Any diaphragm with cracks or pinholes will need to be replaced.

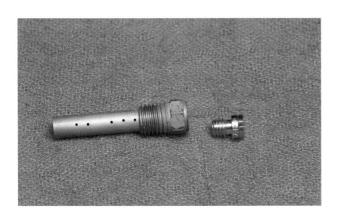

Some jet kits include an emulsion tube. Remove the emulsion tube with an 8-mm socket as you did with the main jet. Don't over tighten the emulsion tube when you install it.

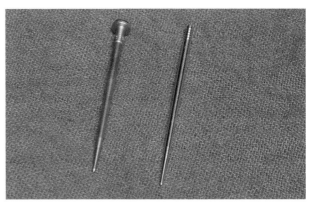

The OE needle (left) has no adjustability, unless you want to shim it up slightly with a washer. The Factory Pro Tuning needle (right) allows you richen or lean out the mixture as your engine setup requires.

Dyno Tuning CV Carburetors

 Time: 2 hours–several days

 Tools: Wrenches, sockets, ratchet, Phillips screwdriver, flathead screwdriver, Allen keys, float-height tool, pliers, drill, rags

 Talent: ▮▮▮▮

 Cost: $–$$$

 Parts Required: Jets of various sizes

 Tip: Finding the best main jet is only the beginning — be patient and finish the job.

 PERFORMANCE GAIN: A bike that carburets perfectly throughout the rev range.

If you've made any changes to your bike that aren't accounted for in an off-the-rack jet kit (like bumped-up compression or cam timing), you'll find that your bike seems to work well . . . or it may run like crap. Regardless, you won't be getting optimum performance from your constant velocity (CV) carburetors until you put your bike on the dyno and do some fine-tuning. Marc Salvisberg, owner of Factory Pro Tuning (www.factorypro.com) in San Rafael, California, has developed jet kits for just about every bike made and has devised a technique for dyno tuning CV carburetors—a technique that is widely acknowledged to be the most thorough and user-friendly. Although you can perform some of the process with the sensors in the seat of your pants, the best results can only be found utilizing an eddy-current dyno and an exhaust gas analyzer.

Dynamometers can be broken down into two general categories: inertial dynos and eddy-current dynos. The dynos found in many motorcycle shops are inertial dynos. The bike's rear tire rests on a large drum, and the bike's horse-power output is measured by how quickly the mass of the drum can be accelerated as the bike's engine runs in a high gear, with the carbs wide open, from low rpm to redline. While inertial dynos are good tools for the type of work most motorcycle dealerships perform (measuring the output of an engine, generating information tuners need to maximize a bike's performance, or verifying that changes worked), inertial dynos have one drawback. Inertial dynos run sweep (or

acceleration) tests in which the readings are taken as the engine makes a run through its rpm range. An entire run through the rpm range on an inertial dyno can take as little as 10 seconds, once the bike is running in top gear.

Eddy-current dynos still place the bike's rear wheel on a large rotating drum, but the dyno gathers information in steps. The engine moves through its rpm range, pausing at regular intervals for several seconds to have the power output measured. At each step, the engine is still running wide open, as with an inertial dyno, but rpm are held constant by the dyno's electromagnetic brake. The power output, as determined by the amount of force required to hold the engine speed constant, is then measured and recorded up to 30 times per second, providing a very accurate picture of what is happening. Aside from gathering extremely accurate data at each step, holding the engine at each rpm step allows the carbon monoxide (CO) output to be measured, giving the tuner one more piece of data hinting at why the engine does or doesn't perform well at a particular rpm.

Salvisberg, who manufactures and sells both inertial and eddy-current dynos, cautions us not to consider the difference between eddy-current and inertial dynos a comparison of which is superior to the other. Instead, they are different tools designed to fulfill different needs, and the eddy-current dyno is designed to gather and sort through the extensive data required for high-end R&D work. Also, since the numbers generated on dynos built by different companies will give slightly different results (due to different manufacturing and calibration specifications), simply comparing dyno numbers without knowing their origin will prove less revealing than comparing baseline and subsequent runs on the same dyno, no matter which type.

From a Baseline Onward

Before you start fiddling with the carburetors, you need to perform baseline dyno runs to determine where your power output is before you make changes. With the baseline data collected, the development process begins, with repeated dyno runs after the carb undergoes incremental, duplicable changes. Every change in jetting creates a change in output, giving some new knowledge about the engine (even if the change made the engine run horribly). You should meticulously record all information, including if the engine misses or backfires. The resulting data is then compared with the baseline and previous runs to determine what the next adjustment should be. Salvisberg stresses that what looks like fooling around—changing the main jet, running the bike on the dyno, and changing the main jet again—is really the way he learns the character of an engine. By concentrating on only the main jet, you make changes with broad strokes (literally moving the fuel delivery curve—the rate at which fuel is delivered to the engine—up and down to see what hap-

No, you won't have one of these sitting in your garage, but the time and effort spent with your bike on a dyno will pay off. *Photo by Andrew Trevitt*

pens) that gradually narrow down on which main jet produces the best peak horsepower. A nice side benefit of these runs (if you're using an exhaust gas analyzer, that is) is that you can also find what exhaust gas readings are associated with the best power delivery throughout the rpm range, making it easier to tune the low- and midrange later.

Once you've found the main jet that makes the best peak power, only then can you begin to address the needle. Why? In order to visualize how the main jet and needle can vary the mixture at different engine speeds, a few basic carburetor concepts must be understood. Air flowing through the carburetor's venturi flows over the discharge nozzle, whose bottom opening rests below the surface of the fuel contained in the float bowl. The low pressure created by the airflow across the discharge nozzle draws the fuel up through the main jet's orifice to be vaporized by the high-speed air. The needle is attached to the slide, which moves up and down, depending on the volume of air flowing into the engine, to keep the airspeed high across the discharge nozzle. As the slide moves up and down, the needle regulates the amount of fuel allowed to vaporize into the airflow. The main jet limits the maximum amount of fuel to enter the airflow at wide-open throttle at high rpm, the only place where the slide will be raised to its highest position out of the airflow (i.e., where the engine's maximum power output will be generated). At all other engine speeds, the needle plays an important part in metering the fuel flow. At low engine speeds the slide is not raised very far, making the diameter of the needle of primary importance. A wider diameter will allow less fuel out of the discharge nozzle than a narrower needle. The point at which the needle's taper begins, and the shape of the taper, can richen or lean the mixture at midrange rpm.

Working the Middle

So, you've installed the best main jets for your engine setup. Now that your top-end power has been sorted, it's time to focus on the midrange power. What you want is the needle shape and height that will give you the most power between 5,000 and 7,000 rpm at full throttle. Since the shaping of needles is a very esoteric skill, you'll be better off ordering a needle from an aftermarket company such as Factory Pro. Your job will be much easier in that you will only be adjusting the needle's height. Starting with the clip in the slot recommended by its manufacturer, make a series of dyno runs in which you either raise or lower the clip. (See Project 72 for more information on needle adjustment.) If you raise the clip in the needle for one run and the power in the midrange improves, raise the clip and make another run. Keep doing this until you get the best power at full throttle in the 5,000 to 7,000 range. If, after your first run, the power drops, try lowering the clip below the starting position and continue testing for the best power.

While you could quit work on the midrange at this point, those who want to make sure that their bike makes the best power it can will also check to see if moving the needle up or down one half-step will make a positive change. After making a run with a washer under the clip of each needle, you can stop if the power improved. If it didn't, try lowering the clip one slot and placing a washer under it. Make one last run. If the results improve, leave the needles as they are. If they don't, remove the washers and move the clips back up one slot.

Winding Up at the Bottom

At this point, you have the best top-end power and strongest midrange you can get out of your current engine setup. Now, you need to finish up with getting the most power you can

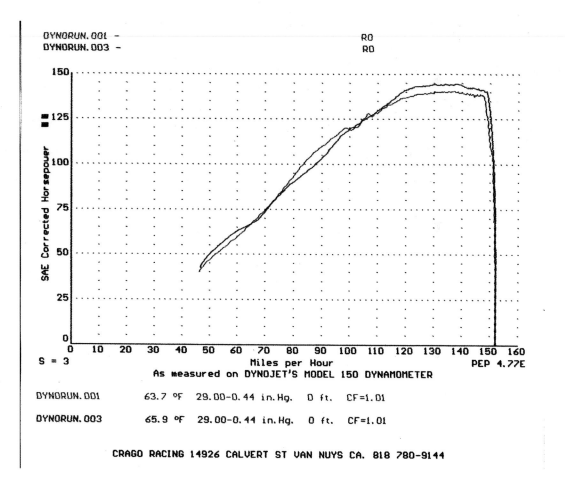

DYNORUN.001 63.7 °F 29.00-0.44 in.Hg. 0 ft. CF=1.01

DYNORUN.003 65.9 °F 29.00-0.44 in.Hg. 0 ft. CF=1.01

CRAGO RACING 14926 CALVERT ST VAN NUYS CA. 818 780-9144

Keep meticulous records while you've got your bike on the dyno. Otherwise, you won't know what changes produced the best power. You need to work in a methodical, organized manner to get the best results in the least amount of time.

out of the bottom end. You're entering an area where few novices ever tread. Consequently, you'll see riders struggle to launch their bikes in traffic. According to Salvisberg, you need to get the engine to accept full throttle in second gear from 2,000 to 3,000 rpm without retching, coughing, spitting, or stumbling. To tune this range to its optimum, you will be listening to the engine as much as you'll be looking at the dyno chart. You'll also need to use a little deductive reasoning to figure out what's going on in the cylinders.

If the engine note is thick, sounding like it has phlegm in its throat that it's trying to clear, and the problem only gets worse as the engine warms up, it is running rich, and the fuel level in the float bowls must be lowered. Try lowering the fuel level by increasing the float height 1 mm. (If this sounds like a foreign language to you, take a side trip to Project 71.) However, if the engine sounds dry and weak with a flat spot between 2,000 and 3,000 rpm, it is most likely lean. Try raising the fuel level a millimeter. Of course, if you've never set the float height on your bike, you should check to make sure that it is within factory specs, anyway.

You're almost done, but not quite yet. You should be familiar with the pilot jet circuit if you've ever installed a jet kit. (Remember the plug you had to remove to access the idle screw?) Begin by setting the screw to the number of turns out from full closed recommended by your factory manual or jet kit instructions. A properly adjusted pilot circuit will prevent rough idling and lean surges at steady-state cruising at low

rpm. Surprisingly, lean surges at high rpm with small throttle openings can also be the result of a pilot problem. For both of these symptoms, richen the mixture by unscrewing the adjuster screw in half-turn increments. The tricky part of adjusting the pilot circuit is that the screws on some carburetors control the flow of fuel in the pilot circuit (fuel screws) while others (air screws) control the flow of air. How can you tell the difference? The more common arrangement locates the fuel screw between the main jet and the engine, while an air screw is between the main jet and the air box. So, richen your mixture by either allowing more fuel or less air, depending on your carburetor type.

Two other symptoms to look for: When blipping the throttle, if the rpm drops down below the idle speed and slowly climbs back up, the mixture is too rich. (These symptoms may also get worse as the engine gets hot.) Screw in the adjuster in half-turn increments until the problems disappear. If the rpm stay high before settling back down to idle speed after the throttle is blipped, it's a sign of a lean pilot mixture. Unscrew the adjuster in half-turn increments. If you can't make the problems go away, you may have a leak in the intake tract you need to hunt down.

While properly tuning your carburetors can be a tedious, time-consuming process, the dividends it pays will be felt every time you throw your leg over your bike. When your friends are bemoaning the flat spots in their jetting, you can simply smile knowingly and tell them how to fix the problem.

176

Setting Float Bowl Height

Time: 1 hour

Tools: Phillips screwdriver, flathead screwdriver, Allen keys, float-height tool, rags

Talent: ʨ ʨ ʨ

Cost: $

Parts Required: None

Tip: Float height is calculated in reverse. Changing from 11 to 12 mm actually lowers the fuel height 1 mm.

PERFORMANCE GAIN: A motor that won't cough or sputter when you whack open the throttle at low engine speeds.

Many riders think that as long as they've chosen the right main jet and needle, their job of fine-tuning the mixture is done. Well, unless you drag-race, your bike doesn't spend all of its time running at redline. Although road racers would rather eat worms than let their engines spin down low, they could still benefit from proper carburetion. Bump-starting a high-compression, big-bore engine at the starting line can be a real bummer. And street riders definitely need carburetion that works between 2,000 and 3,000 rpm, because stoplights and stop-and-go traffic are a fact of life. Also, riders with loud pipes may want to be able to tiptoe past Officer Law's speed trap without attracting attention.

For float height adjustment to have any effect, it must be performed after the main jets and needle settings have been finalized. Otherwise, you're wasting your time. The procedure is relatively simple, but it requires a deft touch. Also, you'll need to have an ear for engine sounds.

Since you should already have the carburetors exposed, disconnect the throttle cables. Separate the carburetors from their boots. Invert the carbs and remove their float bowls and gaskets. Now, for the finesse: With the carb rack standing on end (resting the end on your workbench will make it easier to steady the assembly while you're measuring the float height), tilt the floats until they shift toward the carburetor body. The idea is to have the floats move the valve pin to a closed position—and no further. You don't want the valve spring to compress.

While holding the carb rack in position, measure the float height with Factory Pro's float-height tool. The two arms of the tool should rest on the float bowl gasket surface while the measuring bar gets slid into position so that it just barely touches the highest point on the float (when measured from the gasket surface). You may have to perform several adjustments of the measuring bar to keep it from compressing the float spring slightly.

If your engine is running rich, you need to lower the float height 1 mm to see if that improves the power delivery. In order to do this, since float measurements are backward (from the bottom of the carburetor base down), you want to increase the number of millimeters the float hangs down into the float bowls. So, changing the float height from 13 to 14 mm would lower the fuel level 1 mm. To raise the fuel level in a lean-running engine, you'd change the float height to 12 mm.

Compare the measurement to the height recommended by your jet kit. If you are dyno tuning, base your change on whether you want to lean out or richen the mixture at 2,000–3,000 rpm. One sign that the mixture is too rich is: The engine note is thick, sounding like it has phlegm in its throat that it's trying to clear, and the problem only gets worse as the engine warms up. Leanness is characterized by the engine sounding dry and weak with a flat spot between 2,000 and 3,000 rpm.

To change the height, you need to bend the tang over which the valve's spring loops. A little bend goes a long way, so be careful. You'll find that it's better to move in little steps rather than trying to make large corrections. Your goal is to get the measurements as close as possible to the desired height with a maximum of 0.5 mm difference among all the carburetors.

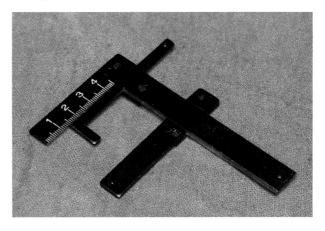

Although it may not look like much, Factory Pro's Float-height tool is precision-machined to allow accurate measurement of float height. It's worth every penny when you're tuning carburetors.

CARBURETION, EFI, EXHAUST, IGNITION, AND ENGINE

The spring on the float valve is easily compressed. When you're measuring float height, you want the pointy end of the valve to just touch the valve seat. If the tip is worn or damaged in any way, replace the valve.

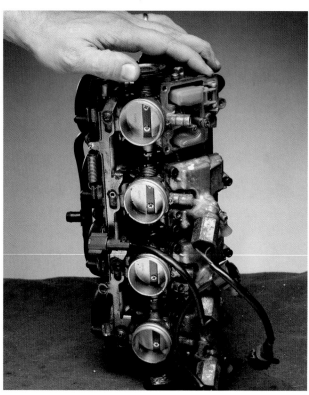

Unless you have superhumanly steady hands, rest the end of the carb rack on your workbench. Then you only have to pivot the assembly back and forth to cause the floats to move.

While you may feel as if you need three or four hands to measure float height, there simply isn't enough room. Patience is the key to successful work here.

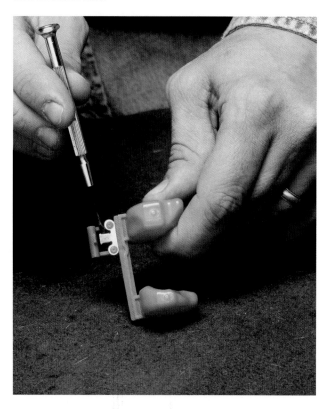

The float tang is a flimsy piece of aluminum (which explains how a good crash can knock your floats out of alignment). Be gentle when adjusting it.

178

Shimming Needles

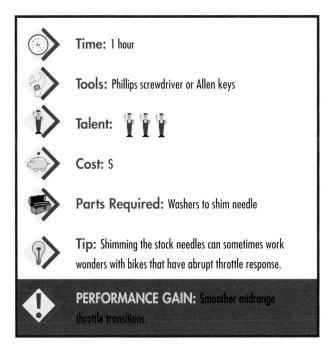

Time: 1 hour

Tools: Phillips screwdriver or Allen keys

Talent:

Cost: $

Parts Required: Washers to shim needle

Tip: Shimming the stock needles can sometimes work wonders with bikes that have abrupt throttle response.

PERFORMANCE GAIN: Smoother midrange throttle transitions.

Some bikes ship from the factory with downright wimpy jetting. Now, before you bemoan the OEMs for selling crappy bikes, you should direct your ire toward the lean, EPA-mandated jetting that the manufacturers must use to pass the federal exhaust sniffers. While cleaner air is a good thing, one has to wonder if a minor needle adjustment to your bike's carburetors to give you better throttle response and, consequently, improved control during cornering (safety!) would be a Bad Thing. Beasts that abruptly shift from deceleration to acceleration as you attempt to begin your roll-on when leaned over in a corner may force you wide at the exit. The last thing you want is for your carburetion to eat up the wrong kind of real estate. Often, a completely stock bike will exhibit a marked improvement in throttle transitions with the installation of a simple needle shim. (Note: Bikes with aftermarket exhaust systems would benefit from a jet kit before you spend the time necessary to adjust the needles. See Project 69 and Project 70 for more information.)

So, leaving the moral dilemmas of altering EPA-mandated jetting behind, we'll turn to adjusting your carburetors' needles. As was discussed in the dyno tuning project, needle adjustments have their primary influence in the 5,000–7,000 rpm range. On many bikes you don't even have to pull the carbs from the boots. If you can access the top of the carbs once you've removed the bodywork, tank, air box, and anything else between you and the mixers, you're golden.

Remove the screws, on one carburetor at a time, with a Phillips-head screwdriver (unless the diaphragm covers have Allen-head bolts). If you have trouble, place the screwdriver in the top of the screw and rap on it with another screwdriver or light hammer to shock the threads. If you strip the screws, they're a bear to get out. When you're loosening the last screw, the cover should pop up because of the spring compressed between it and the slide. Set the spring and cap aside. Remove the slide by sticking a finger into the spring hole and lift out the slide. Watch for small O-rings that are sometimes present.

Once you have the slide out of the carburetor, press the needle up from the bottom of the slide. If the cage-shaped spring holder didn't come out with the spring, it will be the first thing that appears from inside the slide. Next, the needle should appear, and you can pull it out with your fingers. Look inside the slide to make sure a small washer hasn't been left behind. If it has, tap on the slide until it falls free.

Carburetor needles come in two varieties. The stock ones look like nails with a flat head on top and a point below. Aftermarket, adjustable needles have a clip that slips into one of several slots at the top. If the needle has had both adjustments and a washer already, remove the washer and move the clip one slot farther down the needle toward the point. Washers move the needle up one-half the distance of the slots, so why add washers when you can simply move the clip lower and achieve the desired needle raising?

Stock, nail-shaped needles can only be adjusted richer by raising the needle. (If this sounds confusing, read Project 69 for further explanation.) Start with one washer in each carb, reassemble the bike, and go for a test ride. If you feel you still need to richen up the mixture, add another washer.

When reinstalling the slide, make sure that the needle fits into the top of the emulsion tube (the brass opening you can see in the carburetor throat when you look down the slide path). Carefully place the lip of the diaphragm in the groove at the top of the carb body. Any folds or buckles will lessen the vacuum inside the top of the carburetor and prevent proper slide function.

You should now experience smoother acceleration through the midrange with smaller or nonexistent flat spots. Some partial-throttle applications will also improve.

CARBURETION, EFI, EXHAUST, IGNITION, AND ENGINE

Usually you don't need to remove the carbs from the engine to fiddle with the needles.

With the diaphragm cover removed, the slide spring will pop out.

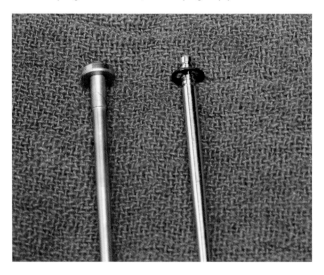

The OE needle (left) has no adjustability. To make the mixture richer, you want to shim it up with a washer or two. The aftermarket needle (right) allows you richen or lean out the mixture, as your engine setup requires, by simply moving a clip. A washer will raise the needle halfway between the slots, adding more adjustability.

Although the slide will only fit in the carb body one way, make it easier on yourself and note the orientation of the slide.

Two variations on a theme. The result in either case is a spring holding both the needle and the slide in position inside of the carburetor body.

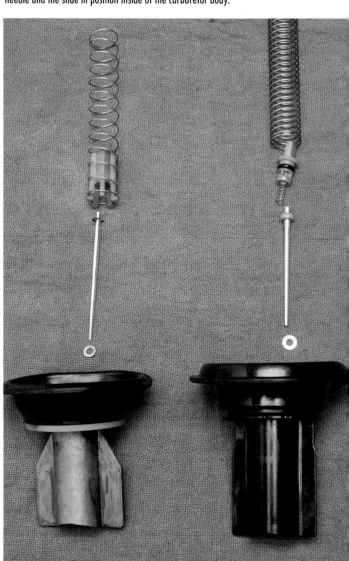

EFI Tuning with Power Commander

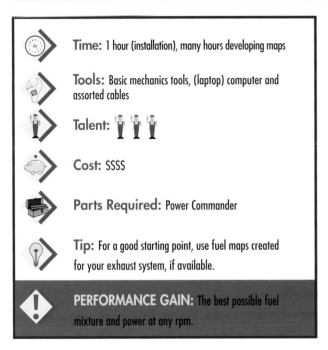

Time: 1 hour (installation), many hours developing maps

Tools: Basic mechanics tools, (laptop) computer and assorted cables

Talent: ▮▮▮

Cost: $$$$

Parts Required: Power Commander

Tip: For a good starting point, use fuel maps created for your exhaust system, if available.

PERFORMANCE GAIN: The best possible fuel mixture and power at any rpm.

The switch from carburetors to fuel injection on sportbikes has opened a whole new door to controlling mixture throughout the rpm range. Gone are the days of jetting's black magic. Instead, we've entered the era of electronic hocus-pocus. With ability to adjust jetting infinitely over the rev range of the engine, fuel injection and its associated maps have given us an infinite number of ways to screw things up. Fortunately, companies such as Dynojet have created magic black boxes that can share the engine management duties with the OE boxes of a similar color and purpose.

Installing a Power Commander is about the easiest bolt-on (or is it plug-in?) process possible. Make sure the ignition is off. Then remove the seat and the pillion/rear cowling to gain access to both the battery and the rear section. Unbolt the tank and simply prop it up out of the way.

Locate the main wiring harness on the frame. Follow the wires from the injector rail to the connector on the main harness. Unhook the connector for use with the Power Commander.

Clean the tray in the rear section with alcohol to remove any grease. Place the Power Commander in position as far rearward as is feasible. This will give you access to the accessory and USB ports while still leaving some room in the trunk for whatever it is you carry in there. Route the Power Commander's wiring harness under the seat-support brace and follow the main wire harness to the injector connectors. While you're running the cables, make sure you keep them clear of any places where they might get pinched by the gas tank, seat, or any of the parts you removed. Make sure

you connect the ground wire to the negative pole of the battery. Attach the plugs from the Power Commander to the appropriate plugs in the wiring harness.

If you are installing the PCIIIr or PCIII-USB (as shown here), you also need to locate the connectors from the pulse cover. On the GSX-R750 featured in the photos, the connectors are easily confused with other ones on the harness. Don't just plug into any old white connector in the area—Bad Things will happen. Check to be sure that the wires have the correct color combinations. In this case, the wires change from green/black to white/green with a white tracer.

Button up your bike so that you can ride it. Running your bike with the Power Commander is now as easy as starting the engine, since you bought it with the base map already installed. If you want to modify the base map, you have two choices. First (and most flexible), hook your Power Commander up to your computer and either manually tweak the maps or download a map from the Dynojet website or your exhaust pipe manufacturer's website. If you're on the road and want to make some adjustments (or don't have access to a computer), you can make mixture changes with the three buttons on top of the Power Commander unit.

With the engine cutoff switch in the run position, depress and hold all three buttons on the Power Commander. Turn on the ignition and wait for the green light to flash on and off. (Note: On some bikes—including this GSX-R750—the fuel injection system powers down if the engine isn't running, requiring a special adapter and a small battery to power the unit.) Choose which rpm range you want to adjust and press the appropriate button once. The LEDs on the unit should show the mixture level. If you press and hold the same button, the mixture will lean out, causing the fuel lights to move down. Pushing and releasing the button repeatedly will richen the mixture and move the lights up the scale. When the two LEDs on either side of the 0 light up, the unit is using its unmodified map.

You don't need to worry if you're not comfortable making changes to your Power Commander's maps. Many bike shops that have dynos also have computers and all the appropriate cables to transfer (or develop) maps to your bike. The beauty of a system like this is that as you modify your bike further, you can create new maps to fit your engine's needs. Also, if you don't like the changes you made to one map, with the push of a button you can revert to your previous one. How about that for twenty-first-century technology?

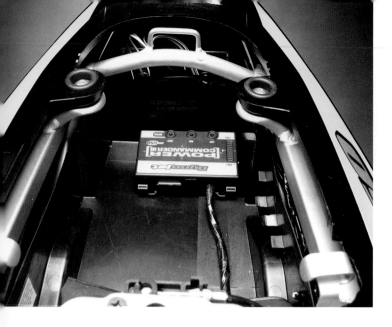

Snugly tucked away in the back of the trunk, the Power Commander leaves plenty of room for access to its USB port without compromising your storage.

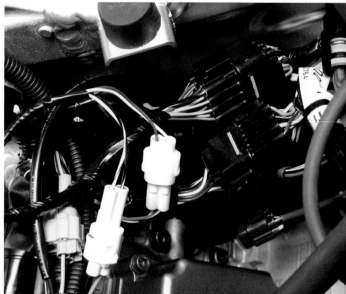

Installations don't get much easier than this. Plug the two black connectors into the wiring harness and select the proper white connectors. Use zip-ties to keep everything in place.

Not too long ago, bulky adapters were required to connect your computer to your Power Commander. Now, it's as simple as plugging in a USB cable.

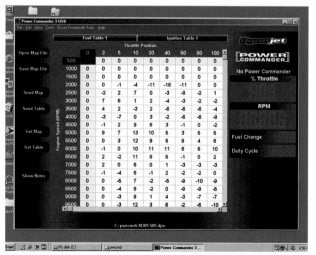

Engine Speed (RPM)	0	2	5	10	20	40	60	80	100
500	0	2	0	0	0	0	0	0	0
1000	0	0	0	0	0	0	0	0	0
1500	0	0	0	0	0	0	0	0	0
2000	0	0	-1	-4	-11	-16	-11	0	0
2500	0	-2	2	7	0	-3	-8	-2	1
3000	0	7	6	1	2	-4	-3	-2	0
3500	0	4	2	-3	2	-6	-6	-6	-4
4000	0	-3	-7	0	3	-2	-6	-6	-8
4500	0	-1	2	9	6	3	-1	0	-2
5000	0	9	7	13	10	5	3	5	5
5500	0	0	3	12	9	5	8	4	6
6000	0	-1	0	10	11	11	6	6	10
6500	0	2	-2	11	8	5	-1	0	2
7000	0	2	0	6	0	1	-3	-3	-3
7500	0	-1	-4	6	-1	2	-2	-2	0
8000	0	0	-5	7	-2	-6	-9	-10	-9
8500	0	0	-4	8	-2	0	-8	-8	-6
9000	0	0	-3	9	1	4	-3	-7	-7
9500	0	0	-3	12	3	6	-2	-6	-10

C: pwrcmdr\389.509.djm

Detail-oriented folks will be in heaven with the Power Commander software. You can twiddle with the fuel and ignition maps to your heart's content. If you're of a Mac persuasion, the application runs fine under Virtual PC.

EFI Tuning with Teka

Time: 1 hour

Tools: Basic mechanic's tools, box fan

Talent:

Cost: $$$$$

Parts Required: Factory Pro Tuning Teka Unit

Tip: Begin with small throttle openings first and then move up the scale.

PERFORMANCE GAIN: The ability to find the best possible power at any rpm without the need for a computer.

Some riders would rather be able to alter the stock fuel injection maps without all the work of installing an additional black box, attaching it to a computer, and downloading fuel maps. The whole injection-tuning process would be much quicker and easier if the curve could be modified real-time without shutting off the bike. Well, Factory Pro Tuning has developed the Teka Suzuki Injection Adjuster for just those reasons. Aside from the initial setup of your bike, you can simply plug the Teka into your bike, adjust the settings, and keep on riding. Dyno tuning can be accomplished in minimal time, since the fuel map can be adjusted and tested immediately. Unfortunately, the Teka isn't the ultimate miracle, since it is only available for some models. So, if you own one of those bikes, consider yourself lucky.

The initial setup of the Teka on a bike begins with setting the stock engine control unit (ECU) back to the OE settings. (The Teka can't read the settings.) The Suzuki Access Port connector needs to be taken out of its hiding place under the seat on the left-hand side of the bike, behind a side panel. Make sure the ignition is off. Connect the Teka to the access port and turn on the ignition. Toggle the engine cutoff switch to run. Once the Teka has powered on, you want to zero out all of the settings. Begin with the Idle Adjustment, and select "All" from the menu. Hit "Enter." Using the left and right arrow keys, set the numeric value to 0. Now, move on to the Run Adjustment menu. Beginning with the 10 percent level, set the value to 0. Repeat this for 25, 50, and 75 percent throttle ranges, setting each to 0.

After the ECU has been zeroed, you'll start adjusting the mixture. Unlike carburetors on which you want to set the main jet size first, setting up the EFI begins at the smallest throttle openings and moves up. Warm up the engine and set the idle speed as low as possible. Select "Idle Adjust" on the Teka and then select "All." Since you've already zeroed the ECU, you can now change the mixture with the right arrow. Set the value to +20 and hit "Enter." The engine note may change as the mixture for each cylinder gets reprogrammed. Fiddle with the adjustments until you get the smoothest-sounding idle at the fastest idle speed. Suzuki inline fours generally end up set between +10 and +40.

The next step is to set the 10 percent throttle range. If you're wondering why you should begin here, consider this: What throttle range are you using when you enter a corner at high rpm? You're starting off closed, and then opening the throttle to move from deceleration to acceleration. Remember how the first couple of generations of motorcycle fuel injection were accused of coming on the throttle abruptly? Now you're starting to get the picture.

So, setting the 10 percent throttle mixture to mimic corner entry is accomplished by tuning for smoothest operation at 9,000 rpm with no load (i.e., in neutral). Still confused? Entering a corner at neutral throttle, or shifting from deceleration to acceleration, requires that your engine run well at high rpm with no load. Move through the menus to the 10 percent adjustment. Now, with the engine in neutral, raise the rpm to 9,000 and hold it steady. The left and right arrows on the Teka will adjust the mixture immediately. You don't need to stop or hit "Enter" until the engine has smoothed out with the rpm increased. Keep a careful eye on the thermostat. You'll ideally want to set the mixture with the temperature between 180 and 190 degrees Fahrenheit—normal operating temperature. Use a box fan to move some air through the radiator.

The remainder of the tuning with the Teka can be done with the dyno that's built into the seat of your pants, or on one of Factory's EC997 Eddy-Current dynos located in race shops around the country. What you'll be judging is the "feel" of the bike as you snap open the throttle. With the engine warmed up, the bike in first gear, and the tach at a steady 5,000 rpm, snap the throttle open a quarter of the way and judge its response. Now, with the Teka, adjust the 25 percent range +20 and repeat the test. Was it better or worse? If it was better, try +40. Dial it back to -20 if it was worse. Keep making these changes until you experience the best response to the throttle snap. When you're satisfied, move on to the 50 and 75 percent tests. Make sure you're wearing your riding gear, since your bike is bound to be pawing at the air on many of these runs.

Finally, for the 100 percent throttle adjustment, you'll want to go out for a real ride. Many riders will mount the Teka to their bike for this series to allow on-the-fly adjustments.

You'll be holding the throttle wide open at high rpm (but not in first gear). Although the track is the best place for this type of testing, you can achieve the same results by testing on the same piece of road, in the same gear, one change after another. Keep making changes to the Teka in steps of +/-20 until you find the sweet numbers.

While this form of performance tuning may seem strange to a generation of sportbike riders—riders who've grown up with dynamometers located within a reasonable riding distance (in most states)—tuning by feel is a noble tradition of motorcycle racing. The beauty of the Teka and fuel injection, though, is that you don't have to tear your bike apart to make each change. You can learn a lot about tuning in a very short period of time, by making—and tracking—multiple changes. Instead of looking at graphs that tell you your bike should feel faster, you've tuned it yourself, literally by the seat of your pants, for maximum drivability so it will launch forward when you twist the loud tap.

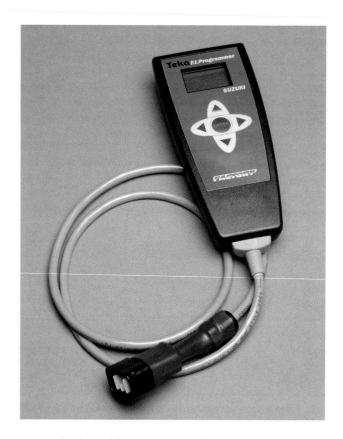

Here it is, the Teka. Good things come in small packages. You can mount it to your bike when you're tuning. Try that with a laptop.

The tuning begins here with the Idle Adjustment. Once you've roughed in the mixture with the "All" function, you can fine-tune each cylinder if it's still not idling smooth enough for you.

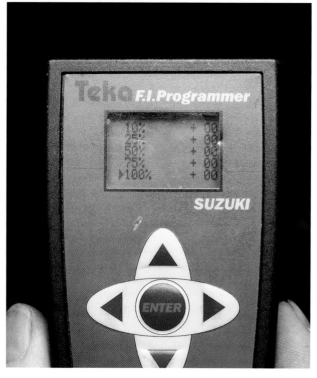

The position of the throttle is of primary importance when tuning with a Teka. Begin at the bottom end and progress to WFO.

EFI Tuning with Yoshimura EMS

 Time: 1–2 hours

 Tools: Allen sockets, sockets, extender, ratchet, torque wrench, Phillips screwdriver, laptop with serial port

 Talent: ▮ ▮ ▮

 Cost: $$$$$

 Parts Required: Yoshimura EMS, Yoshimura EMS hub and accessories

 Tip: For a good starting point, use fuel maps created for your exhaust system, if available.

 PERFORMANCE GAIN: The ability to try three different map sets on the road/track to find the best possible power at any rpm.

Yoshimura has taken its EMS (engine management system) beyond the mere controlling of fuel and ignition maps—as if that weren't enough to begin with. The current-generation Yoshimura EMS features an optional accessory hub for connecting gizmos such as:

- A shift light (to warn you of impending redline),
- A three-position map switch (for instant access to three different, user-adjustable map sets),
- A clutchless shifter (for full-throttle, don't-back-off shifting), a gear-dependent map offset (for tweaking curves based on the gear you're in),
- And an extension cable (to move the data port outside of the bodywork).

Still, at its heart, the EMS' purpose in life is to help your engine put out more power.

As with the Power Commander, installation of the EMS is incredibly easy. In fact, since both systems use OE wiring harness connectors, you should follow the instructions for installing the base unit as outlined in Project 73. Once you have mounted the EMS, you need to verify that the stock throttle position sensor (TPS) is correctly calibrated. If you fail to do this, your EMS may give you an overrich or lean condition, resulting in poor performance. To set the TPS, turn on the ignition without starting the bike. With the throttle completely closed, the LED on the bottom left of the EMS should light up fully. With the throttle open to the stop, the top left LED should light up fully. If you have any flicker of the LEDs, the TPS needs to be calibrated for the EMS via

Yoshimura's software. In the main window of the application, select "Calibrate TP Sensor" from the EMS Utilities menu. By holding the throttle closed and clicking "Set" you tell the software what reading of the TPS' potentiometer equates with a closed throttle. Repeat the procedure for 100 percent throttle. You can now run your bike with the stock EMS maps or begin installing your own with your computer link.

If you're just going to download a prerecorded map for your bike, you can do this pretty easily with your personal computer—assuming you can cozy it up next to your bike. If you're planning on developing maps for your specific setup, you'd probably be better off going to a shop that already knows how to tune via an EMS. Since carrying your laptop around to make adjustments to your maps might be a bit too troublesome, consider adding the multimap switch listed in the accessories above. Using the switch, you can rough the tuning in on the dyno and program three variations, and then hit the track or your favorite road to sample the maps.

This illustrates why you'll want to install the accessory hub to get the most out of your EMS. After plunking down your dough, installation is easy. Simply remove the protective cover on the EMS and plug in the hub's connector, and screw in the keepers. The best place to mount the hub is right on top of the EMS, since the cable is fairly short. Although the hub looks similar to USB hubs for your home computer, you can't just plug an accessory into any port. Specific tools require specific ports.

Installing the Three-Position Map Switch begins with plugging its connector into port number 3. Run the switch wiring along the bike's harness to the triple clamp. Yes, you'll need to remove the tank and the right-hand bodywork. Mount the switch above the front brake lever with the included bolt, route the cable into the frame, and connect it to the wire you ran from the hub. Zip-tie everything down, and you're ready to rock.

If only installing jet kits were this easy. Hook up the connectors to the ones on the wiring harness, and you're done.

Keep everything neat with zip-ties. Make sure the EMS' wires stay clear of anything that could pinch or abrade them.

While the connection to the EMS could be a little more elegant, you'll be glad you sacrificed the trunk space when you begin hooking up the gadgets.

The Three-Position Switch's clean design keeps it out of the way, yet close enough to use at speed. The map changes take place immediately. You could store a street map, a track day map, and a Friday night drag map and switch between them without attaching your bike to a computer.

Installing a Timing Advancer

Time: 30 minutes–2 hours

Tools: Wrenches, sockets, ratchet, gasket scraper, gasket sealer, impact wrench (if required), puller (if required), rear stand (optional)

Talent:

Cost: $

Parts Required: Aftermarket ignition advancer, side-cover gasket

Tip: If the ignition advancer for your bike requires the removal of the flywheel, you must use an impact wrench to loosen the bolt to the crankshaft.

PERFORMANCE GAIN: Snappier throttle response and horsepower increase in portions of rpm range.

Since tuners can no longer just make a simple modification (such as bolting on an aftermarket pipe) to reap double-digit horsepower gains in today's well-designed sportbikes, they resort to making several smaller, incremental changes. Installing an ignition advancer or an adjustable ignition trigger is one such modification that may seem to reap minimal gains. However, when combined with other small gains, you will find that you've made your bike significantly faster.

As I've said before, street bikes are tuned to a compromise since they need to function in a variety of riding styles and situations, including altitude, weather, and performance conditions. The manufacturers also need to factor in things like EPA emissions requirements when setting up fuel and ignition curves for their bikes. Any modifications you make to your bike will also affect the way it responds to the OE ignition settings. Many aftermarket companies make bolt-on ignition triggers to help massage the onset of your spark. While some companies select a uniform advance of 5 degrees from stock, others, such as Factory Pro Tuning, extensively test a range of advancement to find what works best for a particular model. Consequently, some of Factory's kits feature advances of 2, 4, or 6 degrees. For popular models more prone to being hopped up, adjustable timing triggers are also available.

If your bike is relatively stock with, say, just pipe and jet kit/EFI upgrade, go with the advancer created for your bike. If you've bumped up compression or added lumpier or retimed cams, buy the adjustable model and plan on some dyno time to discover what setting works best. Some things to consider about ignition advancers: The improvement in power doesn't come in the same place from model to model. Some improve the low end while others add to the top. Generally, most will improve your throttle response, particularly at partial throttle. According to Marc Salvisberg of Factory Pro Tuning, in stock form, "part-throttle ignition advance is deficient in relation to the optimum." This translates into a bike that feels more willing to roar out of corners, even if the actual horsepower improvement is relatively small. If you're concerned about what power gain you'll see—and where—ask the manufacturer before you plunk down your cash.

Installing an ignition advancer ranges from blindfolded easy to downright maddening. For example, the ZX-6R shown here was a four-step process. Remove the bodywork, the side cover, and the stock ignition trigger. Step four? Reverse. Then you get into bikes like the SV650 or Hayabusa that require the flywheel to be removed, which is a little more involved. Finally, GSX-Rs need to have the pulse coil (the pickup) remounted, which is a good bit more complicated than a simple bolt-on operation.

Begin with your bike on a rear stand. Remove any bodywork necessary to access the side panel. If your bike requires that you remove an engine cover that may spill oil, try leaning the bike over against a wall to send the oil to the other side of the engine. Make sure it is steady before moving on. Remove the appropriate engine cover. Put the engine in gear before unbolting the ignition trigger. Once unbolted, the trigger should slip right off. However, check its orientation before removing it.

Slide the new ignition trigger into position and double-check that it is oriented correctly. Torque the retaining bolt to spec. Carefully clean the gasket mating surfaces on the engine and the side cover. You may find a razor blade helpful in removing troublesome bits of material. Apply just enough nonhardening gasket sealer to the mating surfaces and place the gasket in position. Bolt the cover in place using a crisscross tightening pattern. Button up the bodywork and you're done.

CARBURETION, EFI, EXHAUST, IGNITION, AND ENGINE

Remove the old ignition trigger by unbolting it. If oil collects and drips over the gasket mating surface, make sure you wipe it off before installing a new gasket.

The Factory ignition advancer is in place, and everything is cleaned up for the new gasket.

Installing an Aftermarket Ignition Module

Time: 6 hours

Tools: Standard mechanics tools

Talent: 🔧🔧🔧 – 🔧🔧🔧🔧

Cost: $$$$–$$$$$

Parts Required: Ignition module

Tip: A quick series of dyno runs will tell you which setting works best for your engine.

PERFORMANCE GAIN: More power regardless of the state of tune of your engine.

Owners of older sportbikes may feel a bit left out with all the attention going to the black boxes for the current fuel-injected bikes. Well, your salvation is at hand! Dynatek has developed ignition systems for many popular older bikes. These blue aluminum boxes replace the factory ignition. All of the company's Dyna 2000 systems include five advance curves for various states of basic engine modification. People who have bumped up their engines with turbochargers or big nitrous systems will appreciate the four retard modes.

You also get an adjustable rev limiter. Other features include a test mode for troubleshooting and a safety interlock input to either utilize the OE side stand switch or use as a quick shifter. A digital tachometer output powers your stock or aftermarket tach. Some kits even include sensors for paired cylinders 1–4 and 2–3 to allow for accurate timing of each cylinder pair. High-performance coils are even included in some kits.

Installing the Dyna 2000 takes place in two parts. First, you'll need to install the Dyna unit and its wiring harness. Remove the OE ignition module, mount the Dyna unit on the included bracket, and swap it for the stocker. Attach the Dyna's included wiring harness and route the wires along the stock harness to the components to which they'll connect. You will not be required to modify the stock harness. If your Dyna 2000 kit includes coils, mount them on the supplied bracket, then cut, and assemble the included spark plug wires.

The second part of installing the Dyna involves diving into your engine to replace the stock crank trigger and pickup coils. Replacing the trigger and coils will follow steps similar to those shown in Project 76. However, you'll need to press some of the wires out of the OE pickup harness before removing the pickup. Mount the Dyna crank trigger and pickups to the stock mounts. Align the pickup mounting plate according to the instructions specific to your model bike. Fine-tune the static timing by rotating the crank until the LED on the Dyna unit lights up. Verify in the instructions that the line on the trigger matches the recommended advance settings. If not, loosen the appropriate pickup on the bracket and move it slightly. Rotate the crank again, and repeat until the number 1-4 cylinder pairing is set. Then move on to the registration marks for the 2-3 cylinders and repeat. Button up the engine.

With the static timing set, you can start dialing in the ignition curve. The Dyna 2000 has five advance curves. Curves 1 through 3 are for four-valve engines; the settings are: 1 for stock, 2 for increased compression, and 3 for high compression. Curves 4 and 5 are stock and high-compression twin settings. For special applications, such as turbocharged or nitrous-injected engines, the four retard curves retard the ignition in 4-degree increments, covering 4, 8, 12, and 16 degrees.

Time spent setting up a Dyna 2000 will pay off in horsepower and a stronger-running engine. Even completely stock engines have shown improved power with a Dyna 2000.

This Dyna 2000 kit for the 1998–1999 ZX-9R includes a set of high-power coils and the sexy blue box that performs all the magic.

CARBURETION, EFI, EXHAUST, IGNITION, AND ENGINE

PROJECT 78

Understanding Plug Temperatures

Time: NA

Tools: : Magnifying glass, plug wrench

Talent: 👷👷👷👷

Cost: $

Parts Required: Spark plugs

Tip: You will rarely, if ever, need a plug that's hotter than stock.

PERFORMANCE GAIN: Optimal power output

Other than changing their spark plugs periodically, sportbike owners don't pay much attention to them. Reliability of both the plugs and the ignition systems on modern engines has made them pretty much a nonissue for stock bikes. However, if you start making some big changes to your engine, such as bumping compression, injecting nitrous oxide, or mounting a turbo, you've moved out of the realm of conditions that the original engineers considered when selecting the stock plug temperature.

Since many people struggle with the concept of hotter and colder plugs, let's take a moment to figure out exactly what a plug's temperature means. A hot plug does not make an engine run hotter. Rather, the heat range of a plug determines how hot the plug allows the engine to make it. In most engines, a spark plug's electrode (the center portion of the plug) protrudes slightly into the combustion chamber. When a plug is in the proper heat range for the tune of the engine, the tip of the electrode gets hot enough to burn off any combustion by-products that adhere to it. If a plug is too cold, layers of these chemicals build up as carbon deposits on the insulator. If this happens, the plug gap can gradually get smaller and smaller, until there is no gap for the spark to occur. In this situation, the plug is considered "fouled," and engine performance will be markedly degraded. At the other end of the heat scale, a plug that is too hot will appear white and chalky. It may also display pepperlike spots on the insulator—a sign of detonation (knocking or pinging). A close examination of the electrode will probably reveal a rounding of the formerly sharp edges at the tip. Since sparks prefer to jump from sharp edges, the quality of the spark is hindered.

When a plug is too hot, the primary risk is preignition, in which the glowing-hot plug ignites the charge before the spark does. Often, valuable power is being lost, but riders are unaware of it. Although preignition can *lead* to detonation, preignition should not be confused with detonation, which announces itself with knocking or pinging and can severely damage pistons. Detonation begins with the normal spark, but because of excessive compression and/or ignition advance, the fireball doesn't progress evenly out from the center. Rather, as the burning gases expand outward, the increasing pressure, and heat on the cylinder walls, causes a second, extremely rapid, spontaneous explosion that we hear outside of the engine. If you hear knocking, you should immediately find the source of the problem—be it too lean a mixture, too hot a plug, or too advanced an ignition curve—and remedy it before it damages your engine.

The spark plug's insulator is primarily responsible for determining the heat range. This insulator is not of the thermal kind. Instead, a spark plug's insulator is responsible for making sure that the spark doesn't jump to ground (the plug's threaded exterior), but to the tip of the electrode. However, this electrical insulator is also a thermal conductor, helping to draw heat away from the electrode's tip toward the water-cooled cylinder head. For example, although the tip of a cold plug will protrude into the cylinder the same amount as a hot one, a colder plug has a shorter (and possibly wider) insulator around the electrode where it connects to the outer barrel of the plug. Hot plugs have a longer insulator that leads further up into the plug's body, creating a longer thermal path.

Since your eyes are the tools you'll use for analyzing the subtle colors of your spark plugs, you might want to begin your studies with a more experienced mechanic who can point out the signs for you. To get completely accurate readings, you'll need to use fresh plugs. Just a few dyno runs or laps on the track will write the information you need onto the plugs. You're looking for a nice, even gray or tan on the insulator. The very end of the insulator may still be white, but it should still have the same surface texture as when new. If it shows signs of graininess or wear, the plug may be too hot. Overheating will also take the sharp edges off the end of the electrode, so look for a similar wear pattern. The differences are challenging to discern, but with practice, you'll acquire the knack.

From this angle it is impossible to tell which of these is hot or cold, but the difference could rob you of power. The thermal conductivity takes place inside the plug through the electrode's insulator.

CARBURETION, EFI, EXHAUST, IGNITION, AND ENGINE

Derestricting EFI Suzukis and ZX-12s

 Time: 30 minutes

 Tools: Tools to remove bodywork, No. 2 Phillips screwdriver, pliers, mat knife, wire stripper, terminal crimping pliers, electrical tape, zip-ties or double-stick tape, spade connectors, wire tap

 Talent:

 Cost: $

 Parts Required: Ivan's Performance Products Timing Retard Eliminator (Suzuki), Muzzys Bonneville Box (Kawasaki)

 Tip: The Muzzys Bonneville Box is unfortunately only for 2001 and 2002 ZX-12s

 ⚠ PERFORMANCE GAIN: The ability to go as fast as your bike is capable, plus increased bottom-end power on Suzukis.

A Muzzys Bonneville Box will uncork your stopped-up ZX-12, moving you that much closer to 200 miles per hour. *Muzzys*

Remember the howls of agony when sportbike enthusiasts found out that both the Hayabusa and ZX-12 had their ability to run at top speed neutered? While the limit placed on top speed made big news, Suzuki quietly slipped a different ignition map into the mix for the first four gears of its fuel-injected bikes. The people who noticed the acceleration difference in the first half of the throttle in lower gears still deserve to reclaim their lost acceleration as much as those riders in search of top speed. Fortunately, the aftermarket stepped in with two products. Ivan's Performance Products developed the Timing Retarder Eliminator (TRE) for fuel-injected Suzukis. The clever device tricks the ECU into thinking that the bike is always in fifth gear, so that the first four gears deliver the snappy response they should. A nice bonus is that the speed-limiting ignition curve in both the GSX-R1000 and the Hayabusa is eliminated. And it should be obvious that—in case the name of

Removing some bodywork, plugging in a doodad, and applying a zip-tie can be the quick route to motorcycle nirvana.

the famous salt flats doesn't bring visions of high speed to mind—a Muzzys Bonneville Box frees up the ZX-12's ability to run flat out.

Installing both of these dongles is painfully simple. The TRE installation consists of finding the right location on your particular model Suzuki, unplugging one connector on the wiring harness, and slotting the TRE inline. Finish up by zip-tying the unit securely in place. Want to check to see if the unit is working, without breaking the law? Start the engine and set the rpm at 2,500 with the fast idle control. If the rpm drop when you pull in the clutch, the unit is functional. Easy-peasy.

The Muzzys Bonneville Box requires a little more work but shouldn't take more than 30 minutes. Remove the tool tray under the rear cowl. For ease of access, pop the rubber retainers securing the ECU up and out of the fender. The computer should now pull free. Disconnect the larger of the two plugs on the ECU. (It should be on the right side of the bike when looking forward.) Using a mat knife, slit the tape wrap on the harness to expose about 6 inches of the wiring.

If you're colorblind, you should arrange for an assistant to help you with the next steps. You need to trace out three wires. Choose one of the several black-with-yellow-stripe ground wires that has easy access. Find the solid, light-blue wire. Be careful, because you have four blue wires to select from. Make sure yours is the lightest without a tracer stripe. (Just to confuse things, the correct wire *may* have silver or gold dots on it.) The third wire you'll be working with is yellow with gold dots.

With your wire stripper, cut the yellow wire about 2 inches from the plug and strip about 1/4 inch away from the part still attached to the plug. Crimp a male spade connector to the exposed wire. Fold the remaining yellow wire out of the way back to the harness. On the light-blue wire, press the wiretap onto the wire about 2 inches from the connector. Do the same to the black-and-yellow wire. Now plug the spade connectors in as follows: black to black/yellow, blue to blue, and yellow to yellow. Once you've remounted the ECU, tuck the Bonneville Box into the space to the left. Double-stick tape will keep everything in place.

Now, regardless of which derestricter you've chosen, go set some land speed records.

Shift Light/Digital Gear Indicator

Time: 1 hour

Tools: Basic mechanics tools to remove fairing, wire cutters

Talent:

Cost: $$

Parts Required: Rider Station's Acumen DG8 gear indicator, PD8 shift light, plug-in wiring harness specific to your bike

Tip: If an aftermarket wiring harness isn't available for your bike, you can buy units that splice directly into your stock wiring harness.

PERFORMANCE GAIN: Maximum power that comes from always knowing what gear you're in and when you're approaching redline.

More and more sportbikes are arriving in showrooms with shift lights integrated into the instrument cluster. Once you ride a bike with a shift light, you'll never want to go back to living without one. In performance riding situations, knowing when you're approaching the horsepower peak without having to glance at the tachometer can keep your attention where it should be—out in front of your rapidly accelerating motorcycle. While it might not be as obvious at first thought, having a gear indicator can be vitally useful when riding on an unfamiliar twisty road or racetrack. You'll never have to feel the indignity of letting your rpm drop too low for the exit of a corner again.

Until recently, installing these units required you to splice connections into your wiring harness. Rightfully, many riders who were interested in mounting these informative units to their bikes had second thoughts. Any modifications to part of the ignition system should be approached cautiously to keep unintended Bad Things from happening. Now, you simply order the correct wiring harness from Riderstation.com and proceed with a plug-and-play installation.

Before you begin unbolting parts, decide where you're going to mount the units. The gear indicator simply needs to be in quick-glance sight—probably right beside the instruments. The shift light should be mounted relatively high. On top of the instrument cluster should work for most applications. Consider riding position, too, when making these decisions.

Remove as much bodywork as necessary to access the back of the instrument cluster. On some bikes, such as the R6 shown here, the tank may also need to be tilted out of the way to allow access to the wiring harness. Simply plug the Acumen harness into the back of the instrument pod and route any additional wiring along the main wire harness to the engine compartment. Next, attach the plugs to the back of the Acumen gear indicator and shift light units. Secure the units via Velcro or double-stick tape. Any access wire should be coiled or folded neatly and zip-tied out of the way. Similarly, snug any wires that run into the engine compartment up to the main harness with zip-ties.

Since you need to access the back of the Acumen units with a small key to program them, you might want to leave the bodywork off the bike until you have everything set to your liking. To set the gear indicator, you first need to tell it how many gears your bike has. With the ignition on and the motorcycle in neutral, make sure the unit displays the "N" neutral signal. Insert the programming key in the back of the unit and hold until the "L" for learn is displayed. Release the programming key. Now, press and release the programming key once for every gear (i.e., six presses for six gears). When the correct number of gears is displayed, remove the programming key. In a few seconds the neutral sign will reappear. Note: Leave the ignition on, or you'll have to repeat the previous steps. Put on your riding gear, start the engine, select first gear and ride until the number one changes to three horizontal lines. Shortly after that, the number two will appear. *Slowly*, shift to neutral and then to second. Keep riding in second until the three lines appear followed by the number three. Simply shift to third gear and repeat until you've gone through all the gears. You

The beauty of the Acumen system is that you simply plug the gear indicator/shift light's harness into the back of the speedometer.

CARBURETION, EFI, EXHAUST, IGNITION, AND ENGINE

You change programming modes and enter information via the recessed button on the back of the unit.

don't need to ride fast, you can just putt along changing the gears. Once the unit has learned all of the gears, you can stop and turn off the ignition. Slick, huh?

Setting up the shift light is a little more complicated, since you need to program in both the start rpm for the shift light and the end rpm. However, you'll first need to calibrate the unit to your bike. Start and warm up your engine. With the engine running, press the programming key in the back of the unit for 10 seconds. After the LEDs flash in succession, the unit should stop with the number 1 LED (at about 7:00 on the dial) flashing. Let your engine idle and press the programming key once. The LEDs will cycle again and stop with number 3 flashing. Increase the rpm to 3,000 and hold steady while pressing the programming key. The LEDs will cycle and stop with numbers 1 and 2 lit up.

Now you have 30 seconds to begin to program the unit. While the number 1 LED is on, it means you're inputting when you want the unit to start to function. While the number 2 LED is on, it means you're programming the thousands (of rpm). Press the programming key the same number of times for thousands of rpm at which you want the display to begin. For fun, press it six times for 6,000 rpm. Wait three seconds, and the number 1 and number 6 LEDs will light. With the sixth LED illuminated, the unit is telling you that you are now programming the hundreds for the display. If you press the programming key five times, the unit will begin operation at 6,500—if you followed this example. Wait another three seconds and the number 7 LED comes on, signifying that you are going to program the end of the display. Follow the same steps to set the thousands and hundreds of rpm.

Finally, you get to program the center LED. The center and number 2 LEDs stay on, indicating you can now program the thousands. You get the picture. Once you've set the center LED, the unit will cycle and all of the LEDs will turn off. The unit is now ready for use. But wait, there's more! You can also set the shift light to have all of the LEDs come on at once or have them flash. This is accomplished by pressing and releasing the programming key. You have four options: scrolling with tachometer, flashing while scrolling, all lights on shift light, and all lights flashing shift light. Go ahead, have fun with this multipurpose shift light.

Yes, this bike already had a shift light. Just ignore it and look at how neatly the Acumen units fit in place.

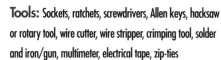

PROJECT 81

Installing Quick Shifter

Time: 4 hours

Tools: Sockets, ratchets, screwdrivers, Allen keys, hacksaw or rotary tool, wire cutter, wire stripper, crimping tool, solder and iron/gun, multimeter, electrical tape, zip-ties

Talent: ▮▮▮

Cost: $$$$$

Parts Required: Techtronics Quick shifter

Tip: Run your wires to their connection points and double-check everything *before* you begin cutting.

PERFORMANCE GAIN: Better acceleration due to less throttle drop between gears.

You may not believe this, but every time you shift gears, you're losing time. Racers know that each shift can cost a tenth of a second. Any time the power isn't being transferred to the rear wheel, you're losing time. The biggest culprit during the shift is the clutch, as it disengages and reengages. Power is wasted here. Since they live by the clock, pro racers have been performing clutchless upshifts for generations as a means of minimizing time lost in gear changes. All they do is preload the shifter and briefly roll the throttle off just enough to unload the transmission cogs before cranking the throttle back to the stops. During that moment when the engine and transmission are essentially freewheeling, the gear change almost magically takes place. When performed correctly, the rider is rewarded with seamless acceleration. When the timing of the events gets messed up, the result can be missed shifts or a loss of momentum.

Quick shifters follow the same theory for unloading the transmission to enable a shift without clutching. The kicker is that, with a quickshifter, you don't even need to roll off the throttle. Depending on which type of shifter you install, a sensor registers either the movement of, or an increase of pressure in, the shift linkage. When that trigger is tripped, the spark is killed for the few microseconds it takes for the tranny to snick into the next gear. The rider merely lifts up on the shifter (or presses down for GP-style race pattern). For the most accurate shifts, the pressure-sensing quickshifters are less prone to false cutouts, since the force of the linkage acting on the shift drum triggers the system. Systems that sense movement of the linkage can time the cutout incorrectly by misinterpreting the taking up of the free play in the linkage with the actual shift.

The most popular pressure-sensing quickshifter on the market, as of this printing, is the Techtronics Quickshifter, manufactured in the United Kingdom. Fortunately, U.S. buyers can pick up these units without the hassles of dealing with import regulations by ordering from Techtronics' exclusive domestic importer, Williamsville Competition.

Installing a Techtronics Quickshifter isn't challenging. It is, however, slow work if you want to do it right. Begin by removing the stock shift linkage. If your bike is one of the lucky models that has male Heim joints, you will only need to cut the 6-mm stud and the spacer tube. Simply hold the stock rod up next to the Techtronics and measure how much you need to shorten it. Next, unscrew the assembly and cut the measured amount off the stud. Don't remove the stud from the sensor unit to cut it. Trim the same amount from the aluminum spacer. Now reassemble the rod and tighten the end cap down with a pair of 10-mm wrenches.

Some bikes, such as the R6 shown in the photos, must have one of the Heim joints replaced. You may need to drill out the pressed-in mount to remove the joint. If your bike has aftermarket rearsets, you may find yourself adding spacers to the shifter pivot or any other components that may interfere with the Quickshifter's assembly. For example, the rod sensor is significantly larger in diameter than the rods used with many rearsets, resulting in interference with the frame.

The Techtronics Quickshifter is manufactured in two varieties. Most bikes press the rod to upshift. However, some bikes, notably the Yamaha R series, pull the rod. You need a sensor for your particular type of shift rod. The two are not interchangeable, so specify what bike you have when you order the part.

Getting your wiring in order is the part that will take your time. Mount the control module in the trunk with either zip-ties or hook-and-loop fastener. Plug in the Quickshifter's wiring harness and route the loose wires toward the engine compartment. The best route is usually the one followed by the stock wiring harness. Decide where you want to install the override switch and drill a 6-mm hole. Separate the various color wires in both the harness and the override switch and run them into the general area of the components to which they'll be connecting. Once you are happy with your routing, cut the wires to length. If you want a clean-looking engine compartment, cover the new wires with the included rubber sheaths and shrink tubing.

Using an eyelet, connect the brown wire to the battery's positive pole. The black wire in the harness goes to the negative pole. The yellow wire connects to the sensor in the shift rod. Some model bikes will require that a ground wire link the other end of the rod to a convenient ground point.

CARBURETION, EFI, EXHAUST, IGNITION, AND ENGINE

194

Tuck the control module safely away in the trunk to keep it out of the elements as much as possible. Make sure that nothing can press on the reset button while the unit is operating!

This stylish shift rod has the sensor built into it. The blue color signifies a sensor that is triggered by pulling. If the wire pigtail could rub or flex against the frame, zip-tie it safely out of the way.

Bikes with individual stick coils for each cylinder require that you find and cut the wire that powers the coils. Using piggyback spade connectors, attach the red wires from both the harness and the override switch to the coil side of the wire you cut. Take the green wires from the harness and override switch and connect them to the other half of the clipped wire in the same manner.

Although the technique is different for bikes with a pair of separate coils, the result is the same. Find and disconnect the positive lead going into the number 1 coil. (If, after consulting your factory service manual's wiring diagram, you're still uncertain, talk to your local bike dealer.) Using piggyback spade connectors, connect this line to two green wires in the harness and override. Attach the red wires to the positive pole of the number 1 coil. Repeat for the second coil with the blue wires linking to the positive lead and the orange wires to the coil.

Now, when the system is enabled, the control module will cut out the spark when you shift. Should the unit ever malfunction, flip the override switch, and you'll have your stock ignition back. Of course, you'll have to use the clutch. To activate the Quickshifter, simply upshift without backing

off the throttle. The shift rod has a sensitivity adjuster to allow you to fine-tune the force required to trigger the shift. To help you dial in the sensor, the control module will beep when it is triggered. With the engine off and the bike in second gear, lift the lever to shift to third. The system should beep after the free play has been taken up and you are pressing on the shift drum. When riding, a sensor that is too stiff will give notchy-feeling upshifts. Too soft a setting, and you may get missed shifts.

The Quickshifter's kill time is also adjustable. From the factory, the unit is set for a 70-millisecond kill. However, if you feel a pause during the shift, you can dial down the time slightly by removing the cap at the top of the module and turning the adjuster very slightly counterclockwise. Be forewarned—shorting the time too much will cause you to miss shifts.

Once you've gotten used to holding the throttle open while shifting, you'll never want to use the clutch again for upshifts. Unfortunately, Quickshifters work best at high rpm. Down low, the unit can cause balky shifts. So, you'll still have to keep your clutch hand in shape.

The piggyback spade connectors make hooking up the system easy. If you're using a crimp tool to mount the spades, make sure the wires are secure. Since you're dealing with the ignition, you should take the time to solder the connectors too.

For normal riding when you won't be using the Quick shifter, turn the unit off with the override switch. Mount the switch where it can be easily reached, yet isn't likely to have its setting inadvertently changed.

Installing a Tether Kill Switch

 Time: 1 hour

 Tools: Allen sockets, ratchet, Phillips screwdriver, wire cutter/stripper, soldering iron, shrink tubing or electrical tape, heat gun or lighter for shrink tubing

 Talent:

 Cost: $

 Parts Required: Tether kill switch

 Tip: The only way to guarantee a permanent connection is to solder the wires together.

 PERFORMANCE GAIN: The ability to "legally" run your bike at drag races (when it comes to your ignition key, now you can take it with you).

So, you want to take your sportbike to the local drag strip for grudge-match night. Although you won't have to make many changes to your bike, many tracks require that you have a kill switch installed to keep your bike from wreaking havoc should you and your bike go separate ways. You could use the tried-and-true method of drilling a hole in the engine cutoff toggle and mounting a bolt secured to a lanyard, but the problem with this setup is that it looks cheesy, and if you forget to take the lanyard off before you dismount, you destroy your engine cutoff switch. Why not mount a real "deadman's switch?"

Many drag-racing outlets sell kill switches similar to the one supplied here by APE Race Parts. Installation begins with finding room on your bar for the switch. Usually, you can slide the brake assembly and the throttle pod slightly to create a space for the kill switch bracket. Although it should be obvious, mount the switch so that the plug and lanyard face the rider to enable them to pull free. Mark where you intend to splice the wires from the kill switch into the wire harness. Next, disassemble the housing containing the OE engine cutoff switch. (Completely removing the switch and unplugging it from the wiring harness will make the next few steps much easier.)

Note the wire colors for the cutoff switch. Trace the wires back to your splice mark. Strip the cover and tape back to expose the wires. Cut either one of the two wires and strip approximately a quarter inch of the insulator off both pieces.

Bare a quarter inch of wire on the kill switch wiring. For those of you who prefer to use shrink tubing instead of electrical tape, slip the tubing over the wires before you solder them together.

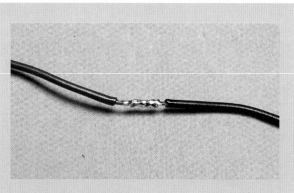

Soldering

Soldering wire connections will provide strong splices that should never fail, even in a vibration-prone environment. If, that is, the joints are properly soldered.

The most common novice mistake when wielding a soldering gun is melting the tip of the solder and then applying it to the wire splice. The difference in temperatures between the wires and the solder hardens the solder immediately just on the surface of the wires, resulting in a weak and chunky-looking connection. What's needed instead is molten solder flowing between the wires of the joint, forming a solid junction. To achieve this, heat the wires themselves with the soldering iron until they are hot enough to melt the solder. When this happens, capillary action actually pulls the molten solder into the spaces between the wires.

When selecting solder, be certain to use a flux-core solder. If unavailable, use plain solder and apply some flux directly to the two wires you are trying to join. Also consider the diameter of the solder and the wires you're joining. For fine-gauge wire, use a fine-gauge solder. Remember, you need to be able to melt the solder with the hot wires.

If these simple steps are followed, you'll end up with soldered joints that look like the photo above. If you've never soldered anything before, practice on some extra wire until you're comfortable enough to do it to wires on your bike.

Although you could use crimp connectors to install the kill switch, applications as vital to your well-being should be soldered. If a crimp connector vibrates loose at speed, your engine could shut down at an inopportune time—like when you're cranked over in a corner on those days you aren't at the drag strip. If you are unfamiliar with proper soldering technique, read the "Soldering" sidebar before moving on. Solder the wires together, making sure you have a solid connection. Cover the bare wire with shrink tubing and heat, or, using electrical tape, securely tape over the fresh connections. To clean up your installation, you can slide the rubber cover on the wiring harness over your new wires for an OE look.

Reinstall the switch housing and the new kill switch, and you're ready for the drag strip!

You'll probably need to move the components a smidgen on your handlebar to make room for the kill switch.

Determine what wires connect to the engine cutoff switch by opening the switch housing.

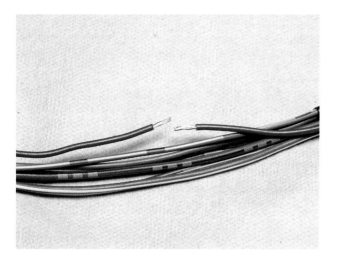

You only need about a quarter inch of exposed wire to solder your connection. Neatness is key here.

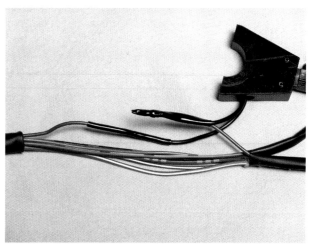

For a sano look, use heat shrink tubing to cover your soldered joints. You can slip a large piece of tubing over the whole wiring assembly as your final step.

Installing a Dry Nitrous System

 Time: 2 hours

 Tools: Allen sockets, ratchet, Phillips screwdriver, wire cutter/stripper, wire crimp tool, soldering iron, shrink tubing or electrical tape, drill, multimeter

 Talent: ▮▮▮

 Cost: $$$$

 Parts Required: Dry nitrous kit; nitrous oxide to charge the tank; Power Commander, Teka or Yoshimura EMS recommended

 Tip: Dry nitrous systems should only be mounted on fuel-injected bikes.

 PERFORMANCE GAIN: Twenty horsepower at the push of a button.

COMPLEMENTARY MODIFICATIONS: Install a full-throttle switch to prevent operation at partial throttle, install an rpm-activated, nitrous kill switch to prevent hitting rev limiter with gas flowing.

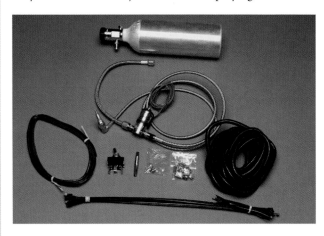

Here is Schnitz Racing's complete dry nitrous kit with a small bottle to hide in your tail section.

If you're looking to pump up the horsepower of your sportbike, nitrous oxide (N$_2$O) probably offers the best bang for the buck around. However, this power doesn't come without its costs. First, unlike fitting big-bore pistons, the power increase can only occur at full throttle. Also, the amount of nitrous you can use depends on the size of the bottle. When the bottle is dry, you're back to the same old engine you've always had (although this could be seen as an advantage for a bike that must also serve commuter duty). Second, if you tune your nitrous system wrong or get too greedy with the power output, your engine may start tossing internal components through its cases.

Nitrous oxide is a molecule consisting of two parts nitrogen to one part oxygen. When exposed to the heat inside the combustion chamber, the bond between the nitrogen and the oxygen breaks down. Since nitrogen is inert (meaning it is nonreactive with other chemicals), its role is over at this point. The oxygen, however, allows more fuel to burn, producing bigger explosions and, consequently, more power. So, look at it this way: Nitrous oxide is essentially more air in the combustion chamber. Why is this important? Because we know that running an engine too lean can do Very Bad Things to the pistons, plugs, and valves. Run an engine excessively lean, and it can blow up from the early detonation of the air/fuel charge.

In the past, nitrous systems required that you inject both the nitrous and extra gasoline into the intake tract to control the mixture when you're on the bottle. These systems are commonly called "wet" systems because of the addition of fuel. The advent of fuel injection on the majority of sportbikes has created a surge in the use of "dry" nitrous systems. In this case, only nitrous oxide is injected. While simplifying the installation and setup of nitrous on a bike, dry systems do have one big drawback: A dry system should only be used to add between 20 and 40 horsepower maximum. Go bigger, and you'll grenade your engine, since the stock fuel injection won't be able to deliver enough fuel to keep the mixture from going overly lean. Once you become addicted to the rush of acceleration from whacking open the bottle, you must resist the urge to add just a couple more horsepower. If you don't have that much self-control, just install the wet system. A final warning: Only buy a dry system from a reputable dealer with a background in drag racing. The system shown here is sold by Schnitz Racing.

A dry nitrous system works in two ways. First, it cools the intake charge, making the mixture much denser. You see, nitrous oxide exits the injector in a liquid state. As it almost instantly evaporates into a gas, it cools the air in the intake significantly. (Don't spray liquid nitrous oxide on your skin. You could get frostbite.) The EFI's temperature sensor in the air box will notice this change and richen the mixture to take advantage of the denser air. Second, it adds a modicum of extra oxygen to the mix.

The nozzle fits nicely into the Ram-Air duct here. The distance from the temperature sensor and throttle bodies ensures that the nitrous completely changes from a liquid to a gas before reaching them.

Begin your installation by stripping off your bike's bodywork, tank, and seat(s). Before you mount anything, think through where you want all the components to go—even plan how you'll route the wiring. To be effective, a dry nitrous system's nozzle needs to be as far upstream in the intake tract as possible. Plumbing the nozzle into the Ram-Air system before the air box is an ideal place. If you don't have room there, mount the nozzle in the very front of the air box, as far away from the throttle bodies as possible. You want the nitrous to have enough time to convert to a gaseous state and cool the air before it reaches the throttle bodies.

Once you've selected the nozzle's mounting point, look for the best way to run the braided steel supply line back to the solenoid that controls the nitrous flow. The best place is usually along the stock wiring harness. If you choose this route, make sure you cover the steel braiding with a spiral plastic brake-line cover or it could wear through and short out your electrical system. Find a convenient place to mount the solenoid. You'll want to zip-tie or bolt it securely in place so that it doesn't rattle around. When you're certain about the route for the nitrous supply line, you can drill and tap the Ram-Air duct or air box for the nozzle.

Tucked safely away under the rear bodywork, the solenoid is secured to the frame with zip-ties. Note the padding between solenoid and the frame.

Deciding where to place the nitrous bottle can be tricky. If you want to be able to completely hide it so that nobody knows you are running nitrous, a preferred location is a clean space in the tail section under the pillion. This, however, will limit the amount of nitrous you can carry. If you want everyone to know you're on the bottle, you can craft a bracket to mount it above the passenger seat or hang it off the side of the tail section. Whichever location you choose, make sure that the bottle is away from any source of heat. As the bottle gets hot, pressure will increase to the point that the solenoid might not fire or—even worse—the bottle's safety valve releases the nitrous into the atmosphere. You need to consider the proper orientation of the bottle. A nitrous bottle has a siphon tube inside it that must be angled to the bottom of the bottle to pick up the liquid nitrous. If you have the tube at the top, you lose much of the benefit of a dry system.

When wiring the system, you want to place the main power switch in a place where it won't be inadvertently bumped. If you honk your horn at someone who pulls out in front of you and accidentally switch the system on, you could be in for a big surprise. Whether you choose to place the main

Stainless-steel lines can saw through wires, or even the frame, so cover it with plastic or tape. This cool wiring cover was provided in the Schnitz kit.

switch in a place that's easy to get to or out of sight depends on whether you want others to know you have a system installed. The simplest way to wire the system is to run a positive, 12-volt switched power to the solenoid. Run the negative pole from the solenoid to the main switch. The remaining two connections to the switch are: the center common ground that goes into the wiring harness for the horn, and the horn ground. What this enables is for the switch to toggle between activating the horn and the nitrous. On bikes that send 12-plus volts to the horn instead of connecting to ground, you can still follow this wiring with the single change of connecting the solenoid to ground instead of a switched power.

Before you attempt to run the system with nitrous, you need to make sure that everything works. With the valve on the bottle *closed*, turn on the ignition and the nitrous main switch. When you press the horn button, you should hear the solenoid click. Never trigger the nitrous system without the engine running. If you do, you could experience a powerful backfire when you start the engine. Your next step should be tuning the system on a dyno that has an exhaust gas sniffer.

Install the smallest nitrous jet that came with your system into the nozzle. When the engine is warmed up, do a dyno run without the nitrous. After this baseline is complete, make a run using the nitrous. Only press the horn button and the nitrous at full throttle. Do not allow the engine to hit the rev limiter with the nitrous flowing. (A quick shifter that cuts the ignition for microseconds while you shift is safe, though.) Both of these could result in a powerful backfire and possible injury. After your nitrous run, look at the exhaust readings to make sure the mixture did not go too lean. If the reading is lean, or even borderline, you will need to richen the fuel curve for wide-open throttle with one of the aftermarket modules. Remember that at speed, the Ram-Air system will be cramming more atmosphere into the air box than when the bike is stationary on the dyno. This means that a lean mixture will get even leaner at speed.

Other items to consider: If you decide you want more power out of your dry nitrous system, select a larger jet for the nozzle, but remember to limit your boost of power to 40 horsepower or less. You should use factory ignition curves when running nitrous oxide. Advancing the timing can cause damaging detonation. Use 90 octane or better fuel to prevent detonation. Never, ever use nitrous in first gear unless you want to smoke your tire or find out what your bike feels like when it's lying on your chest.

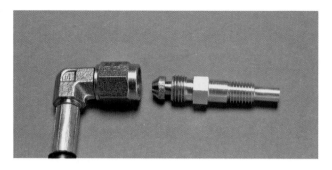

The nitrous oxide jet is installed between the nozzle and the supply line fitting.

A big 2 1/2-pound bottle for lots of nitrous runs! The bottle is angled downward so that the siphon tube will draw every last bit of the liquid nitrous oxide.

Close study of this diagram reveals that the basic dry nitrous system is pretty simple to wire. *Schnitz Racing*

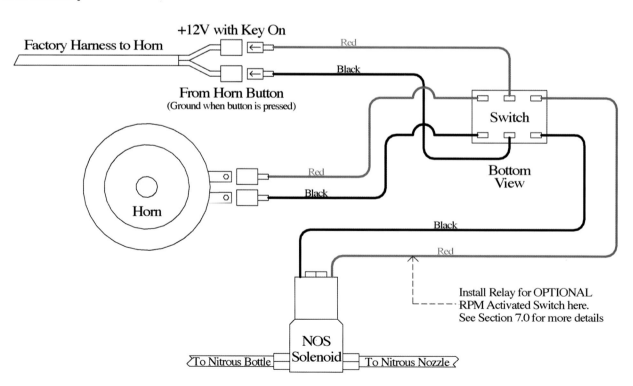

Installing a Wet Nitrous System

Time: 6 hours

Tools: Allen sockets, ratchet, Phillips screwdriver, wire cutter/stripper, wire crimp tool, soldering iron, shrink tubing or electrical tape, drill, multimeter, silicone sealer

Talent: ♛ ♛ ♛ ♛ ♛

Cost: $$$$$

Parts Required: Wet nitrous kit, nitrous oxide to charge the tank, Pingle petcock, silicone sealer, Teflon-based liquid thread sealer

Tip: Wet nitrous systems operate independently of the carburetion or EFI systems..

PERFORMANCE GAIN: Obscene amounts of horsepower at the push of a button.

COMPLEMENTARY MODIFICATIONS: Upgrade cooling system to handle increased heat generated by engine.

So, you're ready for some big horsepower. You read over the dry nitrous installation and knew that you'd never be happy with a mere 20–40 hp boost. Well, this is where you learn how to pump some really sick horsepower out of your engine—be it relatively stock or otherwise. Unlike a dry nitrous system, a wet system functions completely separate from the rest of the fuel delivery system. Thus, you don't have to change anything in the way your bike is running in order to get the most out of your nitrous system. (With a dry system, you are strongly encouraged to richen your fuel map for wide-open throttle to handle the additional oxygen provided by the nitrous oxide.) You will control the amount of fuel fed to your engine during the dyno tuning portion of your installation.

To work its magic, a wet nitrous system needs to inject both the additional fuel and the nitrous between the throttle bodies (either carburetors or EFI bodies) and the cylinder head. The most common place to mount the foggers that accomplish this task is on the boots connecting the carbs to the manifolds. However, what good hot-up doesn't have a little controversy surrounding it? Some tuners swear that mounting the foggers in the boots is fine. Others say that the repeated heat/cold cycles (since nitrous is very, very cold) cause the boots to age prematurely and crack. This, they feel, could lead

to vacuum leaks and/or problems with your nitrous system. How do these folks recommend getting the nitrous and fuel into the engine? They drill and tap the head itself, placing the fogger tip directly into the intake ports. For the average rider, though, the boot method should be tough enough to handle the stress. Still, any time you dive into your engine for maintenance, take a gander at the boots to make sure they're in good condition.

As you're stripping your intake system down to the boots, pause to make sure that you have clearance for the fogger bodies. People usually mount the fogger nozzles on top of the boot, but if there isn't enough room, mounting them below will be fine. Remove the boots and drill a 3/16-inch hole in each. If your kit includes a tap, you can use it to cut threads into the boot. If not, you'll be able to carefully thread in the nozzles themselves. Before you remount the boots, make sure that the nozzle tips are pointing directly down into the engine. Remount the boots and foggers.

Now comes the biggest challenge in the installation. Modern sportbikes have very little room in the engine compartment to mount all the components of a nitrous system. You need to plan carefully so that everything will fit. Since many bikes are fuel-injected with a pump mounted inside the tank, you probably don't think you need to install an auxiliary pump to deliver fuel to the nozzles. You'd be wrong, though. You can't starve the engine for fuel when on the bottle—unless you want to ventilate your pistons. So, unless the nitrous-kit manufacturer says you can get away with using the stock pump, you need to install a pump—just like those folks with gravity-fed carburetors.

Find a place on the bottom of your tank for a Pingle petcock. Make sure that there is enough clearance below the tank. Have a reputable performance shop weld a nipple onto the tank to accommodate the petcock. If your bike has an external pump or no pump at all, you can simply install a T-fitting into the fuel line to run to the nitrous system's pump.

Working back from the fogger nozzles, trace a route for the braided steel lines to a convenient place for the distribution blocks and solenoids. Keep your lines organized. Blue connectors are for nitrous oxide and red are for fuel. Before you attach the lines to the nozzles, be sure to install the recommended nitrous and gas jets into the connector. (The safest approach is to begin with the smallest horsepower increase your kit offers.) Be sure to lube the threads on the fittings with a Teflon-based *liquid* sealer. Do not use Teflon tape. Take care not to allow any dirt into the lines while assembling the system. A clogged nitrous jet will make the mixture overly rich, causing your bike to lose power when you hit the button. A plugged fuel jet will result in a lean condition, with possibly catastrophic results for that cylinder.

The kit provided for this project by Nitrous Express included mounting brackets for the solenoids. To mount

201

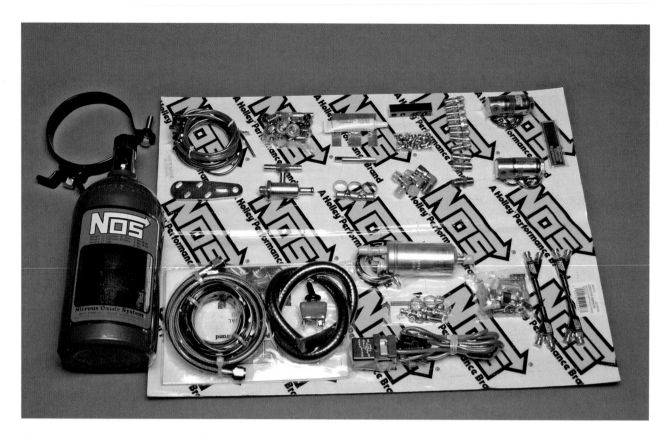

A Nitrous Oxide Systems wet system comes with all these parts and more. Install it correctly, and you'll get the ride of your life only at full throttle.

them, you'll need to drill a hole in the mounting surface. Depending on the location, you can either bolt or rivet the bracket in place. Since the solenoids have directional flow, pay special attention to their labels when you're connecting the lines. Run the nitrous supply line back to where you plan on mounting the bottle. Read the section in the preceding project for tips on properly securing the bottle. Connect the red fuel lines to the fuel pump and run the lines to where they'll connect with the gas tank. Once you have all of the braided steel lines in place, cover all portions of it that run along the wiring harness or any other parts that could be abraded by the metal mesh. (See the preceding project for more on protecting the wires.)

Wiring this Nitrous Express wet system isn't any more complicated than on a basic dry one. First, you need to install the included microswitch in a place that it is triggered only when the throttle is completely open and the nitrous system is powered. When this system is armed, all you have to do is crank the throttle to the stop—and hang on. However, if you prefer to manually engage the system, simply wire a dedicated button (or the horn button) in line with the main power switch. Just make sure that you take the power for the fuel pump from the hot side of the pushbutton, since you want the fuel pump to be up to pressure when you trigger the bottle.

When you activate the nitrous system with the microswitch (or pushbutton, if installed), a relay sends the power from the battery to the solenoids, assuring that the solenoids get full power. So, the relay uses three connections. One goes to the positive pole of the battery. Another goes to the wide-open-throttle microswitch. The last goes to the

positive connections of both solenoids. A fourth wire can connect to an optional fuel pressure kill switch to keep the nitrous from running if there is a problem with the fuel pump.

Before trying your first nitrous shot, you want to test that the system works. Either on the dyno or out on the road, switch the system on. Make sure the nitrous bottle's valve is closed so that none can be released. Now run the engine wide open in third gear. When all the air has been expelled from the fuel lines, the bike will abruptly lose power as the mixture goes way over rich. If this doesn't happen after a couple of passes, check all of your electrical connections and repeat the test. When everything works, you're ready to run the system with nitrous.

Here are two of the three ways you can get your nitrous and fuel mixture into the intake tract. The preferred method (if you have room), is to mount a set of aluminum manifolds. If you don't have room, you can screw the nozzle directly into the rubber boot and add a new inspection to your maintenance routine. *Photo courtesy of Nitrous Oxide Systems*

The aluminum manifolds make for a clean and easy nitrous system installation. *Photo courtesy of Nitrous Oxide Systems*

Many current generation sportbikes don't leave you enough room to install extra manifolds or mount the nozzle in the boot, leaving you to drill and tap the head as on this Hayabusa. *Photo courtesy of Nitrous Express*

When using a wet nitrous system, you need to be careful never to lug the engine. To play it safe, never activate the nitrous below 4,000 rpm. Otherwise, you risk an expensive backfire. The spark plug heat range for nitrous for NGK plugs will have a "9" in the plug number. Most street bikes currently ship with this temperature plug. Also, do not use platinum-tipped spark plugs. The gap is too small, delivering a spark kernel too small to be effective at the pressures nitrous exerts on the cylinder. If you plan on running more than 50 horse-power of boost, you've entered the realm of race fuel. You'll need to use race gas with the highest "Motor" octane level you can find. For the most accurate mixture with a Nitrous Express system, the bottle pressure should be at 1,000 psi. If the pressure is too high, the mixture will be leaner. Too cool and it'll be rich. Riders who really want to know what's going on with their system will install a pressure gauge on the bottle end of the system.

Mount the solenoids on brackets close to the engine compartment. The color coding of all of the lines makes it almost impossible to mix up the nitrous and gasoline.

Engine Break-In

Time: 2 hours

Tools: Ignition key

Talent:

Cost: None

Parts Required: New or rebuilt engine

Tip: Avoid engine damage by not lugging your engine during in the first 1,500 miles.

PERFORMANCE GAIN: Properly seated rings will enable your engine to make maximum power.

When you turn the ignition key for the first time on a new or rebuilt engine, you have a window of opportunity to ensure that the engine makes the best power it can in the future. Paradoxically, the method you use to help ensure your bike's future horsepower output can also improve your engine's longevity. The approaches to breaking in engines are as varied as the owners of the bikes. However, the two extremes of the break-in continuum are represented by the "factory knows best" adherents and the "run it like you're going to race it" supporters. Neither of these approaches is certain to give you maximum horsepower, and one may actually damage your engine. As with many things in life, taking a more middle-of-the-road approach can deliver the power sportbike riders crave while not prematurely aging the engine.

So, what exactly occurs during engine break-in? The metal parts that must work directly with each other soften their hard edges until they mesh more easily. Also, break-in performs a vital heat-treating process. Heat cycling the parts in the confines of the engine—particularly round parts like pistons and cylinders—relieves residual internal manufacturing stresses. Most importantly, proper break-in will give the piston rings optimal seal in the cylinders

Piston rings seal the gap between the piston and the cylinder by using the buildup of pressure in the compression and expansion strokes of the piston. This pressure travels through the space between the cylinder wall and the piston to the ring, which holds itself in place due to its natural springiness. When the gas hits the ring, it presses it down into the bottom of the piston's groove, opening a slight gap between the top of the ring and the groove. The pressurized gases force their way between the top of the groove and the ring and ultimately work their way behind the ring on the innermost point of the groove. Here, as Kevin Cameron puts it in his book *Sportbike Performance Handbook*, "the gas pressure 'inflates' the ring by . . . pressing outward against the cylinder wall."

New or freshened cylinder walls have a crosshatch pattern honed into them that serves two purposes. First, the pattern retains oil to help lubricate the rings. Second, when the crosshatches are fresh they have sharp peaks and valleys that need to be worn down—as does the surface of the rings. In order to get the rings to seat against the cylinder wall, you need to run the engine hard enough to utilize the gas pressure forcing the rings against the walls. If you don't use enough force, the rings don't get worn in well enough to form a tight seal against the crosshatch. Use too much force, and heat builds up on the cylinder walls and rings, preventing a good seal. Cylinders with poor ring sealing will never produce the power of which they are capable, since the explosive charge "blows by" the rings, reducing combustion pressure.

Racers and engine builders will often break in engines on a dyno so that they have complete control over the process, but street riders can do a good job of breaking in a new engine if they follow a couple of simple rules. Fill the engine up to the top of its capacity with cheap, nonsynthetic, name-brand motor oil. You want the oil to be of a decent quality, so go with the big names. However, you're going to dump it really soon, so find it on sale. Next, heat-cycle your engine prior to riding it. Start the engine and vary the engine speed to between 1,500 and 3,000 rpm, so that the engine spins fast enough to pump lots of oil through. If you're breaking in a rebuilt engine, check for oil leaks while it warms up. As soon as the engine hits operating temperature, shut it down and let it return to ambient temperature. Repeat this process once more. The bike is now ready to be ridden.

Warm the engine again before you begin riding it. Avoid riding at a time of day where you will spend excessive time idling or riding at extremely low speeds. You want to be able to accelerate and decelerate without having to worry about other vehicles. Stay out of top gear for now. Out on the road, you want to vary your engine speeds, not holding any one rpm for too long. (One of the worst things you could do is go drone on the interstate at the same rpm for an hour.) Do not lug your engine at any time during the break-in process. Lugging is actually more damaging than excessive throttle at this stage!

When road conditions allow, do some one-half to three-quarter throttle acceleration runs from 6,000 rpm up to about 10,000 rpm. (Note: All of these rpm assume a redline of 15,000. If your bike's limit is lower, then reduce the rpm accordingly. If you're breaking in a twin, you'll need to adjust

No synthetic oil during engine break-in, if you want your rings to seat properly. Use cheap, high-quality motor oil.

engine's idle speed has begun to climb with the loosening of its internals. Adjust it to keep it in the 1,500 to 2,000 rpm range for now.

Now, your engine is ready for some runs to higher rpm. Keep the throttle at about three-quarters for now. (You'll get to go WFO before too long.) Run the rpm up a couple of thousand higher than before, and start from about 5,000 rpm. Continue to follow with that extended, cooling deceleration. Also continue to vary rpm and speed while avoiding top gear. After three or four runs up to 12,000 rpm, you're ready for some full-throttle fun. Beginning at 5,000 rpm, crank the throttle all the way to the stop, letting the engine run up to redline. Cool-close the throttle and let engine braking slow the bike down. Since you're running the engine up to the limit, you can generate some serious speed, so be smart about where and when you do this. Also, do it in lower gears, say second or third. Again, you'll want to repeat these acceleration runs three or four times, with extended cooling in between.

If you follow these steps, your engine should now be broken in. (Remember, this break-in technique is about the progressive loading of the piston rings against the cylinder walls, not a set mileage.) Adjust the idle speed to the factory specification. Dump your oil and replace it with more inexpensive, name-brand motor oil. You can switch to synthetic after 1,500 miles. Some things to remember: Keep varying the engine speed for a few hundred miles and continue to avoid lugging the motor. A smart, conscientious break-in will almost guarantee that your bike will readily accept any modification you make to it.

these rpm further. Begin only going up to about two-thirds of redline and increase the rpm in the same proportions as those listed above.) When you back off the throttle, let the engine decelerate for at least the same amount of time that you were on the gas. This allows the cylinder walls and rings to cool. If you notice smoke in your exhaust during deceleration, don't worry. Smoking on deceleration is common with a new engine. After riding at varied throttle settings for a couple of miles, repeat the acceleration up to 10 grand. Repeat the process one more time (for a total of three acceleration runs). As you're riding, you may notice that the

Heat-cycle your engine by idling it up to operating temperature and then letting it cool back down to ambient temperature. Set the idle speed over 1,500 rpm to make sure the engine runs smoothly.

CARBURETION, EFI, EXHAUST, IGNITION, AND ENGINE

PROJECT 86

Compression and Leakdown Testing

 Time: 2 hours

 Tools: Sockets, spark plug socket, ratchet, breaker bar, torque wrench (foot-pounds and inch-pounds), wrenches, Phillips screwdrivers, contact cleaner, rags, air compressor, compression tester, leakdown tester, rear stand

 Talent:

 Cost: $$

 Parts Required: None

 Tip: Check compression with the engine warm, and check leakdown with it cold.

 PERFORMANCE GAIN: None. Knowledge that cylinders are in good condition.

The old generalization that an engine is just a big pump is a reasonably accurate way of describing how the fuel mixture is drawn into the combustion chamber and spent gases are pushed out (if you ignore the effects of Ram-Air). But what happens to the gases while inside the cylinders? First, they're compressed. Next, thanks to miracle of electricity, boom. The expanding gases push the piston back down the cylinder bore. The efficiency of the engine depends on how tightly sealed the combustion chamber is. A tight seal compresses the charge and transfers most of the explosive power to the piston. A tired engine will allow progressively more of the charge and the expansion gases to pass the piston rings or the valves, resulting in power loss. Two relatively easy tests can give you valuable information about the condition of each cylinder.

A compression test simply measures how much a piston compresses the gases in the cylinder. Basically, you'll be attaching a pressure gauge to each cylinder and taking a reading. What a compression test tells you—once you compare your results to your bike's factory specifications—is how tightly the piston rings and valves are sealing. It can also give you clues as to whether you have carbon buildup in the cylinders. If you suspect that the engine is tired, performing a leakdown test will find a leaking cylinder and give you clues as to where the problem is originating. All you do is fill the cylinders with pressurized air and listen for the leak.

Place your bike on a rear stand. Compression tests should be done with the engine warm. So, to make life easier when you want to check compression, remove any bodywork that prevents access to the top of the engine before you warm it up. If the seat keeps the tank from being tilted back or removed, set it aside too. Start the engine and let it run until the bike is up to operating temperature. Turn the engine off and tilt the tank out of the way. Remove the air box and any heat shielding covering the spark plugs. Label and disconnect the spark plug wires (or stick coils). Blow out the spark plug wells with compressed air to chase out any dirt or grit. (It would be the ultimate irony to introduce abrasives to the cylinders while checking for cylinder wear!) Remove the plugs and set them aside in order. (Now would be a good time to check the plugs. See Project 11 for more information.)

Beginning with the number 1 cylinder on the left side of the bike, screw the appropriately sized adapter into the spark plug hole. Connect the compression gauge to the adapter hose. Either ground the spark plug leads to the engine or install the plugs into the leads and place the threads so that they touch the engine. Hold the throttle wide open and crank the engine over. Once the compression gauge's reading stops increasing, stop running the starter. Write down the compression value and cylinder number on a pad before moving on to the next cylinder. Once you have the stats for all your engine's cylinders, compare them to your factory service manual's standard readings and to each other.

The manual will list the maximum, minimum, and standard compression for your engine in stock form. If one or more of the cylinders reads higher than it should, suspect carbon buildup on the cylinder dome, piston, or valves. Carbon

Screw the plug adapter into the head and snug it down. For an accurate reading, you want to make sure that there are no leaks.

206

Once the needle stops rising with each compression stroke, stop cranking over the engine. Quality compression gauges, like this Craftsman unit, will have a pressure release button, which holds the reading until you've had a chance to write it down.

deposits can heat up to the point that they preignite the fuel mixture much in the way the glow plug in a diesel engine lights the charge. Excessive compression can also lead to engine-eating detonation. Either case is not good for the power or longevity of your engine, so plan on freshening the cylinders. For any cylinders that have a low compression reading, try pouring a teaspoon (or an oil-bottle capful) of oil into the suspect cylinder. A much-improved reading points to worn rings or cylinder bore. If nothing changes, the problem most likely lies in the valves. The valve clearances may simply be too tight, preventing the valve from closing completely and requiring a valve adjustment. A bit of carbon could be trapped between the valve and the seat. The valve seats may be worn, necessitating a valve job. Also, a valve may be damaged or bent. Finally, even if the compression readings for all the cylinders are within the manufacturer's recommended range, the difference between the cylinders should not be more than 10 percent (or specific psi value specified in your manual).

Before you start tearing your engine apart to fix problems hinted at during your compression test, why not find out more specifically what components need your attention? A leakdown test will tell you what's going on in your individual cylinders and what the cause of low compression could be. To perform this test, you'll need a special tool such as Motion Pro's Leakdown Tester and a source of compressed air. After filling the cylinder with a constant pressure, the gauge on the leakdown tester will indicate the percentage of leakage. Then you can listen to various parts of the engine to determine where the leak is occurring, which could save you tons of wrenching time.

As with the compression test, you'll want to begin by placing your bike on a rear stand and clearing your access to the spark plugs. With the engine cold, remove the plug wires or stick coils, blow out the plug tunnels, and remove all of the plugs. You don't want to do this test when the engine is hot because pumping cold air into the engine can warp or damage valves or other components. Install the appropriately sized

adapter into the spark plug hole of the suspect cylinder(s). For the tool to work, you need to get the piston in the cylinder you're testing to top dead center (TDC). Put your bike in top gear, and rotate the rear wheel. If you cover the outlet of the adapter hose, you'll feel the pressure build on the compression stroke. As you pass TDC, the pressure will peak and begin to fall off. Your challenge is to stop before it falls off. If you have trouble with this, you could remove the ignition trigger cover and use the timing marks to find TDC, as well. With the cover off, you could also use a wrench to turn the crankshaft.

Set your pressurized air source to between 70 and 200 psi. (Since most home compressors top out at around 125 psi, 100 psi will probably be optimal by not being at the bottom of the tester's range and not at the top of the compressor's.) Before pressurizing the cylinder, you need to zero out the gauge. Attach the hose from your compressor to the leakdown tester. Pull the regulator valve knob out from the tester body and rotate it to set the gauge at zero. Briefly connect the tester to the spark plug adapter hose and then disconnect. The gauge's indicator needle will swing counterclockwise and return. If it doesn't reach zero, adjust the regulator to move the reading back to zero. Repeat the connect, disconnect, and adjust steps until the needle stays at zero.

In preparation for testing a cylinder, make sure the engine is in gear and someone is pressing down on the rear brake. (Without plugs in the cylinders, the air pressure would spin the crank.) Connect the tester to the spark plug adapter hose to pressurize the cylinder. After a moment, the gauge will settle to its final reading. Engines that are in top condition will have around 5 percent or less cylinder leakage. Six to 14 percent leakage signifies an engine that is in OK condition, but not top-notch. If your engine has from 15 to 22 percent leakage, you've probably noticed some loss of power. Any more leakage, and you might as well be riding a cruiser.

Now that you've pinpointed the condition of the problem cylinder, find out where the sealing problem is occurring. The beauty of using pressurized air to test the cylinders is that you can listen for the leaks. If you can hear the hiss from the carburetor/injector bodies, the intake valves aren't sealing. Noise in the header points toward the exhaust valves. Air exiting the crankcase breather points toward the rings. Bubbles in the cooling system or a rising level in the overflow tank means a blown head gasket, as does hissing in adjacent cylinders.

So, what do you do with this information? If the problem lies with the valves, you need a valve job. While grinding tools are available, this type of project is best left to shops with the proper tools and experience. Head gaskets can easily be replaced with a little patience and a factory service manual. If it's the rings, look to Project 93 to freshen up your rings and cylinder bores.

While using air pressure to tell you when the piston has reached TDC may not be the most precise method, it is plenty accurate for running a leakdown test.

This engine is right where we all hope to find ours. If the leakdown is less than 5 percent, the cylinder is in great shape!

When an engine has less than desirable cylinder leakage, use your ears to figure out where the air is escaping. Put your ear up to the throttle bodies, exhaust headers, and crankcase breather.

Coolant Check and Change

 Time: 15 minutes to 1 hour

 Tools: Sockets, ratchet, wrenches, screwdrivers, funnel, rags, antifreeze tester, drain pan

 Talent:

 Cost: $

 Parts Required: Coolant, new copper drain-plug washer, Water Wetter (optional)

 Tip: When adding water to the cooling system, only use distilled water.

 PERFORMANCE GAIN: With Water Wetter, your engine should run cooler.

Coolant plays a vital role in the health of your engine. Unfortunately, when many riders think of coolant, they only think of "antifreeze." While protecting your engine from freezing during winter storage is important, antifreeze (coolant) also performs several other important duties. The aluminum internals to your engine are prone to oxidizing. Coolant and other products, such as Water Wetter, form a protective coating over the bare aluminum, keeping it from eroding at high-heat areas and from building up on cooler locations, which would reduce the efficiency of the cooling system. Coolant also lubricates the water pump and prevents foaming. If all of this is so critical to a bike's health, why do racing organizations prohibit the use of it? Ethylene-glycol-based coolants have two characteristics that can cause big problems on the track: They are extremely slippery and are tough to clean from pavement.

Street riders, however, would gain nothing from running their engines without coolant. In fact, those living in northern climes would be nuts not to protect their bike from the cold season. Every fall, before the temperatures begin to drop, you should test your antifreeze to make sure it will handle the cold. Changing the coolant every two years is also a good idea. Although the overflow tank is the easiest to access, why not spend the extra time to expose the cooling system filler cap so you can test what's actually inside the engine? So, with your engine cold (a hot cooling system is under pressure and will spew potentially injurious coolant all over the place), remove the filler cap. For the actual testing, you have a couple

of choices. Prestone makes clever throwaway test strips that you dip into the coolant, read the color, then toss into the trash. You can also use a testing tool that measures the specific gravity of the solution and displays the results with floating balls or a needle. While you're at it, check the color of the coolant. If it looks like Mountain Dew, it's probably OK. Other colors, like rust (red-brown) or oil (black) residue, may signal engine problems.

So, what if your coolant didn't pass muster? Perhaps you added straight water to your overflow tank when you noticed it was low, or maybe the coolant is just old. Why gamble? Since it's so easy to replace the coolant, just do it. Then you won't have to wonder if you added enough antifreeze to bring the protection up to the proper level.

Begin with your bike on a rear stand with the lower bodywork removed. Locate the drain plug. (It's usually on the water pump cover.) Place a container, large enough to hold all the coolant, under the plug. If you want to keep the antifreeze off your skin, wear latex gloves. Open the filler cap at the top of the system. Using a wrench, unscrew the plug. Before the plug is completely out, the coolant will start to leak past the threads. So, be prepared. Pull the plug free and let the system drain. As soon as the system is completely empty, reinstall the plug and a fresh copper washer and torque to specs. Next, empty the expansion tank into the catch pan. Pour the used antifreeze into a suitable container for transporting it to a recycling center or auto parts store. For some reason, children and pets have a fatal attraction for this extremely toxic liquid, so get it sealed up and out of reach quickly.

Those who will be filling their cooling systems with a 50/50 mix of coolant and distilled water should mix the solution prior to pouring it into the filler. That way you're certain about the mixture no matter how much liquid the system requires. Also, you'll have a container of the proper mixture if you need to top off the expansion tank in the future. If you are going to run water for track use, buy a bottle of Red Line Water Wetter. The bare aluminum inside the engine will be protected from the corrosive properties of the water, and the system will cool more efficiently. In fact, many performance-minded riders put Water Wetter in systems running ordinary coolant for that very reason. Also, if you truly care about the condition of your engine, only use distilled water. Tap water will have varying levels of minerals (depending on the community) that can create deposits on the engine internals.

Once you've filled the cooling system to the brim, you need to run the engine with the filler cap off. As the engine warms up, you'll see bubbles working their way out of the system. In fact, as the engine circulates the coolant, you may see the level drop quite a way. Keep topping off the system as the level drops. When the engine starts to warm up, the coolant will start to expand out of the filler. Stop the engine and replace the radiator cap. Fill the expansion tank until the

Check your antifreeze every fall, particularly if your bike is stored in an unheated garage. These test strips don't take up any room in your tool box.

level is midway between the two lines. Now, take your bike for a short ride to get it completely up to temperature, then park the bike and allow it to cool off completely. Top off the cooling system and button up your bodywork. You should now be good to go for at least another year.

Coolant usually pours out of the drain plug with a good deal of force, so be prepared. Make sure you have a container that will hold all of your bike's old coolant, or you'll find out how hard it is to clean up antifreeze. Immediately transfer the poisonous liquid to a sealed container. If you're replacing antifreeze with water for a track day, you can save clean antifreeze to reuse in the engine when you return it to street use.

Valve Adjustment

 Time: 6 hours

 Tools: Sockets, Allen sockets, ratchet, torque wrench (foot-pounds and inch-pounds), wrenches, contact cleaner, gasket sealer, rags, oil catch pan, feeler gauge, micrometer, magnet, heavy-gauge wire or large zip-tie, paper tape

 Talent:

 Cost: $

 Parts Required: Replacement shims (if needed), engine cover gasket, cam tensioner gasket (if removed), molybdenum disulfide grease, molybdenum disulfide oil

 Tip: Always recheck the clearance after installing new shims.

PERFORMANCE GAIN: Proper engine breathing

COMPLEMENTARY MODIFICATIONS: Alter cam timing for more power, replace spark plugs, change coolant.

Valve adjustment is one of the most time-consuming items on your service manual's routine maintenance checklist. Fortunately, current sportbikes offer long adjustment intervals. For example, the valve adjustment maintenance interval for a 2000 ZX-6R is 12,000 miles. Other sportbikes can go as long as 26,000 miles. Pity the poor souls who had to dig into their engines every 6,000 miles, which was quite common with the old screw-and-locknut adjusters.

Fortunately, most sportbikes now use some kind of shim-and-bucket arrangement so that the cam lobe can act more or less directly on the valve itself, rather than using a pivoted finger that could exert side forces on the valve and wear it out. Of course, Ducati goes its own way by using the desmodromic system that mechanically opens and closes the valves with rockers. If you're wondering why valves need to be adjusted, consider this. When valve clearances are too tight, they might not close completely, leading to loss of power. If the clearances are too loose, the valve may not open completely, resulting in a power loss. Also, when the clearances are too loose, valves tend to be slapped open by the cam lobes instead

of being ramped open. This can potentially cause mushroomed valve stems as they slam open and closed.

When the time comes to adjust your bike's valves, set aside the better part of a day for wrenching. To work more efficiently, time this chore for when you will be performing other maintenance. Begin with the engine completely cold (or at ambient temperature). Letting it sit overnight is perfect. You need to gain access to the top of the cylinder head, so anything that could get in the way needs to be removed. On many bikes—but not all—you may need to remove the radiator. If the coolant is still good, store it in a place where it won't pick up any dirt and reuse it. Since you must remove the spark plugs, check them too. Label all electrical connectors or take digital photos of the parts as they come off. Remove the valve cover bolts in a crisscross pattern and remove the cover.

There you have it: the engine's top end in all its oily glory. Odds are, however, that the cam lobes aren't in the proper position to measure the valve clearance. So, the cover that gives you access to the crankshaft needs to be removed. Check your factory manual to see which one to remove. You may need to remove yet another cover to see timing marks. Once you have the cover(s) removed, use a breaker bar to rotate the crank in the direction specified by your service manual. If you use a ratchet instead of a breaker bar, you may have trouble stopping the crank in the right position, because the ratcheting function will allow the crank to keep turning slightly. Always turn the engine forward to avoid potential internal damage. When you reach the timing mark indicated (there may be more than one) by your service manual, visually inspect the cam lobes on the cylinder you're measuring. Depending on your bike, you may be measuring the clearances for one cylinder, or multiple ones. Also, some manufacturers

Turn the crankshaft so that the appropriate timing marks line up. Of course, if you've altered your cam timing, you may have to adjust the crank position slightly.

When you're measuring the valve clearance, you'll want to do it on the compression stroke when the intake and exhaust cam lobes on the cylinder you're checking are pointing away from each other. However, some engines will have you measure more than one cylinder at a time for a given cam position.

give you multiple timing marks to use for valve adjustment, while others will give you one and expect you to calculate crankshaft rotation for the remainder of the cylinders.

When checking clearance with a thickness gauge, you want to be able to feel the gauge contact both the bucket and cam at the same time. If you can't, try the next larger size until you do. What you want to feel is the metal of the feeler sliding between the parts as if you were sliding it in and out of a heavy book. If you feel more friction than that, or can't get the feeler in the space, try a smaller size until you do. Record the measurement even if it is within tolerances. Drawing a grid pattern that represents the 16 valve and cylinder locations will make tracking which valve shims you need to change easier. Also, if you keep the chart, you'll have a record for the next time you adjust your valves. Once you've measured all of the clearances, you know whether you need to proceed. If everything checks out, button everything up, relax, and count your blessings, because if even one valve measures out of spec, you've got some work ahead of you.

To get a reading, you slide the feeler gauge between the cam and the bucket. You want to feel about the amount of friction you would experience sliding the gauge in and out of a heavy book. Note how this feeler had to be trimmed to fit in the small space.

Since most sportbikes use shim-under-bucket arrangements these days, the process of adjusting valves has gotten a little harder. You're going to need to remove the cams to gain access to the shims you need to swap out. That's the cost of having longer adjustment intervals. Removing camshafts from an engine isn't as hard as it sounds. Just work slowly and methodically with your factory service manual outlining any specific tricks for your model bike. Generally, the manual will tell you to line up a timing mark to ease reinstalling the cams. If you're planning on replacing or changing the timing of the camshaft sprockets, you'll want to loosen their bolts prior to taking them out of the engine—it's a lot easier that way, because cams can be slippery and you can't put them in a vise. Otherwise, don't worry about those sprocket bolts. (If you have timed your cams and you loosen these bolts, you'll have to retime them. So, beware!) Next, remove the cam chain tensioner. Make sure the gasket comes off because you'll be installing a new one—unless it uses an O-ring. Different engines may or may not require that one or more chain guides be removed.

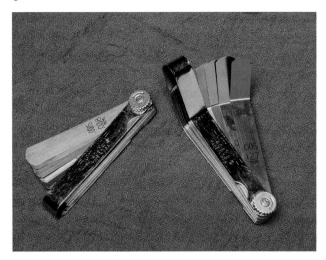

If you can't access the gap between the cam and the bucket without bending a straight feeler, you may not be able to get an accurate reading. Try using an angled feeler.

Loosening the camshaft caps safely requires that you work in a crisscross pattern moving from the outside caps to those in the center of the engine. As an extra note of caution, loosen the cap bolts in stages. (Loosen them all one turn and then repeat with one to two turns in sequence until the bolts come out.) Some of the cam lobes will be pressing against the valves, so the cam will tend to pop up as the caps are loosened. If you let one side get higher than another, you risk tweaking a cam or cap. To prevent having a cap bolt or retaining pin fall into the cam chain tunnel, stuff a clean rag into the tunnel. When you lift the caps free, the dowel pins may stay in either the head or the cap. Remove all the pins and set them aside with the bolts. Lay the caps on a clean rag in the same orientation as they are on the head for ease in reassembly. Temporarily remove the rag and lift the cams free. After you set the cams aside, secure the chain with a piece of wire to keep it from falling inside the engine. Replace the rag so you don't accidentally drop a valve shim into the bottom end.

To ease the re-assembly of the top end, mark the cam sprockets and chain before you remove anything.

Working with one valve at a time, remove the bucket for each out-of-tolerance valve. Getting the shim out of its home may require a magnet. Next, measure the shim with a micrometer. Now, return the parts to position to avoid mixing them up with other valves' pieces. If the valve clearance is too tight, subtract the measured clearance from recommended clearance. Take this number and subtract it from the shim measurement to discover what shim size will be required to bring the clearance to within tolerances. (For the too-loose scenario, reverse the first equation, then add the result to the shim measurement.) Write down this result in the appropriate box on the chart. If you're afraid of math or if you simply want to verify your calculations, most factory service manuals have a chart that allows you to determine what shim you need.

Once you've written down all the adjustments, take your sheet to your local shop to buy shims. Those who are particularly anal may want to take a micrometer to the shop to verify shim sizes before taking the parts home. Either way, don't believe the numbers on the shims. Always double-check the sizes before installing them in the engine. Since a constant number of shims are required in an engine, see if the dealer will allow a slight discount on the price of the new shim with the exchange of the old one. Kawasaki ZX-7 shims range from 2.50 to 3.50 mm in increments of 0.05 mm (approximately 0.002 inch). Yamaha's R6 shim sizes range from 1.20 to 2.40 mm in 0.05-mm

Removing the cams to access the buckets and shims requires close attention to detail.

increments. So, it is likely that no single shim will result in the optimum clearance. In those situations, choose the shim that will net the next-closest clearance.

When installing the new shim in the bucket, make sure you put the side with the printed numbers on it facing up against the bucket. Lube the shim with molybdenum grease before inserting it. Coat the outside of the bucket with molybdenum oil prior to reinstalling it in the head. The bucket should turn smoothly by hand once inserted. If not, remove it and add more lubricant.

Once all the new shims have been installed, you need to reinstall the cams. Using engine oil, lubricate all camshaft bearings, journals, and lobes. Verify that the crankshaft is still aligned with its timing mark. Install the exhaust cam first by pulling the timing chain on the exhaust side tight. Slip the exhaust cam sprocket into the chain in position so that the timing mark on the sprocket aligns with the edge of the cylinder head. While holding the chain taut from the exhaust cam to

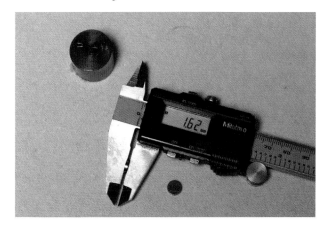

Don't trust the numbers printed on top of the shim. Always verify the thickness by measuring it with a micrometer.

the intake side, install the intake cam with the timing mark properly aligned. Temporarily place a rag in the timing chain tunnel. Insert all of the dowel pins in the head. When mounting the camshaft caps, make sure that you have them in the proper position and in correct orientation. They will be labeled in a manner described in the service manual. Don't forget to install any chain guides you had to remove. Install the timing chain tensioner per the manufacturer's instructions. Again, tighten the cam cap bolts in steps, working from the center of the engine out in a crisscross pattern. Finish by torquing the bolts down in the same pattern.

Rotate the crankshaft until its timing marks line up. Now verify that the marks on the cam sprockets are in alignment with the edge of the head. If they don't line up exactly, try skipping a tooth on the tensioner side. If that doesn't work, remove and reinstall the cam. Once you've checked the timing, now you need to remeasure the valve clearance on the valves that have new shims. The clearance should be perfect. If not, disassemble the top end again and remeasure the shims to be certain you have the right size. When you have the clearances right, you can button up the engine, remount all the parts you had to remove, and go ride with confidence that your valves are good for another x-thousand miles.

Adjusting Cam Timing

Time: 8 hours

Tools: Sockets, Allen sockets, ratchet, torque wrench (foot-pounds and inch-pounds), pry bar or big flathead screwdriver, gasket sealer, timing wheel, heavy wire pointer, dial indicator and mount, piston stop

Talent:

Cost: $

Parts Required: Slotted cam sprockets

Tip: Modifications to the engine components will determine the range of changes you can safely make to the cam timing.

PERFORMANCE GAIN: More power where you want it.

CARBURETION, EFI, EXHAUST, IGNITION, AND ENGINE

If you've spent any time reading the projects in this book, you're pretty familiar with the fact that many components and settings on a stock sportbike result from a manufacturer's compromise—to produce the most versatile motorcycle possible. Also of concern for the factories is the need to meet emissions restrictions. Consequently, more power can be derived from an otherwise stock engine by timing the cams. As with many performance modifications, what the wrench giveth, the wrench taketh away. Simply put, you can massage where you want the maximum benefit of your cam timing, but you will have to compromise in other areas. When you tune for improved midrange, the top end may suffer. Conversely, if you want to get the absolute biggest peak horsepower figure

A piston stop threads into the spark plug hole to provide a consistent point for halting the piston's trip up the cylinder. Using some simple averaging, you determine the exact location of TDC.

out of your engine, the bottom will take a hit. However, you can increase both midrange and top end with cam timing, but neither will achieve the absolute maximum available. There's that old compromise again.

With relatively inexpensive horsepower there for the taking, why don't more riders take advantage of it? Because cam timing is an exacting process best undertaken by a pro—it's not for the faint of heart. More is at stake than just changing the precise point at which the valves open. Get your timing wrong, and the pistons and valves will try to occupy the same space at the same time. The engine will grenade, the owner's heart will break, and the credit card companies (and parts retailers) will make lots of money. So, before attempting to perform this modification by yourself, consider observing an experienced mechanic who has done the job a few times. Maybe entice him (with food and drinks) to observe you as you muddle through your first timing experience.

Another issue you might want to consider about cam timing is that the numbers you get from other riders or the Internet or a shop may not be the right ones for you—if you're looking for maximum power. All engines are different and require slightly different tuning. So, when you get timing numbers from someone, make sure that their engine is in a mechanical state of tune similar to yours. Any modifications like raised compression (be it by pistons or milling engine parts) will have an effect, not just on the timing numbers, but also on the numbers you're able to safely use without fear of metal-on-metal contact. (A side note about increasing compression by milling the head or removing the base gasket: These modifications change valve timing. Consequently, you must retime your cams just to get back to stock timing.) So, with all these variables in play, consider this project more of an overview on cam timing rather than a step-by-step explanation.

Although it is possible to time the cams with the engine in the chassis, the tight working space makes this tough job tough. Having the engine mounted in a stand or on a bench will ease the process. You'll also want the valve cover and spark plugs removed. If you haven't set the proper valve clearances, do this before attempting to alter timing. Maintenance always comes before upgrades. Check to make sure that the OE timing marks for the crankshaft and cam sprockets line up before proceeding. This check will usually set your engine to top dead center (TDC) for the number 1 cylinder. When the crank is in this position, attach the timing wheel. Mount the sturdy wire pointer somewhere else on the engine. A nearby side-cover bolt will usually work. Bend the wire so that it aligns with the 0 (zero) on the timing wheel.

Finding the actual TDC on the piston will be the first step. Because this involves turning the crankshaft both forward and backward, you will first need to loosen the cam sprocket bolts then remove the cam chain tension adjuster and the cams. (Look to the valve adjustment project for more information.)

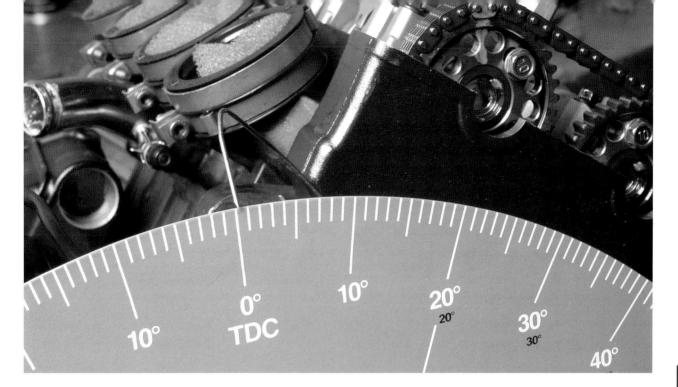

Setting the timing wheel on the crankshaft and mounting a sturdy wire pointer are imperative for accurate cam timing. If you bump the wheel or pointer, you will need to verify TDC before continuing with the project.

Once you have the cams removed, hold the timing chain to remove its slack and rotate the crank approximately 90 degrees forward. Insert a piston stop into the number 1 cylinder's spark plug hole. Rotate the crankshaft forward until the piston contacts the stop. Write down the number the pointer indicates on the timing wheel. Now, turn the crank backward until it contacts the stop. Note this number. Now add the two numbers and divide by two. With the piston still firmly against the stop, adjust the needle on the timing wheel so that it points to the number you calculated. Remove the piston stop and set the crankshaft at TDC as defined by your now calibrated timing wheel and pointer.

Before you swap the cam sprockets, you need to mark with a pen where the stock sprockets line up with the cams. Remove the sprockets from the cams. If you're installing aftermarket sprockets instead of slotting the stockers, lay the new sprockets over the OE ones so that the center of the slotted hole is over the old sprocket's bolt hole. Line up the teeth on the sprocket, and mark the new sprocket in the same location as your previous pen mark. Line up the new sprockets on the cams and bolt them down. Install the cams according the factory recommendations.

In order to change the cam timing, you need to first calculate where the cams are centered. Set up and zero a dial indicator with its plunger in contact with one of the intake valves' buckets. The indicator should have a range that exceeds the maximum distance that the valve will be depressed. Also, the plunger should be angled as close to parallel with the direction of the valve's movement as possible. Because the initial movement of the valve is difficult to measure, mechanics generally measure the crank rotation required to lift the valve 1 mm.

Once the dial indicator is set, slowly turn the crankshaft forward until the dial indicator reads a 1-mm lift. Stop and note the number on the timing wheel. Now, continue to rotate the crankshaft forward. You will need to count the number of times that the indicator's needle circles the gauge before reversing direction as the valve starts to close. Count down the same number of turns on the indicator until the closing height is at 1 mm. Write down this number. Give the numbers a logic check to make sure that what you've recorded makes sense. An intake valve will open before top dead center (BTDC) and close after bottom dead center (ABDC). Exhaust

The dial indicator needs to be solidly mounted to the engine. Make sure that the plunger moves parallel to the valve and has enough range to track the valve through its maximum extension.

To alter the cam lobe's center, you need to loosen the sprocket bolts and move the crankshaft slightly.

valves will open BBDC and close ATDC. (Note: Some mechanics will turn the engine backward to measure the point where the valve is 1.5 mm from closed, then turn the crank forward until the valve is at the 1-mm testing height. By turning the engine backward, you must account for any possible free play in the timing chain or you'll risk incorrect readings.)

Now get out your calculator to find the cam lobe centers. Total the valve opening and closing numbers plus 180. Divide this number by 2. Finally, subtract the smaller of the measured numbers from the quotient. If the valve opening number is the smaller of the two measured numbers, the equation would look like this:

$$((V_{open}+V_{closed}+180)/2)-V_{open}=\text{Cam Lobe Center}$$

If your numbers for the intake at 1-mm lift were 30 BTDC open and 68 ABDC closed, your equation would work like this: 30+68+180=278, 278/2=139, and 139-30=109. The intake lobe center is at 109 degrees. Although you can't go wrong subtracting the smaller number from the quotient, just for clarity's sake: The smaller number on an exhaust cam will be V_{closed}.

By calculating where the cam lobe centers are, you now have the tools needed to begin altering the timing. The most common method for altering timing is to adjust the intake and exhaust cams as a pair. Doug Meyer of Muzzys Performance Products sums up the primary options pretty succinctly in his tech article "Cam Lobe Centers Explained" when he writes: "Advancing the intake and retarding the exhaust ('closing up the centers') increases overlap and should move the power up in the rpm range, usually at the sacrifice of bottom end power. The result would be lower numerical values on both intake and exhaust lobe centers. Retarding the intake and advancing the exhaust ('spreading the centers') decreases overlap and should result in a wider power band at the sacrifice of some top end power." So, now that you have the location of your engine's lobe centers, you can guesstimate what those magic numbers could do to change your power band.

Any changes you make to the cam timing should be small ones, as adjustments of even 1 degree can have profound effects on your engine's performance. Only alter one cam at a time by taking it through all of the measurements prior to

Loctiting the bolts down. To make the changes, simply loosen the cam sprocket bolts on a cam and then shift the crankshaft slightly. Tighten the bolts and recalculate the lobe center.

Regardless of whether you are trying to develop your own cam timing numbers or are using the hot setup recommended by a fellow mechanic, you must check your valve clearance with the piston before you crank over the engine. The most critical valves are the intakes, but you should also check the exhaust. Checking at 10 degrees before and after TDC will give you a good idea of how close you've cut it. (Some mechanics will go the extra mile to make sure that everything is safe by checking at 5, 10, and 15 degrees before and after TDC.) For intake valves you want no less than 1.25-mm clearance. On the exhaust side keep it to 2 mm. To measure the clearance, simply set the crankshaft to the appropriate degree. If you encounter any solid resistance while turning the crank, stop and determine what the problem is. Don't force it. With the dial indicator set up on the valve bucket as it was for the timing, take a pry bar or large flathead screwdriver and press the valve down until it contacts the piston. Note the reading. If the intake clearance is too tight, you will need to retard the timing until you reach a safe point. If the exhaust clearance is too tight, you will need to advance the timing until you reach a safe point. You only need to check one intake and one exhaust valve, since the others should all be the same.

When the timing is set to its final values and you've checked the valve-piston clearance, you'll want to remove the cam sprocket bolts one at a time. Clean the threads of any oil. Apply Loctite to the threads and torque the bolt to the cam. Remeasure the timing once more after you've locked all of the bolts to make sure that nothing changed. Once you're happy with the valve timing for the engine, all you have left to do is close up the engine and reinstall it in the frame—easy work, compared to adjusting the timing.

To make sure that the valves aren't going to butt heads with the piston, you need to measure the valve-piston clearance at 10 degrees both before and after TDC.

Installing Manual Timing Chain Tensioner

 Time: 2 hours

 Tools: Sockets, Allen sockets, ratchet, torque wrench (foot-pounds and inch-pounds), breaker bar, contact cleaner, gasket sealer

 Talent: ★★★★

 Cost: $

 Parts Required: Manual cam chain tensioner, gasket for crankshaft cover

 Tip: If your engine's idle speed drops after you've set the manual tensioner, it's too tight.

 PERFORMANCE GAIN: Spot-on valve timing at extremely high rpm.

The timing chain tensioner plays an important role in the operation of your sportbike's engine. Aside from the annoying clatter of a loose cam chain, you can have other issues with a faulty tensioner. Bikes that have hydraulic tensioners (such as those on many Hondas and Suzukis) can experience some problems unique to this setup. For example, the tensioner can overload the chain, causing wear when running extreme high engine speed/high oil pressure. Also, if the throttle is chopped at high rpm, the sudden loss of oil pressure can cause the hydraulic tensioners to loosen up and allow the cams to briefly go out of proper timing. The results can be bent valves or other engine damage.

Fortunately, American Performance Engineering (APE) has a history of making sturdy manual cam-chain tensioners. The benefit of a manual tensioner is that, once it's set, the tension stays the same. The disadvantage of a manual tensioner is that you need to check it periodically to make sure that the setting is still appropriate. Depending on what type of OE tensioner is installed on your bike, this modification can be done in as little as an hour. Mechanical adjusters simply get unbolted from the engine.

Hydraulic adjusters require a little more work. The oil line leading to the adjuster must be removed, and the oil galley feeding the line needs to be permanently plugged. When blocking off the galley, use a flanged bolt with the same

thread size that is no longer than the threaded portion of the oil banjo bolt. If the bolt is longer, it could crank into the delicate internals of the engine, possibly cracking the oil galley. Assure a tight seal with a fresh copper washer for an oil line. Common sense dictates that the engine not be cranked over with no tensioner in place, right?

To install the APE manual tensioner, back the tensioner bolt out until it is the same length as the stock tensioner in its retracted position. Install the included gasket and torque the tensioner to factory specifications for the stock bolts (usually between 7 and 10 ft-lbs). Although installation is straight-forward, adjusting the tensioner has a plethora of options.

APE's directions recommend stripping your bike down to expose the cams as you would to measure valve clearance *before* you remove the OE tensioner. Then press down on the timing chain at the midpoint between the cam sprockets. Note the measurement, which should be approximately 0.25 inch. Install the manual tensioner and tighten it until you have the same deflection of the chain. The problem with this is that if your current tensioner is faulty, you could be measuring the wrong amount of deflection.

Clever mechanics have come up with a pair of alternative methods of setting the tension. A word of warning, though: Both require a degree of finesse, and you could set the wrong tension if you're not careful. For the necessary feel required for these methods, the rubber O-ring that seals the tensioner below its locknut needs to be away from the adjuster's. So, back the locknut all the way out to the end of the bolt and roll the O-ring up the threads to the locknut.

The first method recommends that you tighten the tensioner in until you feel the resistance of the cam chain guide pressing against the chain. Start the engine and let it idle. You should hear the familiar clatter of a poorly adjusted timing chain. Some people call this a "diesel" sound. Slowly tighten the adjuster until the clatter stops. You've gone too far if the idle speed drops. In this case, back the adjuster out until the clatter resumes and try again. Some clicking is normal, but you still want to try to minimize it. Once the tension is set, shut off the engine, roll the O-ring down to the adjuster body and tighten the locknut.

Tuners who think the previous method of adjusting the tension is too risky have an alternate version. You need to gain access to the crankshaft. Since the chain guide on the valve cover adds preload to the timing chain, only use this method of setting the tension when the cover is in place. Turn the adjuster in, using your fingers on the threaded part of the shaft, until it feels snug. Turn the engine forward by hand with a socket and breaker bar. While rotating the crankshaft, tighten the tensioner a little more. The reason you're using your fingers on the shaft and not the bolt head is that you don't want to crank the adjuster in with a bunch of torque, and keeping your fingers on the threads prevents that. Now,

217

The APE manual tensioner bolts to the engine in place of the OE piece. Note how the O-ring is well away from the tensioner body, preventing it from limiting feel when tightening the adjuster.

rock the crankshaft about 5 degrees to take up any slack on the back side of the timing chain. Rotate the crank forward while tightening the tensioner. You're trying to feel the free play in the chain. Keep tightening the adjuster until only the tiniest bit of free play remains. You should only be able to rotate the crankshaft about 2 degrees with the correct amount of free play. Hold the adjuster in place while you move the O-ring and locknuts into position.

Now that the manual tensioner is installed, you have a new maintenance item to add to your list. APE recommends giving the timing chain a close listen after every oil change. If you hear any noise, tighten the adjuster a quarter turn. Depending on how hard you run your engine, you should perform a check of the tension in the same way you initially set it every time you measure valve clearance, at the very minimum. A better interval would be at the halfway point in the valve adjustment interval or 10,000 miles, whichever comes first.

Rock the crankshaft back and forth to get an impression of the free play in the timing chain. When this rocking yields only 2 degrees of movement, the tensioner is set.

PROJECT 91

Clutch Replacement

 Time: 2 hours

 Tools: Sockets, Allen sockets, ratchet, torque wrench (foot-pounds and inch-pounds), picks, contact cleaner, gasket sealer, rags, oil catch pan, grease pencil or marker, scraper, sandpaper, solvent

 Talent:

 Cost: $

 Parts Required: Clutch kit (fiber plates, steel plates, and clutch springs), clutch cover gasket

 Tip: Fine-tune your clutch engagement with a combination of stock and aftermarket springs.

PERFORMANCE GAIN: Positive clutch engagement.

COMPLEMENTARY MODIFICATIONS: Install aftermarket clutch basket and hub

Most riders rarely think about their bike's clutch, if at all. Sure, they use it every time they ride. They may even do the right thing by adjusting and lubricating the cable occasionally. But do they ever consciously think about the clutch? Never. That is, until it becomes grabby or starts to slip. (Been drag racing, have you?)

Even if you haven't been drag racing, your bike's clutch wears every time the plates slip over each other as the clutch is engaged or disengaged. At the first sign of clutch failure, you should replace it. Don't wait until your clutch fails completely and takes more expensive engine components with it. The signs of clutch wear include: slipping under power, loss of clutch "feel," grabbiness, or some other marked change in clutch function. Although you can often get away with only replacing the clutch's fiber plates, performance-minded folks replace all the plates and springs to assure that everything is within specs. Barnett Tool and Engineering conveniently sells kits for most sportbikes.

When you order replacement fiber plates, you may be faced with the choice of either carbon fiber or Kevlar friction material. Carbon fiber plates can handle more abuse, which makes them ideal for racing situations. That additional strength used to come at the expense of being slightly more abrasive to the steel plates, wearing them out quicker. So Barnett offered the less abrasive (and slightly less durable) Kevlar plates for street riders—since they tend to both abuse and replace clutches less frequently. Now, according to the company, it has refined the carbon-fiber compound to give the same abuse tolerance as Kevlar without the additional abrasiveness. Consequently, Barnett's entire line of fiber plates will be moving exclusively to carbon fiber in the next couple of years. So, consider carbon fiber the future of clutch materials.

Start by leaning the bike away from the clutch side so that the oil won't leak out when you get the clutch cover off. (If you're replacing the clutch after it failed, you should change the oil and filter, since they're most likely contaminated with clutch-plate particles.) Next, using the appropriate socket, loosen all of the clutch cover bolts in a crisscross pattern. Pick a point on the cover (mark it with a grease pencil if you're forgetful), remove the bolts one at a time in either direction, and place them in order on a clean shop rag. You may find that the bolts vary in length, so maintaining their orientation will be vital on reassembly. Position a pan to catch any oil that may leak out when you remove the cover. Tap the cover along its edge with a rubber mallet or dead-blow hammer to loosen the gasket sealer. Pull the cover free. If the cover still won't pull free, locate the pry tabs on the clutch cover and gently pry the cover free of the case with a screwdriver or pry bar.

To clean up the cover, get rid of any remnants of the old gasket with a knife or gasket scraper. Be careful not to score the sealing surface. Sometimes little bits of the sealant will refuse to relinquish their hold on the surface. You can use

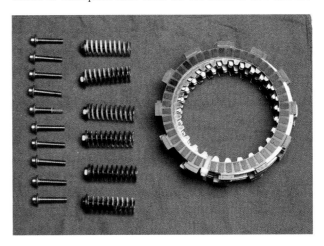

The importance of carefully setting parts aside can't be overstated. Zip-tie the clutch plates together to maintain their order. If fasteners are arranged neatly and logically, reassembly of the clutch pack and covers will be much easier.

CARBURETION, EFI, EXHAUST, IGNITION, AND ENGINE

219

The springs play the key role of holding the pressure plate against the clutch plate. Measure the free length of each spring to make sure it is within manufacturer's specifications, or, better yet, play it safe and replace the springs along with the clutch plates.

some very fine (600-grit) sandpaper to vanquish these last bits of crud. Chemical strippers, like naval jelly, can help in particularly tough cases, but be careful to keep these chemicals away from all painted parts. Make sure all gasket pieces are removed. Clean the mounting surfaces with a solvent such as contact cleaner to make sure no oily residue remains to interfere with gasket adhesion. Covers with O-rings use no sealant, so pay special attention to this step. Remove the five or six clutch pressure plate bolts with a ratchet or air wrench. (Take note of any alignment marks on the clutch pressure plate and basket that may need to be matched on reassembly.) Remove the pressure plate and set it aside. The throwout bearing in the center of the basket may fall out as the pressure plate is removed. If it does, check for alignment marks and place it back into position. Using the tips of your fingers or a pair of curved picks, remove the clutch plates one at a time and stack them in exactly the same order. Note the plate order for installation. Incorrectly stacked plates can cause

After you've removed the clutch plates, inspect the inner and outer hubs where the plates make contact. You're looking for any wear that creates indentations in the basket fingers. If you find any, you'll need to replace the basket assembly. Some polishing of the metal by the plates is to be expected.

premature clutch failure. You may also need to remove an inner steel plate that is secured with a retainer ring on some bikes. Since this plate is usually thicker than the other steel plates, set it aside to avoid mixing the plates.

While the clutch is apart, inspect the clutch basket's inner and outer hubs for wear. If any notches or grooves are visible, the basket may need to be replaced. (See the next project for how to remove the basket.) Installing a new clutch into a worn basket may result in abrupt clutch engagement or clutch chatter.

If you don't plan on replacing the steel plates along with the fiber ones, check the steel plates for any signs of wear, such as discoloration or scoring. Measure the steel plates' thickness to make sure the plates are within the manufacturer's recommended tolerances. Make sure the plates are not warped by placing them on plate glass or another known flat surface. If any of the plates do not lie flush to the surface or can be rocked in any direction, replace the plates as a set.

Slip the fiber and steel plates free of the clutch basket and hub with your fingertips. If you can't reach them, use a pair of picks.

Before assembling the new clutch pack, soak the fiber plates in fresh oil for 5 to 10 minutes. When sliding the plates into the clutch basket, be sure to arrange fiber and steel plates in exactly the same order as the old clutch pack. (This is why zip-tying the old pack together is a good idea.) If you are unsure, the innermost and outermost plates are usually fiber. If your bike's innermost steel plate is of a special thickness, as with this R6, or requires a retaining ring, make sure that you install the correct plate. Also, some OE replacement plates may have color coding to specify the order. Consult your factory service manual. The steel plates are usually made of stamped metal, with one rounded edge and one sharp edge. Some mechanics say to make sure the steel plates are installed with the sharp edge facing the pressure plate or excessive outer hub wear may result. Barnett says that all the steel plates should be installed the same way and that it does not matter if the sharp edges face in or out. In fact, the company's vibratory deburring of the steel plates makes the whole "sharp edge" issue a moot point.

Before you reinstall the pressure plate, clean any surface rust or corrosion off the clutch pushrod to guarantee smooth clutch actuation. A thin film of grease between the pushrod and throwout bearing will help things work more smoothly.

Place the pressure plate over the clutch pack. Remember to match up any alignment marks on the clutch plate and basket. Install the springs into the pressure plate and screw the bolts in until snug. Be sure to install the springs and bolts in a crisscross pattern for even pressure on the plate. Using a torque wrench, tighten the bolts—again in a crisscross pattern—to the manufacturer's specified torque. Although the OE springs may show no signs of wear and exceed the minimum length specifications, choosing to replace them with the Barnett springs is cheap insurance that the plate gets held in place. While the Barnett springs are approximately 10 to 15 percent stiffer and may require a slightly firmer pull at the lever, the company says that the additional tension provided by the springs helps make engagement of the carbon fiber or Kevlar plates more progressive. If you find the increased lever effort objectionable, you can always tune the force by using a mixture of the aftermarket and stock springs—just make sure that you install matching pairs on opposite sides of the pressure plate.

Check your factory service manual for any special allignments between the throwout bearing and the cover. To remount the cover, apply a thin coat of gasket sealant to both gasket mounting surfaces. A pliable, nonhardening sealant works best. If you are unsure of where to apply the sealant, look at the shape of the gasket itself. After allowing the sealant to skin over for a couple minutes, place the new gasket (remember, the $12 you save by reusing the old gasket will seem inconsequential if the cover leaks oil, and you have to take it off again) in position on the engine case. While you're waiting on the sealant, you can install the dowel pins (if any) in the case. The sealant should hold the gasket in position. Reinstall the cover bolts in the same order that they were removed, but do not tighten more than finger tight. Once all the bolts are installed, torque them to the factory specified setting in a crisscross pattern. Don't forget to refill or check engine oil level.

Let the bike sit for a half hour or so to allow the gasket sealant to set before taking your bike out for a ride. Your new clutch will most likely engage in a slightly different lever position, and you may need to adjust the clutch cable free play. Hopefully, you'll also notice how much more positively it engages when compared to the tired old clutch you removed.

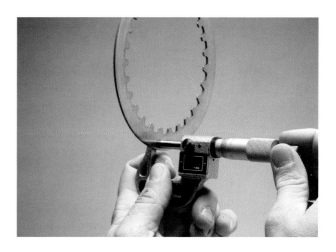

If you're not replacing the steel plates, check their thickness. Inspect them for discoloration or scoring. Finally, make sure they are perfectly flat, using a thick glass surface. Or, save yourself the trouble and buy new ones.

Soak the fiber plates long enough for the oil to completely permeate the porous material. Failure to follow this step will result in a grabby clutch.

Make sure you line up the punch marks if your bike has them. This R6 has indicators on the pressure plate and clutch hub.

Installing a Factory Pro Shift Star

 Time: 2 hours

 Tools: Metric sockets, metric Allen sockets, circlip pliers, air impact wrench, torque wrenches (foot-pounds and inch-pounds), punch, contact cleaner, gasket seal, rags, oil catch pan, grease pencil or marker, an assistant

 Talent: ▮▮▮

 Cost: $–$$

 Parts Required: Factory Pro Tuning shift star, clutch cover gasket

 Tip: You might not be able to complete this job without a rattle gun.

 PERFORMANCE GAIN: Precise, high-rpm shifts.

Although the Suzuki manual will recommend using the factory clutch basket tool to hold the basket in place, placing the bike in gear and using an impact wrench will do the trick. Even with the mightiest breaker bar, loosening this nut by hand is pretty darn difficult—so just use the impact driver.

C urrent sportbikes are great right out of the box, but many would benefit from an upgrade in shifting performance. Positive shifts are important on any bike, but bikes that deliver the horsepower of open-classers need rock-solid shifts, particularly during high-rpm, clutchless upshifts. That doesn't exclude middleweights, either—which generate nearly as much torque as their bigger brothers. It only makes sense that the aftermarket would come up with a solution.

If you're routinely shifting while cranked way over or simply desire the best shifting possible, Factory Pro Tuning has created an easy, bolt-on addition that will be make this dream a reality. All you do is remove the stock shift star and replace it with Factory's version. What makes the stars different? The Factory star's peaks are radiused to a sharper point, and the valleys go just a bit lower—both of which make the spring-loaded detent arm snap home more positively. Factory currently has shift stars available for Honda CBR400RR, 900, 929, 954, F4 and F4i; Kawasaki ZX-6 (from 1995 to 2003 636); and Suzuki's GSX-R600, GSX-R750, GSX-R1000, TL1000 (S and R), and Hayabusa, with more in development.

Begin by removing the lower bodywork. (Note: Most, but not all, of Factory's shift stars require the removal of the entire clutch assembly.) If you don't want to drain the oil, put the bike on its side stand. Remove the clutch cover. Mark the cover under the first bolt you remove, and lay the bolts in order on a clean rag in the order you remove them. Bolts that

have tabs to hold wires or hoses can be stored with the tabs installed so you remember to put them back in the right place. If you're lucky, the cover and gasket will pop off after a tap or two from a dead-blow hammer. Nevertheless, you should have a new gasket on hand. Once you've uncovered the clutch, remove the clutch spring plate and the clutch plates, as described in Project 91.

The toughest part of this installation is removing the clutch basket. The nut securing the basket to the input shaft has been peened to prevent it from spinning loose. If the nut looks like it won't spin off without the help of the impact wrench, straighten out the peen mark as best you can with a metal punch. Put the bike in fifth gear, and have your assistant stand on the rear brake. Using the impact driver, remove the nut. Because of limited clearance within the engine case, you'll need to remove the needle bearing in the basket center before you can remove the basket itself.

Once you have the basket set aside, you'll need to remove the shift linkage from the other side of the engine. A few ounces of oil will leak out of the engine during this step, so place a catch pan under the engine. Now, remove the circlip holding the shift shaft in position. Slide the shaft out until the shift mechanism arm can be rotated down out of the way. Now, you have unfettered access to the shift star. Hold the star in position by placing a plastic screwdriver grip between the detents of the shift star, wedging it in place between one of the neighboring metal components. Loosen the Allen bolt securing the center of the star. This may be tough, as Suzuki used blue locking agent on this GSX-R1000. After the bolt is removed, pry back the detent arm (or pawl) and slide the star free.

Here the shift shaft has been pulled out far enough to let the shift-shaft mechanism hang out of the way. The blue spring holding the pawl onto the star is pretty tough. Pry it away with a screwdriver.

The Factory shift star is keyed so that it will only install in the proper orientation, but be sure to note the orientation of the stock star before removing it. While still holding the detent arm out of the way, slip the star in position. Clean the Allen bolt, apply blue locking agent, and torque the bolt to 104 in-lb. You'll need to wedge the screwdriver handle in place again to keep the star from rotating while you tighten the bolt.

The only tricky assembly remaining is the shift shaft. Hold the circlip in position on the left side of the engine while your assistant slides the shift shaft into place. Don't be surprised if this takes a few tries. Reassemble the shift linkage. Reassemble the clutch basket, making sure that the teeth of the gears behind the basket are engaged properly. You'll know this right away if the basket doesn't slide all the way back against the engine case. Place the bike in fifth gear, have your assistant mash on the rear brake, and torque the clutch basket nut to factory spec (usually around 90 ft-lbs).

All that remains is putting all the clutch parts back together in the order you removed them. Aren't you glad you were careful and laid them out in order? Once the clutch cover is back on the engine, add a few ounces of oil until the level is correct in the sight glass. Put the bodywork back on and go try out your bike's improved shifting.

Here they are: the stock star (bottom) and the Factory modified version (top). The tips of the star have been radiused so that they are pointier, and the detents are slightly deeper.

Engine Freshen Up

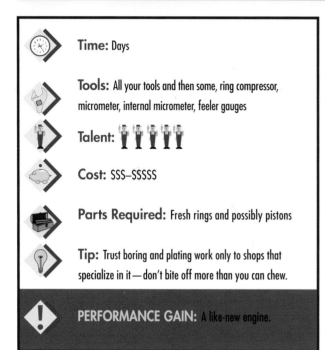

Time: Days

Tools: All your tools and then some, ring compressor, micrometer, internal micrometer, feeler gauges

Talent: 👤👤👤👤👤

Cost: $$$–$$$$$

Parts Required: Fresh rings and possibly pistons

Tip: Trust boring and plating work only to shops that specialize in it—don't bite off more than you can chew.

PERFORMANCE GAIN: A like-new engine.

The relentless march forward in sportbike technology has given motorcycle enthusiasts head-spinning advances in recent years. Who would have thought that Superstock trim motorcycles would be approaching 200 miles per hour on the high banks of Daytona? To achieve such remarkable feats, the manufacturers have focused their attentions on refining engines to get ever more power from less weight. The horsepower numbers have improved along with the end user's experience. Maintenance intervals have been extended (remember adjusting valves every 6,000 miles?) through the incorporation of parts machined to aerospace tolerances and protected with high-tech coatings. One downside to these advances, however, has been limiting the average home mechanic to performing some modifications and maintenance.

Freshening an engine's cylinders is one of the areas where technology has left many amateur mechanics behind. The advent of friction-reducing coatings has pretty much negated the time-honored practice of using a factory overbore kit to give tired cylinders new life. With the old iron cylinder liners, almost every metropolitan area had at least a couple of options for machine shops that could provide quality cylinder boring. However, many cylinder bores are now created directly in the aluminum block and protected with special plating. With the special hones and liner coatings these blocks require, the number of shops capable of matching the tolerances of the factory part—and then plating the bores—is very small. You'll find only a handful in the entire country.

What this means for the average mechanic with a tired engine is that it may be cheaper to buy factory replacement cylinders—even when they're an integral part of the top case—than to send the block/case out to be machined for the first overbore. In fact, many manufacturers are no longer including overbore pistons on their microfiche. But, as always, the people in search of the power that only a big displacement engine can give will always be willing to pay the big bucks to have cylinders set up for some big honkin' pistons.

A word of warning about replacing pistons and rings: Like cam timing, this project involves many precise measurements and assemblies that, if gotten wrong, can leave you with an enormous, expensive paperweight. Novice mechanics should only attempt this project by assisting an experienced builder. Because of all the engine- and model-specific steps involved in cylinder freshening, consider this an overview before you go out and research all that is involved in installing fresh rings in your engine.

So, what's a home mechanic to do if a leakdown test said that the engine's rings aren't sealing well? You can still have the new high-tech cylinders freshened with a hone—if a few key conditions are met. After you tear down your engine and free the cylinders of their pistons, measure the bores themselves to see if the walls are straight. This requires the use of a very precise and expensive micrometer bore gauge. The bores should be measured both side-to-side and front-to-back at several heights in the cylinders. You're checking to make sure that the cylinder is perfectly round. The acceptable difference between these perpendicular measurements is extremely small. For example, the out-of-round limits on a 2003 R6 is 0.05 mm. The taper (the difference between the largest

Careful measurement of the cylinder walls is essential to determining if you need to replace the cylinders or if you can get by with a quick glaze-freeing hone job.

CARBURETION, EFI, EXHAUST, IGNITION, AND ENGINE

Since the cylinders, the pistons, and the rings all interact to seal the combustion chamber, they all need to be checked.

diameter reading at the top of the cylinder and the largest at the bottom) of the cylinder bore is also 0.05 mm. The recommended fix for an engine with iron liners is to bore the cylinders for first overbore pistons. For cylinders that are plated to the aluminum, the factories recommend replacing the cylinders, pistons, and rings as a set.

If your cylinders check out, you're almost halfway home. Now you need to check the pistons with a micrometer. Your factory service manual will tell you where to measure the piston skirt. If the piston is out of specification, you'll need to replace it and the rings as a set. But you're not out of the woods yet. You also need to compare the difference between the largest cylinder diameter reading and the piston skirt diameter. If the difference is outside of specifications (0.055 mm on the aforementioned R6), you'll have to replace the cylinders, pistons, and rings as a set. If not, you're almost good to go. You'll still need to test the piston-ring side clearance and wrist pin/bore tolerances, but you should have escaped the big-money repairs. Cylinder blocks that pass these tests should be sent out to a known race shop that has lots of experience with current-generation cylinders. For example, Crago Racing in the San Fernando Valley performs many engine freshens for local racers and performance enthusiasts. When cylinders pass all of the tests mentioned above, they use a hone with a 400-grit wet/dry sandpaper to simply

knock the glazing off the cylinder walls. The grit also gives a slight crosshatch to allow new rings to bed in properly.

When you have your cleaned-up cylinders back at your shop, your measuring isn't done yet. You'll want to verify that the cylinders and pistons are still within tolerances after the honing. This is rarely a problem, though. Next, measure the piston rings' end gap. Following your manual's recommended depth, push the rings individually into the cylinder into which they will be installed. To assure that they are level in the bore, use a piston to slip them into position. Measure the space between the ends of the ring with a feeler gauge to make sure the gap is correct. If the gap is wrong, replace the ring. You won't be able to measure the oil ring spacer's end gap, but you will be able to check the oil ring rail.

Pay special attention to the orientation of the piston rings when you install them on the piston. The manufacturers have carefully planned out the gap position for maximum combustion-chamber seal. Piston ring compressors simplify the process of installing pistons into cylinders without disturbing the piston ring orientation. Lube your cylinders with nonsynthetic engine oil prior to sliding the pistons into place. Reinstall the head, cams, and valve cover. Insert the engine back into the frame. Hook up the cooling, exhaust, and fuel systems. Mount the bodywork. Carefully break in the freshened engine, following the instructions at the beginning of this section. And you're done. Easy, right? You have just completed one of the most difficult jobs to do on a motorcycle.

Checking the end gap of all rings is essential to proper operation of the engine. If the ends of the rings even touch once while the engine is running, your bore is junk. Although you should use the piston manufacturer's specifications of end gap, a good rule of thumb is 0.003 inch of gap per inch of cylinder bore.

CRASH PROTECTION

You don't have to own a cruiser to want to customize the appearance of your bike. The sad truth about motorcycles is that they sometimes fall down. If the tipover is minor enough, you'll only need to fix some scratches or bent levers. Other times you'll find yourself replacing side covers or repairing the plastic where it was cracked or ground down. However, with some crash-protection products available in the aftermarket, you can help limit the damage to the area of simple cosmetics. If you're turning your sportbike into a track weapon to win races—how about installing some trick fiberglass bodywork?

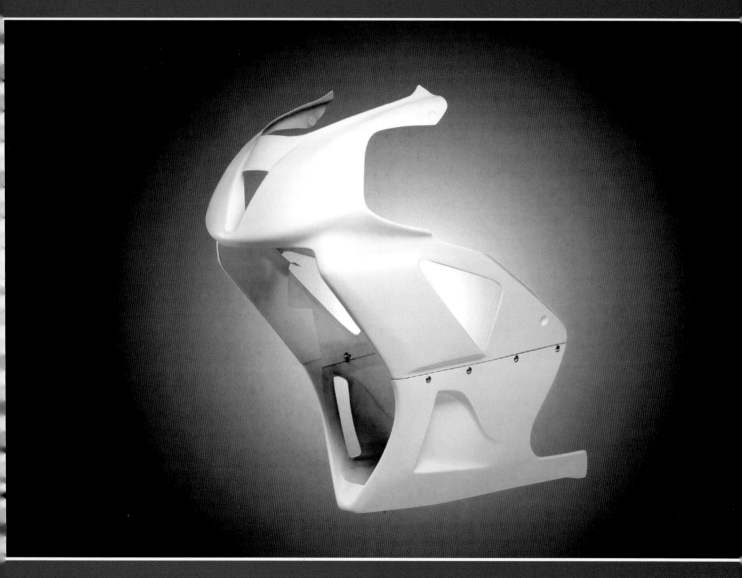

Time: 2–4 hours

Tools: Rotary tool and bits; 80-, 120-, and 220-grit sandpaper; 400-grit wet/dry sandpaper; flexible sanding blocks and/or Craftsman 3D Sander; scissors; plastic spreaders, popsicle sticks, disposable paintbrushes; disposable containers for mixing resins, respirator, latex gloves

Talent:

Cost: $

Parts Required: New or rebuilt engine, fiberglass cloth, fiberglass resin, Plas-Tech repair kit.

Tip: The key to a seamless repair is the final sanding.

PERFORMANCE GAIN: No busted-up seams gumming up aerodynamics.

The swoopy aerodynamic bodywork on sportbikes comes at a cost. As anyone who has had to stand by and watch his or her bike tip over can attest, ABS plastic is not very tough. Other easy ways to wreck ABS are overtightening fasteners or bending or pulling ABS pins out of rubber grommets too quickly. Similarly, the lightweight fiberglass replacement fairings racers use often suffer from pavement abuse. Ruining your expensive bodywork is ridiculously easy.

If you're lucky, cracked or shattered plastic can be easily repaired with minimal visual reminders. In the case of sliding crashes, you're going to have to perform some reconstructive surgery to recapture the fairing's sexy curves. To add insult to already-expensive injury, this type of damage will also require painting. With plastic-repair kits or fiberglass and body filler, the bodywork can look new again— at least from the outside.

ABS Plastic

ABS plastic that has cracked or broken cleanly can be repaired with minimal effort and look almost new again. You do, however, have to assess the damage honestly. If the cracks are thin and no pieces are missing, you'll be able to simply glue it back together with the plastic adhesive included in a Plas-Tech repair kit. If pieces are missing or there are voids to be filled, get used to the fact that you're going to be performing a full repair, complete with sanding and painting—that is, unless you like pink body filler.

Before you attempt to repair the cracks, wash and dry the bodywork to make sure that no dirt or oils can disrupt the bonding process. Then, using a small paintbrush, apply the Plastic Weld Accelerator to both sides of the crack. Let this dry for 15–20 seconds. Next, apply a healthy bead of the Plastic Weld Adhesive Gel to one side of the crack. Press the parts firmly together. Make sure they line up, because the adhesive binds almost immediately. After the gel solidifies, carefully sand away any excess on the outside of the bodywork with 220-grit sandpaper. For a stronger repair, consider applying a layer of tape backing as described below.

Less straightforward breaks in ABS require a little more work. Using 80-grit sandpaper, rough up the back of the broken bodywork. On the seams, sand both sides of the break at an angle so that you expose approximately 1/16th inch of fresh plastic. Make sure that the edges are lower than the surrounding material so that the filler will have someplace to grip. In other words, you want both sides of the fracture to touch, with the sanded angles creating a V as they taper up to the surface of the panel.

You're going to fill in the V you created on the crack. Without something tying both sides of the crack together, the bodywork would easily break at the same location. A coarse fabric tape combined with body filler will help to bind the two pieces together. Wash and dry the bodywork and glue the break together as described above. Sand down any excess adhesive with 80-grit sandpaper until it is flush with the surface. Clean off the dust. Measure and cut the fiber tape to a length that allows approximately an inch overlap on all of the cracks. Damage with big holes to fill should be treated the same as with the fiberglass repairs described below. You'll bind the pieces together and then add a filler coat to fix the hole.

Mix equal parts of the two plastic repair compounds. When the color is uniform, spread it over both sides of the repair. A flexible, plastic spreader will make the job much easier. Make sure the filler extends beyond the break on both sides of the bodywork. Press the fabric tape into the repair compound on the inside of the panel, and then let everything dry. Apply a second coat of plastic repair compound over the fiber tape. Make sure the compound extends at least 1 inch beyond the tape for additional strength.

After one to two hours of drying time, the repair will be fully hardened. Begin sanding with 120-grit sandpaper and follow the instructions for sanding given below. If you find any voids that still need to be filled after the compound has been sanded down, mix up another batch of the filler and spread it thinly over the indentation to fill it. Let it dry, and begin sanding again. Once you've painted the body panel, you shouldn't be able to tell that the plastic was ever damaged.

CRASH PROTECTION

227

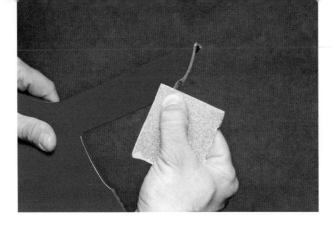

Sand both sides of the edge of the damage with 80-grit sandpaper. Make sure that there are no high points on the break. Do not make the gap wider with your sanding, though.

Fiberglass

So, your efforts to get on the brakes a little bit later and a good bit harder into Turn Three put you on your ear. Now you want to get your race bike looking as good as it did when you first mounted your fiberglass bodywork. Unless you've completely fragged the fairing, fiberglass is a reasonably easy repair.

Begin by cleaning the damaged panels with soap and water. Let everything dry. Now inspect the fractures and abrasions. Places where the panel has worn completely through, leaving only stray strands, should be cleaned up with scissors or a rotary tool. You don't need to grind back

Sand down any excess adhesive with 80-grit sandpaper. Scuff up both sides of the bodywork to prepare for the compound.

Press the reinforced tape into the repair compound on the back of the bodywork. Add an additional layer of compound over the tape.

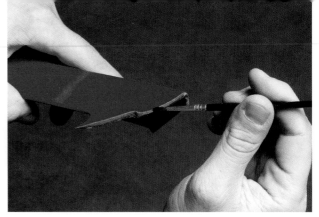

Brushing accelerator onto both sides of the break will help the adhesive hold the parts together while you apply the repair compound.

the solid parts, just clean up the stray threads. If the panel has a fracture that has loose glass threads connecting the two pieces, cut them and clean up the interface between the pieces. You'll be backing the break with fiberglass mesh for strength, and the body filler will make the outside look pretty.

Once the openings are cleaned up, sand both sides of the bodywork to at least an inch beyond all of the openings. You'll want to use 80-grit sandpaper to make sure that the surface offers something for the resin to affix itself to. Failure to do this will compromise the strength of the repair.

The next step in preparing to patch a hole is to cut two patches from fiberglass cloth. You want them large enough to cover the hole with an inch of overlap. If the shape you are trying to fit—say, a corner—requires folding the fabric over in a complicated way, consider cutting a slit to allow the pieces to fold over each other, like the flaps on a box. This will allow the fabric to lie flatter and prevent air pockets. Sometimes the best way to make large patches is to cut the fabric into sections to ease the application. When sizing sectional repairs, don't forget to consider the additional overlap between strips. Clean the areas the patches will cover with either contact cleaner or acetone, and let dry.

Move to a well-ventilated area and wear latex gloves and a respirator for the next steps. Liquid fiberglass is caustic to both skin and lungs. When you mix the resin with the catalyst, you'd rather mix a little too much than risk running out midapplication, so when in doubt, be generous. Mix the resin exactly according to the instructions. If you add too much catalyst, the resin becomes brittle. Don't add more catalyst to speed things up unless you know what you're doing. Remember, you're operating under a strict time limit with fiberglass, so don't dilly-dally.

Rough up the surface of the fiberglass bodywork with 80-grit sandpaper around the repair site. Sand to a minimum of 1 inch around the opening.

Paint the interior of the bodywork with resin prior to mounting the fabric.

Using a cheap paintbrush, paint a thin coat of resin to the inside of the bodywork around the hole. Place the cloth patch on the bodywork and smooth it out on the resin. Smooth surfaces are easier to sand, so any air bubbles between the panel and the patch should be pressed out. When you're happy with the placement, paint the cloth with a thin coat of resin. In tight spaces, dab with the tip of the paintbrush to avoid shifting the cloth. Use just enough resin to wet the cloth. If you saturate the cloth, you will weaken the repair. Wait for the first layer to completely dry, and then add a second.

For cracks that stretch to the edge of a body panel, wrap a small piece of cloth around the edge on the first layer—a half inch should do. Make sure the second fiberglass layer covers the back side of this cloth strip. This will greatly increase the strength of the repair.

Once the patch is completely dry, sand away any bumps or stray threads on the outside with 80-grit sandpaper. Don't sand into the cloth itself. You'll tear the threads and weaken the repair. If the patch is more than a couple of square inches, you should drill a few small holes into the patch to give the body filler a handhold on the fiberglass. Sand the patch and overlap area with 220-grit paper and clean again with contact cleaner or acetone.

When it comes to this type of repair, body filler is the real hero. You can fill and smooth over a variety of ills. Once the sanding is done, the repair can be totally invisible. Body filler should be mixed on a flat surface with a disposable stirrer. Be prepared to act quickly, because body filler hardens in three to five minutes, becoming unspreadable almost immediately. So, only mix what you can reasonably apply in that time. You'll be appplying multiple coats anyway. Flexible plastic spreaders make uniform application of the filler much easier.

Start sanding down the body filler with 80-grit sandpaper or a flexible sanding block when it's hardened enough to hold

Move quickly, or the body filler will harden unused. Don't worry if you can see bumps and lines. You'll be sanding the surface down and applying more filler.

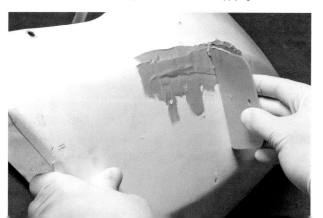

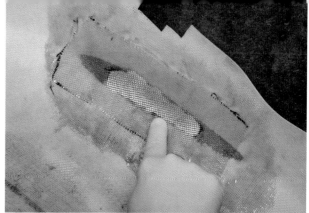

Smooth the fiberglass fabric until it is wrinkle-free. Make sure no air bubbles are visible between the bodywork and fabric.

its shape but will still allow you to make indentations in it with your fingernail. As you're cutting the filler down, don't worry if there are still voids to be filled. You'll get to them on the next coat. When you're happy with the shape, sand with 220-grit and wait for the filler to completely harden—usually 25–30 minutes. Mix up another batch and repeat the filler process until you are happy with the shape.

The final step in bodywork repair is sanding, sanding, and more sanding. Move from 200- to 220-grit, finishing with 400-grit wet/dry paper. The goal is to not be able to feel any seams when you slide your fingers over the patch. When the transition from original surface to replacement is imperceptible, your bodywork is ready to be prepped and painted.

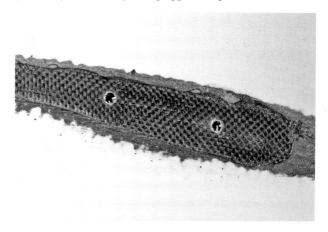

Drill a couple of small holes in the fabric for repairs of more than a couple of square inches. Note how the fabric pattern can still be seen, meaning it wasn't overly saturated with resin.

Although flexible sanding blocks can give you a mirror-smooth surface, the Craftsman 3D Sander is worth its weight in gold when repairing or painting bodywork

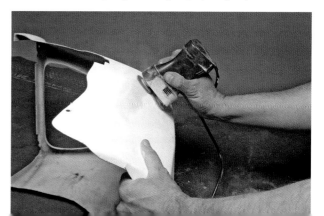

PROJECT 95

Removing Broken Fasteners

Time: Minutes to hours

Tools: Impact driver, air impact gun and compressor, Vise-Grip, left-hand drill bits, rotary tool and bits, Craftsman Drill-Out Power Extractors, Craftsman Bolt-Out bolt/nut removers, drill, hammer, punch, Liquid Wrench, cutting oil, propane torch

Talent:

Cost: $

Parts Required: New nuts and bolts

Tip: Smart wrenching and quality tools will help ensure that you don't strip or break a fastener in the first place.

PERFORMANCE GAIN: None. Busted fasteners: None.

Now you've done it! You told yourself that just a little more effort would get that bolt out. And it did—only you left most of it behind in the hole. You're in what old-timers would call "a pickle." We usually arrive at this situation by ignoring the cardinal rule of wrenching: If you're straining or sweating while removing a bolt, you're probably doing something wrong. However, stripped Allen, bolt, or nut heads can strand us in the same place with very little effort involved.

Before we address this dire situation, let's look at how to keep from arriving here again. Usually, when we encounter a stubborn fastener, we enter into an escalating battle of wills. Before reaching for the "really long ratchet," pause for a moment to take a look at the offending part. Is it corroded? Perhaps you should apply some penetrating oil, like Liquid Wrench, and then shock the threads with a hammer. Could the fastener be held in place by permanent Loctite? Heat, followed by a hammer shock, could help. Is the bolt binding up after turning a little? Treat the bolt like a tap and screw it back in an eighth turn after every quarter turn out until it frees up. Oh, and try penetrating oil.

Back to the broken bolt. If you're really lucky, you're removing something like a brake disc. Simply keep going until you get the part off. Hopefully you've uncovered a good portion of the bolt. Give it a squirt of penetrating oil, and let

it sit for a while. Using a punch, shock the threads with a hammer. This way you'll already have a center mark in the top of the bolt if the next step doesn't work. Using your biggest Vise-Grip, clamp down on the bolt and use the handle's leverage to loosen the bolt.

If these steps fail, you move one step further into your arsenal. Craftsman sells a line of extractors called Drill-Out Power Extractors. What separates these from the love/hate relationship mechanics have had with Easy Outs is that the drill tip on the extractor allows you to center the hole while drilling. In other words, if the tip walks when you first start drilling, you can correct it. The extractors in a Drill-Out set are labeled with what metric sizes they fit, too.

You'll need to set your variable-speed drill to reverse (counterclockwise) for all of these operations. Insert the hex shaft in the drill chuck and tighten it down. Screw the collet so that it rests against the chuck. At the center of the offending bolt, begin drilling at low speed. Stop drilling every 10 seconds or 2 mm to clear out metal chips and add more cutting oil to the hole. If you notice that the initial hole is not centered on the bolt, angle the drill until the hole lines up. Make sure you drill straight down into the bolt. Continue drilling until just before the collet reaches the top of the bolt. You don't want the collet to touch the bolt yet. Clean out the chips and apply more penetrating oil to the bolt threads. Turn the collet five turns clockwise down the extractor. Now for the fun part: Holding the drill securely with both hands, bring the drill to the speed recommended for your bolt size. While making sure the extractor is aimed directly down, in line with the bolt, plunge it into the hole. The shock and force of the drill should remove the bolt. If the drill stalls, remove the Drill-Out from the chuck and try to turn the collet with a wrench. Avoid using excessive force or you could break the Drill-Out. The tool can be removed from the bolt by turning it clockwise.

Liquid Wrench is just one of several penetrating oils that can help free up stuck threads. Use it liberally and often.

Now, let's pretend you've gotten this far and there's still no joy. You're faced with two schools of thought on drilling out the bolt. One says you should immediately begin drilling with progressively larger left-hand drill bits. Why left-hand? Because drilling counterclockwise may cause the bolt to spontaneously unscrew when you've removed enough of the bolt center. The other school says that your aim with a hand drill is not very accurate, so what you need to use is a rotary tool. By allowing you to minutely control the drill bit, the rotary tool will allow you to hollow out the bolt by moving the bit around inside the hole in progressively larger circles. In either case, the bolt should release before you reach the threads.

Mechanics differ in their use of heat for stuck bolts. Some use it early on in their assault on a broken fastener. Others wait until they are in the drilling stage. Whichever category you fall into, remember that you're using heat to try to get the parts to loosen due to their different expansion values. You're not trying to cook the parts to death.

If none of the above methods work, you're going to have to take the part to a machine shop to be drilled and tapped. Or, if you want the bolt size to stay the same, the machine shop can install a Heli-Coil instead of just tapping the enlarged hole.

Having a bolt break isn't the only way for a fastener to stymie your efforts. You can also suffer from the Rounded Edge Syndrome. Although bike manufacturers don't use many Phillips head screws on engines anymore, you can still run into them on occasion. When they get munged up, you can use either an impact driver or Craftsman's Screw-Out. Impact drivers take a hammer blow and turn it into rotational force. So, when you rap it with a hammer, the screwdriver tip is jammed into the screw head at the same time that it attempts to rotate the screw. (Loosening screws this way is oddly satisfying.) The Screw-Out uses a drill turning at super low speed (50–70 rpm) and your pressure to achieve the same goal.

Nuts and bolts can also have their corners twisted off. This usually occurs when using inferior wrenches (like those included in the stock toolkit) or attempting to remove a nut with the wrong tool, say, a pair of Vise-Grips. Craftsman's Bolt-Out uses a clever socket shape to grab onto rounded bolts, and as you crank them out with a ratchet or rattle gun, the socket grabs harder. When you're done, the grip is so tenacious that you will usually have to use a punch to release the bolt.

Next time you find yourself pumping up as you try to loosen a fastener, stop! Take a moment to consider what could be holding the bolt in place, and try a more peaceful method before you end up needing to extract a broken bolt.

Plunging the Drill-Out into the bolt shocks the threads into releasing.

Use a Bolt-Out that just catches the top of the rounded bolt but does not completely cover it. As the socket is turned, the Bolt-Out's unique shape will draw itself further onto the bolt head.

Heating a bolt—particularly one that is stopped by a thread-locking compound—can help to free it up.

Using an impact driver will probably appeal to your inner caveman. A couple of whacks, and the screw will usually submit to your will.

Installing Frame Protectors

Time: Minutes to 2 hours

Tools: Deep sockets, torque wrench, Allen sockets, Phillips screwdriver, drill, hole saw, modeling clay, blue Loctite, Sharpie or color-matched paint

Talent:

Cost: $

Parts Required: Aftermarket frame protectors

Tip: If your frame is black, paint the frame protector spacers black so that they will be visually less intrusive.

PERFORMANCE GAIN: A (hopefully) undamaged frame after a get-off.

Sometimes sportbike fashion can overshadow the original utilitarian purpose of a modification. For example, frame protectors (or frame sliders) definitely have blossomed beyond their club racer roots and into the street market. Face it, club racers don't have the same money for replacing frames that factory teams do. So, as frames became lighter and more exposed, some clever tuners began to attach plastic pucks to bikes in an effort to protect the frame. Well, the go-fast guys on the street decided that it made sense for them too. Now, it seems that almost every sportbike you see has frame sliders.

Unfortunately, in the quest to make installation easier, some manufacturers are selling "street" sliders that don't require the bodywork to be drilled. If you look around, you'll find people who have had those protectors break after something as minor as falling off the side stand. While this doesn't happen with all street sliders, it happens often enough to warrant a little research on your part if you're that afraid of drilling your bodywork. Choose wrong, and you could end up with sliders that will damage the very bodywork you're trying to protect.

Why are people (and many motorcycle shops) reluctant to drill plastic to mount frame sliders? Well, mistakes in locating the holes are painfully obvious, and replacement bodywork is expensive. However, with careful planning and a steady drill hand, you can mount frame protectors in a couple of hours.

If your bike doesn't require that the bodywork be drilled for the sliders, you can install them in three easy steps with your eyes closed. Step one: Remove the stock mounting bolt. Step two: Slide the replacement bolt through the frame slider and spacer. Step three: Apply blue Loctite to the threads and torque to factory specification. See you later, have fun riding.

The rest of us have a little more work ahead of us. The most important part of the whole process is finding the proper location for the pilot hole in the bodywork. People have developed a variety of ways for determining where the center of the mounting bolt lines up on the bodywork. One professional mechanic machined a point onto a spare mounting bolt. Then he simply mounted the bolt in place of the stocker and pressed the bodywork onto the point. The location was marked in the same way that you would use a punch to mark metal for drilling. Since not everyone needs a reusable tool, we'll use the stock bolt but in a simpler manner.

With the bodywork mounted, look to see approximately where the bolt lines up. Remove the bodywork and loosen the bolt until it will almost reach the bodywork when it is in position. Do not loosen the bolt so far that it droops off its usual axis, or you'll risk locating the pilot hole too low. Mash a thin layer of modeling clay or some similar substance to the back of the bodywork. Remount the panel and press it against the bolt. You now have an exact indentation marking the location of the bolt in reference to the plastic.

Remove the panel and inspect the mark. You want a neat, easy-to-see, negative impression of the bolt cap. (If you don't have one, smooth the clay and try again.) Stick a layer of masking or painter's tape over the finished side of the bodywork. Make sure the tape covers the entire area the hole saw will cut. Drill a small pilot hole through the center of the bolt

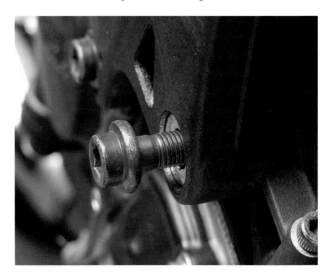

Unscrew the stock mounting bolt until it reaches almost all the way to the bodywork.

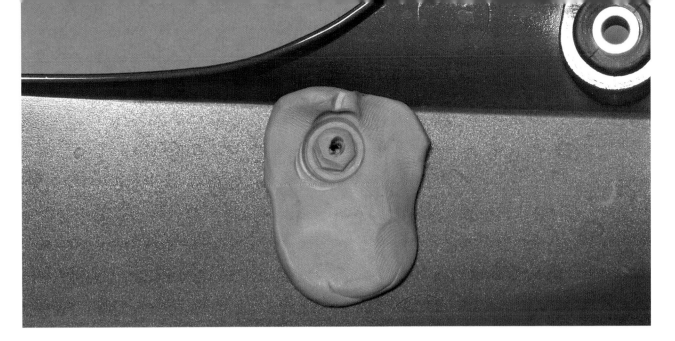

The impression on the clay gives you an easy target for drilling the pilot hole. Check to make sure this hole lines up with the bolt before using the hole saw.

impression. You can now remove the clay. Before you crank up the hole saw and reach the point of no return, remount the panel and check to see that the hole lines up with the bolt. Eyeballing the bolt through the hole isn't very accurate. Instead, try sticking something through the hole and see if reaches to the bolt at the correct angle. If it's long enough, the drill bit would be perfect for this test. Now, it's safe to move on.

When using the hole saw, you'll want to cut from the shiny side, so that the cleanest part of the cut will be what is visible. Only run the drill fast enough to cut the plastic—and no faster. Trying to use a high speed will melt the plastic and lead to a messy installation. When you are drilling, make sure you keep the drill perpendicular to the bodywork. If you let the hole saw cut at an angle, you'll end up with an oval hole with a large gap on parts of the frame slider. Similarly, if the panel makes any radical curves (as the top of this R6 panel does), you may want to angle the hole saw back toward the center of the cut when you're going through the curved portion. This will help keep the hole round as it cuts through the plastic's bend.

Remove the tape. Clean off the plastic burrs with a knife. If any rough spots remain, use a file or a rotary tool (again, at a low speed) to finish neatening up the hole's edges. Temporarily mount the bodywork and the slider to see if the hole lines up perfectly. If you were careful, everything should be perfect. However, if the space is too tight on one side, you can grind away more of the plastic with the rotary tool. Apply blue Loctite to the bolt threads and torque the frame slider in place. If you've got factory touch-up paint, a quick application can help make the inside of the hole disappear. You can also do this with a Sharpie for standard colors like blue, black, or red, but check the color on an inconspicuous place first.

Once everything is remounted and in position, you can add the finishing touch to black frame sliders by giving the silver bolts inside the plastic pucks a spritz of flat black paint. This way there will be nothing bright to draw the eye to the slider. Instead, it will hide in plain sight.

Covering the bodywork with tape and drilling from the outside makes the part of the hole that others will see much cleaner.

Clean up any rough edges with a rotary tool or a file. Work slowly. You don't want to melt or crack the plastic.

Careful measuring and drilling will give you a hole that has an equal distance on all sides of the slider.

If you're lucky, installing frame protectors will be as easy as bolting a bracket in place with no cutting involved. Note how the aluminum spacer stands out against the frame. Some flat black spray paint would make the spacer vanish.

Installing Billet Engine Covers

 Time: 1 hour

 Tools: Sockets, Allen sockets, ratchet, torque wrench, flathead screwdriver, rubber mallet or dead-blow hammer, pan to catch oil, nonhardening gasket sealer

 Talent:

Cost: $$$–$$$$$

 Parts Required: Billet aluminum engine covers (including gaskets)

 Tip: Either drain the oil or lean the bike away from the side cover you're replacing.

 PERFORMANCE GAIN: Engines run better with oil on the inside and dirt on the outside.

Let's face it, sportbikes fall over. Of those mishaps, some of them take place at fairly high speeds. For years, riders have fashioned all manner of devices to protect their engines' side covers. From prehistoric crash bars—big pieces of tubing that stuck out from the sides of a bike just a little further than the engine—to today's machined-from-billet, aluminum engine covers, the intent has always been the same: Give the pavement something tough and easily replaceable to chew on instead of the soft, thin side covers.

Before chassis, suspension, and tire technology advanced to the point where bikes can almost lie on their sides in corners, a steel plate or tube covering the case was enough. The problem is that they decreased cornering clearance and added weight to the bike. So, enterprising racers began to have side covers machined from light but superhard billet aluminum. These covers are usually tough enough to withstand several crashes at speed and don't limit ground clearance. As these parts became more popular on both the track and the street, companies such as Factory Pro Tuning began to look for ways to differentiate their engine covers from everyone else's. Factory's artful addition to the art of creating engine covers was replaceable pucks—like knee pucks and frame sliders—that bolt to the covers. Now, in the event of a crash, those of us who buy the engine covers as much for their looks as for their durability should be able to keep them shiny, even if we've scuffed our bodywork.

Installing one of these covers is as easy as taking the old cover off and putting the new one on. That said, if you've never done this before, you might not quite know where to begin. If you simply take off the existing covers, you'll end up with an oily mess. So, you can either time your project to coincide with an oil change or lean the bike against a wall so that the oil collects on the other side of the engine.

Next, using the appropriate socket, loosen all of the cover bolts in a crisscross pattern. Pick a point on the cover (mark it with a grease pencil if you're forgetful), remove the bolts one at a time in either a clockwise or counterclockwise direction, and place them in order on a clean shop rag. You may find that the bolts vary in length, so maintaining their orientation will be vital on reassembly. Position a pan to catch any oil that may leak out when you remove the cover. Tap the cover along its edge with a rubber mallet or dead-blow hammer to loosen the gasket sealer. Pull the cover free. (If the cover won't pull free, try a couple of more taps with the hammer. As a last resort, carefully pry the cover away with a small flathead screwdriver.) Remove and inspect any dowel (knock) pins you find. If they have even the slightest bit of rust, replace them or you may struggle to remove them the next time you take off the cover.

Clean off any remnants of the old gasket with a knife or gasket scraper. Be careful not to score the sealing surface. Sometimes little bits of the sealant will refuse to relinquish their hold on the surface. You can use some very fine (600-grit) sandpaper to vanquish these last bits of crud. Chemical strippers, like naval jelly, can help in particularly tough cases, but be careful to keep these chemicals away from all painted parts. At any rate, make sure all gasket pieces are removed. Clean the mounting surfaces with a solvent, such as contact

By removing the old gasket with a minimum of damage to the mounting surface, gasket scrapers offer an advantage over using a razor blade.

235

cleaner, to make sure no oily residue remains to interfere with gasket adhesion. Covers with O-rings use no sealant, so pay special attention to this step.

A pliable, nonhardening sealant works best. Apply a thin coat of gasket sealant to both gasket mounting surfaces. If you are unsure of where to apply the sealant, look at the shape of the gasket itself. After allowing the sealant to skin over for a couple minutes, place the new gasket in position on the engine case. (Remember, the $12 you save by reusing the old gasket will seem inconsequential if the cover leaks oil, and you have to take it off again.) While you're waiting on the sealant, you can install the dowel pins (if any) in the case. The sealant should hold the gasket in position. Reinstall the cover bolts in the same order that they were removed, but do not tighten more than finger tight. Once all the bolts are installed, torque them to the factory-specified setting in a crisscross pattern. Don't forget to refill or check engine oil level.

Although you could fire up the engine and go riding right away (just ask any endurance racing team), you should let the bike sit for at least 30 minutes before you use it, just in case. So, take your time replacing the bodywork. Do some more maintenance and go enjoy your new engine covers later.

Apply a thin coat of gasket sealer to the cover's mating surfaces. You need just enough sealer to completely cover the area the gasket contacts.

CRASH PROTECTION

Once the sealer has skinned over, hang the gasket in place. Knock pins make this easier, but the gasket should stay put even without the pins.

Not all engine covers use fiber gaskets that require sealant. This SV650 clutch cover uses an O-ring to keep the oil in. Making sure that the mounting surface is free of grit is vital with O-rings.

When torquing large flat objects like engine covers, you should tighten the bolts in a crisscrossing pattern. Note Factory Pro Tuning's replaceable slider on the cover.

Installing Shark Guard

Time: 5 minutes to 2 hours, depending on mounting method

Tools: Sockets, Allen sockets, socket extenders, ratchet, torque wrench, wrenches, drill, punch, metric tap, tapping oil, blue Loctite, jack or lift, Sharpie, eye protection

Talent: ¡ – ¡¡

Cost: $

Parts Required: Graves Motorsports Shark Guard

Tip: If you need to drill your swingarm, double-check your measurements before boring into the metal. Since holes will weaken the swingarm, you want to get it right the first time.

PERFORMANCE GAIN: None. Body-part loss after get-off: None

CRASH PROTECTION

When metal meets flesh, the softer stuff usually loses. The chain and rear sprocket can do a lot of damage to the errant foot during a tumble. Just look at those teeth! A few years back, some clever builders found a way to direct the hapless rider's foot out of harm's way. A shark guard is nothing more than an aluminum or carbon-fiber bracket mounted to the swingarm in front of the sprocket. The idea is to bounce the fleshy stuff out of the way before the sprocket and chain get an opportunity to close their jaws around it.

While some manufacturers are including tabs on their bikes' swingarms for easy mounting of shark guards, many sportbikes don't have such a nice feature. In these cases, you'll need to drill holes in the flat portion of the swingarm base. So, if your bike has tabs or some other mounting point, count yourself lucky, find the right-size wrench, and bolt the part in place.

If your bike doesn't have that fancy-shmancy mounting bracket, you'll spend a little more time installing the shark guard. With your bike on a rear stand, hold the guard in position in front of the rear sprocket. If you're using one that, like the Graves Motorsports piece, has a curve on the back edge of the part, you'll want to line the back up just slightly in front of the sprocket's leading edge. While this

offers no functional advantage, it looks better when you have a little gap to show off the two similar curves. As you hold the guard in place, make certain you have at least a quarter-inch clearance with the side of the chain. Mark the two mounting points with a Sharpie. Now comes the fun part. Flip back to the suspension section and remove the swingarm as described in Project 48.

Place the swingarm upside down on a workbench. Score the surface with a punch in the center of the Sharpie mark. The size of the bolts you'll be installing will determine the drill bit size. Common bolt and bit sizes are: 4-mm bolt and 1/8-inch bit; 5-mm and 11/64 inch; 6-mm and 13/64-inch. Drill a small pilot hole and follow with the final bit size. Using a tap with the correct pitch, slowly work the tap into the swingarm. Make sure that the tap enters the metal perpendicular to the surface. Also, tapping oil will make the process much easier. To protect the threads on the tap, work the tool into the metal one half turn at a time. Then back the tap out a quarter turn to break the chips free in the tap. Work the tap all the way through the bottom of the swingarm until the threads allow for easy turning. Clean away the grit and oil remnants with compressed air and contact cleaner.

Once the holes are tapped, all you have to do is bolt the shark guard into place. To make sure it stays put, use some blue Loctite on the threads. Reassemble the swingarm, and you're done. Now go take all 10 little piggies to market.

Yamaha thoughtfully provided these tabs for mounting a shark guard on the R6. A wrench and two minutes is all it takes.

This photo shows the ideal position for a shark guard: The leading edge is far enough forward to prevent any possibility of an errant appendage stumbling into the danger zone.

Hold the shark guard in position on the bottom of the swingarm. Once you're satisfied with the placement, mark the bolt holes with a Sharpie.

Patience is extremely important when working with a tap. Get overanxious, and you can break the tap off in the part.

Installing a Fender Eliminator

Time: 1 hour

Tools: Sockets, Allen sockets, ratchet, torque wrench, screwdrivers, zip-ties, drill and bits (for some installations)

Talent: ‍

Cost: $

Parts Required: Fender eliminator, illuminated license plate bolts

Tip: Secure the excess turn signal wires away from anything that could pinch and short them.

PERFORMANCE GAIN: None, but your bike looks faster . . .

COMPLEMENTARY MODIFICATIONS: Install aftermarket turn signals.

All the sportbikes you can ride off of the showroom floor may be inspired by the machinery found in the superbike and GP paddock, but the rear fenders are anything but inspired. Rather, they are required by the Department of Transportation. While the much-maligned rear fender may perform a useful duty in the rain, it is almost universally reviled by anyone who appreciates motorcycle aesthetics. In fact, if you look at the design of many current-generation bikes, the fender mounts seem to be constructed in such a way as to make the removal of the fender easy while not leaving behind stray parts that call attention to the fact that something is missing. Hmmm . . .

Open up almost any aftermarket catalog and you'll most likely find a "Fender Eliminator Kit" of some ilk. They range from the simple practicality of a bracket that relocates the license plate and turn signals (like the Graves Motorsports item shown in this project) to units that include their own directionals and license plate lighting (pictured in the next project). Either way, with just a little work, you can radically improve your bike's looks.

At first glance, you may think that you don't need to go through all the trouble of removing the rear bodywork. Trust me, you'll find it much easier to simply bite the bullet and unbolt the plastic. Both your hands and the bodywork will stand a better chance of finishing this project unscratched. So remove the seat(s) and all of the connectors securing the bodywork. As you try to remove the plastic, you may find that the parts are held in place by pins in rubber grommets. Carefully wiggle the pins free. If you get too aggressive, you may end up with the body panel in your hand and the pin still on the bike. Removing one-piece tail sections is usually simplified by starting with one side and working your way around the part, gradually walking the part off the subframe.

Once you have the bodywork off, you'll be faced with the seat tray and wiring for the rear lights. Carefully disconnect the plugs. Remove the brake light if it's in the way. Locate the fender mounting bolts and remove them. Be prepared for the fender to drop when you loosen the last bolt. Remove the turn signals from the fender and mount them to the fender eliminator bracket. Installation will be easier if you hold off on remounting the license plate until you've got the bracket in position on the chassis.

Using the included spacers and any other special hardware, loosely mount the bracket to the bike. Some kits will allow you to route the wires after the bracket is in place. Others will make you wish for a third hand to hold the bracket while you're hooking up the wires. Use zip-ties to secure the excess wire neatly in place. Tighten up the bolts once all of the wiring and other components are in place. Now you can reinstall the license plate. If your fender eliminator kit doesn't include a license plate light, you can order bolts that have small lights inside them from companies such as Four Strokes Only. Illuminating the plate adds the finishing touch that sets nice modifications apart from hack jobs. Before you return the bodywork to its rightful place on your bike, turn on the ignition and make sure the turn signals and brake light work correctly. Now, go show off your new and improved backside.

Different bikes secure the rear fender in different ways. This R6 requires that four Allen bolts be removed before the fender drops free.

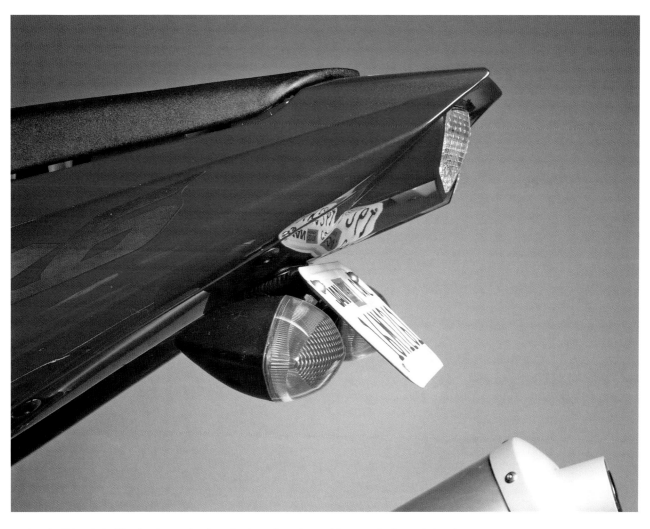

The bike should have looked like this when you bought it. The plate tucks nicely out of the way under the rear bodywork

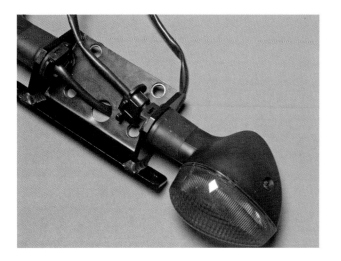

Whether you're mounting OE or aftermarket signals to the bracket, the steps are pretty much the same: Tighten down the signal stalks and run the wires.

These lighted bolts will make your bike stand out (and possibly escape the ire of the local police) by illuminating your vanity plate.

Replacing Stock Turn Signals

Time: 2 hours

Tools: Sockets, Allen sockets, ratchet, screwdrivers, wire cutters, zip-ties, drill and bits (for some installations), soldering iron and solder or connectors and crimping tool, multimeter, electrical tape or shrink tubing, blue Loctite

Talent:

Cost: $

Parts Required: Aftermarket turn signals, turn signal adapter kit, and tail kit

Tip: Consider the visibility of your turn signals from all angles when deciding on what style to install.

PERFORMANCE GAIN: Smaller turn signals are more aerodynamic and look cooler.

COMPLEMENTARY MODIFICATIONS: Install a fender eliminator kit.

CRASH PROTECTION

Motorcycle manufacturers are required to fit turn signals of a certain size at specified distances from the headlight and brake light. Bike owners are under no such restrictions—unless they are given a fix-it ticket by an ornery police officer (usually encountered after seeing very large numbers on a radar gun). Consequently, replacing factory turn signals with smaller items is a popular customizing practice.

While OE indicators are big and ugly, they're there for a reason. Motorcyclists need to be seen in the world where they interact with bigger, heavier vehicles. So, when seeking to mount some svelte signals to a bike, consider how well they can be seen by other road users in front, behind, and beside you. For example, some flush-mount front signals severely limit the forward visibility. Similarly, most brake light "integrator" kits (which flash the individual lenses of the brake light as a turn signal) do a fine job of alerting people to the rear of a bike, but provide no warning to those beside it. Also, while LEDs are a viable option for turn signals, LEDs themselves are quite directional. Well-made LED signals aim the individual diodes or use lenses

to disperse the light over a broad area, as opposed to in a single plane of view. Finally, many smaller front turn signals offer no running light capability, so will limit your conspicuity a bit. Consider all of these issues and be aware of the compromises when deciding on what aftermarket turn signals you plan to install.

Installing new turn signals is an easy undertaking. For the front signals, disconnect the connectors and remove the fairing panels that the signals are attached to. Unscrew or unclip the OE signals and remove them. While some turn signal kits include clip-on-style wire taps, so that you don't have to cut any wires, splicing the new wires to the stock connectors makes removing bodywork for maintenance much easier. So, cut the wires leading to the signals at the midway point.

If the new signals do not have running lights, you will need to find out which wire powers the flasher. Your factory service manual will tell you, but if you don't have a manual you can use a multimeter to find the correct wire. (How did you get this far without a service manual?) Strip the ends of all three wires. The black wire will be the ground. Of the other two wires on each turn signal, one should have the same color on both signals. This is the running light. You can verify this by plugging in one of the connectors and checking voltage between the wire and the black one. (Note: Running lights are frequently on the same circuit as the headlight. If your bike's headlight doesn't turn on until the engine has started, you'll need to start the engine to perform this test.) Cover the running light wire with a little piece of electrical tape.

Before you solder the wires, slip the shrink tubing over them if you're planning on using it. Solder the wires (either two or three, depending on the running lights) and wrap them with electrical tape or shrink tubing. (If you don't know how to properly solder wires, see Project 82 for the proper technique.) If you don't want to solder, wire connectors and a crimping tool will work just fine. Plug in the connector and verify that the turn signal and running light (if applicable) work. Repeat with the other turn signal.

Aftermarket companies selling turn signals are at a disadvantage when comparing the fit and finish of their small signals to the stockers. While some riders loved the bulbous lights, others were turned off by them. Consequently, many riders opted for fairing-mounted versions that covered the hole left behind by the previous signal. A couple of companies stepped up with flush signals for certain models of sportbikes. However, until Targa Accessories devised model-specific signal adapter kits, universal short-stalk turn signals looked universally unfinished on most bikes.

While flush-mount and low-profile turn signals often require drilling mounting holes in the fairing (although some do use high-strength adhesive), Targa's signal adapter plates take a no-mar approach. The bolt that secures the signal stalk to the bike also holds the plates in position. Since the plates are made of aluminum, they can easily be painted to match the fairing. Or, as in the case with the R6 shown in the photos, vinyl-sticker material, color-matched to the OE graphics, can be purchased with a quick trip to a local artist's supply or sign shop.

Cut the sticker slightly larger than the mounting plate so that it seamlessly integrates into the graphic. This actually makes mounting the plate easier, since the sticker will hold the plate in position while you tighten the nut on the inside of the body panel. Don't overtighten the turn signal mounting nut, or you risk cracking the fairing or warping the adapter plate. If you're worried about the nut vibrating loose, place a drop or two of blue Loctite on the threads.

Connect the wires and mount the bodywork, and then stand back to admire how much nicer your sportbike looks. This would be a good time to swap out the rear directionals, so that all four match stylistically.

This low-profile turn signal mounts directly to the fairing and covers the space left by the stock turn signal. It requires drilling the bodywork, though.

The short-stalk turn signal shaft and nut secure the mounting plate to the inside of the fairing. The OE wiring connector has been attached to the aftermarket connector.

This Targa Accessories mounting plate is being held in position by a color-matched vinyl sticker.

The small turn signal really cleans up the bike's lines, but the size doesn't allow for running lights.

Targa's tail kit includes a nifty LED license plate light. The kit's clear-lensed turn signals actually match the brake light lens better than the stock ones.

Installing Race Bodywork

CRASH PROTECTION

 Time: 3 hours

 Tools: Sockets, Allen sockets, ratchet, torque wrench, screwdrivers, zip-ties, drill, Unibit, plastic drill bits, 80-grit sandpaper or rotary tool, several spring clamps, tape measure, caliper (optional), Sharpie, pop rivet gun (for Dzus fasteners, if applicable)

 Talent:

 Cost: $$$$$

 Parts Required: Bodywork, windscreen, Dzus fasteners, well nuts

 Tip: Quick-release fasteners are more than worth the extra installation time they require.

 PERFORMANCE GAIN: Lighter chassis, easier maintenance, and simpler crash repair.

So, you're going to take the big leap and prepare your bike for the track. You've already safety-wired it and replaced the coolant with Water Wetter. Although you can run stock bodywork—and many novice racers do . . . until their first tumble—sooner or later you'll find that, aside from being lighter than stock, aftermarket bodywork is much easier to repair and more cost-effective to install. If you take the time to add quick-release fasteners, you'll also have an easier time accessing your bike's internals for last-minute wrenching in the pits.

The biggest problem many first-time bodywork installers encounter is rushing into the job without thinking. Having a big box (or two) arrive on your doorstep is bound to get your juices flowing. Don't fall victim to drilling holes before you're certain you have parts orientated correctly. You can take practical steps toward installation without marring any portion of the fairing and experience the joy of new fiberglass at the same time, so hold your horses.

Having your bike free of any bodywork is pretty much of a gimme. In determining what parts to remove and what to keep, the big decisions are: Will you use the stock fairing mount and the OE instruments? While lighter brackets are available from many aftermarket companies, most will only accept aftermarket tachometers. So, add a tach and a temperature

gauge to the cost of your bodywork if you plan on using an aftermarket mount. Lots of budget-minded racers stick to the stock stuff until it gets broken. (You can put the money you save into track time—which will help make you go faster than a light bracket will.) As you strip the stock bodywork off, you need to look at what supports the ducting for the Ram-Air system. Often, it connects to the main fairing bracket. Remove any unnecessary brackets and fairing panels.

Before you begin to actually mount the bodywork, you need to make sure that the pieces fit both the bike and each other. Using spring clips, fix the top half of the fairing to the fairing bracket. Hold the part in position and verify that all of the mounting points line up with those on the bike. Clip the lowers into position and check their mounting points too. Pay special attention to where the Ram-Air snorkel(s) meet(s) the bodywork. Note if any electrical connectors need to be relocated slightly to allow for a better fit. (This is more common on the tail section than on the fairing.)

Now, remove the parts and clip them together. Pay special attention to the places where the parts overlap. Well-designed and manufactured bodywork will have the seams line up flush with each other. If you have any problems, now is the time to contact the manufacturer. Once you've marked or cut the fiberglass, you'll have a hard time returning or exchanging the parts. Measure the overlap between the upper and lower. Calculate the midway point and mark the outer panel. You can use a tape measure, but a caliper makes the job of marking easier. Then just connect the dots with a Sharpie. You now have a visual guide that will keep the fasteners in line and guarantee they have enough fiberglass to get a good bite. Decide how many fasteners you will be using per side. With a tape measure, mark the drill points on your line.

The kind of fasteners you decide to use will determine how big a hole you need to drill in the bodywork. Many mechanics recommend cordless drills for bodywork installation since cords can get in the way with the fiberglass. The best drill bit for the job is a Unibit, which has steps allowing you to drill holes incrementally larger with each step. All you have to do is count the steps as it penetrates each panel. Before you drill, ascertain that the overlaps are clipped together in the proper position. Drill through both panels at once. If you are installing Dzus fasteners, you'll also enlarge the hole on the inner piece after you unclip the parts. Don't drill the holes for the chassis mounts until later.

Your next step is also determined by what kind of fasteners you plan on using to secure the panels to each other. Clip-on nuts simply require that you squeeze the clips with a pair of pliers so that they have a tight fit on the bodywork. (A dollop of silicone will help hold them in position after you've painted the fiberglass.) Dzus fasteners require the most work up front, but pay off with quarter-turn disconnection in the future. If you're using Dzus, enlarge the hole on the inner bodywork with the Unibit. Hold the fixed spring in place over the opening and drill two small holes for the pop rivets. Fix the spring to the inside of the panel with the rivets. Slide the D-ring (the most common) Dzus fastener through the outer panel and slip the keeper over the pin to hold it in place. Now, you'll only have to hold the bodywork in position, line up the D-rings, and lock them down with a quarter turn when you want to install the bodywork. Since you'll probably be removing the bodywork five or six times just to finish the installation, you'll be glad you have quick-release fasteners.

The last step before drilling the chassis mounting holes is installing the windscreen. Spring-clip the screen in position on the upper. Be careful not to scratch the delicate plastic. If the screen is predrilled, you simply need to start making the mounting holes, one at a time, moving from the center of the screen out and back. After each hole is drilled, insert a rubber well nut through the fairing and screen. Tighten the nut down to secure the screen. If the screen doesn't already have holes, mark the drill points on the windscreen (while clipped to the fairing), release it from the fairing, and drill the holes with a plastic drill bit—you risk shattering the plastic if you use a regular bit. Once you have the windscreen holes finished, proceed by the same route as with a predrilled screen.

Clip the fairing upper to the instrument brackets and make sure that any other attachment points line up as they should on the chassis. While you may be tempted to use Dzus fasteners on these locations too, the fairing needs to be solidly fixed to the chassis. Quick-release fasteners can vibrate loose. Once you're satisfied with the location of the fairing on the faring bracket, drill the proper-size holes to accept the bolts you'll be using. (Note: Some racers use zip-ties for these mounts to speed fairing removal.)

Now you're ready to drill openings for the other mounting points. Some mechanics like to install the OE grommets to keep the fiberglass from stress or buzzing with the vibration of the bike. A less labor-intensive approach is to drill a bolt-sized hole in the fairing. Next, make a slightly smaller hole in a 1x1-inch piece of rubber mat. By inserting the bolt through the body panel and screwing it into the rubber mat, you create a means to damp vibration and keep the bolt captured when removed from the chassis.

When the fairing is completely mounted, you're in the homestretch. Installing rear bodywork—particularly solo tail sections—is really little more than finding the proper way to wiggle the fiberglass over the subframe and into the right position. Some creative bending and stretching is usually required, though. Just don't force things, or you'll be learning to repair fiberglass before you make it to the track! Prior to getting out your drill, make sure that the seat fits with the tail section in place. If not, determine where you need to grind to get it right. Then just mark and drill the holes.

Finally, fenders take no more than a few minutes to install. You'll drill the holes in pairs. Begin by holding the fender in position with a finger's width of space between its front edge and the tire. Mark and drill the front two holes. Now, loosely bolt the fender in position with those front bolts. Pivot the fender until it has a finger width between its rear edge and the tire. Mark, drill, and mount. You're done!

Now you get to remove the bodywork one last time so that you can prep it for painting. Aren't you glad you used the Dzus?

Before you start drilling anything, clip the bodywork to the bike to make sure everything fits. The mounting points on the bike should closely coincide with those on the fiberglass. Expect to do some bending, though.

Measure the overlap on the inner panel and then mark the halfway point. Although you only need to mark the outer panel, having guides on both pieces makes the process easier. Holding a locked caliper is easier than a tape measure in this instance.

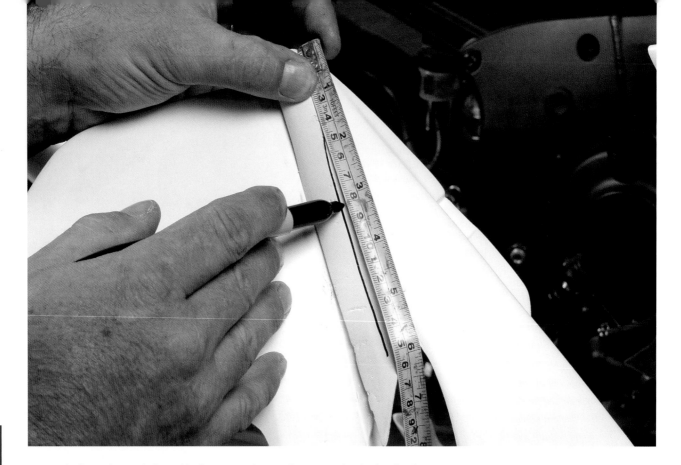

Measure the distance between body panel hardware mounts for even placement. Mark it clearly with a Sharpie.

Before you drill the panel-joining holes, clip the bodywork together. Make sure that the overlaps are lined up properly, so the holes will match when the parts are mounted on the bike.

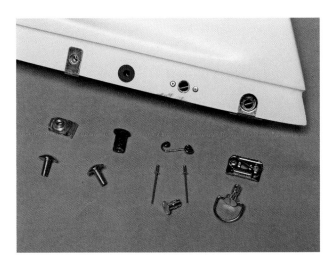

The most common fasteners for joining bodywork panels are (from left to right): clip-on nuts, well nuts (usually reserved for windscreens), Dzus fasteners, and clip-on Dzus fasteners. The Dzus fasteners release in a quarter turn, while the others require unscrewing.

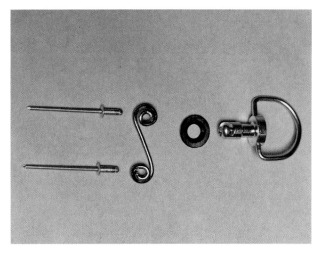

Dzus fasteners consist of a few parts: pop rivets, fixed spring, keeper (to hold the fastener to the bodywork), and the quarter-turn fastener. The fasteners come in several varieties: screw-type (that remove completely like a screw), D-ring fixed (as shown in the picture), and pop-up (which mount to the body panel on a spring-loaded plate).

The Unibit is the best tool for drilling bodywork. The steps on the bit ease the process of varying hole size.

After you've drilled all the holes, you need to deburr the interior of the bodywork, which will allow it to mount more securely.

Before you drill the upper fairing's frame mounts, you need to install the windscreen. Clip the screen to the fairing, making sure it is centered. Start drilling holes in the middle of the windscreen, one at a time. After making each hole, secure the plastic with a well nut before drilling the next hole.

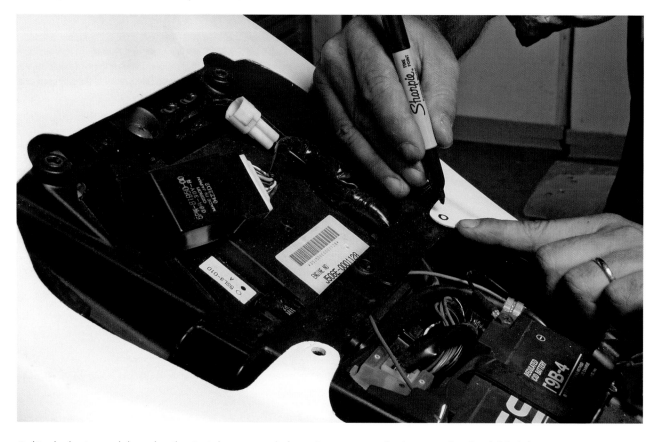

Marking the chassis mount holes on the tail section is the same as on the fairing. Get parts connected and in position first, then drill the holes.

After a couple of hours, your bike should look like this. Now you can remove the bodywork and prep it for painting.

APPENDIX: BUYER'S GUIDE

Aerostich/Riderwearhouse
(800) 222-1994, (218) 722-1927
www.aerostich.com

APE Race Parts
(800) 824-1825, (818) 842-4952
www.aperaceparts.com

Barnett Tool and Engineering
(805) 642-9435
www.barnettclutches.com

Craftsman/Sears
www.craftsman.com

Crago Racing
(818) 780-9144
www.cragoracing.com

Dowco Inc.
(800) 558-7755
www.dowco-inc.com

Dynatek
(626) 963-1669
www.dynaonline.com

Factory Pro Tuning
(800) 869-0497, (415) 491-5920
www.factorypro.com

Finish Line
(see Lockhart Phillips)

Flanders Company, Inc.
(626) 792-7384
 www.flandersco.com

Four Strokes Only
(818) 765-5616
www.fourstrokesonly.com

Fox Racing Shox
(800) FOX-SHOX, (831) 274-6500
www.foxracingshox.com

Graves Motorsports
(818) 902-1942
www.gravesport.com

Home Depot
www.homedepot.com

Ivan's Performance Products
(845) 362-1212
www.ivansperformanceproducts.com

Komoto Draggin Racing
(719) 439-5127
www.komotodraggin.com

Kosman Specialties
(877) 4-KOSMAN, (707) 837-0127
www.kosman.net

Lindemann Engineering
(408) 371-6151
www.le-suspension.com

Lockhart Phillips
(800) 221-7291, (949) 498-9090,
www.lockhartphillipsusa.com

Motion Pro
(650) 594-9600
www.motionpro.com

Motorcycle Mechanics Institute
(623) 869-9644
www.trade-school.org

Motorcycle Safety Foundation
(800) 446-9227
www.msf-usa.org

Motorex
www.motorex.ch

Motul
www.motul.com

Muzzys
(541) 385-0706
www.muzzys.com

Nitrous Express Inc.
(888) 463-2781, (940) 767-7694
www.nitrousexpress.com

Progressive Suspension Inc.
(877) 690-7411, (760) 948-4012
www.progressivesuspension.com

Race Tech Inc.
(909) 279-6655
www.racetech.com

Regina Chains
www.regina.it

Rider Station/Action Station
(888) 922-9269
www.riderstation.com

Roadgear Inc.
(800) 854-4327, (719) 547-4572
www.roadgear.com

Schnitz Racing Enterprises
(800) 837-9730, (260) 728-9457
www.schnitzracing.com

Snap-on
www.snapon.com

Spiegler Brake Systems USA, LLC
(937) 291-1735
www.spieglerusa.com

Sprocket Specialists
(530) 533-0802
www.sprocketspecialists.com

TAW Vehicle Concepts, Inc.
(303) 456-5544
www.tawvehicle.com

Trac Dynamics
(661) 295-1956
www.tracdynamics.com

Two Brothers Racing
(800) 211-2767, (714) 550-6070
www.twobros.com

Williamsville Competition
(716) 537-2309
www.worldbikes.com/wcompetition/

Willow Springs Motorcycle Club
(661) 256-1234
www.willowspringsraceway.com

**Suzuki GSX-R
Performance Projects**
ISBN 0-7603-1546-9

**Ducati Desmoquattro
Performance Handbook**
ISBN 0-7603-1236-2

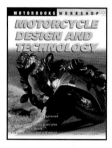

**Motorcycle Design
and Technology**
ISBN 0-7603-1990-1

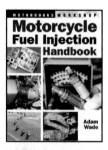

**Motorcycle Fuel
Injection Handbook**
ISBN 0-7603-1635-X

**Sportbike
Performance Handbook**
ISBN 0-7603-0229-4

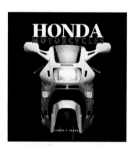

Honda Motorcycles
ISBN 0-7603-1077-7

Total Control
0-7603-1403-9

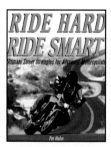

Ride Hard, Ride Smart
ISBN 0-7603-1760-7

Streetbike Extreme
ISBN 0-7603-1299-0